ENVIRONMENTAL LAW FOR NON-LAWYERS

FIFTH EDITION

ENVIRONMENTAL LAW FOR NON-LAWYERS

FIFTH EDITION

by

DAVID B. FIRESTONE
Professor of Law
Vermont Law School

DR. FRANK C. REED
Research Director
Environmental Law Foundation

CAITLIN R. STANTON
Research Associate

SoRo Press
South Royalton, Vermont

ISBN 978-0-9625463-9-6

SoRo Press
1591 Bowman Road
South Royalton, VT 05068
(802) 763-2116

Printed in the United States of America on recycled paper.

PREFACE

Some years ago, I became interested in communicating an understanding of the law to people who are not lawyers but whose professional work involves substantial contact with certain areas of law. It is my belief that there is no need for law to be a mystery understood only by lawyers, and that an understanding of the law by non-lawyers would provide a healthier climate for critical analysis of the law. Sound critical analysis and an understanding of the objectives of the law would hopefully lead to meaningful changes where the law is not doing a good job, as well as less resistance to compliance with the law where it is doing a good job. These beliefs have led me to participate in various educational activities for non-lawyers in the past thirty-five years.

My primary teaching area, as a law school professor and as a teacher of non-lawyers, has been environmental law. I have presented numerous seminars and lectures to non-lawyers from industry and government whose jobs involve environmental law. The feedback from these people has indicated that they have benefitted greatly from being exposed to environmental law in language that non-lawyers can easily understand. I hope this book will further my goal of providing an understanding of environmental law to those who administer it or live under it. Although Frank and I believe this book will also be useful to lawyers who want an overview of the area, our primary addressees are those people who have not had formal legal training. The book will therefore provide the reader with a basic discussion of some general legal concepts as well as environmental law topics. These concepts will be discussed in the context of specific environmental subject areas, e.g., solid waste disposal; however, the reader should be aware that a legal concept discussed in a solid waste context may also be applicable to other subject areas, such as noise pollution or control of radiation hazards.

Before beginning, let me note what we will not be doing in this work. Our role will be that of teacher rather than advocates. We do not view our job as an effort to convince the reader of what is the right or wrong position on any environmental issue. Our job is to present arguments for the alternative positions, and, although it is inevitable that our biases will make themselves known, we do not crusade for a particular point of view.

David Firestone

ACKNOWLEDGEMENTS

This book would not exist without the motivation, follow through, plain hard work, and extremely high level of competence of Laura Gillen. Her help is deeply appreciated. The authors also wish to express their thanks to Vermont Law School for its cooperation and assistance in the preparation of this book.

Special thanks also go to Christine Ryan, Vermont Law School Environmental Law Librarian, and her research assistant, Antonette Palumbo, who wrote part of the How to Find the Law section of Chapter 1 and provided the Additional Readings listed at the end of each chapter. Finally, many thanks go to Ashley Closterman for her highly competent work on the manuscript and to Sara Stanton for her design work, which was used for the cover of the Fifth Edition.

David B. Firestone is a Professor of Law at Vermont Law School, where he has been specializing in the field of Environmental Law for thirty-five years. Prior to teaching law, he was an attorney with the United States Department of Housing and Urban Development. He was also an engineer with the Ford Motor Company and Douglas Aircraft. Mr. Firestone has presented numerous seminars and lectures before industry and professional groups and is thus experienced in providing knowledge of law to non-lawyers. He is a member of the Vermont and Massachusetts Bars and received his JD from Harvard University and a BS in Mechanical Engineering from Wayne State University.

Frank C. Reed received his BS from the State University of New York at Oswego. He then taught high school biology, chemistry, earth science, genetics and geometry in Central Square, New York. Subsequently, he received an MS in Biology and a PhD in Botany from Michigan State University. Dr. Reed has authored numerous papers in ecological journals, including papers concerning acid precipitation and clean air.

Caitlin R. Stanton Vermont Law School class of 2014, was Articles Editor of the *Vermont Law Review*, a student clinician at the Environmental & Natural Resources Law Clinic, and a member of the Moot Court Advisory Board. Caitlin has a B.A. from Brown University and a Masters of Science in Public Health Research from the University of Edinburgh. Prior to law school, she conducted research on policies that affect public health, an area she has continued to examine in the context of environmental laws and regulations.

To our parents for the
environment they provided.

.

CONTENTS

TABLE OF CASES

CHAPTER 1
ENVIRONMENTAL LAW – To What Does It Apply?
Do We Need It? Where It Comes From.
How to Find the Law.

A. TO WHAT DOES IT APPLY?

The environment can be defined in many ways, some highly formal, some very informal. The environment could be said to be the occupation of space through time by definables, or the environment could simply be defined as that which is around us. The environment includes air, water, land, buildings, flowers, snakes and snails. The environment is everything. Most people today have a general sense of what the environment is and agree that it should be protected. What are most often the subjects of dispute are what is the appropriate extent of protection and how fast environmental protection controls should be implemented. The question which needs to be addressed first is how the environment is organized, since that must be examined prior to taking any steps to control or influence the environment.

For our purposes, let us consider the individual of a species as the least complex unit of organization. The person sitting next to you is an individual of the species called humans. All the individuals of the species called humans taken collectively constitute a unit called the species population. The aggregate of all species populations is called the community, and the community, together with the attendant abiotic factors (things that aren't alive) is called the ecosystem. This scheme is presented diagrammatically in Figure 1. At this point, it might be helpful to note that as the complexity of any system increases, the difficulty in establishing cause-effect relationships increases. For example, with respect to the economy and the issue of acid rain, it is easier to define the

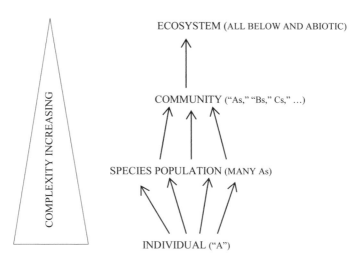

Figure 1. A scheme to help understand one view of how the environment is put together.

economic cause-effect relationship between acid rain and an individual farmer raising a specified crop than the economic cause-effect relationship between acid rain and all farmers raising all crops. In the first case, the question of cause-effect is at the individual level, while the second cause-effect relationship is at the species population level. It would also be easier to define the cause-effect relationship between acid rain and farming than to define the cause-effect relationship between acid rain and all business enterprises which would include not only farming, but also steel production, fishing and automobile manufacturing. The greater the diversity of any system, the more difficult it becomes to define ultimate cause-effect relationships that may be detrimental, since what may cause a negative effect on one population may cause a positive effect on another. Furthermore, the effect that is being investigated will often greatly influence any policy decision being made. In other words, if we want to know the effects of acid rain on the economy, the answer may be much different from the effects of acid rain on human health and survival, and, therefore, any decisions for action will probably be different depending on what effects are being investigated.

Let's move from the general to the specific and focus on one example of what might be called "the environment." Consider Figure 2, along with the following narrative. Suppose you are A, alone (notion 1), and you generate a waste to an external environment, rather than "your" environment. You do not notice, and if there are not too many As, no one will notice. Now suppose that all the As together (species population) collectively send a

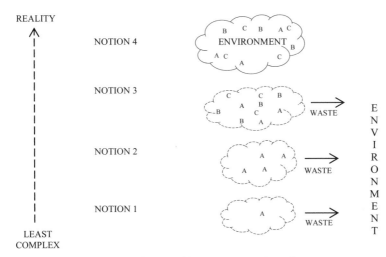

Figure 2. Waste Disposal? You can't always put everything someplace else.

waste to an external environment (notion 2). The "problem" will go unnoticed until there are a lot of As. If the As together with all the species populations (community) produce a common waste, the waste could still go to an external environment and not be a "problem" if a large enough external environment exists (notion 3); however, if we take into account all the species populations, it is highly unlikely that there can be an external environment. The As, Bs and all the other species are no longer able to find an external environment and consequently are putting a common waste directly into the environment of which they are a part—the ecosystem (notion 4). It is in this sense, the ecosystem as a whole, that the definition of environment and the questions of whether or not to control or influence it must ultimately be considered.

B. DO WE NEED IT?

1. From the "Early" Years Towards Today

To a limited extent, environmental law has existed for many years. In the 19th and early 20th centuries, remedies for environmental harms were available. They generally focused on private property damage rather than damage to the public's environment or personal injuries. The remedies usually were just that, remedial, rather than attempting to prevent harm. Today, injury to human health and injury to the environment itself are as significant or more significant than property damage, and extensive statutes covering almost all known subjects of environmental harm seek to prevent harm as well as allow for compensation for harm that happens.

A phenomenal expansion of governmentally imposed environmental controls began in the late 1960's. The degree of regulation with respect to the environment has multiplied many times and has expanded to cover many, many subject areas since then, and the pace of government's environmental involvement shows no signs of slowing down. This portion of the chapter will consider why there has been this tremendous surge of interest in environmental matters and whether the massive network of governmental regulation which has resulted is justified. We will then continue by setting aside, in part, the question of what the involvement of the law should be with respect to the environment, and devote the bulk of this book to an analysis of what the law is and what it means to business, to industry, to people who work for governmental bodies, and to individuals in their everyday lives.

Our analysis of what the law is will include both private law and public law control mechanisms. The private law mechanisms usually consist of the bringing of lawsuits by individuals or corporations. These suits seek monetary compensation or a court order to stop an activity. Neither involves any action by a legislative body. For example, property owners might ask a court to prohibit a factory from polluting the air in their neighborhood because such pollution constitutes a nuisance which a court will act against even in the absence of federal or state air pollution control statutes. The public law mechanism, on the other hand, operates when a governmental body takes some form of initiative, such as enacting legislation. The spectrum of governmental initiatives includes actions such as prohibitions, permit requirements and educational efforts. Examples include: Congress prohibiting the manufacturing of a chemical; a state legislature requiring that a permit be obtained before a factory may discharge a pollutant into a river; or a city council establishing a publicity campaign to educate the public to voluntarily recycle glass and paper.

Having noted some types of environmental control mechanisms which are available for use, let's begin by moving back a step and considering one series of arguments for and against strict governmental control of the environment. These arguments should help us understand why people have reached different conclusions when answering the question: Do we need environmental controls at all and, if so, to what degree?

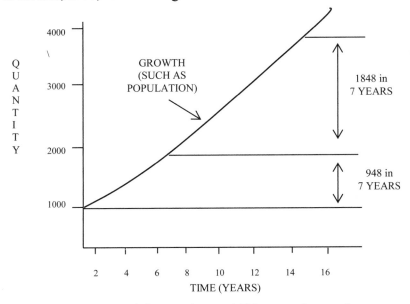

Figure 3. Exponential growth at a 10% annual growth rate.

A study that helped spark widespread interest in environmental protection is called *The Limits to Growth*.[1] A group of researchers

1. Meadows, D.H., et al., *The Limits to Growth* (New York: Signet, 1972).

from MIT used system dynamics computer technology to attempt to predict what future patterns of growth might look like, what limits there might be on such growth, and what the results of various patterns of growth might mean to humans. Concerning patterns of growth, the study found that parameters such as population and industrial production exhibit the characteristic of exponential growth, i.e., growth which increases at a constant percentage rate and therefore increases numerically faster and faster (Figure 3). As one example, consider the meaning of Figure 3 assuming a 10% growth rate and an initial quantity at the beginning of Year 1 of 1000 units:

End of Year 1→   1000 + 10% of 1000 =   1100
(Year 1 Growth = 100)

End of Year 2→   1100 + 10% of 1100 =   1210
(Year 2 Growth = 110)

End of Year 3→   1210 + 10% of 1210 =   1331
(Year 3 Growth = 121)

***   ***   ***

End of Year 7→   1771 + 10% of 1771 =   1948
(Year 7 Growth = 177)

Thus, in seven years, 1000 units has become nearly 2000 units and, in another seven years (the doubling period for a 10% growth rate), we end up with nearly 4000 units. If the growth rate were reduced to 4%, the doubling period would be increased to eighteen years.

The second part of the "Limits to Growth" thesis is that some necessary resources are finite, for example, arable land or the pollution absorption ability of a medium like the air. When those finite resources (limits) are imposed on an exponential growth pattern, the "Limits to Growth" model predicts that the actual behavior of the growth parameters would be in the nature of catastrophic decline. Using population as an example, when exponential population growth reaches the finite limit of arable land, the result is famine and a massive population decrease (Figure

4). In addition, because of the overuse of the arable land resource by the increasing population as the time of a famine is approached, the capacity of the land to sustain population in the future may be severely reduced. If catastrophe is the result of reaching the finite limit rapidly (exponentially), what remedy is prescribed by those who agree with the "Limits" study? The remedy is to have strict control of variables such as population, pollution, and use of natural resources, and, since growth is taking place very quickly (exponentially), strict controls must be implemented very quickly.

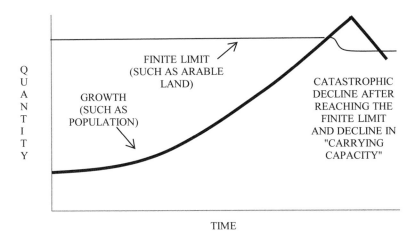

TIME

Figure 4. Catastrophic decline in growth after reaching the finite limit.

The need for early action to avert catastrophe is best illustrated by a children's riddle: A lily plant grows in a pond and the plant doubles in size every day. If allowed to grow freely, it would completely cover the pond in 30 days, killing off all other forms of life. You decide not to worry about checking its growth until it covers half the pond. On what day will that be?[2] With the answer being the twenty-ninth day, there is only one day left for action to avert disaster. Maybe one could effectively control the lily plant in one day, but could population growth or pollution or petroleum use

2. *Ibid.*, p. 37.

be effectively brought under control in a short time period? And, even if last minute control were possible, the drastic nature of the measures which would be necessary to achieve control and the consequences of such measures would be unpalatable and would argue in favor of taking less drastic action at an earlier time.

We should note in passing that the above discussion isolated variables like population and pollution; however, the "Limits" model does consider interrelationships of variables in great detail. Among the dozens of parameters built into the model are land yields, nonrenewable resources, industrial capital availability, pollution generation, and pollution absorption rates. As an example of the effects of the interrelationships of variables, consider population and pollution together. Increasing population might cause increasing pollution, but increasing pollution may cause a decrease in the rate of population growth due to possible deaths or shortened life spans from pollution-related diseases. The "Limits" model attempts to account for the interrelationships among variables and to present a "net behavior pattern" for each parameter evaluated.

Based on their evaluations, the proponents of the "Limits to Growth" hypothesis concluded that, with current growth trends, the limits on growth would be reached within one hundred years, and the likely result of reaching these limits would be a sudden, uncontrollable decline in population and industrial capacity. Furthermore, to return to our lily plant analogy, the point of no return (control possible without needing to use extremely drastic control measures) may occur very soon. Those who accept the "Limits to Growth" type of reasoning would argue in favor of strict governmental controls with respect to the environment and would contend that implementation of those controls should not be delayed. They would say that, without government controls, human society will doom itself by localized environmental degradation just as was allegedly done by the original inhabitants of Rapa Nui (Easter Island) who may have destroyed their society by overexploiting its own resources,[3] and, on a worldwide basis, by

---

3. Hunt, T., "Rethinking the Fall of Easter Island – New evidence points to an alternative explanation for a civilization's collapse," *American Scientist* (Sept.-Oct., 2006) p. 412.

allowing global warming to raise sea levels destroying entire countries or large parts of the population centers of countries.

Having considered one theory with conclusions favoring strict environmental control, let's give equal time to those who are not convinced of the need for massive governmental regulation of our environment by presenting some of the arguments which characterize the "Limits" advocates as "prophets of doom."[4]

One challenge to the "Limits" theory attacks the concept of finite limits. For example, it may be argued that arable land is not finite in amount since technology can increase not only the number of arable acres (by methods such as irrigation), but also technology can increase productivity through means such as the use of new fertilizers or new varieties of plants. Similarly, technology can

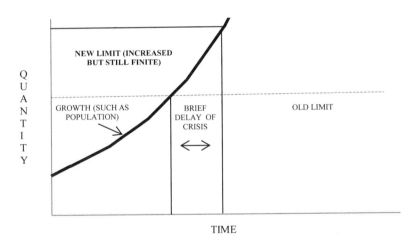

Figure 5. Brief delay of crisis.

increase the availability of resources – petroleum from oil shale; freshwater from seawater. The concept of finite limits may thus be said to be illusory.

The "Limits" proponents might contend that while technology can indeed increase the magnitude of the limits, there still are finite limits, just at a higher level. The result is merely a brief delay in

4. Kaysen, C., "The Computer That Printed Out W*O*L*F," *Foreign Affairs*, 50:660-668 (1972).

reaching the crisis point (Figure 5, above). The critics' response might be that if the growth parameters increase exponentially, technology can also make the limiting parameters increase exponentially. If a "limiting" parameter increases at a rate faster than growth increases, the result is divergence between the limiting parameter and the growth parameter such that no crisis point is ever reached (Figure 6). If the limiting variable increases more slowly than growth demands, then convergence occurs and there is a crisis; however, the crisis point would only be reached when the curves converge, which may be in the very distant future and beyond the level of reliability of our tools of prediction (Figure 7). Thus, those who do not accept a "Limits to Growth" type of reasoning would contend that there is no coming environmental catastrophe to worry about, and, while environmental concerns and the effects of growth should be considered as quality of life issues, there is no need for

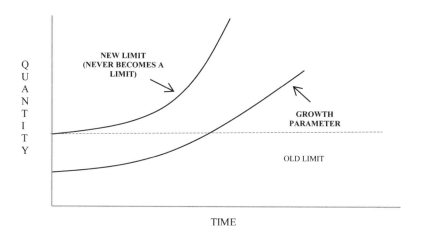

Figure 6. Scenario of never reaching a crisis.

strict governmental controls in areas such as pollution, use of natural resources, or population.

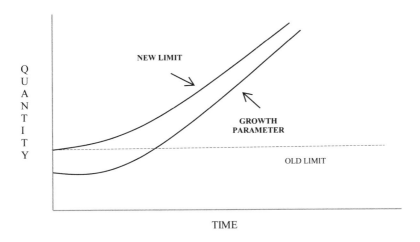

Figure 7. Scenario of long delay in reaching a crisis.

A second challenge to the "Limits" theory might be to attack the concept of catastrophe itself. It may be argued that there are social mechanisms which work in a manner such that as the "limit" is approached, natural decreases in the growth rate take place to keep the system below the limit. For example, as the use of a particular metal grows toward the limit of its availability (i.e., less and less is available due to past use), the price of the metal will rise, and the use will taper off with either the introduction of substitutes or with the less important or inefficient uses being abandoned (Figure 8). The result of the operation of these natural social mechanisms is that growth will not continue to a catastrophic collision with a limit to growth, and thus, while some environmental controls to improve day-to-day living might be justified, there is no need for immediate, strict governmental curtailment of economic growth to avert catastrophe.

The issue of whether one believes in the prophecy of the "Limits to Growth" thesis or dismisses the thesis based on arguments such as those noted above is relevant to one's belief concerning the role of government with respect to environmental issues. Should government take no action at all on behalf of environmental protection; should it take mild action such as educating the public toward voluntary conservation of resources;

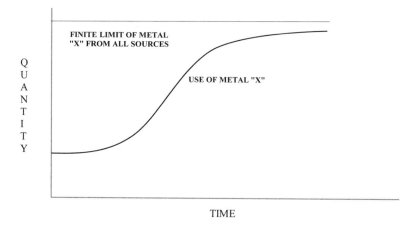

Figure 8. Leveling off of growth as the finite limit of growth is approached.

should it take firm action such as imposing actual limits on the amounts of a pollutant in the air; or should it take drastic measures to stop industrial growth? The debate in the 21st century continues in much the same terms as the discussion above that laid the groundwork for government control of the environment in the latter part of the 20th century. The Proceedings of the National Academy of Sciences (PNAS) concluded that "human demand may well have exceeded the biosphere's regenerative capacity." Humanity's load corresponded to 70% of the capacity of the global biosphere in 1961, and grew to 120% of capacity in 1999."[5] Critics of the PNAS study claimed, however, that it "did not take into account technological advances and better land use practices that can improve efficient use of natural resources. . . ."[6]

2. The Need Today – A Status Report

The rapid growth of environmental law in the form of government regulation continues today. If governmental regulation

---

5. Wackernagel et al., "Tracking the ecological overshoot of the human economy," *PNAS*, vol. 99, no. 14, pp. 9266-9271 (July 9, 2002), available at www.pnas.org.

6. www.eenews.net/Greenwire.htm.

were not succeeding in solving environmental problems, one might conclude that such regulation should be discontinued or its approach drastically altered. Also, if our environmental problems have been solved or are now being fully addressed by mechanisms other than governmentally imposed controls, then those controls should not continue. It is clear, however, that, while government controls have been quite successful, our environmental problems are not even close to being completely solved. The success, but not complete success, with respect to some old problems, coupled with the emergence of new environmental problems, indicates that the continued growth of environmental law by governmental regulation is probably necessary and certainly going to happen. Indeed, the issues debated today no longer focus on the question of whether to have government control, but rather on questions of what is the best type of control mechanism to use, at what level of government should control be exercised, and the time when new controls should become applicable.

Since both the successes and failures of environmental efforts by government seem to point in the direction of increased controls, let us consider examples of the successes of environmental law and examples of areas that need more attention. Notable successes in environmental regulation involve controlling acutely toxic materials. Lead emissions are drastically lower, largely attributable to the phaseout of leaded gasoline and the requirement of catalytic converters in the United States, Japan, parts of Europe, and more recently Mexico. Many state governments have banned the sale of products such as inks, dyes, or adhesives which use heavy metal and encouraged the recycling of lead, especially in batteries. The average blood-lead level in the U.S. population has fallen from 16 micrograms per deciliter in the 1970s to less than 3 micrograms per deciliter.[7]

In the United States, persistent organochloride pesticides like DDT and dieldrin have largely disappeared from use, with the result being sharp declines in the concentration levels of these substances

---

7. Sexton, Ken, et al., "Human Biomonitoring of Environmental Chemicals," *American Scientist*, (Vol. 92, Jan.-Feb., 2004) p. 42; "Adult Blood Lead Epidemiology and Surveillence," Centers for Disease Control, available at http://www.cdc.gov/niosh/topics/ABLES/ables.html.

in human tissues. Polychlorinated biphenyl (PCB) releases are much lower due to a Congressional ban on their manufacture; however, after being in effect for 16 years, a ban on the import of PCB's for disposal by incineration was lifted. Advocates of the policy felt proper disposal in the United States was better than allowing stockpiles of this hazardous material to accumulate along its borders. Other environmental groups accused the administration of succumbing to lobbying pressures from incinerator operators. In 2007, Congress created an exception within the Toxics Substances Control Act to allow PCB imports from overseas bases into the United States for disposal.[8] The exemption was set to expire in 2012, but no action has been taken since issuing the final rule.

Exposure to asbestos is also down substantially. Federal regulations exist with respect to asbestos in school buildings, asbestos emission for buildings being demolished or renovated, and occupational exposure to asbestos. State and local governments have also instituted asbestos exposure standards and, perhaps more significantly, the business community reduced asbestos exposure even when it was not required to do so by law such as in new commercial buildings. This was due to the heightened awareness of the problems of asbestos and the desire of business to protect itself both from possible liability to those who may be injured and from having to redo some of its construction in the event of government regulation of asbestos in commercial buildings. Other nations have also acted to eliminate health risks from asbestos. France prohibited asbestos imports, and the World Trade Organization upheld the ban based on health issues even though import restrictions are generally violations of international trade agreements.[9]

The United States can also claim some success concerning air and water quality. Most of us know of a river or lake that was once too polluted for swimming but that is now considered safe. Annual wetland losses are down, and current policy is focused on not only limiting losses but expanding the wetlands of America.[10] In

---

8. 109 P.L. 364 § 317 amending 15 U.S.C. § 2605(e)(3).

9. "WTO Appellate Body Upholds French Ban On Asbestos Imports," 18 *Int'l. Trade Reporter* 426 (2001).

considering our air, its quality has generally improved with steady reductions of emissions of particulate matter, sulphur dioxide, and carbon monoxide. During a period when the total U.S. population grew by 27 percent, vehicle miles traveled grew by 111 percent, and the gross domestic product grew by 90 percent, the combined emissions of the six principle air pollutants dropped, some, like SO_2 and CO_2 by as much as 75 percent, and total emissions of toxic air pollutants decreased by approximately 42 percent.[11]

Other air pollution efforts have also been relatively successful. The number of areas in the United States failing to comply with EPA standards, known as nonattainment areas, has decreased substantially. As of 2010, there were no violations of the annual standards for SO_2, NO_2, or CO, and from 2001 to 2010, ozone nonattainment areas showed a 9 percent improvement in ozone concentration levels.[12] However, many old air pollution problems still remain, and new problems have arisen. Despite our success in emission reduction for certain pollutants, in 2002 there were still more than 200 classified nonattainment areas, only 30 of which were listed as "severe," "serious," or "extreme."[13] Many of these areas are cities, where smog caused by ozone pollution from automobile exhausts reaches extremely high, health-endangering levels during the summer months. Excessive ozone levels are also being found in rural areas where it is said to be causing crop losses amounting to billions of dollars. These effects are at least partly due to 16,800 annual passenger miles per capita in the 1980s and 1990s. Recent trends show, however, that CO emissions are decreasing—as much as 52 percent from 2001 to 2010—as a result of various national emissions control programs that have reduced emissions as well as annual passenger miles, which have returned to the levels in

---

10. Council on Environmental Quality, *Conserving America's Wetlands 2006: Two Years of Progress Implementing the President's Goal* (April, 2006).

11. "Our Nations' Air- Status and Trends Through 2010," *Environmental Protection Agency* (2011), http://www.epa.gov/airtrends/2011/report/airpollution.pdf.

12. Environmental Protection Agency, *Six Common Pollutants- Air Trends* (2011), http://www.epa.gov/airtrends/2011/report/sixcommon.pdf.

13. U.S. EPA , *The Green Book* (accessed June, 2013), http://www.epa.gov/airquality/greenbook/data_download.html.

the 1970s of under 12,000 miles per capita annually.[14]

We have long been acutely aware of air pollution problems caused by fossil fuel burning power plants and especially by coal-burning electric power plants. Yet the United States has vacillated between a commitment to eliminate the older, more highly polluting plants and an acceptance of their continued existence. One example of this vacillation involves New Source Review (NSR). The Clean Air Act differentiated between existing sources and new or modified sources—requiring NSR for new or modified sources as a way to balance environmental controls and economic growth.[15] EPA subsequently promulgated a rule exempting from NSR modifications for routine maintenance, repair, and replacement of components that do not exceed 20 percent of the replacement value of the entire unit.[16] That rule was, however, overturned by a court decision,[17] and the previous and more broadly applied NSR approach, triggering NSR when expenditures went beyond "routine maintenance," was reinstated.[18]

The adverse effects of ozone and carbon monoxide from automobiles and many of the emissions from fossil fuel power plants are problems that we have been aware of since the inception of air pollution control laws. Other air related pollution problems that required government attention manifested themselves in subsequent years. Among those were acid rain, the depletion of the atmospheric ozone layer, and global warming caused by carbon dioxide emissions. The sources of acid rain are basically sulphur oxides and nitrogen oxides. Sulphur dioxide emissions decreased by about 50% from 2001 to 2010, but still amount to about 4.5 million metric tons per year from coal fired plants alone.[19] Nitrogen oxides,

---

14. Environmental Protection Agency, *Air Trends- NO₂, CO, and SO₂* (2011), http://epa.gov/airtrends/2011/report/no2coso2.pdf..

15. 42 U.S.C. §7411.

16. 42 U.S.C. §7411(a)(4).

17. *New York v. EPA,* 413 F.3d 3 (D.C. Cir. 2005).

18. 68 Fed. Reg. 61248, 40 CFR Parts 51 and 52.

emitted by coal fired plants at about 1.5 million metric tons per year, declined by 33 percent from 2001 to 2010.[20] The Acid Rain Program, established through the 1990 Clean Air Act amendments, requires progressive reduction of SO_2 emissions from electric power utilities using a cap-and-trade system. Whether the Acid Rain Program is a success or not is highly debated. While SO_2 emissions have declined, the Program's fixed legislative goals created barriers to additional necessary federal and state actions and stifle technological innovation. The acid rain problem and the acid rain amendments to the Clean Air Act that are now in effect and that focus heavily on fossil fuel burning electric power plants are discussed in detail in Chapter 3.

An air pollution problem that has met with a high degree of success on a global scale is depletion of the stratospheric ozone layer by chemicals called chlorofluorocarbons (CFCs) and halons. While ground level ozone is a harmful air pollutant, naturally occurring stratospheric ozone is necessary to prevent solar ultraviolet radiation from reaching the earth's surface. Adverse effects of ozone layer depletion almost certainly include an increased incidence of skin cancer and may include depression of the human immune system as well as a decrease in photosynthesis and crop yields.[21] The ozone depletion problem was first widely publicized in 1985. With uncharacteristic speed for international law changes, the Montreal Protocol on Substances That Deplete The Ozone Layer had entered into force by January of 1989, as 29 countries and the European community formally ratified this protocol. The protocol required the halving of CFC emissions. In 1990, the international community reconvened to negotiate the first schedule for a total phaseout of CFCs and halons in industrialized nations by the year 2000 and added two new ozone depleting compounds—the industrial solvents carbon tetrachloride and

---

19. Environmental Protection Agency, *Emissions Tracking Data* (2013), http://www.epa.gov/airmarkets/quarterlytracking.html.

20. Environmental Protection Agency, *Air Trends- NO₂, CO, and SO₂* (2011), http://epa.gov/airtrends/2011/report/no2coso2.pdf.

21. Fleagle, Robert G. "Everybody Talks About the Weather, But Nobody Explains It," *Seattle Post-Intelligencer* (July 18, 1996).

methyl chloroform—to the list of controlled chemicals. Subsequently, it was agreed to phase out methyl bromide in industrialized countries with exemptions for critical use.[22] As a result, worldwide manufacture of CFCs dropped more than 295,000 tons, a greater than 77% reduction over only a six year period from the pre-Montreal Protocol levels.[23] Scientists have said that the ozone-destroying chemicals currently in the stratosphere will likely cause ozone depletion to continue for another twenty years.[24] As discussed in Chapter 8, these reductions should result in an eventual thickening of the overall ozone layer and, hopefully, a return to its original protective capability.

More recently than its recognition of acid rain and stratospheric ozone layer issues, the global community reached a critical period in understanding and responding to the risks of global climate change. A "greenhouse effect" warms Earth when "greenhouse gases" such as carbon dioxide and methane trap infrared radiation reflected from Earth's surface and prevent it from escaping into space.[25] This warming effect is increased when human activities such as burning fossil fuels release additional greenhouse gases to the atmosphere. In 1992, as part of the Earth Summit in Rio de Janeiro, 150 nations, including the United States, signed the Framework Convention on Climate Change. These countries agreed to cooperate in addressing the risks of climate change and established a non-binding aim that developed countries seek to return their greenhouse gas emission to 1990 levels by the year 2000.[26] Without legally binding targets and timetables, the

22. Council on Environmental Quality, *Environmental Quality - 25th Anniversary Report* (Washington, DC: 1996) pp. 194-196.

23. Brown, Lester R., *State of the World 1996: A Worldwatch Institute Report on Progress Toward a Sustainable Society*, p. 14.

24. Environmental Protection Agency, *Repairing the Ozone Layer* (2013),http://yosemite.epa.gov/R10/airpage.nsf/webpage/Repairing+The+Ozone+Layer.

25. Block, B., "Covering Climate Change," 23 *World Watch Magazine* 2 (March/April 2010).

26. Council on Environmental Quality, Environmental Quality - 25th Anniversary *Report* (Washington, DC: 1996) pp. 205.

international efforts following Rio met with little success. Governments were reluctant to enact domestic laws promoting the reduction of greenhouse gases because of the costs of making reductions and because they did not want to give other countries with less stringent greenhouse gas laws competitive advantages such as attracting industry and the jobs created by their presence.

In 1997, a follow-up to the Rio Conference was held in Kyoto, Japan. Recognizing the shortcomings of the prior agreement, a Protocol or Amendment to the Rio framework convention was drafted that set specific targets and timetables for developed, but not developing, countries. Commitment levels were established on a country by country basis. For example, the United States was to reduce its emissions of greenhouse gases by 7% from their 1990 level. Canada was to reduce by 6%, and the European Community as a whole was to reduce by 8%. These reductions were to be accomplished by 2008-2112. While there are now targets and timetables, many questions remain. Among the most significant are the status of the United States, the future of emissions by developing countries, and the degree to which binding commitments and aggressive rhetoric by the European Community will translate into actual reductions in the EU's emissions.

The Kyoto Protocol, entering into force in 2005, is now international law, but it applies only to the 55 nations that have ratified it. In 2012, Parties to the Kyoto Protocol met in Doha, Qatar, and agreed to extend the Protocol until 2020 and to further limit the scope of the proposed reductions. The United States, the largest emitter of carbon dioxide, has signed but not ratified the Protocol, arguing that to do so would be too expensive and inappropriate so long as developing countries are not subject to mandatory targets and timetables. Emissions by developing countries are increasing rapidly, and China is the largest greenhouse gas emitter in the world.[27] While Canada, Japan, and Russia withdrew in 2011, the European Union, a smaller greenhouse gas emitter than the United States or China, is in the process of making commitments that go beyond those required by the Kyoto Protocol.

---

27. "China overtakes U.S. in greenhouse gas emissions," *New York Times* (June 20, 2007), http://www.nytimes.com/2007/06/20/business/worldbusiness/20iht-emit.1.6227564.html.

Fifteen EU member states committed to reduce greenhouse gas emissions by 8 percent by 2012, a figure they met and almost doubled. Twelve additional EU member states committed to 2020 emissions reduction targets, and all but Slovenia are within range to meet this goal.[28] Climate change issues and U.S. law are discussed in Chapter 3. A discussion on the global level is in Chapter 8.

Many other areas of environmental concern also need to be continually addressed by the legal system. With respect to waste, we have not solved problems of finding appropriate disposal sites for our huge volume of waste, of reducing the amount of waste needing disposal by implementing widespread recycling or reuse approaches, and of finding the funds to pay for the cleanup of existing hazardous waste sites. With respect to energy, the quantity of U.S. energy use per capita appears to have stabilized, but total domestic consumption has continued to grow, and problems associated with the individual sources of energy remain. The burning of high sulfur coal and oil is a major contributor to acid rain, the transport of oil by the Alaskan pipeline has reportedly had much greater adverse effects on wildlife habitat and soil erosion than was predicted, and tanker oil spills still create major environmental disasters even though controls have become stricter. New technology has enabled profitable extraction and processing of new sources of petroleum from tar sands and of natural gas and oil deposits, abundant in the U.S. but resulting in potentially severe and unknown environmental effects. Also, our state governments are as concerned as ever about whether to rely on nuclear power with its operating safety hazards and its radioactive waste disposal problems.

The examples noted in our brief status report on the environment indicate that government involvement in environmental controls is certainly still necessary, but that, at least in the United States, significant progress has been made on a wide variety of environmental matters. Also, the vast majority of Americans are increasingly sensitive to the existence of environmental issues and now believe that those issues are of major

---

28. European Commission on Climate Action, *Study shows EU remains on track toward Kyoto emission targets* (Oct. 24, 2012) http://ec.europa.eu/clima/news/articles/news_2012102401_en.htm.

personal concern to them. This awareness is bound to lead to further improvement of environmental conditions in the United States. With regard to other parts of the world, the environmental status is not nearly as good, and the environmental prospects for the future cannot be viewed with the same optimism.

Developing countries are in a poor environmental state today and will need a great deal of help in order to achieve a sound environmental future. World population is growing steadily by roughly 78 million people per year, equal to the population of 10 New York Cities. Today's population of more than 7 billion is projected to grow to around 9.5 billion by 2050, and is expected to be overwhelmingly urban. Perhaps of greatest significance is the fact that while population growth could end in some developed countries, [29] the population of the 48 least-developed countries is projected to double by 2050,[30] and one study finds that global population may soar to 11 billion by 2100 as African population quadruples. [31] With rare exception, all the cities with the worst air quality are in the developing countries. A huge percentage of all illness in the developing world can be traced to unsafe or inadequate water supplies and sanitation, and HIV/AIDS is highly concentrated in some of the poorest nations. The developing countries also have environmental problems not often even thought about in the developed countries—food, clothing, and shelter. Although the 1972 Declaration of The United Nations Conference on The Human Environment called for the developed countries to make efforts to reduce the gap between themselves and the developing countries, that gap continues to exist and likely is widening.

The financial resources simply do not exist in the developing

---

29. For example, Germany's population has fallen (Daley, Suzane, "Germany Fights Population Drop," *New York Times* p. A1 (Aug. 14, 2013).

30. Population Reference Bureau, *Fact Sheet: World Population Trends 2012* (2012), http://www.prb.org/Publications/Datasheets/2012/world-population-data-sheet/fact-sheet-world-population.aspx.

31. Reilly, J., "Global Population to Soar to 11 billion by 2100 as African population quadruples," *Daily Mail* (June 13, 2013), available at http://www.dailymail.co.uk/news/article-2341084/Global-population-soar-11-billion-2100-African-population-quadruples.html#socialLinks.

countries for them to solve their own environmental problems and provide decent living conditions for their people. The developed nations will have to bear the financial burden of improving environmental conditions throughout the world. International cooperation with respect to the global environment has been shown to be possible by the adoption of the Montreal Protocol concerning ozone depletion, and the problems of the developing countries should also be seen as global environmental problems. For example, unchecked population growth produces greater demands for cleared land which results in the burning of tropical rain forests. This adds significantly to the greenhouse effect and exacerbates global climate change. Even without addressing the question of whether it is morally right to allow a large part of the world to be environmentally poor, it is in the self-interest of the developed countries to have environmental conditions in the developing countries improve drastically. Throughout the world, as well as in the United States, there is certainly the need for a significant increase in environmental controls.

3. Population – The Overriding Issue

Having addressed the need for environmental law in terms of the historical need and the current status of the environment, it is imperative that we consider what many people think is the issue that may dominate and clearly has major implications with respect to nearly every other environmental issue—the topic of population. As noted above, about 78 million people are being added to the world each year and population is becoming more and more concentrated in urban areas. The number of people living on Earth more than doubled between 1950 and 2000, from 2.5 to 6.1 billion.[32] Family size in most wealthy nations has declined and they may reverse their population growth eventually, but population in the poorer nations may continue to have a high growth rate. Furthermore, the U.S. population is growing at the fastest rate of any industrial country. Between 1990 and 2010 the U.S. population increased by

---

32. *Ibid.*

60 million people.[33] Its current population of over 300 million is expected to increase to 350 million by 2025 and 400 million by 2050. More people and greater concentrations create added strains on the environment. These range from increased demand for energy and food to increased pollution and greater need for waste disposal facilities. Suppose a city of 3 million people is struggling to at least have its urban air quality be no worse than in 2000. If the city's 2000 population remained constant, then environmental regulation of pollution generating activities would only need to ensure that the same people are doing the same activities as in 2000. In reality, population growth makes environmental regulation increasingly difficult. If, by 2025, our hypothetical city's population increases to 4 million, environmental regulations will need to ensure that people are doing fewer pollution generating activities in order to maintain the urban air quality at its 2000 level. This problem is not unique to air quality regulation—the population problem magnifies all environmental problems—and, in turn, environmental problems create dire consequences for people. Experts have predicted that anywhere between 25 million and 2 billion people may become environmental refugees fleeing worsening environmental conditions.[34]

So what has caused population to grow so fast? Contrary to what might be one's first thought, at least with respect to humans, it has not been simply *increased* birth rates that has stimulated the population to grow, but also *decreased* death rates. Globally, life expectancy at birth is projected to continue to rise from 68 years to 76 years in 2050 and to 81 years in 2100. Modern medicine contributed substantially to the stimulation of population growth by reducing infant mortality as well as preserving the lives of individuals who would have died from diseases such as heritable diabetes or hemophilia. Deaths among children under 5 years

---

33. U.S. Census Bureau, *Population Distribution and Change: 2000-2010* (2011),http://www.census.gov/prod/cen2010/briefs/c2010br-01.pdf.

34. Friedman, L., "Climate Migrants Present a Maze of Unresolved Legal Issues," *Climate Wire* (Apr. 4, 2012), http://stevens.vermontlaw.edu:2088/climatewire/stories/1059962462/search?keyword=environmental+refugee.

declined from 19 million in 1960 to 9.6 million in 2012.[35] Coverage of children immunized against six major childhood diseases increased from 5% in 1974 to 80% in 2012.[36] These people may now live and reproduce. Unfortunately, not all medical developments have resulted in positive trends in the lives of people. Despite recent declines in rates of infection, HIV/AIDS has become a major factor in the reversal of population growth rates in some areas of the world, such as Africa, where life expectancy in 2011 was 56 years[37]—a slowing of population growth, but in a way that no one could rationally consider to be positive. Global inequality among nations with respect to life expectancy has existed for many years; however that inequality has been dramatically exacerbated in recent years by AIDS in Africa.[38]

Other factors that have been implicated in stimulating population growth include religion, increased food supplies, greater mobility of the populace, industrialization, and changes in moral standards. While medicine and food can be viewed as manipulating death rates, religion and industrialization probably manipulate birth rates. Birth rates may also be high in less developed countries because of their lack of a social security system. Parents in these countries need to have more children to provide security for them in their old age. Developed nations also have age distribution issues that involve wanting more younger people in order to provide for the needs of its elderly. Australia has an aging population of about 22 million and attempted to encourage higher birth rates by giving parents a baby bonus of $3000 for every newborn, resulting in an increased population growth rate from 1.7 to 2 percent before the "bonus" was withdrawn in 2013.[39] Whatever one would choose to

---

35. World Health Organization, *Children: Reducing Mortality* (2012), http://www.who.int/mediacentre/factsheets/fs178/en/.

36. World Health Organization, *World Health Report 2012*, www.who.int/en.

37. World Health Organization, *HIV surveillance, estimates, monitoring and evaluation* (2013), http://www.who.int/hiv/topics/me/en/index.html.

38. World Health Organization, *Life Expectancy* (2012), http://www.who.int/gho/mortality_burden_disease/life_tables/situation_trends_text/en/.

39. Sustainable Population Australia, *Baby bonus cut very welcome* (May 15, 2013),

emphasize as the "cause" or "causes" of any perceived population growth problems, the fact is that the human population is increasing and may eventually reach the carrying capacity or finite limit of Earth as discussed in Part B.1 of this chapter.

The population issue is not merely a question of numbers. It is substantively a question of consumption and distribution of consumption. The technology explosion of the twentieth century has allowed people to consume more. Since 1950, the world has consumed as many goods and services as all previous generations combined. This consumption can be directly linked to the increased pollution problems of recent times, such as the increased amounts of air pollutants caused by increased consumption of fossil fuels. From a distribution perspective, the population problem impacts both industrialized and developing countries, but the dramatic consumption increases discussed earlier has occurred primarily in the industrialized nations. While industrialized nations account for only 22 percent of Earth's inhabitants, they also account for two-thirds of consumption. U.S. consumption, with less than 5% of the world's population, produces 23% of all carbon dioxide emissions. While consumption is centered in developed nations, some developing nations are increasing their own consumption and their production of goods for consumption in other countries. This increases their contributions to the world's environmental problems. China surpassed the U.S. as the top carbon dioxide emitter in 2007, although, on a per capita basis, the U.S. is still the biggest emitter.[40] Global population growth, together with increasing global consumption, are putting ever greater pressure on all aspects of Earth's environment.

The complexity of the population growth problem has been difficult to address at both the domestic and international law levels. At the international level, there is very little in the way of law on how to control population growth. At the domestic level, some countries such as China and India have instituted population control

---

http://www.population.org.au/articles/2013-05-15/mr-baby-bonus-cut-very-welcome.

40. Yale Center for Environmental Law and Policy, *Climate Policy and Emissions Data Sheet: China* (2012), http://envirocenter.yale.edu/uploads/pdf/China_Climate_Policy_Data_Sheet.pdf.

measures that have had varying degrees of public acceptance. In the late 1970s, China introduced a strict population control program limiting families to one child and later said that pregnancies involving abnormal fetuses or those with congenital disabilities should be halted.[41] Although the people of China rebelled and the international community responded with outrage to this later position, the one child aspect of China's policy continues to exist. Employment, housing opportunities, and other social measures are used as enforcement tools of that policy. Also in the late 1970s, India had what has been referred to as a "ruthless sterilization campaign." The highly coercive nature of that campaign was subsequently rejected;[42] however India's family planning program remains dependent on female sterilization with 4.6 million tubal ligations in 2002-03 compared to 114,000 vasectomies and only 7% of married women using condoms or birth-control pills.[43]

Viewing the population issue from the positive perspective, the global rate of population growth has declined from its peak of 2.1% per year to under 1.2 percent in 2010, and is projected to decline to less than 0.45 percent by 2050.[44] Women began having fewer children as infant mortality rates declined and modern means of contraception became available and increasingly attractive in most countries. Of potentially great significance, especially in the long term, in September of 1994, the United Nations Conference on Population and Development was held in Cairo, Egypt. After nine days of arguing about sexuality and morals, the conference ended with a broad endorsement of a new strategy for stabilizing the world's population, mainly by giving women more control over their lives. For the first time, a policy was agreed upon by many

41. Mufson, Steven, "China Plans to Restrict 'Inferior' Births; Compulsory Abortions, Sterilization Aim at 'Heightening Standards'" and "China Softens Bill on Eugenics," *Washington Post*, (Dec. 22, 1993) p. A1 and (Dec. 30, 1993) p. A17.

42. Waldman, A., "States in India Take New Steps to Limit Births," *New York Times* (November 7, 2003) p. A1.

43. "For Sterilization, Target is Women," *New York Times* (November 7, 2003) p. A6.

44. United Nations, *World Population Prospects* (2011), http://esa.un.org/unpd/wpp/ Documentation/pdf/WPP2010_Volume-I_Comprehensive-Tables.pdf.

members of the international community that went beyond traditional family planning to include reproductive health care, enabling women to make their own choices, and promoting equality between the sexes.[45] The policy of empowering women has gained momentum over time in countries like India, especially with respect to education and entrepreneurship.[46] That empowerment will hopefully follow the approach begun in Cairo and lead the world to stabilize population at ultimately a lower number than previously predicted and thus reduce the strains on our environment.

Although population, in terms of magnitude, distribution, and related issues of consumption, would appear to be the overriding environmental issue, we will not discuss it directly in relation to each of the environmental topics covered in this book. It is, however, extremely important for us to recognize that population is a significant driving force with respect to aspects of every other environmental topic and the need for environmental controls.

4. Legislative Perspectives

Having considered whether legislative environmental controls are needed, let's briefly note two contrasting points of view about how to regulate various types of activities affecting the environment. Consider the hypothetical "pure economist" and "pure ecologist." Diagrammatically, the resulting legislative alternatives would be:

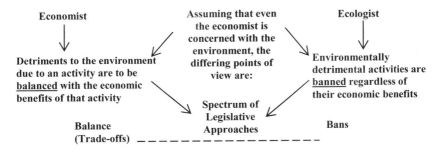

---

45. Cowell, Alan, "U.N. Population Meeting Adopts Program of Action," *New York Times* (Sept. 14, 1994) p. A2.

46. United Nations, *Women's Empowerment and Inclusion* (2013),http://www.undp.org/content/india/en/home/ourwork/womenempowerment/overview.html.

While both are concerned with the environment, the economist would tend to balance environmental concerns with the economic benefits to be derived from an activity and allow environmental harm when it is outweighed by the economic benefits. On the other hand, the ecologist's tendency is to allow activities only if they are not detrimental to the environment: activities which are detrimental to the environment should be banned regardless of their economic benefit.[47]

There is, of course, a spectrum between the legislative poles of always balancing benefits and detriments (allowing trade-offs) and of always banning detrimental activity. The type and magnitude of a particular environmental problem are relevant to where on that spectrum our legislatures should place themselves. Is the environmental problem one of physical health or mostly one of aesthetics? Is a health problem one which has proven, drastic consequences for large numbers of people, or is the health problem speculative, relatively minor with respect to effects, or one involving very few people? Also quite relevant to where on the legislative spectrum a particular legislature will place itself is the degree of governmental control which is politically saleable. How many people would favor a total shutdown of our automobile plants (with the resulting unemployment and economic decline) if the automakers could not meet the requirements of the Clean Air Act? Past extensions of the Clean Air Act deadlines on automakers have been a trade-off clearly mandated by our political process. As we consider various pieces of environmental legislation, we will see that many are quite balance-oriented. For example, emission standards for stationary sources are to be set by EPA based on the "best system of emission reduction" but "taking into account the cost of achieving such reduction"—a balance.[48] Some provisions, however, are on the "ban" side of the spectrum. For example, the Endangered Species Act has been said to be the closest thing to an absolute legislative command in public natural resources law and economic considerations play no role in determining the status of a

---

47. Heller, W., "Coming to Terms with Growth and the Environment," In *Energy, Economic Growth, and the Environment*, S. Schurr, Ed., 3:4-29 (1971).

48. 42 U.S.C. § 7411(a)(1).

species.[49]

With the above introduction, we will leave for the reader's determination the question of whether and to what extent we need government-imposed environmental controls, and, if so, where on the balance/ban spectrum of legislative approaches our government should be on any particular environmental issue. Regardless of our individual viewpoints on what should be the degree of involvement between government and the environment, we do have a substantial body of environmental law in existence at the federal, state, and local levels, and it is to the question of what that law is that we now turn our attention. Let us then begin to consider what the law is by first looking at the sources of power for governmental control of the environment.

C. WHERE IT COMES FROM

The United States Constitution does not, in direct and specific words, give Congress power to control the environment. The Constitution makes no mention of "environment." The basic source of federal power with respect to the environment is found in Article I, Section 8 of the United States Constitution (the Commerce Clause) which vests in Congress the power "to regulate Commerce . . . among the several States . . . ." Historically, this granting to the federal government of the power to regulate interstate commerce (as contrasted to intrastate commerce) was based largely on the idea of preventing states from enacting laws which, although they might be beneficial to one state, would have a detrimental effect on the economic system of the new nation. Tariffs imposed by individual states resulted in adverse economic effects on other states and the nation as a whole. These types of actions contributed significantly to the weakness that the country experienced under the Articles of Confederation. The new Constitution sought to remedy that weakness by giving Congress the authority to regulate interstate commerce.

Although the words have not changed, the past 200 years have seen massive expansion of the scope of the Commerce Clause. That

---

49. Laitos, Jan G., *Natural Resources Law*, (St. Paul: Westgroup, 2002) pp. 188 and 190.

expansion, in the nature of broad powers claimed by Congress, has been found by the courts to be within Congress' power under the Constitution, and today, Congress' power is said to include not only the regulation of interstate commerce, but also activities carried on wholly within one state but which have effects on interstate commerce. The Supreme Court, however, may be changing direction and beginning to tighten the reins on Congress' power under the Commerce Clause.

A few examples of how Congress has and may in the future use its power under the Commerce Clause will illustrate what we know today about its extent and about whether that power has been or may be curtailed. Clearly, a natural gas pipeline from one state to others is a matter of interstate commerce and, therefore, environmental regulation with respect to the pipeline is within the federal power. But what about local rubbish disposal? Consider the following chain of events: the disposal of rubbish at a local disposal site might lead to runoffs after rains; such runoffs might pollute a lake; polluted lake waters have fewer sport fish in them; fewer sport fish means fewer fishermen; fewer fishermen buy less gasoline and fishing equipment; gasoline and fishing equipment are items produced and marketed in interstate commerce. Since Congress has been found to have the authority under the Commerce Clause to regulate activities which affect interstate commerce, Congress has the authority, if it chooses to use it, to regulate local rubbish disposal.

One might contend that the effect on interstate commerce due to what happens at one local dump in rural New England is quite small and that Congress' control does not extend to this small dump. The United States Supreme Court put that contention to rest many years ago when it addressed that argument in the context of a farmer who was growing wheat for consumption on his own farm, but in an amount in excess of his quota under existing federal legislation. The Court found that the aggregate of his excess production along with every other farmer who might then over-produce created enough of an effect on interstate commerce that Congress could regulate the activity.[50] Just as the one small farmer was found to be under

---

50. *Wickard v. Filburn*, 317 U.S. 111, 127 (1942).

Congress' control, so could the one small dump in rural New England be subject to environmental control by the federal government pursuant to the power of Congress under the Commerce Clause of the United States Constitution. In fact, small rural dumps are subject to federal control under the Resource Conservation and Recovery Act, and, pursuant to that act, concerns about run-offs from landfills have led to the requirement that landfills be lined to trap materials that might otherwise leach out of them and enter the groundwater.[51]

If Congress can control a small rural dump, is there any limit to Congressional power with respect to environmental issues? In *United States v. Lopez*, the Supreme Court, by a 5-4 vote, told Congress that the Gun Free School Zone Act, which banned the possession of firearms near schools, was beyond the power that Congress has under the Commerce Clause. The Court said that if the commerce power extended to every effect on interstate commerce, then there would be no limit on the power of Congress.[52] Thus Congress' power under the Commerce Clause seemed to require some sort of relationship, connection, or nexus between the activity being regulated and interstate commerce; however, beyond the fact pattern that gun control near schools does not satisfy the need for such a relationship, the type and degree of the required relationship remained undefined in *Lopez*. *Lopez* was not an environmental case, but the need for a "nexus" was reaffirmed although likely still not clearly defined in *Rapanos v. United States*,[53] a 2006 U.S. Supreme Court case involving the requirement of a permit under the Clean Water Act in order for a developer to fill wetlands. The Supreme Court split 4 to 4 on whether the wetlands were sufficiently connected to a navigable body of water and thus within the scope of the Clean Water Act. The ninth Justice of the Court decided the case by voting to send the case back to the lower court for it to determine whether the

---

51. 40 CFR § 258.40.

52. *United States v. Lopez*, 514 U.S. 549 (1995).

53. 126 S. Ct. 2208.

wetlands had a "significant nexus" to navigable waters. By having the case continue on the issue of whether the wetlands were within the scope of the Clean Water Act, the Court avoided the constitutional question of whether, if Congress intended to control the wetlands through the Clean Water Act, does it have the power to do so under the Commerce Clause. The extent of power given to Congress by the Commerce Clause remains an open issue, but consider, for example, whether the use of a toxic material wholly within one state could ever be found to lack the interstate commerce relationship necessary for Congress to control its use. Unless Congress' environmental control fits within its authority under the Commerce Clause, that control would very likely be unconstitutional.

In addition to the possible limits on the environmental authority Congress derives from its power to regulate commerce, the Supreme Court has also expressed limits on Congress' ability to regulate state activities that might have environmental implications. *Seminole Tribe v. Florida*, which did not involve environmental issues, has been read to say that Congress does not have the authority to abrogate a state's immunity under the 11th Amendment to the U.S. Constitution from being sued by private citizens in a federal court.[54] In *Alden v. Maine*, the Court said that the 11th Amendment did not even permit private lawsuits to be brought in state courts for damages due to violations of federal law.[55] States run facilities that emit air pollutants, discharge water pollutants, use huge amounts of natural resources, and dispose of huge quantities of waste. Might all state activities with environmental effects be held to be immune from federal control? If Congress, acting under its Commerce Clause power, requires by statute that a state do something with respect to an environmental matter and the state refuses, might there be no way to subject the state's environmental action to federal law due to the state immunity the Court found in the 11th Amendment? Yet another limit on the power of Congress appears to come from the Supreme Court's interpretation of the

---

54. *Seminole Tribe of Florida v. Florida*, 517 U.S. 44 (1996).

55. *Alden v. Maine*, 527 U.S. 706 (1999).

10th Amendment. Prior to the *Seminole* case, state power had been protected from Congressional Commerce Clause power in *New York v. United States*,[56] in which the Court struck down Congress' attempt to force a state to take title to nuclear waste if the state had not provided for nuclear waste disposal in line with Congressional standards. The *New York* decision was based on the states' reserved powers under the 10th Amendment to the U.S. Constitution. Some legal commentators have stated that the *Lopez, Seminole, Alden,* and *New York* decisions are the thin edge of an activist judicial wedge seeking to readjust the balance of power between federal and state governments. If that prediction comes true, and if the legal theories of those cases are applied to environmental issues, the power of the federal government to control the environment could be severely curtailed.[57]

Lopez, Seminole, and *Alden* were 5-4 decisions against federal power, and the "plurality" decision in *Rapanos* raised but did not resolve the federal power issue in what was clearly an environmental law context. In the 2004 case of *Alaska Dept. of Environmental Conservation v. EPA*,[58] the Court decided by a 5-4 vote in favor of federal power. EPA had determined that Alaska acted improperly in applying the "best available technology" standard of the Clean Air Act for emissions from a zinc mine, and EPA's decision was upheld by the Court. *Alaska* was a statutory case under the Clean Air Act, not a constitutional power or immunity case, but it did involve federal vs. state regulation. In *Massachusetts v. EPA*, the U.S. Supreme Court went even farther in favor of federal power. The Court held that even though EPA asserted it did not have authority, the Clean Air Act *does* give EPA the authority to regulate greenhouse gas emissions to prevent climate change, and that EPA must develop standards for any

---

56. 505 U.S. 144 (1992).

57. Percival, Robert V., "Environmental Implications of the Rehnquist Court's New Federalism," *Natural Resources & Environment* (ABA Section of Environment, Energy, and Resources, Summer 2002).

58. 540 U.S. 461 (2004).

greenhouse gases affecting public health or welfare.[59] With many cases still to come, with close votes in the past, and with the always present likelihood of changes in Court personnel, there is continuing doubt about the extent of federal environmental power, especially when that power would apply to states.

Some people have suggested that the possibility of a Supreme Court interpretation of the Constitution that would preclude federal control of the environment should be addressed by amending the Constitution to expressly provide for environmental power for Congress. This is an intriguing but potentially troubling approach. A constitutional amendment expressly empowering Congress to control the environment would negate any arguments that such a power, now derived from the Commerce Clause, does not exist. There is precedent for establishing express environmental power in the basic structure of a federal system of government. The original constitutional framework of the European Union (EU—formerly known as the European Economic Community under the Treaty of Rome) did not expressly give the community power with respect to the environment. Instead, like in the U.S., such authority was exerted and held to be valid based on the economic and commerce provisions in the treaty that created the EU. Subsequently, the Single European Act amended that treaty to expressly provide environmental power to the EU. Doubts have been raised, however, concerning whether it would be advantageous to conduct a dialogue about an environmental power amendment to the U.S. Constitution. Since Congress now does have environmental power as evidenced by the vast matrix of federal statutes and regulations, would pursuing such an amendment help legitimize the arguments of the skeptics that an environmental power derivative of the Commerce Clause really does not exist?

In addition to control at the federal level, there exists extensive environmental control at the state and local levels of government. The source of power for environmental control at these levels is the "police power," the power to protect the public health, public safety and the general welfare. The police power is inherent in the sovereign which is the state, and is also delegated by the states via

---

59. 549 U.S. 497 (2007).

enabling statutes and/or State Constitution provisions to the local governments that the states create. There are limits on the exercise of the states' police powers, such as the constitutional prohibitions against the taking of private property without just compensation discussed in Chapter 4. It would be fair to say, however, that the police power gives quite broad authority to state and local governments to establish controls with respect to environmental matters.

D. HOW TO FIND THE LAW

The law on a given question is sometimes unclear. For example, the language in a statute may be subject to more than one reasonable interpretation, or there may be a conflict between two regulations which purport to control the same activity. In most situations, however, the law is quite clear if one can find it. Finding the law is largely a matter of understanding what the sources of the law are, being familiar with a few systems for gaining access to these sources, and going to a law library or other library which has basic legal materials. Table I is a shorthand version of the narrative description for finding the law which follows. Although this description may appear complex, if one proceeds a step at a time through the process, the complexity will rapidly disappear.

One major distinction to be made when considering the sources of law is that between the so-called common law and law by legislation. Law by legislation is law which has been enacted through the legislative process of any level of government. Congress' National Environmental Policy Act (NEPA), the Freshwater Wetlands Act of the State of New York, and the zoning ordinance of the Town of Barnard, Vermont are all examples of legislation. In contrast to legislation, the common law has often been referred to as judge-made law because courts have determined that the facts of a situation are such that they should provide a remedy even though there has been no legislative enactment.

One example of common law action which is often used in environmental matters is the "nuisance" action. An activity of X which causes a substantial and unreasonable interference with Y's use and enjoyment of Y's land will constitute a common law

Table I. Where to Look for the Law (Primary Sources)

	Legislative Law	Administrative Law (Regulations)	Common Law & Interpretation of Legislative & Administrative Law
Federal	• United States Code • United States Code Annotated • United States Code Service • Statutes at Large	• Code of Federal Regulations • Federal Register	• United States Reports (U.S.) • Supreme Court Reports (Law. Ed.) • Supreme Court Reporter (S. Ct.) • Federal Reporter (F., F.2d, F.3d)– Circuit Courts of Appeals • Federal Supplement (F.Supp./F.Supp. 2d) –District Courts • Federal Administrative Agency decisions in publications such as the Public Utilities Reports and agency websites
State	• State Statutes	• State Administrative Codes • State Administrative Regulations	• Regional Reporters • State Reporters • State administrative agency decisions in widely varying types of publications
Local	• Municipal Ordinances	• Local Administrative Regulations	• Local administrative agency decisions in widely varying types of publications

nuisance, and a court will provide a remedy for Y even though no legislation prohibits X's activity or provides Y with a remedy. Both the common law and legislative law exist at the state and federal levels. In Chapter 3, using aircraft noise as an example, we will consider what happens when there is a conflict between state or local law and federal law. A less complicated situation exists where there is a conflict between legislation and the common law at the same level of government. In such a situation, the common law is overridden by the will of the legislative process.

Federal legislative law (also known as "statutory law") is enacted by Congress. At the end of each session, all of the legislation enacted in that session is compiled and published in chronological order in the *United States Statutes at Large*. While these volumes have subject indexes, they are not cumulative, and it would therefore be necessary to search through many volumes to find all of the statutes relating to a given topic. The federal statutes have therefore been codified, which means that they are arranged in a subject-oriented manner under fifty broad topics called titles. The official codification, which is called the United States Code (U.S.C.), is revised every six years and is updated between revisions by annual hardbound supplements. Two major law book publishers, West Publishing Company and LexisNexis, publish unofficial versions known as United States Code Annotated (U.S.C.A.) and United States Code Service (U.S.C.S.), respectively. Both of these sets are updated by the issuance of annual "pocket parts"—supplemental pamphlets which fit into pockets at the back of the hardbound volumes. U.S.C.A. and U.S.C.S. are more useful than the official codification because, in addition to the statutory language, they contain references to court decisions and other valuable research aids. The U.S.C. is available for free online through FDsys http://www.gpo.gov/fdsys/ which provides online access to official Federal Government publications, through FindLaw http://www.findlaw.com/casecode/uscodes/, the Cornell Legal Information Institute http://www4.law.cornell.edu/uscode/, and the Public Library of Law http://www.plol.org/. The U.S.C. is also available through the fee-based services of Westlaw, Lexis, Bloomberg Law, and other services.

If one wanted to find the provisions of NEPA, the National Environmental Policy Act, one might look in the "Popular Name Table" of the General Index of U.S.C.A. or on FindLaw or Cornell LII, and find that NEPA is PL 91-190, Jan. 1, 1970, 83 Stat. 852 (Title 42, §§ 4321, 4331-4335, 4341-4347). NEPA is thus Public Law 91-190 which appears at volume 83 of the *United States Statutes at Large*, beginning on page 852. The provisions of NEPA also appear in Title 42 of the U.S.C., U.S.C.A. and U.S.C.S. in sections 4321, 4331-4335 and 4341-4347. Other access methods are possible depending on what you know and what you are seeking. For example, if the popular name were unknown, but the subject matter was known, one might look in the General Index of U.S.C.A.

under "Environmental Policy" in order to find provisions concerning the subject matter, or do a search in one of the online versions. Once the above-mentioned books are picked up and inspected, finding federal statutory law is quite simple; however, care must be taken to be sure that the law you find is up to date. This is done in the books by checking the supplement volume of U.S.C. or the "pocket part" updates which are found in the backs of the volumes of U.S.C.A. and U.S.C.S. In this way, amendments to NEPA since its original enactment in 1970 may be found.

State statutes may be found using similar tools in the state statute books which are published individually by each state and are available in libraries as well as online through state web sites. Local legislative law is usually available at libraries in the local geographic area or through the local government unit itself.

When we come to finding the common law, the locating system is not much different from that used in finding legislative law. The basic structure and relationship of the federal and state court systems are shown in Figure 9. At both the federal and state level, court decisions are arranged and cited on a chronological basis by volume and page number in a "reporter" which contains the decisions of a particular court. United States Supreme Court decisions may be found in the United States Reports (U.S.), the Supreme Court Reporter (S.Ct.), or the Lawyers' edition of the Supreme Court Reports (Law. Ed. or L.Ed.). Lower federal court decisions are found in the Federal Reporter (Fed. or F. and F.2d or F.3d for the later second and third series of the Federal Reporter) if they are United States Circuit Court of Appeals cases and in the Federal Supplement (F.Supp. and F.Supp. 2d) if they are United States District Court cases. State court decisions appear in regional reporters such as the North Eastern Reporter (N.E.) and the Pacific Reporter (P.) as well as in official State Reporters such as the Vermont Reports. Federal and state common law is also available on Westlaw, Lexis, and Bloomberg Law, and, for recent years online through sites such as:

FindLaw, http://www.findlaw.com/casecode/
Cornell Legal Information Institute, http://www.law.cornell.edu/
The Public Library of Law http://www.plol.org/

Google Scholar http://scholar.google.com/

It should be noted that while legislation is enacted through the legislative process and the common law is made by courts without action by the legislature, courts become involved with legislation by virtue of their role as interpreters of legislation. Thus, the fourth column of Table I shows the location of both the court decisions

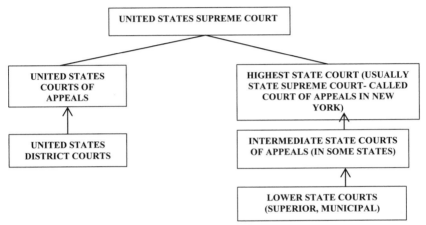

Figure 9. The court structure.

involving the common law and those decisions which provide interpretations of legislative law. Court decisions which contribute to the body of common law and those which interpret legislative law are all reported together and are all cited in the same manner. As examples, the common law nuisance case of *Boomer v. Atlantic Cement Co.* is 257 N.E.2d 870, and *Calvert Cliffs Coordinating Committee v. Atomic Energy Commission*, a case which interprets NEPA, is 449 F.2d 1109. This means that the *Boomer* decision appears in volume 257 of the second series of the North Eastern Reporter and begins on page 870, and *Calvert Cliffs* appears in volume 449 of the second series of the Federal Reporter and begins on page 1109.

If one knows the citation of a case, finding the case is a one-step process. If one knows only the name of the case or does not know of a particular case but wishes to find cases about a given topic, the additional step of consulting a reference tool such as a digest or legal encyclopedia, or of doing a search of the full text versions of the cases online, must be added. There is a *Federal Practice Digest* and there are other digests arranged by region (the *Pacific Digest*), by state (the *Vermont Digest*), and chronologically covering both federal and states cases (the *Decennial* and *General Digests*). These digests provide brief abstracts of cases, as well as case names and citations, under numerous subject headings. The online equivalent of digests are also available on Westlaw and Lexis.

Legal encyclopedias such as *American Jurisprudence 2d* and *Corpus Juris Secundum* can provide one with general discussions of many topics and case citations relevant to those topics. By using these reference tools and their various indices, cases which discuss the topic of one's interest may be located.

Just as we noted with respect to legislation, care must be taken when reading court decisions to be sure to determine whether those decisions are still "good law" or whether they have been overruled or narrowed in applicability by later cases. The analogue to checking the "pocket parts" and supplements in the statute books is to check the cases you have read in a legal citator. The three main legal citators are Shepard's, KeyCite and BCite, which are available online through Lexis, Westlaw, and Bloomberg Law respectively. Shepard's is also available in book format. Look in the volume of *Shepard's Citations* that applies to the court that wrote the decision. *Shepard's* is organized by listing cases by volume and by the page number on which they begin. Under each case citation, all other cases which have cited the case being checked are listed by their volume and page numbers. Abbreviations are used to indicate whether the subsequent cases merely mention the case being checked, follow the case being checked as the controlling case (f), or overrule the case in a subsequent case involving another situation (o). By updating your case in a legal citator, you will be able to determine the current importance of that case as "the law" as well as find additional later cases which may discuss the topic in which you are interested. You can also check online using Westlaw, Lexis, or Bloomberg Law to see if your case is still good law.

Having considered how to find the law as enacted through the legislative process and the common law as made by the courts, we should next consider a second major distinction in sources of law— the distinction between legislation and regulation. Legislation is the product of the legislative process, and it is binding unless it is violative of a constitutional provision. Regulations are usually the product of the administrative agencies, and they have the force of law if there is legislation which authorizes the creation of the regulation and the regulation is consistent with what the legislation mandates. Just as legislation exists at various levels of government, regulations can also be developed at the federal, state, and local levels. At the state and local levels there are different systems for publishing regulations depending on your location.

The system for finding federal regulations is easily described. Many state web sites include regulations. The permanent home of a federal regulation is in the Code of Federal Regulations (CFR). The CFR is organized and cited by title and section numbers. Title 40 is Protection of Environment. Title 10 is Energy. 40 CFR § 1502.4 outlines the major federal actions requiring the preparation of environmental impact statements under the National Environmental Policy Act. The book version of the CFR is completely revised once a year (one quarter of the titles are revised in each calendar quarter), and is also available through FDsys http://www.gpo.gov/fdsys/. An unofficial version is available at eCFR http://www.ecfr.gov/ and updated within days. Prior to finding its way into a revision of CFR, a new federal rule or regulation will appear in the Federal Register (Fed. Reg.) which publishes activities of the federal agencies on a chronological basis. The Federal Register is published each business day, and the contents for the day are shown at the beginning of the issue. Cites to the Federal Register are by volume and page. For example, at 55 Fed. Reg. 10444, on March 21, 1990, the Forest Service established a decision-making framework for the consideration of oil and gas leasing activities on National Forest Service lands, which was codified in 36 CFR § 228.102. On February 15, 2007 (in 72 Fed. Reg. 7391), the Forest Service amended 36 CFR § 228.102 when it issued categorical exclusions from National Environmental Policy Act analyses for drilling in areas where officials do not anticipate negative environmental effects. Both the CFR and the Federal Register are available through FDsys. Administrative regulations may be interpreted by courts or by the agencies themselves. The various locations of interpretations of administrative law may be seen in column four of

Table I.

Additional sources of information concerning environmental law include periodicals and loose-leaf services. Most law schools publish law reviews either annually or more frequently. Articles and Notes in these periodicals usually provide in-depth analysis and commentary on various aspects of the law including environmental law. Some reviews have devoted themselves entirely to publication of articles relating to environmental matters. Law review articles are indexed in the *Index to Legal Periodicals*, *Current Law Index*, *LegalTrac* and *InfoTrac*. Many are also available through Google Scholar. For keeping up-to-date on changes in the law, numerous looseleaf services which provide information on environmental topics can be consulted. A few illustrative examples might be the *Environment Reporter* from the Bureau of National Affairs (BNA), available in book form and through Bloomberg Law, and the Federal Energy Guidelines from the Federal Energy Regulatory Commission. The *Environmental Law Reporter* from the Environmental Law Institute (ELI) is available online. These resources contain material such as current developments, in addition to statutory and regulatory material.

In closing this section on how to find the law, we should note that since law libraries have online research capabilities, finding resources online is a well-established approach to legal research. The fee-based Lexis, Westlaw, and Bloomberg Law legal research systems allow users to obtain the full text of legal documents from numerous databases. These databases include, among others, statutes, regulations, and case law at both the federal and state levels. Databases also contain periodicals such as law reviews and loose-leaf services.

Westlaw, Lexis and Bloomberg Law offer enormous and impressive specialized environmental law sources which contain resources in federal and state primary material including environmental statutes, regulations and cases, as well as environmental law reviews, news, and other secondary sources. These resources are well organized with sophisticated search engines that are often easier to use than free web sites. They may also provide resources not easily available elsewhere.

The databases may be accessed in a variety of ways depending on what you know and what you are trying to find. For example, if you are interested in a subject, asbestos, and you want to find information online about asbestos, you use "asbestos" as your key word. This could result in your getting a huge number of documents, so you would try to narrow your search. If your interest were federal regulations concerning asbestos removal from pipes, as opposed to the medical effects of exposure to asbestos, you could limit your results to the federal regulations database, CFR, and use "asbestos," "removal," and "pipes" as your search terms. One document you would obtain is 40 CFR Part 763, Appendix C to Subpart E. This document provides recommended methods of removal of asbestos containing materials in schools. Of course, if you knew exactly which document you were looking for, then you could simply search by citation.

In addition to finding the law in bodies of materials specifically devoted to the law, many law and law related materials can be found on the Internet. There are an inexhaustible number of sources available. One must be aware, however, that while these sources provide a potentially valuable source of information, the accuracy and reliability of this information is only as good as the organization making the information available. Here are a few specific urls, representing a diversity of environmental perspectives from which one can obtain information. These organizations are EPA www.epa.gov, the Natural Resources Defense Council www.nrdc.org, Mobil Corporation www.mobil.com, and the Environmental Defense Fund http://www.edf.org/. One of the best places to begin environmental law research is at the environmental law resources web page at a law school known for its strong environmental law program, such as Vermont Law School.[60]

---

60. http://www.vermontlaw.edu/Environmental_Law_Resources.htm.

ADDITIONAL READINGS

Carson, Rachel L., *Silent Spring* (Boston: Houghton Mifflin, 1962).

Cohen, Morris L., *Legal Research in a Nutshell* (St. Paul: West, 2010).

Gibbs, Lois M., *Love Canal and the Birth of the Environmental Health Movement* (Washington: Island Press, 2011).

Kunz, Christina L., *The Process of Legal Research: Authorities and Options* (New York: Wolsters Kluwer Law & Business, 2012).

Leopold, A., *A Sand County Almanac* (New York: Ballantine Books Inc., 1949).

Meadows, D.H., Meadows, D.L., Randers, J. and Behrens, W. W., III, *The Limits to Growth* (New York: Signet Publishers, 1972); *see also* Meadows, D.H., Meadows, D.L., and Randers, J., *The Limits to Growth: The 30-Year Update* (White River Junction, VT: Chelsea Green Pub., 2004).

Sloan, Amy, *Basic Legal Research: Tools and Strategies* (NY: Aspen, 2012).

Smith, Zachary A., *The Environmental Policy Paradox* (Boston: Pearson, 6th ed. 2013).

State of the World: A Worldwatch Institute Report on Progress Toward a Sustainable Society (New York: W.W. Norton and Company, Annual).

CHAPTER 2

NATIONAL ENVIRONMENTAL POLICY ACT (NEPA)

A. APPLICABILITY OF THE EIS REQUIREMENT – MAJOR FEDERAL ACTIONS SIGNIFICANTLY AFFECTING THE QUALITY OF THE HUMAN ENVIRONMENT

Although NEPA[1] contains provisions which create the Council on Environmental Quality (CEQ) and require an annual Environmental Quality Report from the President to Congress, the most well-known, most litigated, most harmful or most beneficial (depending on one's point of view), but clearly the single most important aspect of NEPA is the environmental impact statement (EIS) requirement. In contrast to other federal statutes which we will consider later, this operative mechanism of NEPA is addressed primarily to agencies of the federal government—not individuals, not corporations, and not states. We will see that these other entities may be greatly affected by NEPA because of relationships which they may have with the federal government; however, it is only "all agencies of the Federal Government" that are directed to include as part of their "major Federal actions significantly affecting the quality of the human environment, a detailed statement by the

---

1. 42 U.S.C.A. § 4321 et seq.; PL 91-190, 83 Stat. 852.

responsible official on—(i) the environmental impact of the proposed action. . . ."[2] Since NEPA applies to "all agencies of the Federal Government," an EIS may be required not only for activities like the Department of Transportation's funding of highway construction, but also for the Comptroller of the Currency's chartering of a bank.

NEPA applies to all federal agencies; however, an EIS is not required every time an agency undertakes to do something. NEPA requires an EIS only for recommendations or reports on proposals for legislation and other "major Federal actions significantly affecting the quality of the human environment." Whether there is a "major federal action significantly affecting . . ." is a threshold question to be answered by the agency in an "environmental assessment" (EA). If the EA determines that the "major federal action significantly . . ." test has been met, then the agency does an EIS. If the EA determines there is no "major federal action significantly . . .," then the agency issues a "finding of no significant impact" (FONSI) identifying reasons why the proposed action will not have a significant impact on the environment, and no EIS is done.[3] The issues are which actions are major and which actions significantly affect the environment. Let's begin with the words "significantly affecting." Different federal courts in different parts of the country have used different interpretations of these words, but, beginning with the early NEPA court cases, the words have been interpreted broadly. For example, courts have decided that if a project "may cause a significant degradation"[4] or "could have a significant effect"[5] or "arguably will have an adverse environmental impact"[6] or has a "potentially significant adverse effect,"[7] an EIS is required. Today, the CEQ regulations describe

---

2. PL 91-190, § 102; 42 U.S.C.A. § 4332.

3. 40 CFR §§ 1501.4, 1508.13.

4. *Save Our Ten Acres v. Kreger*, 472 F.2d 463, 467.

5. *Minnesota Public Interest Research Group v. Butz*, 498 F.2d 1314, 1320.

6. *SCRAP v. U.S.*, 346 F. Supp. 189, 201.

7. *Hanly v. Kleindienst*, 471 F.2d 823, 831.

"significantly" in terms of "context" and "intensity."[8] The significance of a proposed action may vary depending on its geographical context. For example, if a proposed action is site-specific, significance will likely depend on the effects in the local area as opposed to in the world as a whole. Intensity refers to severity or degree of impact on interests such as public health, unique geographic characteristics, and cultural resources. Consideration should be given to whether the impact of this proposed action taken together with other actions is cumulatively significant. Also, when impacts of a proposal may be both beneficial and adverse, a significant effect may exist, and thus an EIS will be necessary even if the agency believes that on balance the net effect will be beneficial. It should be noted that there are situations where not only is an EIS not required, but also the agency does not have to do an environmental assessment. These are called "categorical exclusions." As recognized in the 2012 case, *Defenders of Wildlife v. Bureau of Ocean Energy Management,*[9] categorical exclusions are "a category of actions which do not individually or cumulatively have a significant effect on the human environment . . . and for which, therefore, neither an environmental assessment nor an environmental impact statement is required."[10] Examples of categorical exclusions include granting helicopter guide permits within national parks[11] and replacing historical bridges.[12]

The word "major" has also been given a broad interpretation by the courts. Numerous different parameters, such as the amount of money to be spent, the geographical size of the area to be covered, and whether the project effects are long-term or short-term, have been used to decide if an action is major. The facts of a particular case are extremely important since they will determine the types of

---

8. 40 CFR § 1508.27.

9. 684 F.3d 1242, 1247 (11th Cir. 2012).

10. *Id.* at 1247; 40 C.F.R. § 1508.4.

11. *Alaska Center for Environment v. U.S. Forest Service*, 189 F.3d 851 (9th Cir. 1999).

12. *Friends of Pioneer Street Bridge Corp. v. Federal Highway Admin.*, 150 F.Supp.2d 637 (Dist. Vt. 2001).

parameters which will be applied. The answer to the question of whether an action is a "major Federal action significantly affecting the quality of the human environment" will depend on which parameters are used, and the CEQ regulations state that "major" reinforces but is not independent of the term "significantly."[13] Perhaps the best way to see what are and what are not major actions with significant effects is to list and compare some cases. No case would be needed to decide if NEPA's EIS provision applied to the trans-Alaskan pipeline, but an EIS was also required in the following less clear situations:

1. adoption of Department of Transportation regulations to permit Mexican trucks to operate within the U.S. pursuant to the North American Free Trade Agreement;[14]
2. a Department of Housing and Urban Development (HUD) loan of $3.5 million to construct a high-rise apartment building in an area containing no other high-rise buildings in Portland, Oregon;[15]
3. the Army Corps of Engineers' designation of a new waste dumping site in the waters of Western Long Island Sound;[16]
4. the trapping of red fox by the U.S. Fish and Wildlife Service in an effort to protect two endangered species of birds;[17]
5. participation of the United States in Mexican herbicide spraying of marijuana and poppy plants.[18]

In contrast, NEPA was found not to apply to:

1. an action by the Secretary of Transportation approving the crossing of an interstate highway by a huge strip-mining

---

13. 40 CFR § 1500.18.

14. *Public Citizen v. Dept. of Transportation*, 316 F.3d 1002.

15. *Goose Hollow Foothills League v. Romney*, 344 F. Supp. 877.

16. *Town of Huntington v. Marsh*, 859 F.2d 1134.

17. *Animal Lovers Volunteers Association v. Cheney*, 795 F. Supp. 991.

18. *NORML v. Dept. of State*, 452 F. Supp. 1226.

shovel;[19]

2. a HUD-insured loan of $3.7 million to construct a 272-unit apartment complex on 15 acres in Houston, Texas;[20]

3. receipt and storage of 157 spent nuclear fuel rods from European countries where facility space remained available;[21]

4. construction of a municipal landfill on wetlands alleged to provide indispensable habitat to the Florida Panther and Eastern Indigo Snake—endangered or threatened species under the Endangered Species Act;[22]

5. the use of aerial surveillance over federal lands for the detection of illegal marijuana.[23]

Let's compare the two HUD examples and analyze why the results with respect to the need for an EIS might have been different in the two cases. First, consider some possible explanations which are largely independent of the substance of the HUD cases. The two HUD cases were decided in different jurisdictions. Issues of interpretation of a statute like NEPA are usually decided by the Federal District Courts or the Federal Circuit Courts of Appeals. There are different courts in different areas of the country, and they often have different ideas on what the law is. Some, but not all, of these differences are resolved by the United States Supreme Court or by Congress. In the absence of a resolution of the conflict by one of these bodies, each lower court opinion is the law within the jurisdiction of that lower court even though the law may thus be different in different parts of the country. It is possible that if the two HUD cases had had identical rather than merely similar facts, the U.S. District Court in Oregon may still have interpreted the "major Federal action" test more broadly than the U.S. Fifth Circuit

19. *Citizens Organized to Protect the Environment v. Volpe*, 353 F. Supp. 520.

20. *Hiram Clarke Civic Club v. Lynn*, 476 F.2d 421.

21. *State of South Carolina v. O'Leary*, 64 F.3d 892.

22. *Fund for Animals, Inc. v. Rice*, 85 F.3d 535.

23. *Carol Van Strum v. John C. Lawn*, 940 F.2d 406.

Court of Appeals in Texas, and an EIS could have been required in Oregon but not in Texas.

Another possible explanation of differing results in similar cases might be that the cases were decided at different times. The country's mood on environmental protection changes and the mood of the courts also shifts with time. In addition, courts often defer to administrative agency determinations, and those determinations can change when there is a change in the political inclinations of the Executive Branch of government. It would not be surprising to find an air pollution case with a given set of facts which was decided against industry in the early 1970s, a case with similar facts being decided in favor of industry in the energy shortage years of the 1980s, and similar facts again going against industry in the more air pollution conscious 1990s. In the 2000s, as noted in Chapter 1, the pendulum of administrative agency decisions began to once again favor industry on a similar set of air pollution facts, but the 2008 and 2012 election results promised closer administrative scrutiny of the activities of industry. While the HUD cases do not represent time periods with great disparity in the nation's level of environmental concern or administrative approaches, a difference in time (1978 vs. 1991) might explain the opposite results in the two marijuana cases. A more likely factual explanation of those cases, however, is that one involved spraying and the other only observation. From a more legalistic perspective, the two marijuana cases are different because some federal activities may be "categorically excluded" by an agency from NEPA. Investigative activities could be categorically excluded unless there were extraordinary circumstances.[24]

Besides explanations based on different jurisdictions or different time periods, the results in the HUD cases can be reconciled because their facts are distinguishable. The dollar amounts in the two cases were nearly the same, but one was a HUD loan and thus involved dollars coming out of the federal treasury. The other case was a HUD-insured loan where the funds would come from private sources, and the only time money would leave the federal treasury would be if the borrower defaulted in repaying the loan. This

---

24. 40 CFR § 1508.4.

second situation arguably involves less in the way of direct federal action and thus might not be a major federal action. Another factual explanation might be that the case in Oregon which required an EIS was dealing with a high-rise building in an area with no other high-rise buildings. Even though the Texas case which did not require an EIS was a proposal to build 272 units on 15 acres, the site was in Houston, which is a city that had many instances of inconsistent land uses and little in the way of land use controls. Which actions are major and require an EIS and which actions are not major is often an "I know it when I see it" situation; however, for most of NEPA's history, the courts tended to resolve the doubtful cases in favor of requiring an EIS. The current trend away from such a broad interpretation of NEPA is best illustrated by the 2004 U.S. Supreme Court decision in *Department of Transportation (DOT) v. Public Citizen.*[25]

In *Public Citizen*, the Court held that an environmental assessment (EA) done by an agency to determine whether its action would be a "major federal action" and thus require an EIS did not need to consider effects of actions over which it had no control. The case involved cross-border operations concerning Mexican motor carriers and safety and registration rules that the agency was issuing. Because the President and not the DOT had the authority to allow or prevent the entry of Mexican trucks, the EA by the DOT did not need to consider the environmental effects arising from the entry of Mexican trucks which would be subject to the safety and registration rules that the agency was issuing.

Let's next turn to another part of the "major Federal action . . ." test and consider the words "human environment." Clearly the human environment involves things such as air pollution, water pollution, and toxic chemicals in our food, but it was also interpreted in *Hanly v. Kleindienst* to include subjects such as housing, unemployment, and crime.[26] Thus, in considering the phrase "human environment," some courts gave a broad interpretation to the words used by Congress. That tendency was limited by the U.S. Supreme Court decision in *Metropolitan Edison*

25. 541 U.S. 752.

26. 471 F.2d 823.

Co. v. People Against Nuclear Energy[27] where a residents' association challenged a decision by the Nuclear Regulatory Commission (NRC) to restart a reactor at Three Mile Island, site of the worst nuclear accident in the United States. The plaintiffs claimed that the NRC failed to take into account the psychological stress on local residents caused by reopening the plant and had thus not complied with NEPA. The Court said that, while effects on human health may include psychological health, NEPA is concerned primarily with the "physical environment." Therefore, the NRC did not need to consider the psychological effects of the existence of a risk before that risk had materialized. This decision led the 8th Circuit Court of Appeals to decide, in contrast to *Hanly,* that alleged effects of increasing crime and halting neighborhood development did not require EIS consideration because they were social changes rather than physical impacts.[28] The effects on the human environment must be physical rather than socio-economic for an EIS to be required, and even physical effects must be related to humans. An agency action which might have a severe effect on something in nature might not be covered by NEPA unless a substantial link to humans and their needs can be shown. Opinions may differ about whether the destruction of a unique habitat for a type of plant or fish is really a significant effect on the human environment, but we should recognize that, in NEPA, Congress' concern was not for the plant or the fish in and of itself. While the plant or fish and its unique habitat may be protected under another statute such as the Endangered Species Act, if the habitat's destruction were not demonstrably connected to the human environment, NEPA might not apply, and an EIS might not be necessary. By way of comparison with respect to the words "human environment," the Washington State Environmental Policy Act, which is nearly a carbon copy of NEPA with words like "Federal" changed to "State," does not contain the word "human" but says "major actions significantly affecting the quality of the environment." Section 43.21C.030 of the Revised Code of

---

27. 460 U.S. 766.

28. *Olmsted Citizens for a Better Community v. U.S.*, 793 F.2d 201.

Washington, Annotated. Fifteen states have enacted "little NEPAs," or State Environmental Policy Acts ("SEPAs") modeled after NEPA. There is variability among SEPAs, such as whether to include substantive mandates, what triggers the EIS requirements, and what standards govern the determination of an EIS's sufficiency.[29] Environmental Statements may also be required by city law and provide "additional environmental protection" or "additional bureaucratic red tape," depending on one's perspective.[30]

Having discussed the words "major," "significantly affecting," and "human environment" in the EIS applicability test, let's consider the word "Federal" and note that, while NEPA is addressed to the federal agencies, courts have applied NEPA beyond situations of pure federal action to include activities of the private sector and of state and local governments. What are NEPA's effects on nonfederal entities? Certainly there are the economic costs of the EIS process, and those costs are borne by all segments of society. Also, the EIS process may result in a substantial delay before a private company receives a license or permit which it needs to conduct its business or before a state or local government receives a federal grant. A less obvious effect of NEPA on nonfederal entities arises when action which is largely that of private business becomes "federal" because the business has contact with the federal government and the private company is precluded from proceeding with its activity until a federal agency prepares its EIS. An example of this situation was a private developer of housing who had a HUD mortgage guarantee and interest grant. HUD could not provide its assistance until an EIS was filed, but the court also found the private developer could be enjoined from going forward with construction on his own property without HUD aid while HUD prepared its EIS. The court's theory for halting the private developer's action was that HUD's initial commitment to

---

29. Schifman, B., *The Limits of NEPA: Consideration of the Impacts of Terrorism in Environmnetal Impact Statements for Nuclear Facilities*, 35 Colum. J. Envtl. L. 373, 403 (2010).

30. DePalma, Anthony, "In Stadium Fight, Both Sides Wield the Environmental Statement," *New York Times* (April 15, 2005) p. B1.

the developer made them "partners" in the undertaking, and, even though he was still only a potential recipient of HUD assistance, the developer had enough contact with HUD so that his action without HUD assistance could be stopped pending a HUD EIS.[31]

The developer in the above situation was seeking government assistance to build housing for low income people. A large number of low income housing developments have been opposed on environmental grounds. The question should be raised of whether plaintiffs in these cases may have sometimes had ulterior motives such as economic or racial discrimination rather than pure environmental protection motives. The further question should be raised that, if it became clear that the motive behind a NEPA complaint was to prevent the construction of housing that would allow poor or minority people to move into a previously all white, middle class community, should a court allow the lawsuit to go forward? On one hand, NEPA was not intended to be a tool of economic or racial discrimination in housing, and if a lawsuit ties up a low income housing development project, the project may become too costly, and it may be stopped. On the other hand, perhaps courts should not look to the motives behind a lawsuit but only consider its merits. If government is providing assistance for a low income housing project, maybe a court should give the same review for environmental compliance that it would give to a proposed highway or a proposed nuclear power plant. It is certainly possible that a plaintiff's motive behind bringing a NEPA action against a proposed nuclear facility is to delay the project and make it so costly that it will be stopped even if, ultimately, it would have been in compliance with NEPA.

Turning to state and local government projects, we see that they, like the private housing project discussed above, can also become "federalized" and subject to NEPA. Where a state needed federal permits and discretionary approval prior to constructing a highway, the court found NEPA applicable because the federal agency had

---

31. *Silva v. Romney*, 473 F.2d 287. A later case enjoined activity by a university pending compliance with NEPA by a federal agency. The court said an injunction against a private party was warranted where the private party's action could not lawfully take place without prior federal agency approval. *Foundation on Economic Trends v. Heckler*, 756 F.2d 143.

authority to exercise discretion over the outcome.[32] Yet not all state projects that have federal involvement become "federal actions" and trigger NEPA applicability. Where a state wanted to construct a light rail project and there was federal funding provided for preliminary engineering studies and a federal wetlands permit, the court said NEPA did not apply.[33] Its decision was based on findings that (1) the preliminary studies were not a commitment to further funding, (2) the federal agency had discretion only with respect to a minor part of the overall project as contrasted to the state highway case noted above, and (3) the relationship of the federal and state governments were not akin to a "partnership" such as in the HUD/private developer case discussed above. We may, therefore, conclude that not all situations of federal agency involvement will result in NEPA applicability, but, beyond some degree of federal participation, the private sector and nonfederal governmental bodies may have their activities impeded until the federal agency does its job under NEPA.

In summary, if a proposal is for a major federal action significantly affecting the quality of the human environment, NEPA requires the responsible federal agency to prepare an environmental impact statement prior to commencing action under that proposal. Although NEPA requires an EIS from the *federal government* in situations of major *federal* action, the private sector and nonfederal governmental entities are very much affected by the EIS requirement. It should, however, be clearly understood that NEPA is not a statute which prohibits any specific activities by the federal government. What it does require is that environmental factors be taken into account in the decision-making process of whether or not to go forward with a project. We will next look at how those factors are taken into account by considering questions involving the content of an EIS.

---

32. *Maryland Conservation Council v. Gilchrist*, 808 F.2d 1039.

33. *Macht v. Skinner*, 916 F.2d 13.

B. CONTENT OF ENVIRONMENTAL IMPACT STATEMENTS

An EIS must consider the effect of a proposed action on the human environment. The EIS is a detailed report by the responsible official on:

1. the environmental impact of the proposed action;
2. any adverse environmental effects which cannot be avoided should the proposal be implemented;
3. alternatives to the proposed action;
4. the relationship between local short-term uses of man's environment and the maintenance and enhancement of long-term productivity; and
5. any irreversible and irretrievable commitments of resources which would be involved in the proposed action should it be implemented.[34]

To accomplish the above task, an EIS is supposed to clearly present the environmental impacts of the proposed action and the alternatives to the proposed action with the purpose of sharply defining the issues and providing a sound basis for the decision-maker to choose among the options.[35] The Council on Environmental Quality refers to the alternatives section as the "heart of the environmental impact statement."[36] Within the alternatives section, the EIS should explore *all reasonable* alternatives including the no action alternative and alternatives that are not within the authority of the agency making the proposal.[37] It

---

34. PL 91-190, § 102(2)(c).

35. An example of the content of an EIS may be seen in Appendix A, which contains the Table of Contents and Summary sections of an actual EIS.

36. 40 CFR § 1502.14.

37. Requiring agencies to consider, in their environmental impact statements, alternatives that are not within their authority is an interpretation of NEPA that was provided by the D.C. Circuit Court of Appeals in 1972 in *NRDC v. Morton*, 458 F.2d 827. Consideration of such an alternative might influence an agency's decision about whether and to what extent to implement its proposal. While the 2004 U.S. Supreme Court decision in the

should then identify the agency's preferred alternative. The EIS must describe the affected area concisely using summarized data indicating the impact. The environmental consequences must be scientifically examined in a comparative manner, and steps to mitigate adverse environmental effects as well as unavoidable adverse impacts should be discussed. The most important considerations are the direct and indirect effects caused by any proposed action or alternative. Such effects might include ecological, economic, historical, aesthetic, or social aspects. Indirect effects relate principally to population-induced changes and resultant uses of land, air, and water.

An environmental impact statement will evaluate the proposed action by considering the environmental consequences of the proposed action and alternatives to that proposed action. A cost-benefit analysis, which includes environmental costs and benefits as well as other costs and benefits, is used to provide a comprehensive evaluation of the desirability of following the proposed course of action. For example, if flood control could be accomplished to varying degrees depending on which one of five alternative dam configurations was selected, one would want to consider the initial construction cost of each configuration, the operation and maintenance cost for each, and the dollar amount of flood damage which each configuration would be expected to prevent. In addition, NEPA mandates that effects such as the destruction of wildlife and losses in commercial and recreational fishing for each alternative be made a part of the decision-making process. These environmental costs must be put into the decision-making balance just as one would add the cost of cement. Also, some dam configurations might provide increased recreational opportunities such as boating. These environmental benefits are a part of the decision-making process just as are the economic benefits of avoiding flood damage. NEPA asks that the federal decision-maker incorporate all the costs and all the benefits in his or her evaluation of a proposal, including those

---

DOT v. Public Citizen case discussed in section A does not appear to directly overrule this requirement because it addressed the Environmental Assessment (EA) aspect of NEPA rather than the EIS process itself, the *Public Citizen* case might indicate a trend of today's courts toward interpreting NEPA more narrowly than it has been interpreted for most of its history.

costs and benefits which are environmental in nature. Of course, not all elements of decision-making can be expressed in terms of dollars. What is the dollar cost of destroying 500 raccoons, 50 deer, or 10,000 starlings? What is the dollar benefit of saving 10 human lives every 50 years? Would saving those lives be worth an extra expenditure of $500, $500,000 or $500,000,000? An administrator's decision-making process, the evidence of which is the EIS, must consider these less quantifiable aspects of our environment as well as those which are more simply expressible in monetary terms.

Besides dealing with the questions of which parameters should be evaluated in the decision-making process and how these parameters should be evaluated, issues arise concerning the required scope of an environmental impact statement. If a federal agency is proposing a program to lease federal lands for energy production, is an EIS required for the leasing of each individual site, for each geographic leasing area, or only for the establishing of the overall leasing program with its rules and regulations? The Council on Environmental Quality has encouraged the use of overall "umbrella" or "programmatic" statements for general programs. The Council believes that programmatic statements foster the desirable end of comprehensive planning and evaluation of long-term environmental goals and effects. The CEQ recognizes, however, that an overall program statement without a particularized statement on, for example, the leasing of site XYZ, may reduce or eliminate consideration of particular environmental problems of special significance at site XYZ. Thus, they have said that individualized statements should also be prepared, in addition to the overall program statement, when the individual actions will have significant impacts not adequately evaluated under the umbrella statement for the whole program. Repetitive discussion of issues that were considered in the general program statement is avoided by "tiering" of environmental impact statements. Tiering says that the EIS for the specific project only needs to summarize any issues which were already discussed in the overall program statement.[38]

A related issue with respect to the required coverage of an EIS is often referred to as "segmentation." Suppose that an agency's

---

38. 40 CFR §§ 1502.4, 1502.20, 1508.28.

long-range planning contemplates a reasonable possibility of a 200-mile highway being constructed over the next 10 years, but current construction and funding is being proposed for only a 20-mile stretch. Should the entire 200-mile corridor be the subject of the EIS or just the 20 miles currently proposed? It would be extremely costly and time-consuming to do the EIS for the whole 200 miles, and if construction is never funded beyond the 20 miles, the EIS work on the rest is wasted. In addition, an EIS done today might be of questionable value with respect to work not to be undertaken for several years. It could thus be argued that the EIS should be limited in scope to the 20-mile segment currently under consideration. The danger of allowing this segmented approach to fulfilling the EIS requirement is that segmenting may undermine objective consideration of environmental issues by unfairly loading the EIS balance in favor of construction. In the diagram below, no significant environmental problems exist in proposed highway segments AB or CD, but a major environmental drawback to superhighway construction exists at point X. If the scope of today's EIS were limited to AB, no environmental problems are present to argue against construction. Once AB is built, the next likely segment to be undertaken by a dedicated superhighway builder is CD, and again no environmental problems present themselves

to inhibit construction of CD. Concerning the construction of BC, an objective evaluation of segment BC by itself might result in a "no construction" decision because, on balance, the costs (including environmental costs) outweigh the benefits of construction; however, if that balance is struck with the added factor of already constructed superhighways AB and CD emptying onto winding country road BC and the resulting traffic problems which may now exist in BC because of AB and CD, a "yes construction" decision may be hard to avoid. The segmenting of the EIS into three parts has undermined the ability to fairly consider the environmental detriment of a superhighway through point X. If an EIS for the whole route, ABCD, had been done prior to construction of the first segment, the problem at point X might have been considered important enough to mandate a different route such as AMND as shown below.

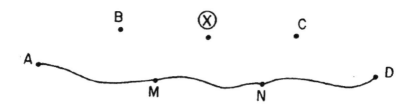

The courts have attempted to resolve the conflicting policies of, on one hand, not wanting to waste time and money on an over-encompassing EIS and, on the other hand, not wanting to allow the objectivity of the EIS balancing process to be jeopardized. The courts have said that if construction of one part of a potentially larger project has "independent utility" and will thus not involve an irreversible or irretrievable commitment of government funds, the EIS may be limited in scope to that one part of the project.[39] If construction of that part alone would still be a sound decision even if no further action were taken beyond the part of the project currently being funded for construction, then the EIS does not need to go beyond the segment of what might someday become a larger project. In this way, the courts have tried to mitigate the argument of "now that we have AB and CD, we need BC to relieve the traffic problems those other segments have caused." AB and CD can only be built without BC and the environmental issue at point X being discussed in the EIS if AB and CD can stand as sound projects on their own without causing detriments which could only be overcome by constructing BC.

C. SUBSTANTIVE POLICIES, PROCEDURAL

---

39. *Conservation Society of So. Vt. v. Sec. of Transportation*, 531 F.2d 637, 640.

REQUIREMENTS, AND THE ROLE OF THE COURTS

NEPA's EIS requirement is a specific procedural step which federal agencies are directed to take. NEPA also makes some broad declarations, somewhat lacking in specificity, concerning the nation's environmental policy and goals and the federal government's responsibility for promoting and attaining them. The analysis of the distinction between NEPA's procedural requirements and its statements of substantive policy was presented in *Calvert Cliffs' Coordinating Committee v. Atomic Energy Commission*,[40] the leading court decision interpreting NEPA. The procedural/substantive distinction serves to define the role of the court system in the EIS process—a process which is directed at the administrative agencies.

The substantive policies and goals of NEPA are found in § 101 of the Act and are broadly worded declarations. They include Congress' desire to "promote the general welfare, to create and maintain conditions under which man and nature can exist in productive harmony . . ." and Congress' direction that the federal government act so that the nation may "fulfill the responsibilities of each generation as trustee of the environment for succeeding generations" and "assure for all Americans safe, healthful, productive, and aesthetically and culturally pleasing surroundings . . . ."[41] The court in *Calvert Cliffs'* noted that Congress required that these substantive goals and policies be pursued by the federal government using "all practicable means." In contrast, Congress directed that the procedural requirement of an EIS, found in § 102 of the Act, was to be followed "to the fullest extent possible." Based on this difference in the language used by Congress in the two sections of the Act, the court found that the substantive aspects of the Act were directives to the agencies which allowed for flexibility and agency discretion and thus provided only a very limited review role for the courts. With respect to the § 101 substantive aspects of NEPA, courts could only interfere with an agency decision when that decision was "arbitrary or clearly gave

40. 449 F.2d 1109.

41. PL 91-190, § 101.

insufficient weight to environmental values." With respect to the §
102 procedural requirements, however, the court found that the
language "to the fullest extent possible" was not highly flexible and
that the language made the courts responsible to reverse agency
decisions which were reached procedurally without the mandated
consideration and balancing of environmental factors. Thus, if an
agency failed to do an EIS where one was required, or did not do a
legally sufficient EIS, or in some other way violated NEPA's
relatively inflexible procedural directives to the federal agencies,
the courts would reverse the agency's decision. Let's consider the
issue of court review of agency decisions under NEPA today in two
contexts: (1) where the agency has done an EIS but the agency's
decision about a proposed project is alleged to be inconsistent with
the § 101 substantive policies of NEPA and (2) where the agency
has decided pursuant to § 102 that an EIS need not be done.

With respect to the court's role of reviewing an agency decision
for compliance with the § 101 policies, even the very limited review
of checking to see if the result was arbitrary, as stated by the court
in *Calvert Cliffs'*, has been placed in doubt. In the United States
Supreme Court case of *Stryker's Bay Neighborhood Council v.
Karlen*,[42] the majority opinion said that an agency's duties under
NEPA are "essentially procedural," and "once an agency has made
a decision subject to NEPA's procedural requirements, the only role
for a court is to insure that the agency has considered the
environmental consequences . . . NEPA requires no more." This
sounds like there is no court review at all of whether a proposed
project is consistent with the substantive policies of § 101. In a
footnote, however, the Court said that if the agency had acted
arbitrarily, it *might* agree that plenary review was warranted. The
use of the word "might" could be interpreted to be less than a full
commitment to, but still an acknowledgment by the Court of, the
position that arbitrary substantive decisions of agencies should be
set aside by a court even if the agency has complied with NEPA's
procedures. Although later cases have not expressly said "no review
with respect to § 101 policy compliance," they continue to focus on
NEPA as a "process" statute and imply that, although the EIS

---

42. 100 S. Ct. 497 (1980).

process is almost certain to affect the environmental substance of an agency decision, there is probably no court review based on § 101.[43] Thus, even the very limited judicial review pursuant to § 101 that was recognized in *Calvert Cliffs'* may have disappeared. There does, however, continue to be judicial review under § 102, and most of the controversies about the role of courts under NEPA have involved § 102. These cases consider the degree to which courts will review the procedural steps an agency has taken to comply with § 102's requirement that an agency must prepare an Environmental Impact Statement. They are the subject of our second inquiry about judicial review under NEPA.

Our second judicial review question is: to what extent will a court review an agency's decision, pursuant to § 102, not to do an EIS or not to supplement an existing EIS. As was discussed at the beginning of this chapter, NEPA requires agencies to prepare an EIS for any "major Federal action significantly affecting the quality of the human environment." As discussed earlier, when an agency is uncertain about whether its proposed action fits this statutory language, the Council on Environmental Quality has said the agency is to prepare an Environmental Assessment.[44] The function of an Environmental Assessment (EA) is to "provide sufficient evidence and analysis for determining whether to prepare an environmental impact statement or a finding of no significant impact."[45] If an agency's EA results in its issuing a Finding of No Significant Impact (FONSI), it does not prepare an EIS. When asked to review whether the agency decision not to do an EIS was in compliance with NEPA, some Circuit Courts of Appeals used the "reasonableness" test—the court itself evaluates whether the agency reasonably concluded that the project would have no significant adverse environmental consequences.[46] Other Circuit Courts provided less in the way of judicial review—the agency decision not to do an EIS would be given deference and would only be set

---

43. *Robertson v. Methow Valley Citizens Council*, 490 U.S. 332.

44. 40 CFR §§ 1501.3 and 1501.4.

45. 40 CFR § 1508.9.

46. *Save the Yaak Committee v. J.R. Block*, 840 F.2d 714, 717.

aside if the court found the decision was "arbitrary and capricious" rather than merely unreasonable when evaluated by the Court. This lesser role for courts of leaving the agency decision stand unless it is arbitrary and capricious was adopted by the U.S. Supreme Court in *Marsh v. Oregon Natural Resources Council* where the Army Corps of Engineers decided not do additional EIS work with respect to building the Elk Creek Dam to control water supply in Oregon's Rogue River Basin.[47]

Those who advocate more court watchdogging of agencies even after the *Marsh* case contend that the arbitrary and capricious standard from *Marsh* need not be applied to agency decisions not to do an EIS because *Marsh* involved an agency decision not to supplement an existing EIS rather than not to do one at all. In *Marsh*, an EIS had been done for the Elk Creek Dam, and the Corps decided not to do an additional supplementary EIS even though new and potentially relevant studies had been done. While this argument may convince some lower court judge to continue to ask if the agency decision was reasonable instead of only non-arbitrary, the language from *Marsh* makes that difficult because the Supreme Court stated in *Marsh* that "the decision whether to prepare a supplemental EIS is similar to the decision whether to prepare an EIS in the first instance. . . ."[48] Still, lower court judges in "first instance EIS" cases who do not want to be constrained by the limited judicial review standard of *Marsh* may accept the argument that the above quoted language from *Marsh* is not necessary to the decision of that case and is thus not part of the "holding" of the case. Since it is only "dictum" and not part of the "holding," it is not binding on lower courts. Regardless of whether one uses the reasonableness test or the arbitrary and capricious test as the standard for judicial review, it is clear that a court will not decide from scratch that an EIS is or is not required. It will only consider whether the agency decision is within the spectrum of either reasonableness or non-arbitrariness.

Our cases concerning judicial review lead to the conclusion that it is the federal agencies who are largely in charge of the NEPA

---

47. 490 U.S. 360.

48. Id. at 374.

process and that NEPA is just that—a process. The substantive goals of NEPA are to be realized through a set of "action-forcing" procedures that require that agencies take a "hard look" at environmental consequences.[49] Although using the procedures (the EIS) will affect the agency's substantive decision, NEPA only prescribes a process—it does not mandate particular results, and it does not mean that environmental values cannot be sacrificed. Environmental values may be sacrificed under NEPA; all that NEPA requires is that environmental values be considered in the balance of the agency decision-making process. The substantive environmental concerns of § 101 are not exclusive goals of an agency, and those concerns may, on balance, lose out. That is allowed under the flexible language of § 101, but the environmental concerns must be given consideration—that is inflexible. Viewed with respect to the balance/ban legislative approaches we referred to in Chapter 1, NEPA is certainly a balance statute—no activity is banned, but environmental values must be balanced with the economic benefits of a proposed agency action. The EIS is the mechanism for reporting on the balancing process, and it is the main procedural requirement of NEPA.

We have determined that the basic operative mechanism of NEPA is the EIS. Does this mechanism work? How does requiring a detailed statement of the environmental impact of a proposed action serve the purpose of fostering proper consideration for environmental values? First, the agency itself, and the human beings who make its decisions, will have environmental concerns and information in front of them for the purpose of writing the EIS. This information will hopefully be considered by the agency, whereas prior to NEPA and the need to write an EIS, environmental information was often never even compiled. Second, the EIS requirement seeks to bring the public and other agencies, in addition to the agency proposing to act, into the picture by informing them of environmental consequences and giving them an opportunity to comment on them and possibly come up with alternatives to the proposed action. Third, if others outside the agency are able to see the agency's statement of the justification for its decision spelled

---

49. *Robertson v. Methow Valley Citizens Council*, 490 U.S. 332.

out in the EIS, an informal pressure is placed on an agency to make a rational decision and to include environmental considerations in that decision. The theory is that better decisions are made when "someone is watching."

The above logic supports Congress' decision to use the EIS mechanism as the procedural tool to implement its substantive policies involving environmental protection; however, there are many who contend that the procedural requirement of an EIS has little or no positive effect on the environment and is just another "red tape/legal technicalities/bureaucratic nightmare" standing in the way of those who seek to have government work to serve the interests of society. The basis of this position is that the preparation of an EIS is a time-consuming chore which adds large amounts of lead time and other economic costs to any project.[50] An EIS can take a year or more to complete and cost over $1 million.[51] Also, the EIS requirement allows a small number of people to tie up a project for long periods of time in a complex litigation process. These arguments might be made by people who would label themselves as being in favor of progress, economic growth, and development rather than being "environmentalists," but many "environmentalists" would join them in attacking the EIS process as undesirable. Some environmentalists claim that as agencies become accustomed to the EIS procedure and to what the courts require for compliance with that procedure, an agency can make any decision look reasonable on paper regardless of whether it is a good balance between the agency's program goals and NEPA's environmental goals. It is the opinion of these environmentalists that the only way

---

50. Some have contended that a court injunction for noncompliance with NEPA led the Corps of Engineers to abandon the "barrier plan" and instead implement the "high-level plan" with respect to levees for New Orleans. They say this resulted in the flooding caused by Hurricane Katrina. Others contend NEPA worked well–a better flood protection approach was implemented at a lower cost. The problem was not NEPA but that the better alternative was poorly constructed. Bligh, Shawna M., "Did NEPA Sink New Orleans?" *Natural Resources and Environment* (Spring, 2006) p. 60.

51. Soraghan, M, "NEPA Reviews Could Stall Return of Offshore Drilling Projects in Deep Water," *New York Times* (Feb. 3, 2011), available at http://www.nytimes.com/gwire/2011/02/03/03greenwire-nepa-reviews-could-stall-return-of-offshore-dr-20907.html?pagewanted=all.

for the § 101 substantive goals of NEPA to really be taken into account is for the courts, being independent bodies without any agency program goals, to be willing to take a close look at the substantive correctness of an agency decision rather than looking only at whether the § 102 procedures are followed. What is needed is for the courts to look more closely at whether an agency decision is right or wrong with respect to the environment rather than to only inquire whether the agency decision was "arbitrary or capricious." It is for you to determine whether you believe that the EIS is a sound mechanism for environmental protection or that the EIS severely handicaps agencies' efforts to work toward a better society or that the EIS can only work to attain NEPA's substantive environmental goals if the courts take a more active role in watchdogging agency actions which affect those goals. The status of the law is that the EIS requirement does exist, but, if the agency complies with the § 102 procedural steps, the courts "might," but are unlikely to, evaluate the substance of an agency decision even to the limited extent of making sure it is not arbitrary with respect to its consideration of the environment.

Having now considered the basic structure of NEPA as established by Congress and as interpreted by the courts, let us digress and see how, in *Calvert Cliffs'*, the leading case that interpreted Congress' intent under NEPA, the Atomic Energy Commission ran afoul of the EIS requirement. In this context, we should think about how a particular set of facts may be influential in shaping the interpretation that courts give to a statute. In *Calvert Cliffs'*, the AEC's procedure for licensing energy-producing facilities was challenged. The AEC made some quite reasonable arguments concerning how NEPA was supposed to be inapplicable to the fact situation in that case because another specific statute precluded NEPA's being applicable. Section 104 of NEPA says:

Nothing in section 102 [the EIS requirement] . . . shall in any way affect the specific statutory obligations of any Federal agency . . . to act, or refrain from acting contingent upon the recommendations or certifications of any other Federal or State agency.

Another statute, the Water Quality Improvement Act (WQIA), had resulted in water quality standards being set by other agencies, and the AEC said it could adopt those standards and did not need to address water quality in its EIS. The AEC, as further support for its position, cited a statement made by Senator Jackson, the sponsor of NEPA, which discussed the relationship between NEPA and the WQIA. Jackson said:

> The compromise worked out between the two bills provides that the licensing agency will not have to make a detailed statement on water quality if the state or other appropriate agency has made a certification pursuant to [WQIA].[52]

The court rejected the AEC's position and found the AEC's EIS must consider water quality because, if it did so, the AEC might decide to impose water quality standards that were stricter than those adopted under the other statute, the WQIA. The court interpreted § 104 to only allow an agency to exclude an issue from its EIS only when its obligations under another statute were "mutually exclusive" with its obligations under NEPA to consider that issue. Considering and adopting stricter water quality standards under NEPA would not violate the minimum standards that had been set under the WQIA, and thus the obligations under the two statutes were not mutually exclusive. The AEC could not simply adopt the WQIA standards without discussing water quality in its EIS. Acceptance of AEC's reasonable and quite well-supported position might have narrowed NEPA's overall applicability and effect, but the AEC's reasonable arguments were rejected by the court. One can only speculate concerning whether that rejection (and thus a broader interpretation of NEPA's scope and greater protection of the environment) was in any way influenced by the following and possibly not-so-reasonable argument which the AEC made.

Under Section 102, copies of the EIS must "accompany" a proposal through the agency review process. The AEC adopted a literal definition of the word "accompany." With respect to some

---

52. 115 Cong. Rec. (Part 21) at 29053.

license application situations, the AEC did an EIS and had the EIS physically "accompany" the application, but the AEC rules precluded the EIS from being considered in the decision-making process of the licensing hearings. The court found that Congress did not intend by use of the word "accompany" to create a situation requiring physical proximity of the EIS but allowing the agency to prohibit its decision-maker from considering the content of the EIS. The court said that "the Commission's crabbed interpretation of NEPA makes a mockery of the Act."[53] The court was clearly outraged by the AEC's approach to its NEPA responsibilities. One may wish to consider what contribution, if any, has been made to the general proliferation of environmental controls and litigation by a few instances of agency or industry recalcitrance or lack of good faith in complying with existing environmental regulations. How much influence have the worst cases of lack of good faith had on the overall scheme of environmental controls?

D. REMEDIES

Having considered when NEPA requires an EIS, what is the content of an EIS, and how courts are involved with reviewing the manner in which agencies comply with both the procedural EIS requirement of NEPA and with NEPA's substantive policies, let's consider the question of remedies for noncompliance by a federal agency with NEPA's EIS requirement. The general remedy is an injunction to maintain the *status quo*—the court orders that the project be halted until a proper EIS is prepared; however, a *status quo* injunction is not granted in all situations of inadequate environmental impact statements. Competing needs may influence the remedy provided by a court. If a delay in continuing the project might result in safety or health hazards or heavy economic losses, and if the environmental harm is not very great, a court may refuse to hold the project in its *status quo* position. Instead, the court may issue a limited injunction which would prohibit certain activities (like site clearance) but allow other project activities to continue (like relocation of people from the site to be cleared). The

---

53. *Calvert Cliffs'* at 1117.

likelihood of a *status quo* injunction with respect to the entire project would appear to be directly proportional to the seriousness of the environmental harm which the project threatens to create. Also, intentional noncompliance by an agency with NEPA may tend to induce a court to grant a broad injunction even though, in the absence of agency bad faith, the factual situation might have led the court to grant only a limited injunction. Although violations of NEPA have not always led to courts being willing to grant injunctions to stop agencies from proceeding until they have complied with NEPA, in most situations of NEPA violation, a *status quo* injunction stopping a project has been the appropriate remedy and has also been enough of a remedy to satisfy the courts that the project will not continue to violate NEPA permanently. Lurking in the background is also the possibility that the court will tell an agency that it has violated NEPA, and, since it should not have proceeded with its project, it must not only stop the project, but it must also undo what has been done. This remedy is rather severe and is thus reserved for extreme situations.

As one example of courts having to consider competing needs in deciding whether to issue an injunction because of agency noncompliance with NEPA, let's consider the interface between national security policy and environmental protection under NEPA. In *Concerned About Trident v. Rumsfeld,*[54] the Navy was involved in the construction of a Trident Submarine Base at Bangor, Washington. The Defense Department claimed that NEPA cannot possibly apply to strategic military decisions and that there is a "national defense" exemption from NEPA. The court found that such a claim "flies in the face of the clear language of the statute" which requires that "all agencies of the Federal Government" prepare an EIS for "major Federal actions significantly affecting the quality of the human environment." There is no national defense exemption. When, however, in *Wisconsin v. Weinberger*, a court was asked to use the remedy of an injunction to stop the Defense Department's expansion of an extremely low frequency submarine communication system due to alleged violation of NEPA, an injunction was denied based on a balance of "the weight of the

---

54. 555 F.2d 817.

alleged NEPA violation against the harm the injunction would cause the Navy and to this country's defense."[55] Historically, an injunction is an "equitable remedy" which means that, even though there has been a violation of the law, courts have the discretion to balance the need for an injunction against the harm it might do. Yet, if a national defense activity is not enjoined when it is in violation of NEPA, do we not have a *de facto* national defense exemption which we were told does not exist under the clear language of NEPA? Although the NEPA/national security interface issue had appeared in federal district court cases such as those discussed above, the Supreme Court addressed the issue for the first time in 2008. In *Winter v. NRDC*, a case involving the Navy's use of sonar during training exercises in the waters off southern California, the Court reaffirmed lower court holdings that there is no national security exemption under NEPA and that whether to grant an injunction for non-compliance with the EIS requirements must be reviewed under a balancing test. The Court concluded that even if the NRDC could show a likelihood of harm, the balance of equities tipped in favor of the Navy. "Even if the plaintiffs have shown irreparable injury from the Navy's training exercise, any such injury is outweighed by the public interest and the Navy's interest in effective, realistic training of its sailors."[56] Three of the nine Justices in dissent disagreed, arguing that harm to the marine mammals was not speculative or insignificant but likely, and that by limiting the availability of an injunction in national security situations, the majority effectively granted *de facto* immunity from NEPA to military projects involving national security.[57]

Another remedy which some people have claimed is available under NEPA is the right of private citizens to bring suit when estimates or predictions made in an environmental impact statement are not adhered to or do not prove to be true once the project is approved and undertaken. Citizens have contended that these

---

55. 745 F.2d 412.

56. 555 U.S. 7, 22-25 (2008).

57. 555 U.S. 7, 53.

situations result in an "implied private right of action" under NEPA. Thus the owner of a bookstore sought an injunction and damages based on NEPA when the noise levels stated in the EIS for a rapid transit project were exceeded after the project was built and operating. The courts have found that Congress did not intend such a remedy to be available under NEPA and have dismissed lawsuits seeking to invoke such a remedy. The courts have said that if this private remedy were available, then decision-makers would receive and report distorted information which was "hedged" to ensure that information used as an estimate or prediction would in fact turn out to be true in practice. This would be inconsistent with the statutory purpose of NEPA which is to provide decision-makers with the best available information on which to base their decisions.[58] A response to the courts' denials of private rights of action might be that, without such potential for actions, agencies can make overly optimistic predictions in an EIS for the purpose of justifying a decision to go forward with a project. Furthermore, one might at least want to consider the argument that if representations made in the EIS as a basis for reaching the decision to proceed with a project are shown to not be coming true as the project is being implemented, the agency should have to reevaluate whether the project should continue based on the new information now available. Such reevaluation might result in a different decision on the project or modifications to the project which would provide greater consistency with the substantive policies that Congress asked be pursued using "all practicable means."[59]

E. CREATIVE APPROACHES TO ENVIRONMENTAL PROTECTION

Although NEPA is limited in that it only applies to actions of the federal government, it is quite broad with respect to the environmental issues it covers. NEPA potentially encompasses all environmental issues, including air pollution, water pollution, water allocation, land use, land pollution, resources conservation, species

---

58. *Noe v. MARTA*, 644 F.2d 434.

59. PL 91-190, § 101.

protection, and protection of our food supply from toxic materials. NEPA may thus be thought of as a "multi-media" or "cross-media" environmental statute, and as it stands in marked contrast to the bulk of our environmental legislation which has been enacted subsequent to NEPA. Those statutes each address a single medium or topic—the Clean Air Act, the Surface Mining Control and Reclamation Act, the Endangered Species Act, the Federal Insecticide, Fungicide and Rodenticide Act. A few multi-media or cross-media environmental protection approaches have been proposed or begun, and may receive greater emphasis as environmental law continues to evolve. Our first two examples, an environmental amendment to the U.S. Constitution and a unified environmental protection statute to address cross-media pollutants, have been proposed but have failed to develop. Our third and fourth examples involve the administrative level of environmental protection. Specifically, EPA uses the cluster approach to environmental management, and nonprofit organizations work to hold agencies accountable to their environmental responsibilities under NEPA.

1. Constitutional Amendment

One type of proposal to amend the U.S. Constitution with respect to the environment involves providing express environmental power to Congress. This would combat any doubt about the existence of the environmental power. Congress now acts pursuant to its implicit/indirect Commerce Clause authority. That topic was discussed in Chapter 1. As long as Congress must depend on the Commerce Clause for its authority, there is the risk that the Supreme Court will hold that Congress' actions to protect the environment are unconstitutional. A second type of amendment would be based on the position that assuming Congress' power is not in doubt, Congress may not exercise that power appropriately. The people themselves (and perhaps nature) should have the right to environmental protection even in the absence of action by Congress to provide that protection or as a limitation on Congress' power in the event Congress acts in a way that threatens environmental protection. The National Wildlife Foundation has proposed that each person has the right to clean air, pure water, productive soils, and to the conservation of the natural, scenic, historic, recreational, aesthetic, and economic values of America's natural resources. Other proposals consist of unenumerated statements such as, "[e]very person has the right to a clean, healthful environment." Still others look beyond protecting people and indeed view people as the threat: "[t]he earth and all its life shall be treated considerately for they are vulnerable to human culture."[60]

Arguments opposing a constitutional amendment to provide for a right to environmental protection include not wanting to undertake additional administrative and judicial costs and burdens, and not wanting to risk the possibilities of misinterpretation and misapplication of a new constitutional provision. A strong argument in opposition is the lack of a need. While not perfect, our environment and our government environmental efforts have had an overall trend of improvement. Also, it has been argued that a constitutional amendment for environmental protection should not be pursued even if it were politically possible. Many people think that the U.S. Constitution should be amended only for reasons involving the basic structure of democratic government—issues like who has the right to vote or how many terms a President can serve. They would contend that the environment is a "social values" issue and not the proper subject for constitutional amendment. Is a healthy environment a proper subject for amending the U.S. Constitution?

At least two states, Pennsylvania and Montana, have environmental rights provisions in their state Constitutions and have used them as the basis to find acts adversely affecting the environment to be unconstitutional as a matter of state law. Constitutional provisions that expressly address the environment have also been enacted outside the U.S. In the European Union (EU), there is express environmental authority in the treaty establishing the European Union. The Treaty of Lisbon, which entered into force in December 2009, forms the constitutional basis of the EU. The treaty reaffirms the EU's commitment to

---

60. For a discussion of these and other amendment proposals, see *Environmental Amendment Circular No. 4*, The Comprehensive Environmental Amendment Project (Thornton, Colorado: June, 1991).

environmental protection and recognizes the EU's role in combating climate change.[61] The treaty established shared control of environmental issues between the EU and Member States.[62] Articles require the EU to "work for the sustainable development of Europe based on ... a high level of protection and improvement of the quality of the environment," and call for efforts to "promote measures at [the] international level to deal with regional or worldwide environmental problems, and in particular combating climate change." These Articles underline the legally binding force to the principles of sustainable development and of the integration of environmental requirements into other EU policies. Ecuador has also enshrined environmental protection into its Constitution by approving a constitutional provision granting inalienable rights to nature with hopes to "change the status of ecosystems from being regarded as property under the law to being recognized as rights-bearing entities." The Constitution grants nature "the right to exist, persist, maintain and regenerate its vital cycles, structure, functions and its processes in evolution."[63]

2. Unified Environmental Protection Act

The primary advantage claimed by proponents of a unified statute to protect the environment is definitional. It would be a unified or single law to deal with all environmental issues or at least with all forms of an environmental topic like pollution. The Conservation Foundation's study which led to a document titled "The Environmental Protection Act" discusses having one statute to replace the Clean Air Act, Clean Water Act, and seven other statutes which comprise the bulk of the activities of the

---

61. *In depth: The Treaty of Lisbon - Implications for the Environment*, http://www.europarc.org/news/in-depth-the-treaty.

62. *Treaty of Lisbon: Amending the Treaty on European Union and the Treaty Establishing the European Community*, Official Journal of the European Union, 50 (2007).

63. Revkin, A., "Ecuador Constitution Grants Rights to Nature," *New York Times* (Sept. 28, 2008) available at http://dotearth.blogs.nytimes.com/2008/09/29/ecuador-constitution-grants-nature-rights/.

Environmental Protection Agency. In this way, "[R]egulatory priorities, budget allocations, and research initiatives could be considered for the entire [proposed] Department of Environmental Protection (DEP)."[64] While a more integrated approach to environmental protection probably makes good sense, it is not very likely that the massive existing statutory framework of single-media legislation will be dismantled anytime soon.

3. The Cluster Approach to Environmental Management

EPA's general organizational structure is single-media. Different parts of EPA deal with each medium—air, water, land. This has often resulted in industry being subjected to duplicative and sometimes conflicting regulations. It has also led to some issues "falling through the cracks" because each section of the regulatory process may leave the issue for another section to handle. In addition, the effort to mitigate adverse effects on one medium may create adverse effects on another medium. EPA has promoted numerous multi-media initiatives for environmental regulation for many years,[65] and multi-media approaches continue to be advocated in many situations.[66] In the 1990s, EPA initiated its "cluster approach" and began applying it to the pulp and paper industry—one of the largest industries in term of the quantity of toxic chemicals it releases to the air, water, and land.

The pulp and paper industry releases are covered by many different statutes and were thus under the control of multiple program offices of EPA. To provide better integration of control, EPA established a cluster team to approach the problems holistically rather than from a program-by-program perspective. Thus air and water regulations for the pulp and paper industry

---

64. From the "Rationale and Summary" introduction to the proposed "Environmental Protection Act," The Conservation Foundation, Washington, D.C.

65. Mank, Bradford C., "The Environmental Protection Agency's Project XL and Other Regulatory Reform Initiatives: The Need for Legislative Authorization," 25 *Ecology Law Quarterly* (1998) p. 1.

66. Morriss, A.P., et al., "Water Use Symposium: Principles for Water," 15 *Tulane Environmental Law Journal* 335 (2002) p. 338 and fn.10.

would be developed jointly to seek the optimal combination of technologies to meet statutory requirements, avoid cross-media pollution transfers, and reduce industry compliance costs through coordination of action.[67] EPA has formed other clusters which focus on a specific economic sector like petroleum refineries, on a pollutant like lead (regardless of which medium the lead is affecting), on an environmental resource like ground water, or on other logical multi-media groupings of activities.[68] But, in order to be effective, the cluster approach will have to overcome institutional inertia in areas such as single media approaches to budgeting and setting statutory deadlines. It will also have to cope with power struggles among entrenched bureaucrats. Clusters do, however, have great potential to give us faster and better solutions for environmental problems—better in terms of both environmental protection and the costs of that protection.

4. Nonprofit Organizations and Agency Accountability

Federal agencies are accountable under numerous statutes and administrative regulations protecting the environment, but those provisions are only meaningful when they are enforced. Environmental nonprofits are organizations that work to hold federal agencies accountable for their actions affecting the environment. For example, the Environmental Integrity Project (EIP) increases the likelihood that environmental laws are actually enforced by making environmental data locally relevant and making it accessible to the public for use in their advocacy efforts.[69] It also helps the public voice their concerns in the media, legislature, and environmental agencies. EIP works toward accomplishing these goals by combining research, reporting, and media outreach to

---

67.   Cleland-Hamnett, W. and Retzer, J., "Crossing Agency Boundaries," *The Environmental Forum* (March - April, 1993) p. 17.

68. Sandalow, D.B., "EPA Clusters: A New Approach for Environmental Management," *The 22nd Annual Conference on Environmental Law* (American Bar Association, Section on Natural Resources, Energy, and Environmental Law, 1993) Tab 14.

69. <http://www.environmentalintegrity.org/>

expose both violations of environmental laws and political intimidation of enforcement staff. It encourages federal and state agencies to take enforcement action to stop violations of environmental laws. Similar efforts to ensure the integrity of our environmental laws hold agencies accountable while educating the public and making them better able to demand compliance and enforcement. In the future, such an approach has the potential to involve more players in the agency's process of considering the environment.

F. THE FUTURE OF NEPA

While the Supreme Court has decided seventeen cases regarding NEPA, each time they have come down in favor of the government.[70] However, there have been many environmental victories within those losses which have played important roles in NEPA's continued service as one of the nation's primary environmental statutes.[71] For example, in the 2010 case, *Monsanto Co. v. Geertson Seed Farms*, the Supreme Court expanded standing to sue to those with a "reasonable probability" of injury. The Court held that the substantial risk of contamination was enough to cause harm, even if no contamination occurred, and such harms are "sufficiently concrete to satisfy the injury-in-fact prong of the constitutional standing analysis."[72] A second example of "environmental victory" in an otherwise losing case against the government came in *Norton v. Southern Utah Wilderness Alliance*,[73] where the Court held that the Bureau of Land Management (BLM) did not violate NEPA by failing to prepare a supplemental EIS considering the significant increase in off-road

---

70. Patrick Parenteau, Discussing NEPA during Vermont Law School's "Constitution Day," Sept. 17, 2012.

71. Lazarus, R., *The National Environmental Policy Act in the U.S. Supreme Court: A Reappraisal and a Peak Behind the Curtains*, Geo. L.J. 1507 (2012).

72. 130 S.Ct. 2743, 2755 (2010).

73. 542 U.S. 55, 60 (2004).

vehicle use in a wilderness-study area,[74] but said that a supplemental EIS would be required if BLM's plan was amended or revised.[75] Let's consider NEPA's future in the context of two highly contentious environmental topics: climate change and energy supply.

1. Climate Change, Greenhouse Gases and Cumulative Impacts

NEPA requires an EIS for major federal actions significantly affecting the quality of the human environment. However, even insignificant levels of greenhouse gas emissions from one agency action can combine with multiple other agency actions, resulting in a significant effect—global warming. This is generally known as "cumulative impacts." In 2010, the CEQ advised federal agencies to consider the impact of all levels of greenhouse gas emissions on climate change in their EIS's, and furthermore, suggested they take measures to reduce greenhouse gas emissions when possible.[76]

There is no consensus among courts as to whether NEPA is an appropriate tool to address climate change, but courts continue to interpret the meaning of "significant" in greenhouse gas emission situations. For example, in *Center for Biological Diversity v. National Highway Traffic Safety Administration*, the Ninth Circuit held that the "cumulative impact" analysis requires more than quantifying expected emissions, it must also evaluate the "incremental impact" that these emissions will have on the environment more generally, including the "individually minor" effect an action may have on the environment, as well as any "collectively significant actions taking place over a period of time."[77] Instead of quantifying the increase relative to existing

---

74. *Id.*, at 60.

75. *Id.*, at 73.

76. Petition of International Center for Technology Assessment, et al. to CEQ (Feb. 28, 2008); National Environmental Policy Act Draft Guidelines, 75 Fed. Reg. 8046 (Feb. 23, 2010).

77. 538 F.3d 1127, 1216 (2008) ("stating the total miles of roads to be constructed is similar to merely stating the sum of the acres to be harvested—it is not a description of the *actual* environmental effects").

emissions, an EA must include an estimate of total emissions in light of other past, present, and reasonably foreseeable actions, because any increase might cause a tipping point; even small increases in emissions may be grounds for requiring a supplemental EIS.[78] However, two years later, in *Hapner v. Tidwell*, the same Ninth Circuit held that while NEPA requires a qualitative discussion of climate change, the depth required is minimal when the activities are of a "minor scale so that the direct effects would be meaningless."[79] Other courts have recently held that when there is a question as to whether an action emitting greenhouse gases will significantly affect the human environment, the agency must prepare an EIS because the impact of greenhouse gases on climate change is "precisely the kind of cumulative impacts analysis that NEPA requires agencies to conduct.[80] For example, in *Mid-States Coalition for Progress v. Surface Transportation Board*, the Eighth Circuit held that all foreseeable emissions of greenhouse gases require an EIS, because greenhouse gases always significantly affect air quality.[81] It remains to be seen whether the future will find courts utilizing NEPA to lessen the aggregate or cumulative impact of greenhouse gas emissions on climate change.

2. Using NEPA to Promote Sustainable Energy Practices

As reliance on domestic natural gas and oil increases, the importance of environmentally sound energy development has also

---

78. Taylor, P., *Judge's ruling tests early success of collaborative restoration*, E&E reporter (July 17, 2012).

79. 621 F.3d 123, (9th Cir. 2010) (The court concluded that the Forest Service adequately considered the project's impact on global warming when it authorized the commercial logging and prescribed burning of national forest, because the EA took a "hard look" at environmental consequences of the project, even though it failed to address whether forest thinning actually reduced wildfire intensity).

80. *Center for Biological Diversity v. National Highway Traffic Safety Administration*, 538 F.3d 1127, 1217-19 (2008).

81. 345 F.3d 520, 549 (8th Cir. 2003).

increased. The rise of natural gas production, which involves hydraulic fracturing, or "fracking," brings with it many environmental hazards.[82] Fracking relies on pressurized fluids that allow oil or natural gas to flow through cracks in rock, a process requiring large amounts of water and toxic chemicals. Of great significance, the process produces methane, a greenhouse gas twenty times more harmful to the climate than carbon dioxide. EPA is divided about whether and how to increase regulation of fracking.

The federal government regulates some but not all the risks associated with fracking.[83] Even though EPA set standards to control emissions of toxic and greenhouse gases resulting from the process, Congress exempted fracking under the Safe Drinking Water Act (SDWA).[84] EPA originally exempted fracking after concluding it "poses little or no threat to drinking water," despite the fact that the process involves toxic chemicals that leech into the groundwater.[85] Natural gas companies have exemptions from some federal laws protecting air and drinking water from the processes of industry. For example, coal mining operators cannot inject toxic fluids into the ground without federal permission, but fracking operations can do so without permission. In addition to any federal efforts, states have attempted to control fracking in ways that fit the states' particular geology, ecology and citizen concerns. This has resulted in a patchwork of regulations. Many states require disclosure of the chemicals used, while some states allow operators to store toxic wastewater in open pits, risking surface or groundwater contamination. Still other states lack the knowledge or

---

82. Reitze, A., *The Role of NEPA in Fossil Fuel Resource Development and Use in the Western United States*, 39 B.C. ENVTL. AFF. L. REV. 283, 332 (2012).

83. Freeman, J, "The Wise Way to Regulate Gas Drilling," *New York Times* (July 5, 2012) http://www.nytimes.com/2012/07/06/opinion/the-wise-way-to-regulate-hydraulic-fracturing.html?_r=0.

84. Urbina, I, *"Wastewater Recycling No Cure-All in Gas Process,"* *New York Times*, p. A1 (March 1, 2011); Urbina, I, "Pressure Limits Efforts to Police Drilling for Gas," *New York Times,* p. A1 (March 3, 2011).

85. Urbina, I, "Pressure Limits Efforts to Police Drilling for Gas," *New York Times* p. A1 (March 3, 2011).

resources to enforce standards at all. Perhaps federal regulation is necessary to establish uniformity, especially since pollutants do not always stay within state boundaries. EPA has investigated water-well contamination in Wyoming, where fracking is widespread, even though the agency might not have jurisdiction for such an investigation, and has made efforts in Texas, where it overrode state regulators when a fracking operation was suspected of water contamination.[86]

Having noted the haphazard nature of efforts to control the environmental effects of fracking, let's look specifically at the role NEPA might play with respect to fracking. NEPA was designed to ensure federal agencies consider environmental issues when taking action, and non-governmental organizations have used NEPA to encourage development of sustainable and environmentally friendly energy while opposing energy development with harmful or unknown environmental effects. Without more data on the environmental effects of fracking, courts have been slow to determine whether fracking "significantly affects the human environment" to trigger an EIS. Little is known about the environmental effects of fracking, and agencies do not have enough information to ensure natural gas is produced as cleanly as possible.[87] For example, the New York Attorney General filed a complaint against the EPA and other agencies seeking an EIS for a fracking project in the Delaware River Basin because NEPA applies to projects and programs financed, assisted, conducted, regulated or approved by federal agencies.[88] A federal judge found the complaint premature in light of the speculative nature of the risks of

---

86. Urbina, I, "Pressure Limits Efforts to Police Drilling for Gas," *New York Times* p. A1 (March 3, 2011).

87. Zeller, T, "Studies say natural gas has its own environmental problems," *New York Times* (Apr. 11, 2011) http://www.nytimes.com/2011/04/12/business/energy-environment/12gas.html?pagewanted=all&_r=0.

88. Vaidyanathan, G, "Judge dismisses N.Y. AG's suit seeking enviro reviews in Delaware River Basin," *E&E reporter* (Sept. 25, 2012); Hurley, L, "N.Y. Natural Gas Fracking Lawsuit Raises NEPA Questions," *New York Times* (June 1, 2011) http://www.nytimes.com/gwire/2011/06/01/01greenwire-ny-natural-gas-fracking-lawsuit-raises-nepa-qu-12192.html.

fracking.[89] Without scientific data about the impacts, there can be no assessment of "cumulative impacts." Some fracking projects have, however, been found to violate NEPA, like the Bakken Shale field in North Dakota, by failing to include proper analysis in their EIS.[90]

Because technological advancements have resulted in continuously changing environmental impacts, the effects of fracking are unknown.[91] This, combined with outdated resource management plans, has led the Bureau of Land Management to begin work on a nationwide fracking rule that would require public disclosure of chemicals used in hydraulic fracturing on public land and set standards for well design and wastewater disposal.[92] Absent such a rule, fracking projects continue to be approved with inaccurate EIS's, but NEPA has the potential to be a strong tool to prevent or delay fracking projects until environmental effects can be ascertained.

89. Hurley, L, "N.Y. Natural Gas Fracking Lawsuit Raises NEPA Questions," *New York Times* (June 1, 2011) http://www.nytimes.com/gwire/2011/06/01/01greenwire-ny-natural-gas-fracking-lawsuit-raises-nepa-qu-12192.html.

90. Fact Sheet, "State Dept. Releases Draft Supplemental Environmental Impact Statement on the Proposed Keystone XL Pipeline," *U.S. Dept. of State* (2013) available at http://www.state.gov/r/pa/prs/ps/2013/03/205547.htm.

91. Streater, S, "BLM rules haven't kept up with technology, conservation groups charge," *E&E reporter* (Aug. 10, 2012).

92. *Ibid.*

ADDITIONAL READINGS

Duit, A., *State and Environment: The Comparative Study of Environmental Governance* (MIT Press, 2014).

Eccleston, C., *NEPA and Environmental Planning: Tools, Techniques, and Approaches for Practitioners* (CRC Press, 2012).

Ferlo, A. et al., *The NEPA Litigation Guide* (Chicago: American Bar Association, Section of Environment, Energy, and Resources, 2nd ed. 2012).

Greenberg, M., *The Environmental Impact Statement after Two Generations: Managing Environmental Power* (Routledge, 2012).

Hanna, K., *Environmental Impact Assessment: Practice and Participation* (Don Mills, Ont.: Oxford University Press, 2nd ed., 2009).

Lawrence, D., *Impact Assessment: Practical Solutions to Recurrent Problems and Contemporary Challenges* (Wiley, 2012).

Luther, L., *The National Environmental Policy Act: Background and Implementation* (2013).

Murrill, B., *Hydraulic Fracturing and the National Environmental Policy Act* (CRC Report for Congress, 2012).

Pearson, E., *Environmental and Natural Resources Law* (LexisNexis, 2012).

Toppert, K., *A Citizen's Guide to the NEPA: Having Your Voice Heard* (Penny Hill Press Inc., 2013).

CHAPTER 3
POLLUTION

A. DEFINING THE PROBLEM

Before we address specific pollution problems, we need to consider some basic ideas about what constitutes an ecological system so that we will better understand how pollution becomes a problem. In the simplest sense, all things are connected. We will begin by examining the connections in an ecosystem using Figure 1 as a guide. The figure is representative of common ecosystems, and follows the flow of water from the atmosphere through to the bedrock. In the figure, A represents the surface of the earth, B represents the atmosphere, C represents a lake, D represents flowing water, E represents the boundary between unsaturated soil (F) and saturated soil (G), H represents the boundary between the soil (G) and the bedrock (K), I represents cracks in the bedrock (K) and J represents a deep rock well.

A represents the land, where human activities take place. These activities include manufacturing, mining, agriculture, electrical generation, silviculture (logging), fishing, and just plain living. B represents the layer of air directly above the surface of the earth, known as the troposphere. This air carries various materials, like gases, metals, and dust, which come from both naturally occurring and anthropogenic (man-made) sources.

Material from land activities are washed into the lake basin, C. In the lake basin, water levels are a function of both D, water flowing from rivers and streams, and E, the boundary between the saturated and unsaturated soils. The lake basin is like a teacup at the bottom of a funnel: it catches all the water running over the land

and downhill, and constantly exchanges water with the saturated and unsaturated soil (G and F). Lake basins therefore collect materials that have run off from the land, fallen from the sky, and entered through the soil.

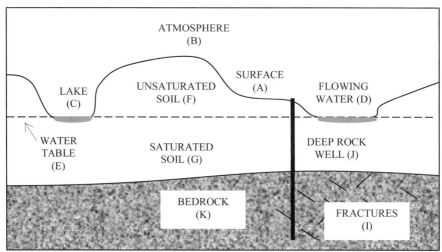

Figure 1. A diagrammatic representation of how the ecosystem is put together.

Water flow in C and D are a function of E, the boundary between saturated and unsaturated soil. E varies depending on rainfall, soil composition, temperature, and land use patterns. When E breaks the surface of the earth, there is a body of water. The rate of water flow in the soil dictates the movement of chemicals; unsaturated water flow is faster than saturated flow. H delineates the boundary between the soil and the bedrock, K, which contains fractures (holes), I, which accumulate and store water. Wells (J) are generally drilled into the bedrock, which, depending on the depth of the bedrock, recharge (water replacement) after drawdown (water removal) pretty quickly. Essentially, wells get their water from the surface after it permeates the soil and reaches a level saturation (G) or an area of storage (I).

Although subsurface conditions vary from one geographic location to another, we can safely say that where water goes, the chemicals and materials in the water are carried through the ecosystem. The connectedness in the ecosystem is therefore established by the flow of material, like water, through parts of the ecosystem.

A more specific example of the interconnectedness can be found in Figure 2, where we examine a simplified version of the nitrogen cycle. The figure follows the structural forms of nitrogen, a nutrient important to all protein, and demonstrates how materials cycle through processes that change their chemical makeup. If we start with organic nitrogen, we can follow the nitrogen cycle in Figure 2. Organic nitrogen in plants is converted to ammonium after plant death, which converts to atmospheric nitrogen and is taken back up by other plants.

Having demonstrated the interconnectedness of ecosystems, we now turn to pollution and the problems it presents. There are multiple types of pollution, including air, water, aesthetic, and noise, but the dominant forms are water and air pollution.

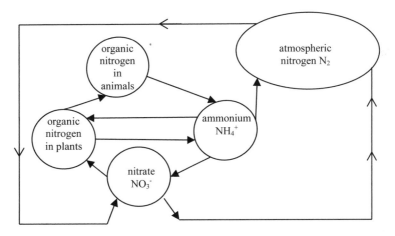

Figure 2. A simplified view of the nitrogen cycle.

1. Water Pollution

Water pollution is broadly defined under its principle environmental statute, the Clean Water Act. "Pollutant" includes solid waste, sewage, garbage, chemical wastes, biological materials, heat, and a host of other materials.[1] Courts have recognized the

---

1. 33 U.S.C. § 1362(6).

expansiveness of this definition and interpreted it to include virtually any material.[2] The Act operates on a discharge prohibition premise, namely that the discharge of a pollutant to navigable waters is prohibited unless EPA or a delegated state agency has issued a permit allowing the discharge. The Act then establishes multiple permit programs, each covering a different type of pollutant source.

Later in this chapter we examine the control mechanisms of this statute. For now, let's focus on which water pollution sources are covered by these permitting programs and which are not. We begin with the National Pollutant Discharge Elimination System (NPDES) permit program which provides permits to direct dischargers from a point source. A "point source" is a discernible, confined, and discrete conveyance from which pollutants may be discharged.[3] Since every public and private facility that discharges any potential pollutant directly into waters of the United States is required to get a permit that describes discharge limitations for specific materials and imposes other conditions on the permittee, we have presumably isolated and identified these point sources. Industrial point source users of water include dairy products processors, sugar processors, textile mills, cement manufacturers, soap and detergent manufacturers, petroleum refiners and electric power generators.[4] What happens to their used water? A large portion of it is treated by various methods to remove identified pollutants, and it is then directly discharged into our watercourses. Public water users discharge primarily through a municipal sewage treatment plant, also known as a publically owned treatment works (POTW). Under its NPDES permit, the POTW tests for pollutants like other direct dischargers. It is also required to implement at least the secondary treatment level of waste removal which removes about 90% of oxygen-demanding substances and suspended solids. Furthermore, those entities who send their waste water to a POTW—i.e. indirect

---

2. *See e.g.*, *U.S. v. Hamel*, 551 F.2d 107, 110-12.

3. 33 U.S.C. § 1362(14).

4. 40 CFR Part 401 *et seq.*

dischargers—have limitations imposed on them. The permit program imposed on these indirect dischargers is known as the pretreatment program because it controls the quality and quantity of water that sewer system users can send to the POTW. Thus, we either treat industrial wastewater separately or pretreat it before it flows to a municipal sewage treatment plant. Industrial treatment or pretreatment is used to recover metals such as silver and cadmium and to remove toxic chemicals such as carbon tetrachloride, trichloroethylene, and other organic as well as inorganic chemicals before discharge.

After treatment, dischargers are often required to test for the presence of pollutants such as biochemical oxygen demand (BOD), suspended solids (SS), total coliform (TC), fecal coliform (FC), phosphorous, nitrate, and pH.[5] The things we test for are good indicators of the types and levels of pollution we wish to control. For example, BOD is a measure of the oxygen demand of microorganisms in the water as they break down organic material. This demand for oxygen reduces the amount of oxygen available for fish and other water creatures. If the BOD is too high, the dissolved oxygen in the water will be too low to support fish such as trout, which require at least 5 parts per million of oxygen in water. SS is a measure of particles in the effluent. If SS is high, aquatic life can be killed when breathing spaces are plugged. Also, sunlight is prevented from penetrating the water, resulting in plants dying and increasing the BOD as they decompose. TC and FC are monitored as indicators of human pollution in water and as a test for chlorination effectiveness in effluent from municipal treatment plants. Maximum levels are established to ensure no adverse effects from disease-causing bacteria. Testing for phosphorous and nitrate can also be required because these two nutrients stimulate aquatic plant growth to such an extent that few other organisms are able to survive at the low dissolved oxygen (DO) level caused by plant decay. The NPDES and pretreatment permit programs offer fairly comprehensive coverage over point source dischargers. Of course, the stringency of a permit's conditions and a permit holder's compliance also play a role in the Clean Water Act's ability to

---

5. 40 CFR Part 133.

regulate pollution from these major sources.

A second major source of pollutants in our waterways is from non-point sources of pollution. Non-point sources include agriculture, construction, silviculture, urban runoff, mining, livestock operations, and home septic systems. Specific examples include soil from erosion and manure from livestock. The major pollutants from these sources are suspended solids from erosion and nutrients such as nitrogen and phosphorus. Each year, billions of tons of soil are eroded by water and wind. About half of this eroded soil is deposited in watercourses. Substantial pollutant contribution to these watercourses comes not only in the form of the soil itself but also from the tons of fertilizers spread over the vast agricultural fields lining our rivers and streams and over each of our gardens and lawns. These sources are not the defined, discrete conveyances regulated by the NPDES permit program, but many of the nutrients in the fertilizers such as nitrogen, phosphorous, and potash end up in runoff to our waterways. Construction is another significant contributor of sediment from erosion, and one bared acre of land can contribute over 150 tons of such sediment each year. Silviculture may cause landslides, and certainly extensive erosion results from poor logging practices. Urban runoff (storm drains) carries metals and toxics as well as suspended solids into our watercourses. Mining operations—mainly strip mining for coal—have exposed over 400,000 acres of unreclaimed soil surface in Ohio alone. Water washing across these surfaces turns acidic before entering a watercourse. In Pennsylvania, reduced pH levels from acidic runoff has resulted in the destruction of many good trout streams.

Another significant non-point source of water pollution is manure from livestock, both unconfined and those kept in feedlots. Would you support the position that concentrated animal operations constitute a point source of pollution to our waterways and should therefore be subject to the permitting process? If so, how would a permit limit these operations and how would compliance with a permit be monitored? One approach is to not focus on the discharge, which is difficult to measure, but to require better management practices from the operators.[6] Yet another non-point source of water pollution is the approximately 20 million homes that are serviced by septic tanks, presumably with leach fields. Many of these are poorly maintained and serviced only when a noticeable problem develops, which is usually long after soil water has been contaminated.

To recap, when water (polluted or not) comes in contact with any material it can physically or chemically carry, it will carry that material. Very undesirable material may end up in a very inappropriate location. The NPDES and pretreatment permitting programs under the Clean Water Act seek to limit and monitor—but not prohibit—the addition of pollutants to our waterways from point sources. Non-point sources, however, also play a significant role in contributing to water pollution and non-point source control is left largely to the states under the Clean Water Act,[7] and the results have been mixed.

Having considered the nature and sources of water pollution, we next turn to air pollution. In that context, we should keep in mind that pollutants in the air also reach and pollute water even if the water is far removed from the air pollution source. We thus have a distinct connection between water pollution and air pollution. That connection will also be explored when we discuss acid rain in Section C.

2. Air Pollution

The federal government has defined "air pollutant" as any physical, chemical, biological or radioactive matter that enters the air.[8] Historically, we dumped pollutants into the air, using tall smoke stacks, thinking that "dilution is the solution to pollution." What we did not understand was that material placed into the air eventually gets washed out of the air when it rains, and into the

---

6. EPA has shown interest in this approach, See the Agency's discussion of "Concentrated Animal Feeding Operations," available at www.epa.gov/npdes.

7. 33 U.S.C. § 1329.

8. 42 U.S.C.A. §7602(g).

water and soil. As more and more sourced pollutants were created (more utility plants, more industrial facilities, more cars on the road), more pollutants were discharged into the air. The overall quantity of pollutants in the air increased, and eventually we began to notice them both in the air and the rain. One example is the production in the atmosphere of acid rain when sulfur dioxide (SO_2) emissions combine with water to produce sulfuric acid (H_2SO_4).

In order to address the overall quality of the air around us, we have ambient Air Quality Standards under the Clean Air Act (CAA) for six common air pollutants.[9] These pollutants, also known as "criteria pollutants," are particle pollution (often referred to as particulate matter), ground-level ozone, carbon monoxide, sulfur oxides, nitrogen oxides, and lead. Exposure to these pollutants is associated with numerous effects on human health, including increased respiratory symptoms, hospitalization for heart or lung diseases, and even premature death. Table I shows the National Ambient Air Quality Standards.

The CAA also controls the amounts of individual pollution that are emitted from various pollution sources. Four of these pollutants (carbon monoxide, lead, nitrogen oxides, and sulfur oxides) are emitted directly from a variety of sources. Ozone is not directly emitted, but is formed when oxides of nitrogen and volatile organic compounds (VOCs) react in the presence of sunlight. Particulate matter can be directly emitted, or formed when emissions of nitrogen oxides, sulfur oxides, ammonia, organic compounds, and other gases react in the atmosphere. The sources of emissions can be grouped into eight major source sectors: agriculture, dust, fires, fuel combustion, industrial processes, mobile, solvent and miscellaneous. For example, agriculture includes crops and livestock dust, fertilizer application, livestock waste; industrial processes include cement manufacturing, pulp and paper storage, oil and gas production. How emissions from specific sources are controlled will be discussed in section C.

---

9. 42 U.S.C.A § 7408.

Table I. National Ambient Air Quality Standards[10]

Pollutant	Averaging Time	Primary Standard	Secondary Standard
Particulate matter $PM_{2.5}$	Annual	$15 \ \mu g/m^3$	$15 \ \mu g/m^3$
	24-hour	$35 \ \mu g/m^3$	$35 \ \mu g/m^3$
Particulate matter PM_{10}	Annual	$15 \ \mu g/m^3$	$15 \ \mu g/m^3$
	24-hour	$150 \ \mu g/m^3$	$150 \ \mu g/m^3$
Sulfur oxides	24-hour	0.14 ppm	-
	Annual	0.030 ppm	-
Carbon monoxide	1-hour	34 ppm	-
	8-hour	9 ppm	-
Nitrogen dioxide	1-hour	100 ppb	-
	Annual	53 ppb	0.053 ppm
Ozone	1-hour	0.12 ppm	-
	8-hour	0.075 ppm	-
Lead	3-month average	$0.15 \ \mu g/m^3$	$0.15 \ \mu g/m^3$
	Quarter	$1.55 \ \mu g/m^3$	$1.55 \ \mu g/m^3$

B. PRIVATE LAW REMEDIES – NUISANCE AND NEGLIGENCE; INJUNCTIONS AND DAMAGES

One method of analytically describing and evaluating the tools that the legal system uses for pollution control is to separate them into private pollution control mechanisms and public pollution control mechanisms. For our discussion, private control mechanisms will include lawsuits instituted by individuals (or other entities, such as corporations or states) against a polluter where the lawsuit is based on a common law wrong such as negligence by the polluter or the polluter maintaining a nuisance. Remedies for common law wrongs can be provided by the judicial system, even though no legislature has prohibited any specific actions or provided remedies for wrongful actions. By contrast, public pollution control, which we consider in Section C, is based on the enactment of legislation—federal or state statutes, or local ordinances—which is intended to directly affect pollution.

---

10. 40 CFR § 50.4 et seq., 42 U.S.C.A. § 7409.

1. Nuisance

Consider this example: Assume that a cement plant is located near where you live, and it is discharging dirt and smoke into the air. You want to stop the pollution, so what might you do? You might hope for a statute or administrative regulation that would prohibit the pollution and bring with it a governmental enforcement scheme or at least provide you with the opportunity to bring a citizen's suit to enforce the prohibition. In the absence of such a statutory or administrative prohibition, you might initiate a private lawsuit against the cement company and ask the court for an injunction ordering the cement company to stop polluting and/or to order payment of damages for the harm they have done to you. Your case would be a tort case claiming "nuisance." This action basically claims that the cement company has a duty not to unreasonably interfere with your peaceful enjoyment of your land, that it is so interfering, and that it is thus a nuisance. The common law (judge-made law from previous court cases) recognizes this tort of nuisance and allows judges to enjoin the action causing the nuisance and to provide monetary compensation for harm. This private control mechanism also operates as a deterrent—e.g., manufacturers who cause damage by polluting and are held liable for payment for that damage may be deterred from polluting, and others who learn of the liability may also be deterred from similar conduct.

This cement company situation is similar to the precedent setting New York case of *Boomer v. Atlantic Cement Company.*[11] In *Boomer*, the plaintiffs were successful in establishing that there was a nuisance. The question that was raised for the appeals court concerned the appropriate remedy to be given to the plaintiffs. The alternative remedies considered by the court were: (1) to issue an injunction prohibiting the cement company from maintaining the nuisance (stop polluting or close down) with a postponement of the injunction for eighteen months to allow the company an opportunity for technical advances to eliminate the nuisance, or (2) to in effect allow the company to continue operating as it had been on the

---

11. 309 N.Y.S. 2d 312, 257 N.E. 2d 870.

condition that it pay permanent damages to the plaintiffs which would compensate them for the total existing and future economic loss to their property caused by the cement company.

In deciding between these two potential remedies, the court considered that the plaintiffs' economic harm was relatively small compared to the consequences of an injunction. An injunction could have resulted in the closing of a $45,000,000 plant with over 300 employees. In addition to the magnitude of the economic harm to the company and, perhaps of greater significance, to the community, the court was influenced by the fact that the company was up to date in air pollution control technology and eighteen months would not result in meaningful technical advances. Furthermore, the court believed that the making of technical advances should be an industry responsibility rather than the responsibility of the defendant company. As for the deterrence of pollution, the court believed that the risk of being required to pay permanent damages would be a sufficient incentive for research by cement plant owners for improved techniques to minimize pollution. The court thus opted for permanent compensatory damages. This was a major change in the law because prior to *Boomer*, if there was a nuisance, then an injunction to stop the activity was almost automatic. In *Boomer*, plaintiffs were paid for past and future harm, but the pollution was allowed to continue.

A dissenting opinion was filed in *Boomer*. The dissenting judge contended that by letting the cement company pollute if it paid damages, the court was licensing a continuing wrong. The company could do what the law said was wrong so long as it paid a fee. Perhaps the court could be accused of supporting or helping establish a societal norm of accepting polluted air because it had placed an official stamp of approval on pollution-causing activity if the polluter paid for the harm done. Which result would you favor given the factual circumstances—stop the pollution or just make the company pay for the harm? Maybe paying for the harm negates the "polluting," and because there is no pollution, the benefits from the cement plant outweigh the detriments. Full compensation essentially erases the harm, and, without harm, perhaps there can be no such thing as pollution. Regardless of the readers' position, the difference between the philosophies of the majority of the New

York high court and the dissenting judge is basic to the continuing environmental debate—should an activity which causes harm be stopped, or can it continue if it pays for the harm it causes? It can be argued that if the company can produce the cement, pay for the pollution damage, and still make a profit by asking and getting a high enough price for the cement to cover the damages it has to pay, then the utility to society of the cement outweighs the harm which its manufacture creates.

While the court in *Boomer* chose compensatory damages over enjoining the nuisance, other cases have resulted in the issuance of an injunction. It is possible that these different results are due to the fact that states vary with respect to what their body of common law contains; however, an attempt at explaining differing results based on factual differences rather than jurisdictional differences is worthwhile. First, we should note that *Boomer* may have been an example of "good guys or bad guys" law. What was in fact the proper remedy in *Boomer* may be said to be a reasonably debatable question. In close cases the court may tend to give the benefit of the doubt to a defendant with a good track record. Perhaps the result in *Boomer* might have been different if it had not been found that the most modern dust control devices available had been installed in the defendant's plant and that it was unlikely that the defendant itself could develop improvements in the near future. Second, we should consider what factual situations have led other courts, as opposed to the *Boomer* court, to enjoin the operation of facilities that were causing nuisances by polluting.

One case in which an injunction prohibiting the operation of a polluting facility was issued was *Spur Industries, Inc. v. Del E. Webb Development Co.*[12] That case involved a cattle feedlot, which had been operating lawfully but became a nuisance when nearby land was developed for residential purposes (Del Webb's Sun City in Arizona). The odor and flies from the feedlot were at the least annoying and perhaps also unhealthy for the nearby residents. Del Webb's request for an injunction against Spur's operation was granted by the court. The court raised some factors which, if present in a given situation, may lead courts to be willing to grant an

---

12. 108 Ariz. 178, 494 P. 2d 700.

injunction. If a large number of people or an entire neighborhood is affected by the nuisance rather than a small number of persons, a court might be more likely to enjoin the nuisance instead of providing damages as a remedy. In *Spur*, the court also emphasized the type of injury, health rather than property damage, as a factor in its decision. A breeding ground for flies which are capable of transmitting disease had been declared dangerous to the public health by the Arizona legislature. Another factor possibly supporting the granting of the injunction may have been the harshness of the injury to the developer, Del Webb. Its parcels of land were difficult if not impossible to sell. Factors like a large number of victims and health effects have led courts to find that the nuisance is a "public nuisance" rather than a "private nuisance" and to be more willing to enjoin it. Note, however, that a remedy based on a finding of "public nuisance" is still within the realm of private pollution control because it is a court-made remedy which does not need to be based on legislation intended to directly affect pollution.

In the *Spur Industries* case, Spur's operation of a feedlot was found to be a nuisance and, for the above reasons, the operation was enjoined; however, Spur did not come away from court as a total loser. The court recognized that at the time Spur established its feedlot there was no indication that a new city would spring up alongside it in what had been a rural, agricultural area. The court said that Spur was enjoined not because of any wrongdoing on its part but because of the court's regard for the rights of the public. The court also found that Del Webb was not blameless with respect to the problem. It had taken advantage of the lower land values and the availability of large tracts of rural land. Del Webb's land would almost certainly skyrocket in value without the nearby feedlot. The court thus required Del Webb to indemnify Spur Industries for damages to Spur occasioned by the injunction that required Spur to either cease operation or move its feedlot.

The court itself noted that the result in *Spur* "may appear novel," and the court also carefully limited its decision to cases where a developer has, with foreseeability, necessitated the granting of an injunction against a lawful business by coming into a previously agricultural or industrial area—coming to the nuisance. This novel decision raises some interesting questions. The court clearly finds that a polluting nuisance should be stopped, but it also acknowledges that when the issue is preventing someone from continuing to engage in a lawful activity because of changes in circumstances, consideration should be given to preventing the lawful enterprise from suffering economic loss brought about by the changed circumstances. If XYZ Steel Company has been operating in a lawful manner for years, and the public decides that air pollution problems require stricter emissions standards and hence installation of pollution control equipment by XYZ Steel, should the public compensate the company for costs brought about by the public's demands, or should the costs fall to the shareholders or customers of the company? Perhaps, although XYZ Steel had been using the public's air before the new emissions standards were in effect, that prior use does not give the Company a financially protected interest to continue to use the air without meeting the new restrictions. An effort to reconcile this response with the *Spur Industries* case runs into problems. In the operation of its feedlot, Spur was not confining itself to its own land and the air above it. Odor and flies appeared on or above land owned by others. For a period of years no one complained, but when new needs of the public required that the odor and flies be halted, the court appears to have found that Spur's prior use was relevant to giving it an interest which was to be financially protected when its continued use of the surrounding air was inconsistent with the public interest. If Del Webb was simply asking that its land and property rights not be interfered with by others in a way which is prohibited by the common law of nuisance, then why should it have to pay to have that prohibited interference stopped? If Spur is the one causing the pollution, it would appear that Spur should bear the costs of stopping the pollution rather than the cost being placed on Del Webb, which was merely making sound business use of land which it owned. The "novel" *Spur Industries* case may be an example of the judicial system working at its best and taking the unusual approach of reaching a compromise solution to a problem which is the fault of no one and the costs of which are better shared than placed on one party. Yet, what would the court have done if many residents surrounding the feedlot had bought and built there individually rather than buying from a land developer? Would the court have required them to indemnify Spur for Spur's losses due to the injunction, or would the court have refused to issue an injunction? Should the result in the case have depended on the fact that Del Webb was a convenient corporate treasury which was both allowed and required to "buy an injunction"?

The relationships between neighboring property owners in agricultural situations like that in the *Spur Industries* case continue to be the subject of nuisance litigation, and the results have been varied. For example, in 2012, the Seventh Circuit held that when the character of the area changes gradually from commercial, industrial or agricultural to residential, the homeowners can seek to abate those uses as private nuisances.[13] Also in 2012, however, the Illinois Court of Appeals held that further development of an existing residential property did not transform a neighboring cattle operation into a nuisance because the property was residential when the defendants began their cattle operation.[14] State legislatures have intervened on the issue of agricultural activities and nuisance, and all 50 states have adopted some form of a Right-to-Farm Act intended to protect agricultural producers from nuisance actions. The Acts preclude nuisance suits to varying degrees, based on factors like whether the residential development expanded into traditionally agricultural lands, and whether the nuisance existed prior to the residential development.[15] For example, a Vermont statute states that: "Agricultural activities conducted on farmland, if consistent with good agricultural practices and established prior to the non-agricultural activities, shall be entitled to a rebuttable presumption that the activity does not constitute a nuisance. . . ."[16]

---

13. *Guth v. Tazewell County*, 2012 WL 4901159 F.3d (7th Cir. 2012).

14. *Toftoy v. Rosenwinkel*, 356 2d. 267 (Ill. 2012).

15. *Alpental Community Club, Inc., v. Seattle Gymnastics Soc.*, 111 P.3d 257 (Wa. 2005).

16. 12 V.S.A. § 5753(a); *Trickett v. Ochs*, 2003 Vt Lexis 273 discusses the application of "right-to-farm" statutes in a number of states.

2. Other Private Law Mechanisms

In addition to nuisance actions, there are other legal mechanisms which are not based on pollution control statutes and which parties have sought to utilize for pollution control purposes or to obtain compensation for harms which may have come to them due to the conduct of a polluter. Since these private law mechanisms are applicable to fewer pollution situations and/or have met with less or more indirect success than the tool of a nuisance suit, some but not all of them will be noted here, and our consideration of them will be relatively brief.

If your drinking water supply became polluted because of someone's unintentional but careless discharge of a toxic water pollutant, you might bring a negligence suit against the discharger of the pollutant and seek monetary compensation for the harm done. This suit is like a negligence suit brought against a driver who struck your car in the rear because the driver was acting carelessly by following you too closely. Negligence suits may be contrasted to nuisance suits by noting that negligent conduct can generally be described as a "one-shot deal" rather than the continuing conduct and continuing harm which forms the basis of a nuisance suit. Thus monetary compensation for harm is usually the appropriate remedy because there is not continuing wrongful conduct to enjoin. Although a negligence suit does not stop the polluting event from taking place (it has already happened), negligence suits can deter pollution in addition to providing compensation for pollution's harms. At least in theory, the potential liability of a polluter for its negligence will result in greater care being taken by people. That should deter negligent conduct and thus reduce pollution. The practical effect of this deterrence mechanism is dependent on factors such as the added costs to the potential polluter of greater care compared to the costs of paying for damages caused by negligent conduct. Furthermore, the utility of negligence suits as a pollution control tool is attenuated by factors such as the cost and bother for a victim to bring a lawsuit. The magnitude of the harm may not be worth the effort of the suit, or the victim's insurance may cover the loss. Chapter 6 contains additional discussion of the theory of negligence suits and the difficulties which a victim may face with respect to winning such a suit.

Some of the other approaches to private pollution control may be illustrated by the examples of suits based on the federal antitrust laws, the federal securities laws, and provisions of the federal constitution. While these suits are not common law actions, they are discussed here as private pollution control because the statutes or constitutional provisions being invoked were not specifically directed at pollution problems.

One attempt to invoke the antitrust laws to combat pollution involved a suit wherein plaintiffs alleged that automobile manufacturers had conspired to eliminate competition among themselves with respect to the development, manufacture, and installation of automotive air pollution control devices.[17] The plaintiffs asked the court to find that: (1) there was a conspiracy; (2) the conspiracy was a violation of the Clayton Act's prohibition on conspiracies that restrain competition; and (3) the automobile companies should be required to retrofit their automobiles with effective air pollution control devices. The court found that while "the invitation to provide an innovative solution to it [smog] is tempting," the only purpose of the antitrust laws is to prohibit restraints on competition in order to guarantee a free marketplace in which an unsophisticated consumer can be assured of the best possible product for the least possible expense. Even assuming that there was a conspiracy, the court found that retrofitting automobiles with pollution control devices would not further the purpose of the antitrust laws and that the antitrust laws do not provide a remedy for pollution.

Federal securities laws provide another example of indirect pollution control through awareness and deterrence mechanisms. These laws promote the disclosure of facts about a publically traded company that a reasonable investor would want to know. This allows investors to inform themselves about companies they are considering for investment and protects against market manipulation by a handful of investors who might be privy to non-public information. Disclosure is ensured under these laws by

---

17. *In re Multidistrict Vehicle Air Pollution*, 481 F. 2d 122 (1973), 367 F. Supp. 1298.

imposing liability on anyone who makes false statements or omissions in connection with the financial filings that a publically traded company is periodically required to make with the Securities and Exchange Commission ("SEC").[18] Investors can then use these filings as a reliable source of information with regard to a company. Additional disclosure requirements were mandated by Congress after the scandals involving Enron and other corporations,[19] but few specific provisions exist for disclosing environmental liabilities. As a result, not only are the regulations rarely enforced, but the liabilities are rarely taken into account by financial analysts when they are assessing companies. This is mostly because it is difficult to calculate potential liabilities, especially considering long-term trends like global warming that do not fit into the quarterly reporting schedule.[20]

From an environmental perspective, consider two effects of these disclosure requirements on a publically traded company. First, in order to submit its required filings with the SEC, a company will need to periodically audit its compliance with federal, state and local environmental laws. This process raises the awareness level of the company and its investors as to environmental issues. Moreover, the awareness is not just with regard to past environmental compliance. The securities regulations also require the company's reports to look forward and include financial estimates of anticipated expenditures for items such as pollution control devices.[21]

A second effect of the environmental disclosure requirements found in federal securities laws is the corresponding desire for a company to want to limit the environmental issues that it must

---

18. Calland, D. and Babst, C., "S.E.C. Gets Vigilant on Corporate Environmental Liabilities Disclosures," 35 Pa. L. Weekly 48 (December 2, 2002); 15 U.S.C.A. § 7266 (Enhanced review of periodic disclosures by issuers).

19. Corporate and Auditing Accountability, Responsibility and Transparency Act of 2002. Pub. L. No. 107-204, 116 Stat. 745.

20. Cortese, A., "As the Earth Warms, Will Companies Pay?" *The New York Times*, available at http://www.nytimes.com/2002/08/18/business/business-as-the-earth-warms-will-companies-pay.html?pagewanted=all&src=pm.

21. 17 CFR §229.101 (c)(1)(xii).

disclose. For example, suppose you are an investor considering a purchase of stock in a soap manufacturer. You only want to invest in one soap manufacturer, so you have to choose between Company A and Company B. You pull up financial reports for each company on the SEC's webpage[22] and learn that Company A has an enforcement action pending with EPA for alleged violations of its NPDES permit. Company A's environmental disclosures indicate that a quick resolution of the matter is anticipated with a possibility of monetary penalties. Company B's financial reports indicate that it has been equally successful in the soap manufacturing business, but there are no significant environmental disclosures provided in Company B's recent reports. Since you know that securities laws require Company B to list the environmental concerns that a reasonable investor would want to know, you take this to mean that Company B has been more successful at environmental compliance. As a "green" investor, you may be more likely to choose Company B. As an investor who is not interested in "green," you may also be more likely to choose Company B because you think there is less risk of environmental disaster and financial loss or ruin in the future. The potential for investors to choose a company for investment based, at least in part, on its environmental record creates an incentive for companies to address rather than avoid environmental issues. It deters non-compliance because non-compliance will deter investors.

Attempts have been made to directly invoke the United States Constitution to remedy pollution problems without resorting to statutory or common law remedies. In *Tanner v. Armco Steel Corp.*, the plaintiffs claimed that the Ninth Amendment included a right to a healthy and clean environment.[23] The Ninth Amendment states: "The enumeration in the Constitution of certain rights, shall not be construed to deny or disparage others retained by the people." The court determined that this residual retention of rights by the people would not be interpreted to embody a legally assertable right to a healthful environment. While neither the Ninth Amendment approach nor the antitrust approach discussed earlier was

---

22. <www.sec.gov>

23. 340 F. Supp. 532.

successful, they have been noted here to raise the question of whether, if the facts of a case were compelling enough, and if resort to some non-environmental body of law were necessary to provide a remedy for a wrong, a court might accept an invitation to provide an innovative solution to an environmental problem.

In the realm of constitutional environmental protection, better potential may exist at the state level for success in bringing constitutional provisions to bear directly on the environment without resorting to statutory or common law mechanisms. Some state constitutions have provisions that speak expressly of environmental concerns. For example, Article 1, Section 27 of the Pennsylvania Constitution states: "The people have a right to clean air, pure water, and to the preservation of the natural, scenic, historic and esthetic values of the environment. . . ." In an appropriate case, a court may be disposed to invoke such a state constitutional provision, in and of itself, as the basis for a remedy. Since these state constitutional provisions deal specifically with the environment and are not a part of the common law, from the point of view of the organization of this chapter they may really a part of our next section—Public Pollution Control.

C. PUBLIC POLLUTION CONTROL – STATUTES AND REGULATIONS: FEDERAL, STATE, AND LOCAL

As an introduction to our discussion of pollution control mechanisms, which are established through legislation, intended to directly affect pollution, we should note that the legislation addresses various subject areas such as pollution of the air and water and pollution by noise, heat, and even light. These subject areas are often interconnected, yet legislative enactments have usually separated them and treated them individually. While for purposes of analysis, this section will also tend to treat these subjects individually, we should not completely forget their interrelationships. In addition, the reader should be aware that some issues that will be discussed here in one context, such as air pollution, are relevant to other pollution subject areas such as water or noise. The discussion of similar issues will not be repeated for different subject areas; however, the reader is encouraged to consider how an issue raised under water pollution might apply to air pollution.

1. Air Pollution – Control Mechanisms and Economic Costs of Control; Stratospheric Ozone Protection; Acid Rain; Climate Change

The main tools for air pollution control are found in the Clean Air Act.[24] The Clean Air Act vests the EPA Administrator (the head of the federal Environmental Protection Agency) with information gathering, research, and planning functions, but of more significance to us are the direct operative control mechanisms that the statute establishes. The act segregates automobiles and aircraft as "moving sources" of air pollution and requires administrative promulgation and enforcement of emission standards for these sources. Moving sources are certainly of great importance, but, because of space constraints, we will emphasize the parts of the statute that establish quality standards for the air around us (ambient air quality standards) and emission limitations for nonmoving or "stationary" sources.[25] At the end of this section we will, however, note some recent developments with respect to the Clean Air Act's applicability to automobile emissions of "greenhouse gasses."

Leaving the moving sources aside, and postponing acid rain control until our next section, we can think of the Clean Air Act as having three focuses: (1) the medium (air), (2) the sources of pollution, and (3) the pollutants. With respect to the medium, the act provides for establishment of and compliance with ambient air quality standards for various pollutants. This mechanism states that regardless of where the pollutants come from, there may only be certain levels of them present in the air. With respect to the sources of pollution, the act says that regardless of whether the air around us is clean or dirty, there is no justification for allowing stationary sources of pollution (like factories or power plants) to emit higher

---

24. 42 U.S.C. § 7401 et seq.

25. Reducing air pollution from automobiles by encouraging the use of alternative fuels is discussed in Chapter 7.

levels of pollutants than necessary so long as we take into account available control technology and the cost of such technology. Thus emission standards are established for stationary sources. With respect to the focus on the pollutants themselves, Congress decided that some air pollutants are so hazardous that especially strict emission limitations, and perhaps prohibitions, are necessary. Also, production of the specific chemicals that destroy the stratospheric ozone layer is to be halted regardless of cost or availability of substitute products. Let's consider the "pollutant" focus of the Clean Air Act (CAA) first.

Under the 1970 CAA, Congress defined a "hazardous air pollutant" as one which may "reasonably be anticipated to result in an increase in mortality or an increase in serous irreversible or incapacitating reversible, illness" and directed EPA to set emission standards for these pollutants to provide "an ample margin of safety to protect the public health."[26] No mention was made of the costs which might be incurred in achieving this strict standard, although EPA was specifically directed to take costs of emission reduction into account in setting emission standards for "nonhazardous" air pollutants in other parts of the CAA. One could thus conclude that the sole factor of relevance in setting emission standards for hazardous air pollutants was health, and cost could not be considered. EPA contended, however, that Congress had not intended to preclude the use of cost as a factor, and, in *Natural Resources Defense Council v. EPA*,[27] the court found that, while Congress was primarily concerned with health in the hazardous air pollutants part of the statute, the history of the legislation did not indicate an intent by Congress to preclude EPA from using cost as a factor in setting hazardous air pollutant emission standards.

Even with cost as a legally allowable factor, EPA was presented with a statutory quandary. Emission standards were required to provide an ample margin of safety to protect the public health, but most hazardous air pollutants are potential carcinogens with no known threshold below which emission levels would be considered

---

26. 42 U.S.C. § 7412 prior to 1990 amendment.

27. 824 F.2d 1146.

"safe." Yet if EPA were to set emission levels at zero, the effect on industry and the economy would be significant. As a result, between 1970 and 1990, EPA had listed only eight hazardous air pollutants and set emission standards for only seven of them.[28]

In the 1990 amendments to the CAA, Congress, dissatisfied with EPA's slowness in listing and limiting hazardous air pollutant emissions, took the unusual step of specifically listing 189 hazardous air pollutants, a task usually left to an agency and its expertise.[29] Congress did, however, continue to leave the setting of the emission standards in the hands of EPA, but it provided a new framework for doing so. EPA is directed to promulgate emission standards that require the maximum degree of emission reduction achievable for new and existing sources of hazardous air pollutants, taking cost, public health, environmental impacts and energy requirements into consideration.[30] This standard cannot be less stringent than the emission control achieved by the "best controlled similar source." Analogously, emission standards for existing sources may not be less stringent than the average of the few best performing existing sources. If costs to industry will allow for them, EPA may establish even stricter standards, but the best in the industry is now Congress' benchmark for emissions of "hazardous air pollutants."

The scope of hazardous air pollution control has broadened from being solely directed at protecting human health in 1970 to include protection of the nonhuman environment from significant and widespread harm in the 2000s. Even stricter emission standards will be set if necessary to provide an ample margin of safety to protect the public health or to prevent an "adverse environmental effect." "Adverse environmental effect" includes significant and widespread adverse effects on wildlife, aquatic life, or other natural resources. Also, the "best in the industry" approach of the amendment is intended to constantly reduce emissions by providing

---

28. Marchant, G. and Danzeisen, D., "Acceptable' Risk for Hazardous Air Pollutants," 13 *Harv. Envtl. L. Rev.* 535 (1989).

29. 42 U.S.C. § 7412(b).

30. 42 U.S.C.A. § 7412(2).

incentives for development of new emission control technology. If you develop technology to make you the "best controlled similar source," no one can enter the market to compete with you unless they develop still better technology or pay you to use your technology.

The "pollutant" focus of the CAA is also manifested in the sections of the amendments that control by name those pollutants that contribute to the destruction of the stratospheric ozone layer. The pollutants are the chlorofluorocarbons (CFCs) and halons. The adverse effects resulting from use of these chemicals, including increases in skin cancer, and the worldwide concern about ozone layer depletion that led to the international treaty known as the Montreal Protocol, are noted in Chapter 1. The 1990 Clean Air Act restricted United States production and consumption of CFCs and halons by providing for a phasing out of these chemicals by the year 2000. In each year from 1991 through 2000, decreasing percentages of production levels from a baseline year (1986 or 1989 depending on the chemical) were allowed.[31] While Congress apparently thought this phaseout schedule would probably be sufficient to address the ozone depletion problem, it authorized an acceleration of the phaseout if scientific information showed that a more stringent schedule was necessary to protect human health or the environment.[32] In response to new scientific data showing major ozone depletion likelihood in highly populated northern hemisphere areas including the U.S., the President accelerated the phaseout by ordering that CFC and halon production halt entirely by the end of 1995.[33] As noted in Chapters 1 and 8, the international effort, the U.S. cooperation in that international effort, and renewed commitment to the phaseout of the harmful chemicals in developing nations will hopefully lead to a successful resolution of the stratospheric ozone layer depletion problem.

---

31. 42 U.S.C. § 7671 and § 7671c. The less harmful "hydrochlorofluorocarbons" are phased out on a different schedule (see 42 U.S.C. § 7671d).

32. 42 U.S.C. § 7671e.

33. *Weekly Compilation of Presidential Documents* (Washington, DC: Office of the Federal Register, Feb. 17, 1992) p.249.

Having outlined the "pollutant" focus of the Clean Air Act (the approach used to control hazardous air pollutants and CFCs), let's next consider the control mechanism that focuses on the "medium" (the air)—the ambient air quality standards. Congress has said that the quality of our air should be protected and enhanced to promote the public health and welfare. The Administrator is thus directed to study the effects of pollutants having negative impacts on the public health and welfare and to establish national primary and secondary ambient air quality standards based on that study.[34] The national primary ambient air quality standards are those the attainment and maintenance of which, allowing an adequate margin of safety, are requisite to protect the "public health." The national secondary ambient air quality standards are those the attainment and maintenance of which are requisite to protect the "public welfare" from known or anticipated adverse effects. Effects on welfare are said to include, but not be limited to, effects on items such as soils, water, crops, animals, climate, property, economic values, and personal comfort. The list is very broad, but even if one could think of something adversely affected that is not on the list, the "but is not limited to" clause would allow its inclusion.

In EPA's setting of the primary ambient air quality standards, the issue of cost again became relevant. The CAA instructs EPA to set primary standards that are requisite to protect the public health with an adequate margin of safety. Cost is not mentioned as a factor in the section of the CAA involving the primary ambient air quality standards, although it is mentioned in other sections with respect to other types of standards. The statute requires EPA to review and make appropriate revisions to the ambient standards every five years. In 1997, EPA revised the standards for ozone and particulate matter and did not consider cost. Industry challenged the standards in court, arguing that the words "requisite" and "adequate margin" mean EPA should have considered cost. In a 2001 case that had a number of issues and was a broad industry challenge to the CAA, the U.S. Supreme Court unanimously decided that Congress did not intend cost to be a factor and that the CAA "unambiguously bars

---

34. 42 U.S.C. §§ 7408 and 7409.

cost considerations from the NAAQS-setting process."[35]

The setting of the ambient air quality standards is done at the federal level, but the implementation of the federally set standards is placed in the hands of the states.[36] The attainment or implementation phase of the ambient air quality standards mechanism is a good illustration of the fact that many environmental statutes are political compromises between those who favor state control and those who favor federal control, either because of differing beliefs about which level of government can best perform a task or about which level should be in control of local geographic areas. The Air Quality Standards are set by the federal government, but each state has the opportunity to implement the standards and to choose its own methods of doing so. Thus one state may choose to implement the standards by being more restrictive with respect to automobiles, while another may choose instead to emphasize limiting industrial growth. The states submit their state implementation plans (SIPs) to EPA, which may approve or disapprove a plan or any portion thereof depending on whether it meets requirements listed in the statute.[37] If a state does not submit a plan, or EPA disapproves of a submitted plan, the state must either submit a new plan or face sanctions, and federal courts have ordered that after a certain point, EPA must step in and promulgate a Federal Implementation Plan (FIP).[38]

With respect to the ambient air quality standards, a major issue that emerged is known as Prevention of Significant Deterioration (PSD). PSD ensures that the Ambient Air Quality Standards do not let states that are within the standards ("attainment standards")

---

35. *Whitman v. American Trucking Association*, 531 U.S. 457, 471.

36. 42 U.S.C. § 7410.

37. 42 U.S.C.A. § 7410(a) (Requirements include items such as having monitoring and enforcement programs, showing the capability of attaining the air quality standards within the time frames set by the statute, and containing provisions to prohibit any stationary source within the state from emitting pollutants which will prevent another state from attaining the ambient air quality standards).

38. *Assoc. of Irritated Residents v. U.S. EPA*, 686 F.3d 668 (9th Cir. 2011).

allow their air to degrade to the upper limits of the standards.[39] EPA established the primary standard to protect the public health and the secondary standard to protect the public welfare from any known or anticipated adverse effects.[40] Those in favor of allowing the air quality to deteriorate "up" to the level of the standards argue that there is no reason for air to be cleaner than the standards. Unindustrialized areas of the country would argue that they should not be penalized for failing to industrialize before the CAA, and that it would be unfair to prevent them from allowing a limited amount of deterioration if it enabled more industry and jobs and a potentially better standard of living.[41] They should not be required to forever be America's "clean air paradise" dependent on low wage tourism jobs from those who live in more economically prosperous locations.

Those in favor of preventing deterioration argue that because the standards are the product of factual and political/philosophical compromises, it is better to err on the side of caution and keep clean air at its existing level of cleanliness. This is often known as the precautionary principle. Factually, scientific experts disagree on the standard necessary to protect the public health and welfare, and the standards are likely to be a compromise between those who are very worried about the adverse effects of air pollution and those who are less concerned. From the political or philosophical perspective, people will disagree about the significance of data, for example, the level of certainty required to say something is an anticipated adverse effect. Disagreement among those involved in the decision-making process may well result in a compromise on numerical standards.

The United States District Court examined PSD in *Sierra Club v. Ruckelshaus*,[42] and held that the words "protect and enhance" in

---

39. *Sierra Club v. Thomas*, 828 F.2d 783, 785 (D.C. Cir. 1987).

40. 42 U.S.C.S. § 7602(h).

41. This position is also taken on a global basis by the less developed nations who argue that any internationally set environmental standards should be not as strict and/or not applicable as soon for the less developed countries.

42. 344 F. Supp. 253.

the CAA's evidenced Congress' intent to improve air quality and prevent deterioration rather than allowing deterioration. The court concluded that an SIP allowing areas with air quality cleaner than the ambient air quality standards to degrade down to those standards would be contrary to Congress' intent. The issue was taken to the U.S. Supreme Court, which split equally on the issue. The split underlines the legal and political division that existed on the issue.[43] In response, Congress amended the CAA, requiring that SIP's prevent "significant deterioration" of air quality in areas where the air is cleaner than the ambient air quality standards.[44] While Congress generally permits agencies to set standards, Congress itself defined "significant deterioration," and stated a maximum allowable increase in particulate matter for clean air areas (attainment areas). It should be emphasized that the allowable increases do not permit ambient air quality standards to be exceeded.

The last operative mechanism of the Clean Air Act that we will consider focuses on the "sources" of pollution. We have noted that the act uses separate approaches for dealing with moving vs. stationary sources and we will here discuss the "stationary source standards."[45] As we said earlier, the stationary source standards mechanism of the act is based on the premise that stationary sources of pollution like oil refineries, power plants, and cement plants should only be allowed to emit levels of pollutants that they cannot prevent with available control technology. Even if the ambient air meets the federal standards, stationary sources should control their emissions. The main thrust of the stationary source emission standards is on new stationary sources with EPA setting emission standards based on the best available emission reduction technology but taking into account the cost of using that technology. Although existing stationary sources may become subject to emission limitations, standards of performance for existing stationary sources

---

43. *FRI v. Sierra Club*, 412 U.S. 541.

44 42 U.S.C.A. §§ 7479(2)(C), (D).

45. 42 U.S.C. § 7411.

may be less restrictive than for new sources and may take into account the remaining useful life of the existing source. Perhaps the justification for treating existing sources more leniently than new sources can be analogized to the court's requirement in the *Spur Industries* case (discussed above in Section B) that the preexisting polluter be indemnified for its losses when it was ordered to stop its polluting activity.

One issue that has been raised in connection with the stationary source standards is whether it is unfair discrimination to have different stationary source standards for different industries—e.g., one set of standards for cement plants and less strict standards for power plants. One way of supporting the position that different standards create unfair discrimination is to argue that if the level of emission control is based on the available technology, then those industries that voluntarily developed technology prior to the statutory requirements would be punished for their good faith efforts in the past. They are saddled with a higher standard because the technology is available to them, while those industries that were the "bad guys" and never developed control technology voluntarily are rewarded with looser standards since technology is not available to them. When this issue was presented in court, the court's response was that Congress intended to clean up the air in whatever ways the available technology would allow, and that uniformity of standards for all industries was not required.[46] Furthermore, it can be said that comparisons between industries should not matter since, as long as the standard is the same for all competitors within one industry, none are disadvantaged. The only time that comparisons between industries should be relevant is when the industries produce substitute or alternative products. In those situations, failure to at least take the inter-industry competitiveness into account would be a failure to take into account the economic costs of achieving the new stationary source emission standards, and the words of the statute require that when EPA sets emission reduction standards, there must be a "taking into account the cost of achieving such reduction." The need for inter-industry comparisons in such competitive situations was recognized by the court in the

---

46. *Portland Cement Association v. Ruckelshaus*, 486 F. 2d 375.

case noted above.

A second issue concerning the Clean Air Act's stationary source standards involves what is known as NSR (New Source Review). As noted above, emission limitations for existing stationary sources are less stringent than for new sources; however, at what point might modifications made to an existing plant trigger New Source Review and result in the existing plant being considered a new source and thus being subject to the stricter emissions limits for new sources? The 2007 U.S. Supreme Court case of *Environmental Defense v. Duke Energy Corporation*[47] found that increasing the annual amount of discharge of a pollutant from an existing plant that has been modified might make the plant subject to the stricter new stationary source standards even though the hourly rates of emissions from the plant did not increase. The Court appeared to be supporting the notion that, while Congress recognized the need to have existing power plants continue in operation and not be subject to the stricter emission standards for new sources, it might not be appropriate for the existing plants to continue in operation forever without becoming subject to the stricter standards. When major modifications are made that will likely extend the life of a plant, that plant should be considered a new plant for purposes of imposing emission limitations. That policy also found support in the 2006 decision of the U.S. Court of Appeals, D.C. Circuit, in *New York v. EPA*[48] where the court invalidated EPA's "20% rule" which would have allowed existing sources to avoid New Source Review when replacing equipment that did not exceed 20% of the replacement value of the whole unit. Under the 20% rule, an existing power plant could have totally rebuilt itself in 5 years and not become subject to the stricter new source emission limits.

An air pollution topic that has received increasing attention is the use of economic incentives to achieve air pollution targets. Congress has used economic incentives to foster environmental goals, which we will discuss in the context of energy production in Chapter 7. The economic incentives provided by cap and trade programs are often seen as the lowest-cost solution to domestic air

---

47. 549 U.S. 561 (2007).

48. 443 F.3d 880.

pollution problems and to the global air pollution problem of climate change (and an easier sell than a tax on fossil fuels).[49] EPA provided for "marketable emission reduction credits," where a company that has reduced its emissions below what is required by the law, can sell the surplus as a credit under EPA's Emission Trading Policy.[50] When facilities can sell their credits for a higher price than it cost to make the extra emission reductions, it creates an incentive to make cost effective emission reductions beyond those that are mandated. Those industries that cannot control their emissions at as low a cost will be the ones buying the credits.

One criticism of emission credit trading is that it does nothing to reduce the total amount of emissions. EPA does, however, discount the emission credits, and a 100 ton surplus reduction may only be worth 80 tons to the purchaser of the credit. A company may also choose to return their unused credits to the government rather than selling them, either because they believe that reducing emissions is environmentally responsible business behavior, or they seek the positive publicity created by returning rather than selling emission credits, or they simply want the tax deductions associated with selling them back to government.[51] Another criticism is that when new technology results in emission reductions, instead enabling that user to sell his credits to someone not using the same technology, EPA should mandate that everyone use the emission reducing technology. The CAA itself supports this contention when it requires that new stationary sources of pollution use "the best system of emission reduction which...has been adequately demonstrated."[52] Yet, in the Clean Air Act Amendments, Congress approved EPA's market incentive approach by legislatively authorizing the transfer of the SO_2 allowances, which Congress

---

49. Broder, J., "From a Theory to a Consensus on Emissions," *New York Times* (May 16, 2009), available at http://www.nytimes.com/2009/05/17/us/politics/17cap.html?pagewanted=all.

50. 47 Fed. Reg. 15076.

51. Ackland, P., "Hutchinson No Longer Holds Its Nose," *New York Times* (Feb. 3, 1991) p. D1.

52. 42 U.S.C. § 7411(a)(1).

enacted to control acid rain.[53] In 2003, the Clear Skies Initiative expanded pollution trading systems for sulfur dioxide and nitrogen oxides, and introduced a new trading system for mercury.[54] It has been claimed that rather than reducing emissions, the Clear Skies Initiative instituted weak emissions standards for three of the major air pollutants—NO_2, SO_2, and mercury— and permitted an additional 8 million tons of NO_2, 34 million tons of SO_2, and 163 tons of mercury than would have been released under regular enforcement of the Clean Air Act in the absence of the Clear Skies Initiative.[55]

Having talked about air pollution in general, there are two specific areas of concern that require a more detailed discussion: 1) acid rain and 2) climate change. We begin with a discussion about acid rain, which arose prior to the public's awareness of climate change, and was addressed in policy and law before climate change.

a. Acid Rain – A Hybrid Form of Pollution

Acidic metal-containing precipitation (acid rain or acid deposition) is a hybrid form of pollution. It is really a water pollution problem downwind from emissions of air pollution. Sulfur oxides and nitrogen oxides are produced from stationary and mobile point sources when fossil fuels are burned. Acid rain results when these sulfur oxides and nitrogen oxides form sulfuric and nitric acid and fall to earth as rain. In addition, acid rain often contains heavy metals such as cadmium, lead, and zinc. The damage done by acid rain includes possible respiratory disease in humans, loss of profits from farming, accelerated building deterioration, and numerous negative impacts on our lakes, rivers, and forests. For example, the

---

53. 42 U.S.C. § 7151b(b).

54. Lee, J., "E.P.A. Plans to Expand Pollution Markets," *New York Times* (Dec. 15, 2003) p. A21.

55. Clean Air Act: Hearing on S. 385, Before the S. Comm. on Environment & Public Works, Subcomm. on Clean Air, Climate Change, and Nuclear Safety 108th Cong. (2003) (statement of David G. Hawkins, Director of the Air and Energy Program, Natural Resources Defense Council), available at http://epw.senate.gov/108th/Hawkins_040803.htm.

increased acidity can kill all the fish and other life forms in lakes and, in ways not fully understood but being studied extensively, the combination of acidity and metals in the soil reduces growth or kills some species of trees. At the ecosystem level, this may result in altered species composition and succession because resistant species may be favored while sensitive species decline. In our discussion of acid rain, we will first consider some historical aspects of the phenomenon. We will then examine why past approaches to regulation were seemingly inadequate and how Congressional action that specifically focuses on acid rain is designed to solve the problem.

Acid rain is, as far as we can determine, a phenomenon of recent origin. After World War II, the people of the United States indicated dissatisfaction with the particulate emissions from industrial facilities that burned fossil fuels. Precipitators were installed at the facilities to remove most of the particulates (soot), and, while this provided a solution to one problem, it created another. Particulates had acted to neutralize sulfur dioxide emissions and essentially prevent the formation of atmospheric sulfuric acid that might eventually fall to earth. At the same time, we built a lot of tall smokestacks to help remedy the local pollution situation by dispersing the pollutants over a wide area, an undertaking that likely contributed to the regional problem we faced later. Around 1950, the automobile industry introduced the high compression engine and with it a combustion product of much greater magnitude than previously experienced, nitrogen oxides. Thus, in our effort to be more efficient in one case (automobiles) and less polluting in another case (precipitators and tall stacks), we allowed two oxides into the air. In the atmosphere, these oxides can be transported long distances and can be chemically altered to form sulfuric and nitric acids, the components of acid rain.

For many years there was not sufficient evidence to convince everyone that acid rain was indeed causing the harm that was being attributed to it. Today, research and debate have shifted to the severity of the effects of acid rain, and the question of causation is a settled one. Few scientists or politicians currently doubt the serious threats acid rain poses to the public and the environment; however, the significant economic costs and political fallout from efforts to control acid rain stood in the way of Congress and EPA directly attacking the acid rain problem until 1990. Prior to 1990, the Clean Air Act recognized what turned out to be the main sources of acid rain—sulfur oxides and nitrogen oxides. It set both emission limits and ambient air quality standards for these oxides, but the emission restrictions and ambient standards were designed to insure that the public health and welfare were protected locally, without regard for the impact of the emissions on other regions through acid rain. The problem of acid rain was finally specifically addressed by Congress in the 1990 Amendments to the Clean Air Act.

The CAA amendments retained the original scheme for controlling acid rain but added an entirely new subchapter titled Acid Deposition Control.[56] The new provisions focus on the major source of acid rain causing pollutants: power plants that burn fossil fuel. In 2002, 80% of SO_2 emissions came from fuel combustion, and most of that came from the electric utility industry.[57] Again, Congress acted with a degree of specificity normally left to the administrative agencies, perhaps as an indication of legislative frustration with EPA, legislative concern about having waited a long time to control acid rain and not wanting to have more time spent in the administrative agency process, or legislative awareness about foreign affairs and the deteriorating goodwill between the U.S. and Canada over the issue of U.S. caused acid rain in Canada. For whatever reason(s), Congress listed by name 111 power plants, sometimes called the "big dirties," and the individual generators at those plants and provided numerical "allowances" for each in tons of SO_2 which may be emitted annually. Part of Table A from 42 U.S.C. §7651c(e) is shown in Figure 3.

These allowances are Phase I of the control program, with applicability as of January 1, 1995; Phase II, applicable as of January 1, 2000, reduces the Phase I allowances and also applies to smaller, cleaner plants. In Phase II, a national "cap" on SO_2 emissions from power plants limits their aggregate annual

---

56. 42 U.S.C. § 7651 et seq.

57. National Emission Trends, Fig.2-54, available at www.epa.gov.

TABLE A. AFFECTED SOURCES AND UNITS IN PHASE I AND
THEIR SULFUR DIOXIDE ALLOWANCES (TONS)

State	Plant Name	Generator	Phase I Allowances
Alabama	Colbert	1	13,570
		2	15,310
		3	15,400
		4	15,410
		5	37,180
	Gaston	1	18,100
		2	18,540
		3	18,310
		4	19,280
		5	59,840
Florida	Big Bend	1	28,410
		2	27,100
		3	26,740
	Crist	6	19,200
		7	31,680
Georgia	Bowen	1	56,320
		2	54,770
		3	71,750
		4	71,740
	Hammond	1	8,780
		2	9,220
		3	8,910
		4	37,640
	J. McDonough	1	19,910
		2	20,600
	Wansley	1	70,770
		2	65,430
	Yates	1	7,210
		2	7,040

Figure 3. Part of the list of power plants and their SO_2 allowances.[58]

emissions to 8.9 million tons.[59] While a plant must have one allowance for each ton of SO_2 to be emitted each year, SO_2

---

58. 42. U.S.C. § 7651c(e).

59. 42 U.S.C. § 7651b(a).

allowances are transferable.[60] With respect to NO_x emissions, Congress was more traditional. It directed EPA to establish regulations that would reduce annual power plant NO_x emissions by a total of approximately 2 million tons, but left to EPA's expertise the setting of the emission standards based on emission rates achievable with low NO_x burners. The transferable allowance system, which will be discussed more thoroughly in the context of climate change, has resulted in impressive reductions in SO_2 emissions at costs far below the original estimate. Despite this progress, pollution "hot spots" remain. Emission trading allows the pollution allowances to concentrate in some areas.[61]

EPA has addressed the smog-forming nitrogen oxide pollutants and health-threatening sulfur dioxide that drift eastward from Midwestern power plants three times in the last eight years, and twice it has been overruled by the United States Court of Appeals for the District of Columbia. The only successful mechanism to prevent emissions from crossing state lines was the cap-and-trade program for sulfur dioxide SO_2 under Title IV of the CAA. EPA's second attempt, the Clean Air Interstate Rule (CAIR), was less successful. In 2005, EPA expanded the cap-and-trade market in an attempt to reduce or eliminate the impact of upwind sources on out-of-state downwind locations by creating an optional interstate trading program.[62] The Rule required states to reduce their emissions to account for the drifting pollutants from a nonattainment state, and in 2008, the D.C. Court of Appeals held that EPA lacked the authority to terminate or limit Title IV allowances through a trading program.[63] EPA's third attempt, the

---

60. 42 U.S.C. § 7651b(b).

61. Altman, D., "Just How Far Can Trading of Emissions Be Extended?," *New York Times* (May 31, 2002) p. C1.

62. Nelson, G., "EPA Orders Power Plants to Clean Up Interstate Emissions," *New York Times* (July 7, 2011), available at http://www.nytimes.com/gwire/2011/07/07/07greenwire-epa-orders-power-plants-to-clean-up-interstate-87138.html.

63. Wald, M., "Court Blocks E.P.A. Rule on Cross-State Pollution," *New York Times* (August 21, 2012), available at http://www.nytimes.com/2012/08/22/science/earth/appeals-court-strikes-down-epa-rule-on-cross-state-pollution.html; *North Carolina v. EPA*, 531 F.3d 896 (D.C. Cir. 2008).

Cross-State Air Pollution Rule, known as the Clean Air Transport Rule, would have required power plants to cut their SO_2 emissions by 73% and their NO by 54 percent from 2005 levels.[64] The court held that the trading system violated the CAA because it imposed federal standards before the states could develop their own State Implementation plans.[65]

b. Climate Change

A discussion about air quality must consider climate change, because the two are intrinsically linked. Climate change is caused by gases that trap heat in the atmosphere. These gases are known as greenhouse gases, and include carbon dioxide, which enters the atmosphere through burning fossil fuels, solid waste, trees and wood products; methane, which is emitted during the production and transport of coal, natural gas, and oil, as well as livestock and other agricultural practices and by the decay of organic waste in municipal solid waste landfills; nitrous oxide, which is emitted during agricultural and industrial activities, as well as during combustion of fossil fuels and solid waste; and fluorinated gases, which are emitted from a variety of industrial processes.[66] Human activities, including the burning of fossil fuels for electricity, heat, and transportation, have been the biggest contributors to the increase in greenhouse gases in the atmosphere.

There is a strong consensus that the climate will continue to change and the planet will continue to warm as long as concentrations of greenhouse gases in the atmosphere continue to increase.[67] There have been several attempts to slow or stop this

---

64. Nelson, G., "EPA Orders Power Plants to Clean Up Interstate Emissions," *New York Times* (July 7, 2011), available at http://www.nytimes.com/gwire/2011/07/07/07greenwire-epa-orders-power-plants-to-clean-up-interstate-87138.html.

65. Editorial, "Another Rebuff for Cleaner Air," *New York Times* (Aug. 22, 2012), available at http://www.nytimes.com/2012/08/23/opinion/another-rebuff-to-the-epa-for-cleaner-air.html.

66. <http://www.epa.gov/climatechange/ghgemissions/gases.html>

67. Gillis, J., "Study Affirms Consensus on Climate Change," *New York Times* (June 22,

process, including global conventions setting limits on emissions. The U.S. is a signatory to the United Nations Framework Convention on Climate Change (UNFCCC), a treaty developed at the Earth Summit in Rio de Janeiro in 1992 and entered into force in March 1994. The treaty established a framework for intergovernmental cooperation to address global climate change, resulting in the 1997 Kyoto Protocol, but sets no mandatory limits on greenhouse gas emissions for individual countries. Approximately 137 developing countries, including India and China, have ratified the Kyoto Protocol, and while the U.S. is a signatory, it did not ratify the Protocol, and it is therefore not binding on the U.S. The U.S. has taken other measures to address climate change, but lacks an overarching federal law explicitly requiring mitigation of impacts on climate change.

i. Federal Climate Change

There is no provision in the CAA granting EPA express authority to regulate climate change or other federal legislation explicitly addressing climate change. Regardless, the federal government has taken steps to regulate greenhouse gas emissions by increasing energy efficiency and decreasing dependency on fossil fuels. In 2007, the government enacted the Energy Independence and Security Act. The Act included provisions to increase the production of clean renewable fuels and lower energy costs to consumers.[68] While many provisions of the 1990 CAA Amendments were aimed at controlling smog, acid rain, and other pollution problems, until recently, EPA has not attempted to regulate greenhouse gas emissions. The potential for regulation depends on whether Congress conferred the authority to regulate greenhouse gases on EPA under the CAA. In *Massachusetts v. EPA*, with a 5-4 majority, the U.S. Supreme Court held that Congress did confer the authority to regulate greenhouse gases on

---

2010), available at http://green.blogs.nytimes.com/2010/06/22/evidence-for-a-consensus-on-climate-change.

68. 42 U.S.C.A. § 17001.

EPA, but only required EPA to either issue a finding of "endangerment" that greenhouse gases "cause, or contribute to, air pollution which may reasonably be anticipated to endanger public health or welfare," or explain why CO_2 emissions cause no danger.[69] In response, EPA issued a finding that the six most significant greenhouse gases constitute a threat to public health and welfare. Such a finding is a prerequisite for EPA to regulate emissions from sources linked to climate change.

Two programs under the CAA, New Source Performance Standards (NSPS) and New Source Review (NSR) have the potential to reduce greenhouse gas emissions from both new and existing facilities. NSPS establishes emissions limitations for any source that causes or contributes to endangerment of the public health or welfare and requires stationary sources to use technology-based controls to limit pollution in both newly constructed and existing sources when a modification would increase the rate of discharge of pollutants measured in kilograms per hour.[70] In 2011, EPA began requiring permits for new *and* modified facilities under the New Source Performance Standards (NSPS).[71]

EPA has also ruled that the combined emissions from motor vehicles causes and contributes to climate change, and as a result, it raised corporate average fuel economy (CAFE) standards for automobiles for the first time since 1975.[72] Several courts have examined the scope of this authority. The D.C. Court of Appeals upheld both the endangerment finding and the fuel economy vehicle

---

69. *Mass. v. EPA*, 127 U.S. 1438.

70. 42 U.S.C.A. § 7411(a)(2); *U.S. v. Alabama Power Co.*, 6 F. Sup.2d 1292 (N.D. Alabama 2008).

71. Nelson, G., "GHG Scholars Suggest New Clean Air Act Approach to Curbing Greenhouse Gases," *New York Times* (Oct. 14, 2010), available at http://www.nytimes.com/gwire/2010/10/14/14greenwire-scholars-suggest-new-clean-air-act-approach-to-61330.html (last visited Nov. 30, 2012); Greenhouse, L., "Justices Say E.P.A. Has Power to Act on Harmful Gases," *New York Times*, www.nytimes.com/2007/04/03 (Tailpipe emissions from cars and trucks account for 27% of the U.S. emissions of "greenhouse gases," the heat-trapping gases including carbon dioxide that cause global warming).

72. Pub. L. No. 110-140, H.R. 6.

standards, finding that EPA was "unambiguously correct" when setting limits on industrial and automotive emissions of greenhouse gases after properly concluding that the gases were pollutants endangering human health.[73] Also, Federal courts in California and Vermont have rejected challenges to state imposed greenhouse gas emissions requirements for new automobiles. California enacted new greenhouse gas emissions standards in accordance with the CAA, and Vermont proposed to adopt California's regulations. In both cases, auto dealers and manufacturers argued that states' emissions standards could likely only be met by increasing automobile fuel efficiency. They claimed the emission standards were preempted by the 1975 Energy Policy and Conservation Act (EPCA), because EPCA requires the National Highway Traffic Safety Administration (NHTSA) to set minimum CAFE standards for a manufacturer's fleet of new vehicles at the "maximum feasible average fuel economy level,"[74] and EPCA expressly preempts states from adopting laws that regulate fuel economy. Federal district courts in California and Vermont considered and rejected this argument. In both *Green Mountain Chrysler Plymouth Dodge Jeep* and *Central Valley Chrysler-Jeep* the U.S. District Courts concluded that the regulations were not preempted by the EPCA's fuel standards, and that states are not precluded from promulgating emission control regulations that effect fuel economy.[75]

The above developments and several other provisions of the CAA reduce emissions of greenhouse gases. For example, controls of acid rain, interstate air pollution, and mercury from power plants encourage energy conservation and renewable energy, thereby indirectly reducing the growth in fossil fuel-derived greenhouse gas emissions. Although the U.S. does not have a comprehensive climate change statute, in 2012, EPA finalized new source

---

73. *Coalition for Responsible Regulation, Inc. v. EPA*, 684 F.3d 1-2, 113 (D.C. Cir. 2012).

74. PL 94–163 (1975).

75. *Green Mountain Chrysler Plymouth Dodge Jeep v. Crombie*, 508 F.Supp.2d 295 (D.Vt. 2007); *Central Valley Chrysler-Jeep, Inc. v. Goldstene*, 529 F.Supp.2d 1151 (E.D. Cal. 2007).

performance standards for natural gas production, which while not directly regulating, indirectly cut methane emissions.[76] Also, in 2013 the President issued an Action Plan on climate change to reduce overall emissions by 17 percent by 2020 by establishing federal limits on carbon dioxide emissions for new power plants.[77]

ii. State Climate Change

Despite slow progress on a federal level, several states have moved forward with their own plans to address climate change. Almost half of the 50 states have active legislative commissions and/or advisory groups to develop recommendations or implement measures to reduce state greenhouse gas emissions; more than three dozen states have developed or are developing climate change "action plans" outlining strategies for reduced emissions; almost two dozen states, primarily in the Northeast and West, have set emission reduction targets; at least a dozen states have adopted the California greenhouse gas standards for motor vehicles; and over 40 states have adopted measures designed to encourage the development and use of bio-fuels.

States have imposed their own controls, like limiting carbon dioxide emissions from automobiles, or creating cap-and-trade programs.[78] California's Assembly Bill 32 (AB 32) established a range of statewide programs to reduce greenhouse gas emissions and promote energy efficiency. Specifically, AB 32 requires that the California Air Resources Board (CARB) establish a statewide cap-and-trade system to limit greenhouse gas emissions.[79] In developing

---

76. "Oil and Natural Gas Sector: New Source Performance Standards and National Emission Standards for Hazardous Air Pollutants Reviews," *Federal Register* (Aug. 8, 2012), available at https://www.federalregister.gov/articles/2012/08/16/2012-16806/oil-and-natural-gas-sector-new-source-performance-standards-and-national-emission-standards-for#p-3.

77. Justin Gillis, "Taking a Risk Over Climate Change," *New York Times* at A1 (June 26, 2013).

78. Hakim, D., "Challenge to Emission Rules Is Set to Start," *New York Times* (April 10, 2007) p. A.19.

79. Cal. Health & Safety Code §§ 38500 *et seq*. (Only one other state caps CO_2

regulations to achieve the required reductions, CARB considered various factors, including cost effectiveness, and established a cap-and-trade system. In 2012, a California state appellate court overturned a lower court and held that CARB had not been arbitrary and capricious in developing the cap-and-trade program, but did so pursuant to legislative intent.[80] In October 2012, CARB held its first auction, selling 23.1 million allowances.[81] Even if some attempts by states to regulate greenhouse gas emissions are invalidated for one reason or another, many state controls would survive legal challenges. This would result in numerous different controls with which industries would have to comply. That potential result may well mean that the strongest advocates for mandatory federal controls on greenhouse gas emissions will be industry because it may be much more to their advantage to have one uniform set of controls than a patchwork of different controls from state to state.

iii. Regional Compacts

In addition to activities by individual states, collaborative efforts to reduce greenhouse gas emissions have resulted in the development of regional compacts for cap-and-trade programs. Because greenhouse gases travel across state lines, regional compacts seek to equalize reductions of emissions over a larger area than a single state. The Western Climate Initiative (WCI) is a collaboration between several western U.S. states, Canadian provinces, and parts of Mexico, and it plans to implement a cap-and-trade program in 2014.[82] The Regional Greenhouse Gas

---

emissions, Illinois, *See* http://www.epa.state.il.us/air/erms/).

80. *Association of Irritated Residents v. California Air Resources Board*, 143 Cal. Rptr.3d 65, 69 (Ct. App. 1st Dist. 2012).

81. Barringer, F., "A Market in Emissions Is Set to Open in California," *New York Times* B5 (Nov. 14, 2012); Barringer, F., "California's CO2 Has a Price, but a Low One," *New York Times* (Nov. 20, 2012), available at http://green.blogs.nytimes.com/2012/11/20/californias-co2-now-has-a-price-but-a-low-one/ (Each allowance for one metric ton of CO2 emissions sold for $10.09 at the initial auction).

82. <www.westernclimateinitiative.org>

Initiative (RGGI) is another collaboration between ten northeastern and mid-Atlantic states. RGGI established the first mandatory, market-based CO_2 emissions reduction program in the country.[83] Each member is capped and is committed to reduce CO_2 emissions from power and utility facilities by 10% by 2018.

iv. Local Policies and Non-Governmental Organizations

Overarching federal policies and regional compacts have the potential to create uniform regulations, but local governments can create policies based on local geographic and political capabilities that reduce energy consumption and carbon emissions. For example, they can incentivize higher density through zoning or building regulations or initiate mechanisms that reduce emissions, like providing bikes or electric buses as alternatives to private cars. Cities have implemented many local policies that promote renewable energy, energy efficiency, and clean technologies. EPA has sought to facilitate these activities with the State and Local Climate and Energy Program,[84] which provides technical assistance, analytical tools, and outreach support to state, local, and tribal governments. San Francisco set goals to be a zero waste city by 2020, and currently recycles or composts 77% of its waste, avoiding tons of planet-warming methane gas emissions. Phoenix established the Phoenix Energy Conservation Program promoting recycling, water conservation, and energy efficiency. Dekalb County, Georgia captures landfill gas to generate green electricity and address environmental challenges. The project produces approximately 22.5 million kilowatt-hours, enough to power 2,000 homes annually. Similar programs have emerged across the country, and continue to enhance large-scale efforts to reduce emissions. Some local governments have gone as far as to regulate the private sector. For instance, a handful of cities and smaller municipalities have passed

---

83. <www.rggi.org> (Connecticut, Delaware, Maine, Maryland, Massachusetts, New Hampshire, New Jersey, New York, Rhode Island, and Vermont. Ontario, New Brunswick, Quebec, Pennsylvania and the District of Columbia are observers to RGGI).

84. <http://epa.gov/statelocalclimate/>

zoning laws mandating green building requirements, and San Francisco has established a carbon tax on commercial businesses.[85]

Public policy is not the only way to reduce climate change. Non-profit organizations have also developed programs, like the Sierra Club's Cool Cities project,[86] which helps cities implement clean energy solutions that save money, create jobs, and help curb global warming, and Carbon Engineering,[87] an industrial scale plant designed to capture carbon dioxide from the air for possible commercial use. There are also private individuals working to slow climate change, including David Keith, who uses solar engineering to counter rising temperatures by reducing the amount of sunlight that reaches Earth.[88] Non-profit organizations, including the World Wildlife Fund, have created various certifications to help consumers choose "green" products and services. These certifications are propelled by concern about consumer views and pressure from activists groups and shareholders, essentially removing consumer "guilt by association."[89] Green Seal is another independent non-profit organization that promotes the manufacture, purchase, and use of more sustainable products and services.[90] Green Seal uses an "eco-label" award to certify products or services that are safer for human health and the environment and have met a high level of functional performance. These mechanisms, combined with government action, have the potential to increase awareness and reduce emissions of greenhouse gases.

---

85. Navarro, M., "City Council Is Set to Encourage Greener Buildings With Zoning Changes," *New York Times* (Apr. 26, 2012), available at http://www.nytimes.com/2012/04/27/nyregion/new-york-council-is-set-to-encourage-greener-buildings-with-new-zoning-rules.html.

86. <http://coolcities.us/>

87. < http://carbonengineering.com/>

88. < http://www.keith.seas.harvard.edu/geo.html>

89. Zeller, T., "When Green Becomes Inc.," *New York Times* (October 8, 2008).

90. <www.greenseal.org>

c. Federal Preemption of State and Local Policies

Climate change is a global issue, and a federal standard would ensure that every state contributes to reductions in greenhouse gas emissions. However, if and when federal climate control legislation is implemented, it will bring with it the issue of preemption. Preemption is derived from the Supremacy Clause of the U.S. Constitution, Article VI, and establishes federal priority when federal and state laws conflict. There are three situations that give rise to preemption: (1) express preemption, where a federal law explicitly declares it supersedes state laws; (2) implied preemption, where federal regulation is so pervasive that it invalidates state action; and (3) conflict, where following both state and federal law would be impossible.

Certain states have imposed their own limits on carbon dioxide emissions from automobiles. If the only way to limit carbon dioxide emissions from automobiles is to increase the miles per gallon obtained from the car, then perhaps the federal law that establishes average fuel economy standards preempts a state from indirectly establishing its own fuel economy standards. Section 209(a) of the CAA generally preempts states from establishing their own motor vehicle emissions standards, but § 209(b) provides for a waiver for any state motor vehicle emissions standards adopted prior to March 30, 1966, as long as the state has determined that its emissions standards are "at least as protective of public health and welfare as applicable federal standards."[91] In 2007, EPA denied waivers for 17 states to set their own emissions standards for motor vehicles.[92] The California standards are the only ones qualified to obtain a waiver under 209(b), and EPA originally denied California's request for a waiver, even though its standards were stricter than the standards set by the federal government. EPA justified its denials based on the

---

91. 42 U.S.C.A. § 7543.

92. Broder, J., and Barringer, F., "E.P.A. Says 17 States Can't Set Emission Rules ," *New York Times* (Dec. 20, 2007), available at http://www.nytimes.com/2007/12/20/washington/20epa.html (Including California, New York, New Jersey, Connecticut, Maine, Maryland, Massachusetts, New Mexico, Oregon, Pennsylvania, Rhode Island, Vermont, Washington, Arizona, Colorado, Florida and Utah).

global nature of greenhouse gases, stating that the challenge posed by greenhouse gases "is not exclusive or unique to California" and therefore differs from California's prior waiver requests.[93] California sued to overturn EPA's waiver denial, and EPA eventually granted the waiver in 2009.[94] We will discuss the preemption issue in further detail in the section on Noise Pollution.

d. Comparison Between Acid Rain and Climate Change

While both acid rain and climate change are results of air pollution, the two are dissimilar and control efforts have resulted in different reductions in the effects of acid rain and climate change. Perhaps most notably is the difference in the speed at which controls were established. Congress responded to scientific data about acid rain relatively quickly, imposing limits on utility emissions to reduce the amount of acid components entering the atmosphere. It was relatively easy to place these limitations, because emissions were from relatively few sources. On the other hand, pollution leading to climate change comes from a greater number of sources and is a global issue rather than an issue internal within the United States. Regulating climate change within the U.S. is not only more politically difficult, it is also more expensive, and there are a large variety of sources of greenhouse gases. Acid rain comes from emissions from Midwest utility plants, and regulations on those plants results in reduction in acid rain. However, greenhouse gases contribute to climate change on a global scale. Reduction of emissions in the U.S. will decrease aggregate global levels, but will not likely result in any benefit to the U.S. unless major developing nations like China and India act decisively to reduce their greenhouse gas emissions.

---

93. Dec. 19, 2007 letter from EPA Administrator Stephen L. Johnson to California Governor Arnold Schwarzenegger, available at www.epa.gov/otaq/climate/20071219-slj.pdf.

94. Galbraith, K., "EPA Allows California Emissions Standards," *New York Times* (June 30, 2009), available at http://green.blogs.nytimes.com/2009/06/30/epa-allows-california-emissions-rules/.

2. Water Pollution–Control Mechanisms, Federal Jurisdiction, Thermal Pollution

We have just concluded a detailed analysis of the Clean Air Act's mechanisms for air pollution control and some of the issues raised by those mechanisms which required court interpretation or Congressional clarification. Similar issues of interpretation have been raised over the years with respect to the Clean Water Act and continue to be the subject of litigation. Let's compare the structures of the Clean Air and the Clean Water Act, address cases involving statutory interpretation, and raise the topic of the power of Congress under the U.S. Constitution.

a. Comparing the Clean Air Act and the Clean Water Act

The Clean Air Act's approach of addressing the medium being polluted, the sources of pollution, and the nature of the pollutants themselves is also utilized in the Clean Water Act.[95] Thus the ambient air quality standards (the medium focus) have their counterparts in the use of water quality standards and state implementation plans under the Clean Water Act. The counterpart of the stationary source standards for air pollution can be said to be the effluent limitations for point sources (discernible, confined, and discrete conveyances, like a pipe), and industrial and municipal facilities must obtain National Pollutant Discharge Elimination System (NPDES) permits if their discharges go directly to surface waters.[96] The CWA also singles out toxic water pollutants for special control efforts following the CAA pattern of providing a separate control mechanism for hazardous air pollutants.

Although similar in the above ways, the two statutes are significantly different in terms of the emphasis placed on the various control mechanisms. While the CAA made substantial use of SIPs to achieve ambient air quality standards, the CWA leans very strongly toward pollution control by limiting discharge from

---

95. 33 U.S.C. § 1251 et seq.

96. 33 U.S.C.A § 1342.

the source by requiring permits. The permit limits the amount of discharge, which is based on both available control technology and costs.[97] If, however, water quality standards are not being met using technology-based effluent limits, more stringent water quality-based limits are established.[98] These limits are called "total maximum daily loads" (TMDL),[99] and limit the amount of a pollutant that can go into a body of water per day without violating the water quality standard. The TMDL is allocated among the dischargers, and that allocation is their limit for effluent discharge.

b. Interpreting the Clean Water Act

If water already polluted with phosphates from urban and agriculture runoff that would drain into the ocean is instead pumped into a wetland, is this an "addition of any pollutant to navigable water from any point source," or is the pumping station more of a conduit?[100] If the wetland is connected to the ocean, was there an addition? If there is a "discharge of pollutants," a permit would be required, and the phosphates might never enter the Everglades. If not, no permit would be required, and the likely result would be massive amounts of phosphates being pumped into the wetlands and massive ecosystem damage. The U.S. Supreme Court found that a point source conveying a pollutant to navigable waters, merely introducing the pollutant into the waters of the United States, does require a permit, but that because the canal and wetland were indistinguishable parts of a single water body, pumping water from one into the other does not require a permit.[101] In a separate decision, the Court created another exception for NPDES permit requirements. In *Decker v. Northwest Environmental Defense*

---

97. 33 U.S.C.A § 1316.

98.. 33 U.S.C. § 1311(b)(1)(C).

99. 33 U.S.C. § 1313(d)(1)(C).

100. 33 U.S.C. § 1362(12)(A).

101. *South Florida Water Management District v. Miccosukee Tribe of Indians*, 124 S.Ct. 1537, 1545 (2004).

Center, timber companies in Oregon discharged stormwater from ditches along logging roads in state forests without NPDES permits.[102] The Court held NPDES permits are only required for discharge of channeled stormwater runoff "associated with industrial activity" (such as factories); discharges not associated with industrial activity are exempted.[103] EPA interpreted the regulation to exempt non-traditional industrial activity, and the Court deferred to EPA's interpretation. Deference is required when an agency interprets its own regulation unless the agency's interpretation was "plainly erroneous or inconsistent with the regulation."[104] Because it is plausible to interpret the Industrial Stormwater Rule as exempting discharges of channeled stormwater runoff from logging roads from the NPDES permitting scheme, the Court upheld the exemptions. Technical distinctions with respect to interpretation of the Clean Water Act and agency regulations under it have long frustrated proponents of water quality protection and arguably undermined the protection Congress intended when it enacted the Clean Water Act.

c. Federal Jurisdiction

In this section, we raise the topic of the federal government's power to deal with pollution matters. For this, we begin by looking at *United States vs. Holland*,[105] a case that, early in the history of federal water pollution control efforts (1974), tested the authority of the federal government. The *Holland* case involved defendants who admitted that they were discharging pollutants into man-made mosquito canals and wetlands without a permit which the government said was required under the Clean Water Act. The defendants claimed that they did not need a permit because they were discharging into waters that were not within the federal

---

102. *Decker v. Northwest Environmental Defense Center*, 133 S.Ct. 1326, 1336 (2013).

103. 33 U.S.C. § 1342(p)(2)(B); the term is defined in the Industrial Stormwater Rule, 40 C.F.R. § 122.26(b)(14) (2006).

104. *Auer v. Robbins*, 519 U.S. 451, 461 (1997).

105. 373 F. Supp. 665.

jurisdiction. Their argument had two distinct parts. One part was that Congress never intended that the Clean Water Act be applicable to the canals and wetlands and, secondly, even if Congress did want to assert jurisdiction or control over the waters at the point where defendants were discharging, it did not have the Constitutional authority to do so.

To answer the question of whether Congress intended to control the waters into which the defendants were discharging, the court looked at the statutory language that Congress had used which said that the statute applied to "navigable waters." The court went on, however, to say that what was meant by "navigable waters" was not necessarily what it would mean in the technical sense or in average usage but rather what Congress intended it to mean. In the statute itself, Congress had defined "navigable waters" to be "waters of the United States," and the legislative history of the statute from the House and Senate clearly indicated that Congress intended that the statute apply to "all waters of the United States." The court thus found that Congress had intended to control the waters into which the defendants were discharging even though they were wholly unsuited for navigation and even though the statute said it applied to "navigable waters." Thus an important lesson concerning the reading of statutes is that the words used do not necessarily mean what they appear to mean. At least in situations where a term is used in the statute and specifically defined in that statute, the term's meaning may not be its ordinary language meaning. Rather, the term will mean what the statutory definition says it will mean. In the Clean Water Act, "navigable waters" means "waters of the United States" and, according to the court in the *Holland* case, the legislative history added the gloss of "all waters of the United States."

The second issue for our consideration in *Holland*, that of whether Congress has the constitutional authority to regulate pollution of non-navigable canals and wetlands, has more far-reaching implications and an interesting history that bears on the answer. As we noted in Chapter 1, Congress' power to regulate concerning environmental matters comes from the Commerce Clause of the United States Constitution, which gives Congress the power "to regulate Commerce . . .among the several States . . . ."

We also noted that the scope of the Commerce Clause power has been interpreted to include the power for Congress to act with respect to matters which have an effect on interstate commerce. The court in *Holland* said that it is beyond question that water pollution has a serious effect on interstate commerce, and Congress can thus regulate activities which cause pollution such as the dredging and filling in which the defendants were engaged. The court used the "effect on interstate commerce" approach to find that the pollution causing activities at the defendant's site would have serious effects on interstate commerce. If it had not been able to use the "effect" approach, one can speculate that the court may well have taken another step in the historical expansion of Congress' power with respect to bodies of water. That expansion was detailed by the court as follows.

The court noted that since much of 19th century commerce was carried out on the water, Congress' power "to regulate Commerce" had early been held to necessarily include the power over navigation.[106] If you are to effectively regulate navigation, you must have the power to keep navigable waters open and free, and Congress was found to have that power also.[107] Subsequent steps in the expansion of Congress' authority included the authority to regulate waters over which commerce is or *may be* carried on with other states;[108] waters capable of commercial use, not merely those in actual use;[109] waters with a history of commercial use;[110] and waterways which could be made navigable by reasonable improvements.[111] Few bodies of water could escape from the Congressional power under these expanded interpretations of what the Commerce Clause supposedly authorized Congress to control. If mosquito canals and wetlands could escape, and if the "effect on

106. *Gibbons v. Ogden*, 22 U.S. 1 (1824).

107. *Gilman v. Philadelphia*, 70 U.S. 713 (1865).

108. *The Daniel Ball*, 77 U.S. 557 (1870).

109. *The Montello*, 87 U.S. 430 (1874).

110. *Economy Light and Power v. United States*, 256 U.S. 113 (1921).

111. *United States v. Appalachian Electric Power Co.*, 311 U.S. 377 (1940).

interstate commerce" approach were not available to bring them within Congress' jurisdiction, it would not be difficult to imagine the court taking the next step and somehow further expanding its interpretation of the Commerce Clause to include those bodies of water also. The question after the *Holland* case might be whether, in light of the above described scope of Congress' power under the Commerce Clause, there are any bodies of water (or land, or air, or minerals or...) over which Congress does not have the Constitutional power to act? Can Congress control what you do with a temporary puddle that forms in your backyard or basement after a rainstorm? Is it likely that the people who drafted the United States Constitution would have approved of such power being in the hands of the federal government?

The result of the *Holland* case and the preceding questions need to be revisited in light of our discussion of recent Supreme Court cases about Congressional power in Part C of Chapter 1 and in light of the U.S. Supreme Court decision in *Solid Waste Agency v. Corps of Engineers*.[112] The *Holland* case involved landfilling operations for real estate development. The *Solid Waste* case also involved landfilling, but for waste disposal. It raised the question of whether, pursuant to the Clean Water Act, a permit was required to landfill an abandoned sand and gravel pit that had evolved into permanent and seasonal ponds that were visited by a number of migratory bird species. The issues, as in the *Holland* case, were did Congress intend the Clean Water Act to apply and, if so, did it have the Constitutional authority to do so. The court in *Holland*, a Federal District Court, had answered yes to both questions. The Supreme Court in *Solid Waste* found that Congress did not intend to exercise authority over the pits and ponds. It, therefore, avoided the constitutional question of whether Congress would have the power to control. The lower court in the *Solid Waste* case had held that Congress did have the power to control under the Commerce Clause, as had the court in *Holland*, but, in view of the doubts about Congressional power raised in our discussion of recent Supreme Court cases in Chapter 1, the question of the extent of Congress'

---

112. 121 S. Ct. 675.

Commerce Clause power with respect to water pollution control appears to remain in doubt. While avoiding the issue of power in the *Solid Waste* case, the Supreme Court did state it was avoiding "significant constitutional and federalism questions."[113] The issue of Congress' power in the water pollution context was avoided yet again by the U.S. Supreme Court in *Rapanos v. United States* in 2006 when the Court decided a wetlands case similar to *Holland* on the grounds of whether the wetlands in that case were intended by Congress to be within the scope of the Clean Water Act rather than by asking whether, if the wetlands were within the CWA, did Congress have the power to put them there.[114]

d. Thermal Pollution

Thermal pollution could be an air pollution problem as well as a water pollution problem, as anyone who has stood in heavy traffic on city pavement on a hot summer day can verify. Today's most significant thermal pollution problems are, however, water-related, and the Clean Water Act provides for thermal pollution control for bodies of water. Thermal pollution problems result from the fact that even minor changes in water temperatures can affect the reproduction, migration, and metabolism of cold-blooded heat-sensitive aquatic animals. Heat also causes adverse effects on aquatic plants, and the death of a body of water could result due to heat-caused oxygen depletion.

A major cause of thermal pollution is the electric utility industry. Other sources include steel mills and pulp processing plants. In order to control thermal pollution problems, Congress has included "heat" within the definition of "pollutant" under the Clean Water Act, and thus water quality control measures like effluent limitations are to include thermal discharge standards. While Congress has recognized thermal pollution as a problem, it has also recognized that the characteristics of heat make its effects more temporary and localized than many other pollutants. With this in mind, the Clean Water Act provides that thermal discharges should

---

113. *Ibid.*, p. 684.

114. *Rapanos* is further discussed in Section C of Chapter 1.

not be subject to any limits more stringent than necessary to assure the protection and propagation of a balanced, indigenous population of shellfish, fish, and wildlife in and on the relevant body of water.[115] Some examples of mechanisms which have been used to control thermal pollution are allowing only limited rises in the temperature of a plant's outlet water over its inlet water, holding down the size of the water's "mixing zone" to prevent the formation of migratory barriers, and keeping the dissolved oxygen level sufficient to support local species.

Although heat is generally viewed as a pollutant of water and the law has sought to regulate it in at least a limited way, thermal discharges may have a positive side. Projects are under way to explore the commercial possibilities of aquafarming of species like freshwater shrimp and rainbow trout using the heat from cooling water discharged by operations such as power plants. A pollutant could therefore become something from which a benefit could be derived and perhaps the better the control of the pollutant, the greater the enhancement of the benefit. That would be a highly desirable result for other pollutants as well as for heat.

3. Noise Pollution

We will conclude our discussion of public pollution control by considering what some people believe will soon become a major issue in the area of pollution control—noise pollution. While air pollution and water pollution problems have been coming under control to a large extent, noise pollution problems may be moving in the opposite direction. Noise is thought to be a possible contributing factor to diseases such as heart disease, arthritis, and diabetes, and to have adverse effects on children's development.[116] Some research has also indicated a possible relationship between noise levels and the human body's ability to cope with being in the presence of toxic materials. Huge numbers of toxic substances are in common use in industry and business, and there is some

---

115. 33 U.S.C. § 1326.

116. Moore, C., *Silent Scourge* (New York: Oxford University Press, 2003) pp. 156-193.

indication that the body's intake of toxic substances may be increased under the stress of high noise levels.

Besides the above "possible problems," there are the well-documented hearing loss problems which are derivative of noise and the plain fact that noise is often unpleasant regardless of whether it is unhealthy. Studies indicate that noise levels at subway and bus stops could easily exceed public health recommendations and have the potential to damage hearing with significant exposure.[117] Job-related hearing loss affects many, and excess noise in the workplace is said to have the potential of harming millions of American workers. Regulations established pursuant to the federal Occupational Safety and Health Act (OSHA)[118] have sought to limit the permissible exposure of workers to noise. While workers are reasonably well protected in occupational environments, noise outside the workplace is not actively regulated by EPA, and local and national authorities have stepped in to implement local action plans.[119] State statutes are only preempted by the federal Noise Control Act when the statute regulates an issue explicitly covered by the Act.[120] Despite constitutional claims, the Eleventh Circuit upheld a noise ordinance that a Florida city enforced against a nightclub, finding it did not violate the First Amendment right to free speech or Fourteenth Amendment rights to due process.[121] A recent noise pollution issue, the emergence of "wind turbine syndrome," illustrates the overlap between noise pollution and nuisance. Wind turbines have been reported to cause health problems, including diabetes and balance problems, but there is no

---

117. Robyn Gershon, et. Al, "Pilot Survey of Subway and Bus Stop Noise Levels," 83 *Journal of Urban Health* 5 (2006).

118. 29 U.S.C. § 651 et seq.

119. Wassener, B., "Trying to Dial Down the Volume of Noise Pollution," *New York Times* (Aug. 15, 2010), available at http://www.nytimes.com/2010/08/16/business /energy-environment/16iht-green.html?pagewanted=all.

120. *S. Pacific Tansp. Co. v. Public Utility Com'n of State of Oregon*, 9 F.3d 807 (9th Cir. 1993).

121. *Da Mortgage, Inc. v. City of Miami Beach*, 486 F.3d 1254 (11th Cir. 2007).

clear evidence to suggest they actually result in negative health effects. Some courts have affirmed permits for turbine development because there was insufficient evidence to support a finding that wind turbines caused negative health effects,[122] while others have granted injunctions to prevent construction of wind turbines, finding that the noise constituted a nuisance.[123]

The question before Congress and courts is not so much whether there should be permissible levels established, but rather what those levels should be. While prevention of overexposure to noise may be a sound goal, achieving noise control means accepting the costs inherent in control. The usual related questions are present. Is noise reduction to be achieved while taking into account the costs of achieving the reduction, or are the evils of noise sufficient in some circumstances to require reduction regardless of cost? Also, from a factual point of view, what is the noise level above which a certain type of harm will occur? As with most factual questions, opinions concerning the answer are often widely divergent. Our emphasis in the noise control area will be to consider the mechanisms for noise control established by or pursuant to the Federal Noise Control Act[124] and then to discuss the question of whether state and local control of one type of noise, aircraft noise, is allowable or prohibited.

Just as we saw that there are mechanisms in the Clean Water Act that closely parallel those in the Clean Air Act, so too are there parallels between the Noise Control Act and the Clean Air Act. The Noise Control Act directs the EPA Administrator to establish levels of environmental noise the attainment and maintenance of which are requisite to protect the public health and welfare. This control mechanism (which might be called "ambient noise levels") could be thought of as analogous to the ambient air quality standards under the CAA since it seeks to address the medium which is polluted without regard to the source of the pollutant. A critical difference

---

122. *Martha A. Powers Trust v. Board of Environmental Protection*, 115 .3d 127 (M.E. Sp. Ct. 2011).

123. *Burch v. Nedpower Mount Storm, LLC*, 647 S.E.2d 879 (W. Va. 2007).

124. 42 U.S.C.S. § 4901 et seq.

exists, however, with respect to the utilization of those "ambient" standards or levels. While ambient air quality standards are required to be implemented by state or federal implementation plans, there is no mandatory implementation of the noise levels. Clearly, Congress is reflecting the view of the American people that noise levels are not, at least yet, bad enough to require mandatory implementation.

A second parallel between the noise statute and the air statute is that both provide control mechanisms that focus on the source of pollution. The CAA has its stationary source standards, and the Noise Control Act requires the Administrator to publish noise emission standards with a goal of protecting the public health and welfare by attaining the degree of noise reduction achievable by the best available technology but also by taking into account the cost of compliance.[125] Standards are set for products distributed in commerce, such as construction equipment, motors, and engines, and for railroads and motor carriers. These standards are to protect the public health and welfare, and they are to take into account the magnitude and conditions of use of the products. For example, maximum noise emission levels have been established for street motorcycles, and they vary depending on factors such as year of manufacture and engine size.[126] Motors used for short periods of time in unenclosed spaces may be subjected to a less strict standard than those used continuously and in enclosed areas. The manufacturer of each applicable product is to warrant to the ultimate purchaser and subsequent purchasers that the product conforms to its noise emission standard at the time of sale. In

---

125. Appendix B illustrates the typical statutory and administrative relationship for environmental matters, in this case regulating motor carrier noise. The statute imposes the duty on the Administrator to regulate motor carrier noise and provides general standards such as "best available technology," "taking into account the cost of compliance," and "assure appropriate consideration for safety." The Administrator must abide by the statutory direction and guidance; however, there is a substantial amount of administrative discretion allowed in the setting of the standards. The detailed standards, such as how much noise, at what speed, and measured how far from the vehicle, are contained in the administrative regulations. The reader is encouraged to study Appendix B not necessarily for its substantive content but to become acquainted with the relationship between statutes and regulations.

126. 40 CFR § 205.152.

addition, enforcement of the noise emission standards may take place through citizen suits, and willful or knowing violation of the emission standard regulations may result in criminal penalties. The noise emission standards are to be promulgated as a result of a balancing by the Administrator similar to the balancing that leads to new stationary source emission standards under the CAA.

In addition to the mandatory control mechanism that applies to certain noise-emitting products (the noise emission limitations), the Act also provides for a control mechanism of consumer education. Products which emit noise capable of adversely affecting the public health or welfare, or which are sold on the basis of effectiveness in reducing noise, are required to give notice to the prospective user by labeling the product with information on the level of noise the product emits or its effectiveness in reducing noise. Thus even without mandatory controls, purchasers should be able to factor noise levels into their decision-making process regarding which of competing products should be purchased. Given the legislative mandate of the Noise Control Act, EPA promulgated regulations providing for the certification of low-noise-emission products and the identification of products as suitable substitutes for federal procurement.[127] The federal government may purchase "low-noise-emission" products—those that emit noise in amounts significantly below the levels specified by the noise emission standards—in preference to other products of its type so long as its retail price is no more than 125% of the least expensive product for which it is a substitute, hoping that this will encourage the development of such products that will also become available for purchase by the general public. The Office of Air, Noise & Radiation of EPA established noise emission criteria for a number of federally procured products such as motorcycles, trucks, and air compressors. Despite the hope of Congress and the efforts of the EPA, industry did not find the financial incentives of the program attractive enough to apply for low-noise-emission status.[128] Interestingly, the Air Force purchases

---

127. 40 CFR § 203.1 et seq.

128. Telephone interview with the former Director of the Noise Regulatory Program in EPA's Office of Air, Noise and Radiation.

thousands of portable air compressors for starting their jets and incorporates into their procurement specifications noise emission standards that meet low-noise-emission criteria. It is important to note that not all mechanisms enacted by Congress achieve their anticipated results. Low-noise-emission certifications have not been pursued, and the EPA office which administered the Noise Control Act was renamed the Office of Air and Radiation due to a lack of activity regarding the statute. Most of the attention focusing on low-noise-emission product procurement is now found at state and local levels with "buy-quiet" programs being implemented by cities including New York, Chicago, and Salt Lake City.

An area of federal noise control that has seen greater federal regulation than the subject areas covered in our above discussion of the Noise Control Act is aircraft noise. The Federal Aviation Administration has the authority to provide for control and abatement of aircraft noise and sonic boom.[129] Our inquiry in the area of aircraft noise will consider whether, given the large federal role, there is also a nonfederal (state/local) role in aircraft noise regulation. Our starting point will be the United States Supreme Court case of *Burbank v. Lockheed Air Terminal*.[130]

In the *Burbank* case, the City of Burbank had enacted an ordinance that made it unlawful for jet aircraft to take off from the Hollywood-Burbank Airport during certain hours (11 p.m. - 7 a.m.). The validity of the ordinance was challenged based on the Supremacy Clause of the United States Constitution (as discussed previously in relation to state and federal regulation of climate change). The Supremacy Clause, found in Article VI, says that the "Constitution, and the Laws of the United States . . . shall be the supreme Law of the Land; . . . anything in the Constitution or Laws of any State to the Contrary notwithstanding." Two theories which might possibly invalidate a state or local law are derived from the Supremacy Clause. The first is conflict—where state or local law and federal law address the same subject matter and are structured such that they cannot stand side by side. If, for example, state law

---

129. 49 U.S.C.A. § 44715.

130. 411 U.S. 624.

required an aircraft to have blue lights and federal law said no lights other than red lights are allowed, one could not possibly comply with both state and federal law. There is a conflict, and the state law is invalid pursuant to the Supremacy Clause. The Supreme Court did not address the conflict theory in *Burbank* but based its decision on the second theory derived from the Supremacy Clause—federal preemption.

If federal law set a 95 decibel (dB) maximum noise level for aircraft, and local law set a 90 dB maximum level, there would be no conflict since one could comply with both laws. Operation at 90 dB or anything less would satisfy both laws. As previously discussed in the context of climate change, the preemption theory says that even though both laws could stand side by side since they create no direct conflict, if Congress intended to fully take over or "preempt" the field of regulation of certain subject matter, then the nonfederal law concerning that subject matter is invalid. No express preemption existed with respect to aircraft noise control; however, the Supreme Court found that Congress' intent to preempt the field of control was evidenced by the "pervasive nature of the scheme of federal regulation of aircraft noise." The Court said that the pervasive control authority vested by Congress in federal agencies left no room for local curfews or other local controls. The Court further pointed out that if local ordinances such as Burbank's were allowed and other localities followed suit, the federal government's flexibility in controlling air traffic would be severely limited with potential problems such as increased air traffic congestion resulting in decreased safety and possibly increased noise levels. The Burbank ordinance was thus invalidated as having been preempted.

When the New York Port Authority sought to prevent the flight of the Concorde supersonic airplane into New York City due to noise (*British Airways v. Port Authority*),[131] wasn't that a clear case of federal preemption and the Port Authority could not act? The answer is that the federal preemption finding in *Burbank* did not apply to the Port Authority because the *Burbank* case involved an ordinance of a governmental unit (a city) controlling a private

---

131. 558 F.2d 75.

airport. The Supreme Court specifically stated in *Burbank* that it was not addressing the issue of the power of a proprietor of an airport to regulate aircraft noise. Although the Port Authority was a governmental unit, it was also the proprietor of the airport, whereas the City of Burbank was not the proprietor. The Second Circuit Court of Appeals decided that, as the proprietor of the airport, the Port Authority was fully within its power to regulate aircraft noise. The reasoning behind what might appear to be a strange distinction (allowing regulation by a proprietor but invalidating regulation by a local government) was: (1) that Congress never intended to preempt aircraft noise control by proprietors—this statement of "intent" came from the legislative history in the form of House and Senate Reports, and (2) that proprietors of airports are liable for harm to others which may result from noise of aircraft using the proprietor's facility. Thus the proprietor must have the right to protect against this liability by restricting the use of its airport. The "proprietor" exception to the *Burbank* preemption rule resulted in the Port Authority having the power to regulate aircraft noise. The viability of the position that airport proprietors are liable for aircraft noise was reinforced in *Greater Westchester Homeowners Association v. City of Los Angeles.*[132] The California Supreme Court in fact expanded the proprietor's liability in that nuisance case to include not only the traditional nuisance liability for property damage but also liability for injury to the person. Although public law with respect to pollution has relegated private law like nuisance cases to a secondary status, the *Greater Westchester* case indicates that private law remedies in the pollution area continue to be available and even adaptable to current needs.

D. SPECIALIZED ENVIRONMENTAL MEDIATION AND DISPUTE RESOLUTION

We have previously discussed two general approaches to resolving environmental issues and disputes. The first was private law court cases such as nuisance actions. The second was the

---

132. 603 P.2d 1329.

legislative process. In general, the legislative process is invoked in a situation where there are large-scale environmental issues affecting large numbers of people. Legislative solutions to problems have advantages such as more uniform results than private law court cases and the ability to be "preventative" rather than "remedial" with respect to problems. Disadvantages of the legislative process include it being a cumbersome mechanism that tries to serve many divergent interests and, therefore, often takes a long time to implement and often results in compromises that are based on political power rather than solely on the environmental and economic merits. Also, the legislative process does not lend itself very well to resolving disputes between individual people or business entities. For these, the private law court case mechanism continues to be widely used. That mechanism is an adversarial process that generally results in a winner and a loser even though each party often has some justifiable basis for its position. In addition, the "all or nothing" result often comes after the expenditure of much time and money. Approaches for improving on environmental dispute resolution include using more specialized courts and avoiding the court process entirely by using some form of alternative dispute resolution.

Court cases involving environmental issues might provide better results and be more efficient if the courts had specialized expertise. A science court[133] could be used for making factual scientific determinations, and an environmental law judge could be appointed to bring environmental expertise to bear on resolving environmental

---

133. Jurs, A., "Science Court: Past Proposals, Current Considerations, and a Suggested Structure," 15 *Va. J.L. & Tech.* 1 (2010) (Science courts were first proposed in the 1970s, but have made little progress since. A specialized science court would allow the federal judiciary to better handle, both procedurally and substantively, the most difficult scientific questions).

issues.[134] Alternatives for keeping cases entirely outside the court system that have grown significantly in both amount of use and areas of application include arbitration and mediation. The mediation process attempts to bring together all parties involved in a dispute to try to reach a solution that is legally supportable by and fundamentally acceptable to all parties. This type of undertaking requires trust among the parties, truthfulness and openness, and a commitment to abiding by the result of the collective process. Professional mediators will often be needed in such instances. Central to the idea of using mediation is the necessity of compromise and having an issue that is capable of resolution by compromise. What mediation also provides is a less costly means of "solving" a problem. What mediation does not provide is a winner, nor does the process necessarily create a binding result; however, the use of environmental mediation and other types of alternative dispute resolution (ADR) have grown dramatically in recent years.[135] Because judges do not resolve disputes, but adjudicate and impose binding decisions, ADR and negotiation provide the parties with the opportunity to collaborate and resolve the environmental conflict. Environmental disputes are often initiated in court, but resolved by attorneys during a pre-trial settlement. If attempts at settlement fail, ADR is often the next step either voluntarily or compelled by the court.

---

134. 4 V.S.A § 1001 (The Vermont court system has an environmental court with an environmental judge); Administrative Office of the Trial Court, The Massachusetts Court System, Land Ct. Dep't, www.mass.gov/courts/courtsandjudges/courts/landcourt/ (last visited Mar. 7, 2012) (Massachusetts has a land court); *See generally* Enforcing Environmental Laws, New York State Dep't of Envtl. Conservation (last visited Mar. 7, 2012), www.dec.ny.gov/regulations/391.html (New York has a state administrative environmental tribunal within their Department of Environmental Conservation); EPA, www.epa.gov (last visited Mar. 7, 2012); Dep't of Interior, www.doi.gov (last visited Mar. 7, 2012) (At the federal level, there are specialized tribunals in the U.S. Environmental Protection Agency (EPA) and the Department of the Interior (DOI)).

135. Christie, E., ed., *Finding Solutions for Environmental Conflicts: Power and Negotiation* 4 (Northampton, MA: Edward Elgar 2008).

ADDITIONAL READINGS

Ayma, E., *Planet or Death: Climate Justice Versus Climate Change* (Verso, 2014).

Burns, W., Osofsky, H., *Adjudicating Climate Change: State, National and International Approaches* (Cambridge Press, 2011).

Dietrich, E., *Pollution Limits and Polluters' Efforts to Comply: The Role of Government Monitoring and Enforcement* (Stanford Economics and Finance, 2011).

Domike, J., Zacaroli, A., *The Clean Air Act Handbook* (American Bar Association, 2013).

Lincoln-Oswalt, J., *Better Air: Benefits and Costs of the Clean Air Act* (Nova Science Publishers, 2011).

Markowitz, G., Rosner, D., *Deceit and Denial: The Deadly Politics of Industrial Pollution* (California/Millbank Books, 2013).

McGuire, C., *Adapting to Sea Level Rise in the Coastal Zone: Law and Policy Considerations* (CRC Press, 2013).

Osofsky, H., McAllister, L., *Climate Change Law and Policy* (Aspen Elective, 2012).

Perez Henriquez, B., *Environmental Commodities Markets and Emissions Trading: Towards a Low-Carbon Future* (RFF Press, 2012).

Ryan, M., *The Clean Water Act Handbook* (American Bar Association, 2011).

CHAPTER 4
LAND USE

A. CONTROL VS. NONCONTROL

1. The Uses of Land

Nearly 60% of the land in the United States is privately owned (1.35 billion acres). The federal government owns 29% (635 million acres), state and local governments 9% (198 million acres), and Indian trusts 3% (66 million).[1] The major uses of land in the United States and the approximate number of acres allocated to each use are indicated in Table I. The recent available data seems to indicate a continuing increase in special use land and a decrease in cropland but a reversal of the declines in the amounts of grassland and forest land.[2] Of note, land-use patterns vary by region. For example, cropland accounts for 54% of all land in the Corn Belt but only 12% in the Northeast; almost two-thirds of North Dakota is cropland, versus 41 percent in South Dakota.[3] Having noted the longer and shorter views of land use trends, let's take a closer look at specific land uses.

---

1. Nickerson, C., Ebel, R., Borchers, A., Carriazo, F., "Major Uses of Land in the United States," *U.S. Dept. of Ag.* (2007) www.ers.usda.gov/publications/eib89.

2. U.S. Dept. of Agriculture, "Trends in Major Uses of Land," *Economic Information Bulletin No. (EIB-14)*, May 2006.

3. U.S. Dept. of Agriculture, "Agricultural Resources and Environmental Indicators," *Economic Information Bulletin No. (EIB-98)*, p. 4 (2012).

a. Private Land Use

Cropland is a resource used not only to produce much of the food consumed either directly or secondarily in the United States, but also as a food resource for other parts of the world. Currently, the United States contains about 400 million acres of cropland.[4] Each year millions of these acres are converted to development or become nonproductive after isolation by development. Conversion and isolation are but two mechanisms by which cropland is lost. Two other mechanisms are erosion and loss of fertility. Loss of fertility is a relatively newly recognized form of cropland conversion. Since the discovery of the Haber process, it has been possible to make synthetic fertilizer containing nitrogen at a low cost. Having an inexpensive source of fertilizer made from various synthetic chemicals has allowed farmers to dispense with green manure or animal manure as a source of nutrients for crops. These synthetic chemicals have proven both effective and reliable for farmers in terms of dependable production. However, the application of these chemicals also enhances the breakdown of organic matter in soil and consequently alters soil structure, making the soil more susceptible to flooding and water erosion as well as wind erosion. Additionally, the soil's binding ability for nutrients and water is decreased. Thus, the fertility of the soil itself is being lost, and much agricultural soil has become merely a holdfast for crops while they are fed nutrients so that they may produce. Eventually, all of the above mechanisms could deplete our cropland resource.

As rural land use declines, the use of land for development is expanding very rapidly as population increases and as the demands of society for these land uses increase. There has been an average annual increase of 1.4 million acres in urban land since 1990, and acreage has quadrupled from 1945 to 2007, twice the rate of population growth.[5] Land in urban areas was estimated at 61 million acres in 2007, up 17 percent since 1990 with an average

---

4. Nickerson, C., Ebel, R., Borchers, A., Carriazo, F., "Major Uses of Land in the United States," *U.S. Dept. of Ag.* (2007), available at www.ers.usda.gov/publications/eib89.

5. *Ibid.*

annual increase of 1.4 million acres since 1990. While this phenomenon in and of itself may give some cause for alarm, it is the type of land selected for use under this category that is even more troublesome. It is easier to develop land that is flat. Croplands are therefore prime targets.

Table I. Major Uses of Land in the United States, 1959-2007 (in millions of acres). [6]

Year	Cropland[7]	Grassland Pasture & Range	Forest Land[8]	Special Use[9]	Misc.[10]	Total*
1959	458	633	728	123	329	2271
1964	444	640	732	144	306	2266
1969	472	604	723	141	324	2264
1974	465	598	718	147	336	2264
1978	471	587	703	158	345	2265
1982	469	597	655	270	274	2265
1987	464	591	648	279	283	2265
1992	460	591	648	281	283	2263
1997	455	580	642	286	301	2263
2002	442	587	651	297	288	2265
2007	408	614	671	313	258	2265

* In millions of acres.

Note: Much of the large increase in "special use" land and decrease in "miscellaneous" uses between 1978 and 1982 as shown above are due to definitional changes in classifying land in Alaska by the Department of Agriculture.

Special and miscellaneous land include wetlands and wildlife areas, but they also include the lands that we often refer to as

6. "Major Land Use Database" (U.S. Dept. of Agriculture) and *Major Uses of Land in the United States*, 2007/EIB-14, Economic Research Service/USDA (Dec. 2011).

7. Includes idle & pasture that could be cropland.

8. Excluding special uses like state parks.

9. Transportation, rural parks, defense & industrial, etc.

10. Other: Urban, wetland, tundra, etc.

developed land, including rural transportation, national/state parks, wilderness and wildlife areas, national defense and industrial areas, and farmsteads and farm roads. These land uses have increased nearly threefold since 1959, and from 2002-07, special-use areas grew by more than 16 million acres (6%). This is mainly due to a reclassification of "miscellaneous" land, which resulted in a decline of 30 million acres (14%) over the same period.[11]

b. Federally Owned Land

Approximately 650 million acres of land are owned by the federal government. Additional acreage is controlled through the federal government holding various interests in land that do not amount to an ownership interest. The resources of this vast amount of land include water, timber, minerals, wildlife and plants for grazing. Other significant attributes of the land include its scenic, recreational and cultural values. Our discussion here will focus on forest land and wildlife habitat. Use of federal land for energy production is discussed in Chapter 7.

Federal timber land not reserved in parks, wildlife areas, or other uses consists of about 158 million acres.[12] About 41% of all forest land was government-owned in 1997—33% owned by the federal government.[13] In 2007, there were 127 million acres of grazed forests in the U.S., excluding an estimated 80 million acres in parks, wildlife areas, and other special uses. Forest-use land increased 20 million acres (3%) from 2002 to 2007, reversing a 50-year downward trend largely due to forest-use land reclassified to special-use areas. Currently, 51% of timber in the U.S. is less than 50 years old, and only 5% is more than 175 years old.[14]

---

11. Nickerson, C., Ebel, R., Borchers, A., Carriazo, F., "Major Uses of Land in the United States," *U.S. Dept. of Ag.* (2007), available at www.ers.usda.gov/publications/eib89.

12. "Major Land Use Database" (U.S. Dept. of Agriculture) and *Major Uses of Land in the United States*, 2007/EIB-14, Economic Research Service/USDA (Dec. 2011).

13. *Ibid.*, p. 24.

14. *Ibid.*

Management of timber lands has received various forms of attention over the years, but many people believe that a comprehensive approach to the management of forest land is yet to come. Maximum growth-sustained yield was and is one concept that forest management has championed. This concept emphasizes harvesting trees at a time that achieves maximum productivity of the forest rather than allowing trees to reach their mature growth size (see Figure 1). While this approach would keep forests actively growing, it does not allow for old age stands useful for wildlife habitat as well as aesthetics and soil rejuvenation. It could also eventually lead to the management of forests totally for commercial production, with the selection of only fast growing, highly marketable tree species for cultivation. This could eliminate tree species considered unprofitable and consequently the gene pool of such species. Once this extinction occurs, the species cannot be retrieved. A significant question is what role, if any, government should play in preventing the conversion of cropland to developed land and forest land to cropland.

A combination of the Forest Reserve Act of 1891,[15] authorizing national forests, and the Organic Administration Act of 1897,[16] which limited the purposes for which national forests could be established, resulted in the designation of national forests (1) for the protection of the forest, (2) for securing favorable waterflows, or (3) to furnish a supply of timber. While these were the only purposes allowed by law as the basis to establish a national forest, once a national forest was established, the practice was to manage it for other purposes also, such as for grazing and recreation. In the Multiple Use-Sustained Yield Act,[17] Congress addressed itself to the question of what in fact were to be the allowable uses for national forest land. The statute declared that, in addition to the previously authorized purposes for establishing national forests, the national forests were to be administered as well as established "for outdoor recreation, range, timber, watershed, and wildlife and fish

---

15. 26 Stat. 1103, as amended 16 U.S.C. § 471 (1946).

16. 30 Stat. 34, as amended 16 U.S.C. § 475 (2012).

17. 16 U.S.C. §§ 528-531.

purposes." The Secretary of Agriculture was instructed "to develop and administer the renewable surface resources of the national forests for multiple use and sustained yield of the several products and services obtained therefrom." The multiple use approach to forest land management was thus codified by Congress with the five above-quoted purposes being the allowable multiple uses.

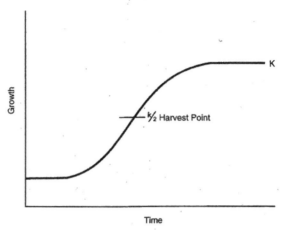

Figure 1. Harvest point of trees in relation to growth, where K equals the minimum size a tree would reach.

The Multiple Use-Sustained Yield Act gives us an example of how Congress often provides guidance to an administering agency but still leaves much in the way of how the statute will actually work in the control of the agency and, in part, in the hands of the courts that will interpret Congress' intent in its statute. The statute requires management for a sustained yield of products and services and defines sustained yield in terms of striving for perpetual output. Under the Act, "multiple use" management means "making the most judicious use of the land for *some or all* of these resources or related services."[18] Therefore, when the Forest Service promulgates a rule that "develops and administers the renewable surface resources of the national forests for multiple use," it does not necessarily need to permit all uses in the statute, including "for outdoor recreation, range, timber, watershed, and wildlife and fish

---

18. 16 U.S.C.A. § 531(a).

purposes."[19] This grants the Forest Service broad discretion to determine the proper mix of uses permitted within specific forest lands.

The statute speaks of managing the resources in the combination that best meets the needs of the American people, while recognizing that some of the land may be used for less than all of its resources. The combination of uses selected for each piece of forest is to take into account competing uses by considering the relative value of the various resources, but the use pattern is to be "not necessarily the combination of uses that will give the greatest dollar return or the greatest unit output." Perpetual output management; a combination of uses; not necessarily maximizing dollar return or unit output— these are reasonably clear boundaries set by Congress within which the agency must work, but the statute also says that in administering the national forests, "due consideration shall be given to the relative values of the various resources in particular areas." What is "due consideration?" This question is not clearly answered by Congress since the statute just says "due consideration." It has been argued that due consideration means equal consideration of the various competing uses, and that a use plan that is formulated by giving anything less than equal consideration to any potential use is invalid. The courts have, however, taken the position that "due consideration" means merely "some consideration," and that "the decision as to the proper mix of uses within any particular area is left to the sound discretion" of the administrative agency.[20] The courts have thus adopted an interpretation of the statute that, even with the boundaries discussed above within which the agency must work, allows substantial agency discretion in the actual determination of what uses will be emphasized for our national forest land. The Ninth Circuit held that "due consideration ... to the relative values of the various resources in particular areas" requires a "hard look" at the environmental impacts and consequences of the action during the NEPA process.[21]

---

19. *Wyoming v. U.S. Dept. of Agriculture*, 661 F.3d 1209, 1269 (10th Cir. 2011).

20. *Sierra Club v. Hardin*, 325 F. Supp. 99.

21. *Wyoming v. U.S. Dept. of Agriculture*, 661 F.3d 1209, 1269 (10th Cir. 2011).

One use of our nation's forests that is expressly provided for in the Multiple Use-Sustained Yield Act is timber harvesting. Timber harvesting is probably the most contentious topic when dealing with federal forest land. Federal timber land not reserved in parks, wildlife areas, etc. consists of about 109 million acres. There is tremendous economic pressure to harvest this timber; however, the Act mandates that forests shall be used for uses in addition to timber sales, including the protection of wildlife. The Forest Service, therefore, must reconcile the inherent tension that exists between these competing uses, and a combination of agency regulations and federal statutes serves to constrain the harvest of timber throughout the national forest system. Let's consider some examples.

The Forest Service has established broad wildlife management regulations requiring that viable populations of wildlife be maintained in national forests by insuring that adequate supporting habitats exist and are well distributed.[22] An example of how the regulation works is found in the case of the northern spotted owl. A Forest Service committee of biologists proposed permanently dedicating 5.3 million acres of forest to habitat conservation areas in which no harvesting or other conflicting uses would be allowed. In effect, this proposal, made pursuant to the regulations, would make protection of the spotted owl the dominant use in these areas, perhaps consistent with or perhaps contrary to the approach of multiple uses. Besides agency regulations, federal statutes also constrain the harvest of timber in national forests. The National Environmental Policy Act[23] requires that the Forest Service, with considerable public involvement, prepare an environmental impact statement (EIS) to examine the consequences of proposed tree harvests. In addition, NEPA may permit environmental public interest groups to contest timber sales based on potential inadequacies in the EIS. A second federal statute constraining

---

22. 36 CFR § 219.19-219.20.

23. 42 U.S.C. § 4321 et seq.

timber harvests, the Endangered Species Act,[24] requires that virtually all other federal laws yield to its mandate. Section 1536 of this act provides that Forest Service activities must not jeopardize species of wildlife identified as endangered or threatened. This limitation is implemented for each proposed timber sale through interagency consultations with the U.S. Fish and Wildlife Service. The consultations are designed to determine whether such species will be jeopardized by the proposed activity.[25] As a result, efforts to protect wildlife including the red cockaded woodpecker in the southeast, the caribou in Maine, the grey wolf in Minnesota and Idaho, and the Mexican spotted owl in the southwest, have limited the harvest of timber on federal lands. A third federal statute that places constraints on timber harvesting on federal land is the National Forest Management Act.[26] This act requires extensive planning for any proposed timber harvest and makes it clear that the multiple use approach must be implemented—not simply the objectives of highest dollar return or highest volume of timber production.

While the above examples of regulatory and statutory provisions certainly have made it such that maximum timber harvest and/or maximum profit have not been the only use of federal timber land, the economic pressures will always be present to increase timber harvesting. The Healthy Forests Initiative pursued both legislatively and administratively in 2002-2004 has been championed by its advocates as designed to "help prevent catastrophic fires that devastate communities, kill wildlife and burn away millions of acres of treasured forests." A key aspect of the initiative is to make it easier to remove "hazardous fuel accumulation" from forests by excluding activities related to hazardous fuel reduction from the National Environmental Policy Act's Environmental Impact Statement process.[27] Critics, however,

---

24. 16 U.S.C. § 1531 et seq.

25. 50 CFR § 402.01 et seq.

26. 16 U.S.C. § 1601 et seq.

27. Alphonso, G. et al., "Fire, Wood, and Water: Trends in Forest Management Requirements," *Natural Resources and Environment* pp. 18-20 (Summer 2003).

contend that this would allow timber to be harvested for private sale without review of environmental impacts and that the initiative is a thinly disguised effort to drastically increase our use of federal forest land for timber sales.

Both Congress and the federal agencies must constantly deal with the issue of how to appropriately resolve the need to protect wildlife and other environmental interests in the face of continuing pressure for increasing timber harvests on federal forest land. Whether to allow clear cutting practices in the national forests or even any logging in the nation's old-growth forests involves many factors. Among them are: thoughts about the near total destruction of the existing environment on a huge amount of acreage; the effects of replanting a monoculture of trees; aesthetics; the probability of unemployment and major changes in lifestyle for loggers and their families; and how possible increases in the cost of building materials might affect the ability of people to afford decent housing. These interests may not always be reconcilable, and some of the above factors are illustrated in the photographs at the end of this chapter.

In addition to federal timber lands, the federal government also owns millions of acres of wildlife habitat. Prior to 1966, the wildlife refuges run by the federal government were administered as many separate administrative units and by different federal agencies. With the passage of the National Wildlife Refuge System Administration Act,[28] these units were consolidated into the National Wildlife Refuge System which today consists of over 550 refuges and 150 million acres of federal land.[29] Under this statute the Refuge System is to be administered by the Secretary of the Interior to

> permit the use of any area within the System for any purpose, including but not limited to hunting, fishing, public recreation and accommodations, and access whenever he determines that such uses are compatible with the major purposes for which

---

28. 16 U.S.C. § 668dd.

29. "Annual Report of Lands Under Control of the Fish and Wildlife Service," *U.S. Fish and Wildlife Services* (Sept. 30, 2012), available at http://www.fws.gov/refuges/land/LandReport.html.

such areas were established. . . .

This statutory standard for administration adopts the management concept of "dominant use" as opposed to "single use" of the land in the Refuge System. Wildlife is the dominant use, but it is not the single use to which the land can be put since other uses "compatible with" wildlife are allowed. The dominant use management approach appears to provide for a more efficient use of land; however, it also raises the issue of when other uses are compatible and when are they not. With the pressures that are often applied to use land for economic yields such as recreation or grazing, use as wildlife habitat is subject to being compromised in ways that could not happen under single use management. In enacting the dominant use approach, Congress decided that the administrative tool of requiring "compatibility" of other uses with wildlife is sufficient protection, and that to go beyond the compatibility level to protect wildlife would be an unwarranted waste of land resources. In the 1997 Wildlife Refuge Improvement Act, Congress retained the "dominant use' system but added provisions to insure to a greater extent that human uses are compatible with wildlife conservation. It also specified that wildlife conservation includes sustaining and, where appropriate, restoring and enhancing, populations of animals and plants.[30]

The protection of wildlife as the dominant use for Wildlife Refuge land was called into question by the federal appeals court case of *Schwenke v. Secretary of the Interior*.[31] In *Schwenke*, which originated in Montana, the Department of Interior argued that grazing was permitted on the Charles M. Russell Wildlife Refuge only to the extent it was compatible with wildlife values. Reductions in the existing grazing levels were proposed by the Department because of evidence of overgrazing and destruction of wildlife habitat. Cattle ranchers contended, however, that grazing on the Russell Range should be administered under the Taylor

---

30. 16 U.S.C. § 668dd(d)(3) and 668ee(1)-(4).

31. 720 F.2d 571.

Grazing Act[32] rather than the Wildlife Refuge Act, and that management of the refuge ought to give equal priority to livestock and wildlife. Though the cattle ranchers won at trial, the government prevailed on appeal, and the appellate court determined that the refuge land must be administered under the Refuge Administration Act. The court held that, given the goals of maintaining specific numbers of various wildlife species including antelope and sharptail grouse, a limited priority in favor of wildlife existed. Only when the designated wildlife populations have been achieved, can wildlife and livestock grazing have equal priority in access to the resources of the range. Thus, wildlife is the dominant use under the Refuge Administration Act itself, and it may also be dominant over other uses established by other specific federal statutes such as the Taylor Grazing Act.

2. The Need to Control

The above discussion of land and its uses has been largely about land use problems related to topics like the relationship of development to agriculture, forestry and wildlife. There are many additional land use problems that are of greatest significance in areas that are already highly developed and heavily populated. One example of these problems might be the question of whether retail stores should be located in numerous small clusters within residential areas or kept out of residential areas and instead grouped into one huge shopping center area. Another example is whether a 25-acre suburban housing development should have 25 one-acre building lots or 25 houses clustered on 10 acres with 15 acres of common open space. Major issues have also emerged as a result of the changing uses of land. Land use changes occur for a variety of reasons, including changing commodity and timber prices, agricultural and natural resource policies and, more recently, energy policies prompting private landowners to shift land to uses that maximize economic returns. Also, land near urban areas is subject to pressure from residential, commercial, and industrial

---

32. 43 U.S.C. § 315.

development. Once converted to an urban use, land rarely transitions back to less intensive agricultural or forestry uses.[33] As previously mentioned, increases in population result in demand for land, and consequently changes in land uses. This demand has resulted in increased pressure to develop the flat and inexpensive wetlands. Wetlands are reservoirs for water, breeding grounds for various forms of wildlife, and feeding areas for other kinds of wildlife. Viewing the choice of what land to develop from another perspective, even though people want to live in a given location that does not mean that such a place can support them in terms of needed resources. Witness the migrations to the sunbelt areas of the Southwest. While the climate is hospitable in many ways, the demands for water have all but eliminated any sustained supply and have necessitated the proposal of various large-scale engineering masterpieces to transport water to these water-impoverished areas. This type of solution, even if technically and economically feasible, masks the problem, and may be only a short-term solution. Marshes, deserts and tundra also deserve consideration as natural resources. Humans have and continue to use these areas without an understanding of their role in nature. These areas are not simply there to be developed; they are areas that support various gene pools of plant and animal species that may be very necessary for the continued functioning of the ecosystem even though we may not today fully understand their utility. A discussion of the uses of land often focuses only on uses made by people. One should at least pause and consider that land in its natural state, unused by humans, is also a use of land.

The rest of this chapter will focus on various approaches to land use control. These land use control mechanisms most often, but not always, come into play when pressures are created by population growth in a specific location. As a further introduction to our sections on control mechanisms, we note that when considering the need for land use controls in any context, one could contend that control is necessary only when things get "out of hand." When is the point at which things are "out of hand" is an issue upon which

---

33. "Agricultural Resources and Environmental Indicators," *U.S. Dept. of Ag. Economic Information Bulletin No. (EIB-98)* p. 4 (2012).

reasonable people could differ. Also, most people are of the opinion that land use issues should be resolved before they become major problems rather than later. Thus we will see that many of our "control" mechanisms will really be land use "planning" mechanisms that try to prevent problems rather than remedy them.

B. PRIVATE LAND USE PLANNING AND CONTROL: NUISANCE, EASEMENTS, COVENANTS, AND INCENTIVES

In Chapter 3 we discussed the doctrine of "nuisance" that prevented landowner X from using his land in a way that would unreasonably interfere with the peaceful enjoyment by landowner Y of landowner Y's land. The common law of nuisance thus exists as a minimum degree of restriction that society has placed on what one can do with his land. It is also the minimum level of protection that a landowner has available against those who interfere with her use of her land. This level of control is imposed by society, but it is a "private" mechanism since it merely gives victims the opportunity to seek a remedy if they so choose.

Beyond this private control mechanism created by society, there are private planning and control mechanisms that can be created by individuals themselves. These privately created control mechanisms are called easements and restrictive covenants. If one is the owner of an easement, it can be said that she holds an interest in someone else's land. If your rural neighbor has a good water source on her property and you want to use it to supply your pond, you might purchase the right to use that water source and to go on her land to lay and repair the pipe to bring the water to your land. Your neighbor would convey this right to you by deeding you an easement on her land for the stated purposes. The benefit of that easement would pass to subsequent owners of your land unless the easement were created for the personal benefit of the holder ("easement in gross") rather than to benefit the land owned by the holder of the easement ("easement appurtenant to the land"). Easements also exist with respect to government owned land. Payment from private parties to the federal government for easements jumped from $213 million in 2005 to $294 million in

2007.[34] Most easements are created by voluntary transactions between the parties, but easements can sometimes come into existence in other ways. For example, if you were to use your neighbor's water source for a long enough period of time (often fixed by statute), in an open, visible, and continuous manner, without her consent, and adverse to her interests, you may acquire a "prescriptive easement" to use the source.

Covenants, unlike easements, do not give one landowner the ability to make active use of another landowner's land. Rather, a restrictive covenant will give to A an interest that allows A to restrict how B will use B's land. These restrictions by covenant go beyond limits that would be imposed by the nuisance doctrine and beyond public controls such as zoning. Thus if A owned fifteen adjoining lots that were zoned to allow either single-family or multifamily residential housing, A might sell one lot to B, and others to other buyers, with restrictive covenants that the lots be used only for single-family housing. In general, if the parties who agree to a restrictive covenant intend that the restrictive covenant shall bind subsequent owners, it can be written to do so, i.e., to "run with the land."

While restrictive covenants are generally enforceable and are well accepted as private land use planning tools, we should note some circumstances where the law has precluded their use. The clearest situation in which restrictive covenants may not be used is where the covenant would lead to the exclusion from housing on the basis of race. *Shelley v. Kraemer*,[35] a United States Supreme Court case decided in 1948, held that racially restrictive covenants could not be enforced by courts because to do so would violate the equal protection clause of the Fourteenth Amendment to the United States Constitution. The equal protection clause makes it unconstitutional for a *state* to "deny to any person within its jurisdiction the equal protection of the laws." In *Shelley,* the court decided that for a state to use its court system to enforce covenants that provide restrictions

---

34. Nickerson, C., Ebel, R., Borchers, A., Carriazo, F., "Major Uses of Land in the United States," *U.S. Dept. of Ag.* (2007) www.ers.usda.gov/publications/eib89.

35. 334 U.S. 1.

based on race would be *state action* denying persons equal protection of the laws.

The prohibition on the use of racial restrictions with respect to housing and some of its related facilities has gone far beyond *Shelley v. Kraemer. Shelley* prohibited state action to enforce a racially restrictive covenant. What about situations where there is no state action, but a completely private land use restriction mechanism operates in a racially discriminatory manner? In *Sullivan v. Little Hunting Park, Inc.,*[36] a 1969 U.S. Supreme Court case, a corporation had been formed to operate recreational facilities for the residents of a subdivision. A homeowner could have a share in the corporation that entitled him to use the facilities, and that share could be assigned to a tenant but only with the approval of the corporation's board of directors. The board refused to approve an assignment to a Negro tenant, and the court held that the tenant had a right to the assignment. Even though no state action was involved, a statute that had been enacted by Congress, the Civil Rights Act of 1866,[37] prohibited private individuals from discriminating in housing on the basis of race. The Civil Rights Act of 1866 states: "All citizens of the United States shall have the same right . . . as is enjoyed by white citizens . . . to . . . purchase, lease, sell . . . real . . . property." The Court had earlier held that Congress had the constitutional power to prohibit private as well as public racial discrimination with respect to the sale and rental of property, and that Congress' words in the statute meant just what they said: all racial discrimination, both private and public, in the sale or rental of property is prohibited.[38]

While the invalidity of racially restrictive covenants is very clear, a less clear situation in which restrictive covenants are limited in their validity involves the law's long adhered to policy against "restraints on alienation." This policy is based on the belief that restrictions on the ability to transfer one's interest in land inhibits

---

36. 396 U.S. 229.

37. 42 U.S.C.A. §§ 1981, 1982.

38. *Jones v. Alfred H. Mayer Co.*, 392 U.S. 409.

economic development and is adverse to the interests of society. Thus a covenant that kept a property owner from selling his land except to members of a designated property owners association was unenforceable.[39] There are, however, policies that compete with that of free alienability of property. One such policy is freedom of contract—courts enforcing the terms of an arrangement into which the parties have voluntarily entered. Some courts have adopted the position that covenants that restrict the alienation of property are invalid only if they are unreasonable. Possible factors bearing on the reasonableness of the restriction might be how long it lasts or whether it is absolute in that it makes no provisions for hardship situations. Thus a covenant prohibiting a condominium owner from leasing his unit was found reasonable and therefore valid since provisions were made for hardship situations and the duration of the restriction was not necessarily forever.[40] Other courts have, however, held that covenants are a contract involving valuable property rights, and reasonableness of a covenant is not relevant so long as it does not violate public policy. Thus, a restrictive covenant that prohibited trailers in a subdivision was found valid, and a factual inquiry by a court into its reasonableness could not take place.[41]

But for the possible need to resort to the courts to enforce them, restrictive covenants and easements are wholly private land use planning tools. Let us next look at a quasi-private mechanism. We call this quasi-private because, although it is not mandatory and is utilized on the initiative of private parties, government has created the mechanism for use by the private parties, and it is in the nature of a financial incentive rather than a limitation. The mechanism advances the goal of keeping land from being built upon by providing an income tax incentive to the owner to act in ways which will keep the land perpetually undeveloped.

Assume that Ms. Rich is in the 50% tax bracket for income tax

---

39. *Mountain Springs Association v. Wilson*, 196 A.2d 270.

40. *Seagate Condominium Association v. Duffy*, 330 So.2d 484.

41. *Aragon v. Brown*, 2003 N.M. App. Lexis 80, 78 P.3d 913.

purposes.[42] For every dollar of taxable income she receives above the upper limit of the next lowest tax bracket, she pays fifty cents of that dollar as income tax. Ms. Rich owns a large and valuable piece of real estate in a rural area. Adjacent to that real estate is a parcel owned by someone else. That parcel is about to be subdivided into 100 lots with a house to be put on each lot. Ms. Rich does not like this subdivision from an environmental point of view and, possibly, because she also believes it will reduce the value of her real estate holding. The owner of the 100 lots is willing to sell them all together for $500,000 which is their value as land for a housing development. What action can Ms. Rich take to prevent the subdivision and what will it cost her?

First, she could just buy the adjacent parcel for $500,000 and keep it from being developed. She will have protected the environment (and her other property and its value) from the development at a cost to her of $500,000 minus whatever comparatively small income she can obtain from the property in its undeveloped state. Of course, she would also own the parcel for its future value as an investment. Let us see if we can help Ms. Rich preserve the undeveloped land by making it less costly for her to do so. Under Section 170 of the Internal Revenue Code, Congress has provided that individuals may deduct from their income the amount of a "charitable" contribution that they make to a qualifying "charitable" organization. A "charitable" organization is much more broadly defined than merely those that give help to the poor. An organization whose purpose is to keep land from being developed may qualify under Section 170, with the result that gifts that are made to it are tax deductible. These organizations are usually called "land trusts." Ms. Rich can buy the proposed development for $500,000 and donate the land to the land trust. The land trust will

---

42. The numerical results in this example depend on the tax rates in existence, and those change from time to time. For ease of calculation, we are assuming a 50% rate for combined federal and state income tax purposes. Similarly, the treatment of capital gains, restrictions on the extent and/or timing of deductions, and many other aspects of income taxation are constantly subject to change. We make assumptions with respect to those as well. Regardless of the current details of income taxation and the exact amount of financial help "Ms. Rich" would receive in trying to achieve her environmental and/or personal goals, the § 170 charitable contribution deduction in the Internal Revenue Code has the potential to greatly reduce the costs for a "Ms. Rich" to achieve those goals.

then sell the land for a lesser amount, but with restrictions that allow it to be used only for such activities as agriculture or forestry. Ms. Rich takes the value of her donation to the land trust, $500,000, as a tax deduction, and she removes the adverse effects of the development at a cost to her of $250,000 rather than $500,000. This is because on $500,000 of her very high income she would have paid income tax of $250,000. By giving the $500,000 to the land trust and taking a deduction, she saves having to pay $250,000 in income tax. Of the $500,000 donation she gave to the land trust, only $250,000 is a net out-of-pocket cost to her—the other $250,000 is money that she has just chosen to send to the land trust instead of to the United States Treasury. Ms. Rich has now accomplished her objective at a cost to her of $250,000 rather than $500,000. Can we do still better for her?

Instead of having Ms. Rich give all 100 lots to the land trust after she buys them, let us have her keep ten of them. Since she paid $500,000 for the whole parcel and is donating 90 out of 100 lots, her tax deductible charitable contribution is 90/100^{ths} of $500,000 or $450,000. Being in the 50% tax bracket means she saves paying taxes on $450,000 at the 50% rate. She thus saves $225,000 in taxes. She has spent $500,000, saved $225,000 in taxes, and is therefore out-of-pocket $275,000—but she still owns ten building lots for which she paid $5000 apiece. These ten lots are now surrounded by 90 lots that the land trust has perpetually restricted from development, and, since these ten building lots will be *forever* surrounded by open space instead of by 90 houses, their value is greatly increased over the $5000 that was paid for each of them. Ms. Rich sells these prime building lots for $35,000 each and receives $350,000. On this sale she has made a profit of $300,000 (paid $5000 each and sold them for $35,000 each). Assuming that she kept them for more than one year after she bought them, her profit would be taxed as a capital gain, which means she would pay tax at a lower rate than her 50% tax bracket rate. If the capital gain rate were 25%, she would pay 25% of her $300,000 profit— $75,000. She has taken in $350,000 on the lots she sold and pays a tax of $75,000, leaving her with $275,000 on the sale. Her donation of $450,000 to the land trust left her out-of-pocket $275,000 as we saw above. The donation and the sale taken together have left her with a minus $275,000 and a plus $275,000.The 100-lot subdivision that threatened the environment and Ms. Rich's other real estate has been reduced to ten prime building lots, and the cost to Ms. Rich has been zero.

The reader may want to question the justification for Congress allowing and even encouraging the above actions by Ms. Rich. On one hand, Congress' environmental and land use objectives of preserving agricultural and forest land are furthered, and the rich are the ones with the capital and the risk taking ability that can help Congress achieve its land use objectives. Also, the charitable contribution deduction is an incentive for wealthy landowners to keep land they already own from being developed. On the other hand, it can be argued that the United States Treasury (all taxpayers) is subsidizing Ms. Rich's achieving her objectives of protecting the value of her real estate and preferring to have undeveloped land with a few high priced residences instead of a large number of lower priced residences. Furthermore, even if we look only at the environmental objective that Ms. Rich may have and not at her property value objective, should Ms. Rich's environmental desires be heavily subsidized by the treasury when someone named Ms. Poor will not be subsidized to anywhere near the same level to accomplish those things that she believes are environmentally important? That is because the lower the donor's tax bracket, the less is the percentage of the donation that actually is provided by the treasury instead of by the donor. A $1 donation by someone in the 50% bracket is really 50 cents of her money and 50 cents of money that does not get sent by her to the treasury. A $1 donation by someone in the 20% bracket is 80 cents of her money and 20 cents of money that she does not have to send to the treasury. Is then the proper perspective from which to view the above-described tax mechanism: (1) "should more government money be spent on the environmental goals of the rich than on those of the poor?" or (2) "should government accomplish its environmental objectives by encouraging the use of privately initiated voluntary methods wherever possible?" Congress has decided to use the charitable contribution deduction incentive to help protect farm and forestry land from development and the system is in widespread use. From 1990 to 2000, the amount of land protected by land trusts grew from 1.9 million acres to 6.2 million acres—a 226% increase.[43] By 2010, the amount of land protected by land trusts grew to 47 million—an increase of 10 million acres since 2005 and 23 million since 2000.[44] The land is kept open and protected from development; however, it may be that other land prices and thus the cost of housing increases. The land trust approach is perhaps most justified when preserving large amounts of land from development is coupled with providing affordable housing on part of that land or on other land. Some land trusts have begun to view assisting in the construction of reasonably priced housing as a very significant part of their mission.

C. PUBLIC PLANNING AND CONTROL; THE "TAKING CLAUSE" LIMITATION ON CONTROL

While the federal government exercises some control over how privately owned land is used, most public planning and control of privately owned land is done by local governments under authority given to them by the states. The degree to which states get directly involved in land use control varies from state to state. Some states do very little. Vermont, however, has a Land Use Development Law[45] that mandates, in addition to local requirements, a state permit for developments which might have significant environmental impact. We will focus on local land use controls and then look at the extent to which the "taking clauses" of the United States and state constitutions limit public control of land use.

1. Zoning and Local Control

The dominant local land use planning and control mechanism is

---

43. Liegel, K. and Duvernoy, G., "Land Trusts: Shaping the Landscape of our Nation," *Natural Resources and Environment* (American Bar Association, Fall 2000) p. 96.

44. Chang, K., "Land Trust Alliance, 2010 National Land Trust Alliance Census Report," 5 (Rob Aldrich & Christina Soto eds., 2011), available at http://www.landtrustalliance.org/land-trusts/land-trust-census/national-land-trust-census-2010/2010-final-report.

45. 10 V.S.A. § 6001 et seq.

zoning. There are numerous different forms of zoning controls and numerous purposes for enacting them. The most well-known type of zoning is "use zoning." Use zoning categorizes different activities which people may seek to undertake on land and prescribes which activities can be conducted on which parcels of land within the local government's jurisdiction. For example, a suburban city may have its land allocated for five types of "uses" and thus call its use zones R-1, R-2, R-3, C-1, and C-2. R-1 could be single-family residential, R-2 could be two-, three-, or four-family residential buildings, and R-3 could be apartment buildings of 5 or more units. C-1 areas might be for light commercial operations providing consumer goods and services on a retail basis, while C-2 might be for heavy commercial operations conducted at the wholesale level. Some of the possible purposes for segregating these uses to different areas might include keeping heavy traffic out of places where people live, protecting property values by assuring people that a movie theater will not be built next door to their ranch house, or facilitating the efficient provision of city services like trash collection or police protection.

The uses designated for a given zone may be "permitted uses," which are activities that are allowed in that zone as a matter of right, or "conditional uses," which may be allowed in the zone if the user meets certain conditions. These conditions may either be stated in the zoning ordinance itself, or the ordinance may authorize a local body such as a Zoning Board of Adjustment to impose conditions in a discretionary manner. Our C-1 zone described above could provide that all uses allowed in it are permitted uses unless the use will involve more than 30 people being on the premises at any one time. If more than 30 people will be there, the use may be conditioned on the landowner providing a specified number of off-street parking spaces.

In addition to the distinction between permitted and conditional uses, we should note the distinction between two other terms, exclusive zones and cumulative zones. If a zone is established as an exclusive zone, only the activities specified for that zone may take place there. If a zoning scheme provides for cumulative zoning, then, in addition to the activities specified for a particular zone, any "higher" (i.e., less intensive) use may also take place in that zone.

Thus under cumulative zoning, a light commercial zone could be used for residential use but not for "lower" (i.e., more intensive) heavy commercial activities. Exclusive zoning can be said to have the advantage of better serving the health and safety protection purpose of zoning by ensuring that people cannot choose to live in a heavy traffic commercial area or in an industrial area with high air pollution. Also, if residential uses are allowed in an area zoned for industry, industries that want to locate there may be deterred from doing so because they could be subject to liability as a nuisance to the residential landowners. Cumulative zoning, however, has the advantage of flexibility and diversity. Perhaps people should be able to choose to live in a commercial area if rents are lower there, if it is simply more convenient for them, or if they like living in an area where nonresidential activity is happening. Depending on the character and planning objectives of a city, it may choose to have some of its zones be cumulative and some exclusive.

Many other types of zoning ordinances exist besides use zones. Maximum height limitations may be provided for purposes such as added fire safety, aesthetics, or to ensure adequate availability of light. Distances may be established as a required "setback" of a building from a street for reasons such as planning for possible future widening of streets or to provide greater visibility at street corners. Communities may establish agricultural zones to preserve the character of the community by protecting it from invasion by intensive development. Regardless of the type of zoning that a local government may want to enact, it must get its authority to impose its zoning scheme from the state, since local governments are the creations of the state.

The zoning power is a part of the state's police power—the power to protect the public health, public safety, and general welfare. Usually, the states have delegated the zoning power to local governments, with the most common mechanism for the delegation being zoning "enabling acts" which enable or permit local governments to zone but do not require them to do so. Whether the zoning power was a valid part of the state's police power was questioned in the 1926 U.S. Supreme Court case of

Village of Euclid, Ohio v. Ambler Realty Co.[46] A landowner contended that a "use" and a "height and minimum area requirements" zoning scheme that restricted his use of his land and thereby reduced its market value was not a valid exercise of the state's police power. The Court found that a comprehensive zoning ordinance bears a rational relationship to the public health and safety and is therefore a valid exercise of the police power. *Euclid* thus clearly established the validity of comprehensive zoning, but that is not to say that all attempts at zoning are necessarily valid. One type of zoning where the trend has been in the direction of invalidity is exclusionary zoning.

Exclusionary zoning was the subject of a New Jersey case, *Southern Burlington County N.A.A.C.P. v. Township of Mount Laurel.*[47] The Township of Mount Laurel had a zoning ordinance that provided for varying minimum lot sizes, widths, and dwelling unit sizes for each of its residential zones. There was very little available land in the zones with the least restrictive requirements. Most of the available residentially zoned land required a minimum lot size of about one-half acre. Although the New Jersey Supreme Court noted that Mount Laurel's requirements were not as restrictive as those in many similar municipalities, it said that a developing municipality may not, by a system of land use regulations, make it physically or economically impossible to provide low and moderate income housing in the municipality and thereby exclude people from living within its confines because of the limited extent of their income and resources. The result of such a system would be presumptively contrary to the general welfare and therefore outside the scope of the zoning power.

Two other factors that tend to attenuate harsh results which may otherwise flow from the exercise of the zoning power should be mentioned briefly. These are variance and nonconforming use provisions often contained in local zoning ordinances. A variance will allow someone to put her land into use in a way which is not allowable under the zoning ordinance as it applies to her land. The purpose of having a variance procedure is to account for special

---

46. 272 U.S. 365.

47. 336 A.2d 713.

situations involving the property itself, rather than its owner. Because of the characteristics of the property itself, fairness or good sense should result in the property not being required to be used in compliance with the zoning laws. This might include situations where a lot is so small that to enforce compliance with minimum lot size requirements would preclude putting a building on the lot and make it useless. Another example might be where a restaurant will be located near ample public parking facilities. A variance from zoning requirements for off-street parking for restaurants would appear to be in order. As a matter of practice, zoning variances are often given where the legal criteria for a variance have not been met. In the absence of significant adverse effects on neighboring property or on the public, a variance is often issued even though the property has nothing in the way of physical characteristics that make it different from other property that is zoned in the same way.

Nonconforming use provisions also attempt to mitigate possible hardships by allowing a use to continue in violation of the applicable zoning ordinance if it lawfully existed prior to the adoption of that zoning. The nonconforming use provisions do reduce hardship to the landowner, yet, if the use has been made unlawful for the public benefit and would not be allowed had it not already been there, is not that public benefit being partly sacrificed by allowing the nonconforming use to be there just because it was there before the zoning enactment? Might not a better remedy for any unfairness to the owner be to compensate the owner for losses due to his having to give up his nonconforming use?

Besides zoning, local governments have other land use control mechanisms available to them. State statutes often authorize local governments to require local approval of subdivisions of land. In exchange for providing this local approval, local governments have sometimes sought "exactions" from developers who want to subdivide. For example, if a developer wants to subdivide her land for residential use, the local government may require that she dedicate land to the community for park or recreational purposes. Such exactions have been found valid for reasons such as, using the above example; an influx of new residents brought in by the subdivision will increase the need for park and recreational facilities. The subdivision will also make the developer's land more valuable. Part of her gain can be required to be used to provide for the local needs she will be creating.[48] The subdivision approval mechanism has also been used to regulate the rate of growth of a community by restricting the number of subdivision permits that will be issued within a given period of time. The town of Ramapo, New York, sought to alleviate population growth pressures by enacting an ordinance to control the growth of the community. Ramapo's ordinance tied development by residential subdivision to the availability of municipal facilities. Before a permit to subdivide would be issued, certain municipal facilities would have to be available. The facilities were to be provided in accordance with an 18-year plan or capital program. Growth would thus be allowed, but it would be slowed down to the pace at which facilities were provided. Ramapo's ordinance raised the general question of whether a town should have the right to control its growth, but in the *Ramapo* case the question was whether the town did in fact have that right. The town's ordinance was attacked on the grounds that it was a "taking" or confiscation of private property by the government without the just compensation required by the constitution and also that Ramapo's action was an unjustifiable exclusion of people from the community.

The court's answer to the taking without compensation argument was that the restriction on any individual piece of property was only temporary rather than permanent because the property would be able to be subdivided sometime during the 18 years. Also, the property could be used prior to its qualifying for a subdivision permit—it just could not be subdivided. A detailed discussion of what is an unconstitutional "taking" without just compensation is in the next subsection of this chapter. It is there shown that what will be called a "taking" by the courts may be very narrow, and that governments such as the Town of Ramapo have a great deal of latitude in regulating and controlling the use of land and ultimately controlling population through land use controls. On the issue of whether the ordinance amounted to an unjustifiable exclusion of people from Ramapo, the court said that the ordinance was not exclusionary but was merely the implementation of

---

48. *Associated Home Builders v. Walnut Creek*, 484 P.2d 606.

sequential development and timed growth. The court said it would not countenance exclusion, but that timed growth was acceptable. Since timed growth is only a temporary exclusion and results in fewer people in an area for only a period of time, governmental control over the size of the population within its boundaries was found to be allowable at least to some extent.[49]

The source of power for the local land use planning and control mechanisms discussed above is the police power. Another source of power to control land use is the eminent domain power, which is the power of government to take private property for public use. Rather than being an explicitly stated power, the eminent domain power is an inherent power of the sovereign—either the federal government or the state government and its authorized offspring, the local governments. Acknowledgment of the existence of the eminent domain power comes by way of limitations on that power that are expressed in the United States Constitution and, in various forms, in state constitutions. The "taking clause" of the Fifth Amendment to the United States Constitution reads: "nor shall private property be taken for public use, without just compensation." Thus the taking of private property by government is acceptable so long as it is taken for a public use and just compensation is paid to the owner. If a local government wanted to establish a park, it could "take" or condemn private property and use it for a park. Similarly, if a local government wanted certain land to be used only for agriculture, it might, instead of zoning it for agricultural use only, "take" or condemn the land and resell it with restrictions that it be used only for agriculture. The key difference between accomplishing these local government objectives by using the eminent domain power, as opposed to the police powers of zoning or subdivision exactions discussed above, is that when government is acting under the eminent domain power, it must pay "just compensation." While in many instances government will voluntarily act under its eminent domain power to handle a land use situation, since regulation under the police powers does not require payment of compensation to the landowner, there is a strong inclination for government to

---

49. *Golden v. Planning Board of Town of Ramapo*, 285 N.E. 2d 291.

"regulate" rather than to "take." Landowners who have found themselves subjected to uncompensated regulation often have contended that government has gone beyond the scope of its police power authority and either does not have the power to do what it seeks to do at all or, if it can act, it can do so only under the eminent domain power and with the payment of just compensation. Suits brought by private landowners alleging that an attempt to "regulate" is really a "taking" and that just compensation should be paid, are called "inverse condemnation actions."[50]

2. The "Taking Clause" Limitations on Land Use Control

Eminent domain, the power of government to take private property for public use, is an inherent power of the sovereign—either the federal government or the state government—and its authorized offspring, the local governments. Acknowledgment of the existence of the eminent domain power comes by way of limitations on that powers that are expressed in the United States Constitution and, in various forms, in state constitutions. The "taking clause" of the Fifth Amendment to the United States Constitution reads: "nor shall private property be taken for public use, without just compensation." Thus the taking of private property by government is acceptable so long as it is taken for a public use and just compensation is paid to the owner. If a local government wanted to establish a park, it could "take" or condemn private property and use it for a park. Similarly, if a local government wanted certain land to be used only for agriculture, it might, instead of zoning it for agricultural use only, "take" or condemn the land and resell it with restrictions that it be used only for agriculture. The key difference between accomplishing these local government objectives by using the eminent domain power, as opposed to the police powers of zoning or subdivision exactions discussed above, is that when government is acting under the eminent domain power, it must pay "just compensation." While in many instances government will voluntarily act under its eminent domain power to handle a land use situation, since regulation under the police powers

---

50. *Fulton County v. Wallace*, 393 S.E.2d 241.

does not require payment of compensation to the landowner, there is a strong inclination for government to "regulate" rather than to "take." Landowners who have found themselves subjected to uncompensated regulation often have contended that government has gone beyond the scope of its police power authority and either does not have the power to do what it seeks to do at all or, if it can act, it can do so only under the eminent domain power and with the payment of just compensation. Suits brought by private landowners alleging that an attempt to "regulate" is really a "taking" and that just compensation should be paid, are called "inverse condemnation actions."[51]

In trying to define the line between a police power regulation and an eminent domain taking, a realistic beginning point is the United States Supreme Court's opinion in *Goldblatt v. Town of Hempstead*.[52] The Court acknowledged that the line is a fuzzy one: "There is no set formula to determine where regulation ends and taking begins." Instead, a court will engage in an *ad hoc*, fact-oriented inquiry to examine several potentially significant factors relating to the taking question.[53] Let us then look at some of the factors that have been used by courts to determine whether a government action is a compensable taking or a noncompensable regulation.

Goldblatt concerned a town ordinance that placed restrictions on mining excavations. Those restrictions included fencing requirements, prohibitions on further excavation below the water table, and filling any existing excavations below that level. The landowner had operated a gravel pit on his property for many years and contended that the ordinance was not regulatory but completely prohibitory and confiscated his property without compensation. The Court said that, although a beneficial use of the property had been prohibited, that does not mean that the ordinance is beyond the scope of the police power and thus a taking. The owner was not

---

51. *Ibid.*

52. 369 U.S. 590.

53. *Keystone Bituminous Coal Assn. v. DeBenedictis*, 480 U.S. 470.

disturbed with respect to his control or use of his property for other purposes, and his right to dispose of his property was not restricted. Besides factors of control, disposability, and use, the *Goldblatt* opinion also referred to how onerous the government action might be in terms of decreasing the value of the property. A comparison of property values before and after the government action was said to be relevant but by no means conclusive.

This type of analysis, or balancing test, in which the court weighs several factors including the governmental interests being advanced and the effects on property values, has repeatedly been used in "taking" cases. In addition to examining the character of the government action and the nature of the different rights of property ownership that are restricted or retained, courts may consider the extent of the economic impact and the degree of interference with the owner's reasonable investment-backed expectations. These factors formed the basis for the United States Supreme Court's decision in *Lucas v. South Carolina Coastal Council.*[54] Lucas had purchased two beachfront lots intending to build houses. After his purchase, but before construction, the state enacted the Beachfront Management Act designed to preserve South Carolina's beaches from erosion. Under the provisions of the Act, construction on the Lucas lots was prohibited. Lucas's property was rendered valueless, and Lucas claimed a taking requiring compensation. The Court stated that: "Where the State seeks to sustain regulation that deprives land of all economically beneficial use, we think it may resist compensation only if . . . the proscribed use interests were not part of his title to begin with." Thus only if common law principles of nuisance and property law would have prevented construction, can construction be prohibited without compensation. If these principles had prohibited construction, his title to the land would not have included a right to construct on it. The Court further noted that such principles rarely support prohibition of the "essential use" of land. It appears that, while historically ingrained aspects of the public interest like nuisance may be used to prohibit construction without paying compensation, areas of the public interest that have

---

54. 112 S. Ct. 2886.

become of concern more recently, such as beach erosion and wetlands preservation, may only be protected if government is willing to pay private landowners for losses—at least if those losses are the total value of the land.

The *Lucas* case may be thought of as a *per se* rule: if government control will deprive a landowner of all the economically beneficial use of the property, it is a taking and requires the payment of compensation. The total loss of all beneficial use of property is likely a rare situation, and likely even rarer in view of the 2002 U.S. Supreme Court opinion in *Tahoe-Sierra Preservation Council v. Tahoe Regional Planning Agency*[55] where it was held that a temporary prohibition on the use of land was not a taking. Apparently, there must be a permanent loss of all value of the property for the *Lucas per se* rule to apply. *Tahoe* involved a 32-month moratorium on development, although, in fact, the moratorium had gone on for decades. Given that full loss of value will not always be a usable test and that the Court in *Tahoe* indicated that it, at least where there was not a full and permanent loss, a balancing of factors is what will determine whether there has been a taking, let's consider some other factors besides loss of property value.

Actual physical use by the government or the public may be a taking, whereas prohibiting uses by the owner may not be a taking. A United States Supreme Court opinion held that "a permanent physical occupation authorized by government is a taking without regard to the public interests that it may serve." Therefore, a New York statute that required landlords to allow installation of cable television facilities on rental properties was a permanent physical occupation and was thus a taking for which just compensation was required.[56] Another analytical possibility is a sliding scale approach to the taking/regulation distinction. This may be used to say that the higher the type or degree of public interest, the greater the infringement on property rights that should be allowed without there being a taking. For example, action X should be a taking if

---

55. 535 U.S. 302.

56. *Loretto v. Teleprompter Manhattan CATV Corp.*, 458 U.S. 419.

government does X for historic preservation purposes, but the same action X should not be a taking if done to protect what might be considered a more important interest of the public health. The *Lucas* case contains language that appears to contemplate possible use of this sliding scale approach.

Let's note three additional elements that may be relevant when determining if the payment of just compensation is required. For short, these may be called "reciprocity," "nexus," and "temporary taking." First, there may be a land use regulation that prohibits a landowner from causing a nuisance to her neighbors, and that regulation may also protect the landowner from her neighbors imposing a nuisance on her. This "reciprocity of advantage," by simultaneously restricting a landowner's use of her land and conferring a benefit to the landowner, may persuade a court that no taking has occurred.[57] Second, if a government regulation is not sufficiently related to the public purpose it purportedly is designed to further, a court may determine that the regulation is an improper exercise of the police power and amounts to a taking. For example, if a privately owned ocean front lot was between two public beaches, a municipality could attempt to condition a building permit for the private lot on the landowners' granting the public an easement to pass from one public beach to the other across their lot. If the purpose of the easement is a desire to protect the public's ability to *see* the beach, then the restriction requiring public access *along* the beach is not related to the public's "visual access" to the beach. The easement would not improve the public's view. Thus there was no "nexus" between the requirement of the easement and the alleged purpose of the easement—the view and the landowners must be compensated for a "taking" if the easement is required.[58] Finally, consider the notion of a "temporary taking." When an attempted regulation is determined by a court to be a taking, the government may repeal the regulation or amend the regulation to permissible standards for non-compensable regulations. Nevertheless, even if the municipality repeals or modifies the regulation, payment of just compensation may be required for that

---

57. *Keystone Bituminous Coal Assn. v. DeBenedictis*, 480 U.S. 470.

58. *Nollan v. California Coastal Commission*, 483 U.S. 825.

period of time that the taking was in effect.[59] Note the difference between this "temporary taking" and the *Tahoe* case discussed above. If there is a taking for a temporary period of time, that "temporary taking" requires compensation for that period. However, a temporary prohibition on use of land will not necessarily establish that there has been a taking.

Regardless of the factors that have been used by individual courts to draw the taking/regulation line, it is fair to say that the result has been that government can go a long way in restricting private property rights and reducing private property values by those restrictions without needing to pay compensation. To the extent that Americans believe that they are secure from their government acting in ways that reduce their property value from $200,000 to $100,000 without paying compensation, that feeling of security is a myth. Yet there is a limit. Beyond some ill-defined point, and one that appears to shift from time to time in court opinions, government action that adversely affects private property will be a taking and constitutionally require the payment of just compensation.

One might want to consider the wisdom of allowing government to act in ways that substantially reduce individual property values without compensating the owners for the loss. Would it not be better to say that when government acts for the public benefit, all citizens should pay the price for that benefit rather than having the cost fall on one property owner or a small group of property owners who stand to bear the cost because of fortuitous circumstances? Thus, perhaps all government action that results in a substantial loss in property value should be compensated, and the question of whether there has been a "taking" or a "regulation" should not be relevant. Furthermore, should compensation be limited to losses related to land use? For example, if a company has been operating lawfully for 20 years and even been encouraged to expand its operation by federal income tax incentives, should new pollution laws enacted for the public benefit be allowed to put this company out of business or reduce its profitability without compensating its owners? Are there compensation systems for land or other property

---

59. *First English Evangelical Church of Glendale v. Los Angeles County*, 482 U.S. 304.

value losses that might be workable and yet be fairer than the taking/regulation distinction? If one looks for them, one will find many possibilities.[60] For example, some land use decisions by government, like rezoning, will increase the value of some private property. Government action has thus added value to that property. This could be viewed as a windfall to its owner. Perhaps some of that windfall added value could be captured by government and used to compensate other property owners whose property has lost value due to government action but who are not constitutionally entitled to compensation because there has not been a "taking."

If government were required to pay compensation for property value losses brought about by environmental regulations, which would present a significant and perhaps financially insurmountable challenge to our nation's principal environmental laws. That challenge has manifested itself in the form of increasingly successful lawsuits against the U.S. Government in the United States Claims Court. When the government is ordered to pay a million dollars to a mining company for restricting its activities which would have destroyed wetlands or created water pollution, basic environmental protection laws may become too expensive to enforce.[61] Indeed, the willingness of the United States Supreme Court in the *Lucas* case described above to require that government pay compensation when it acts to protect parts of the public interest such as beachfronts, wetlands, and endangered species, may be a big step in putting some environmental protection measures out of the realm of budgetary possibility. This will be especially true if the Court were to go one step beyond its *Lucas* decision and require compensation for property owners who would have very substantial but not total economic loss of their land. Even without an expansion of property owners' rights to compensation under the federal or a state constitution, state legislatures or state ballot initiatives may

---

60. Hagman, D., and Miczynski, D., *Windfalls for Wipeouts* (Chicago: American Society of Planning Officials, 1978); Epstein, R.A. *Takings, Private Property and the Power of Eminent Domain* (Cambridge, MA: Harvard University Press, 1985); Berger, M. "Tahoe Sierra: Much Ado About—What?" 25 *Hawaii Law Review* 295 at 320 (2003); Clune, M., "Time for a New Look at 'Windfalls for Wipeouts'?" *Natural Resources and Environment* (Spring, 2006).

61. *Florida Rock Industries v. United States*, 21 Cl. Ct. 161.

expand property owners' rights to compensation and thus inhibit efforts to prevent sprawl, preserve farmland, protect vistas and achieve other similar environmental goals. For example, the Oregon voters approved a ballot measure that requires government to either compensate owners for reductions in property values due to regulations or to waive the restrictive regulation.[62]

Our last topic in this section concerns the reasons for which government can take private property even if it will pay just compensation for it. The taking clause says: "nor shall private property be taken for public use, without just compensation." There is thus recognition that while the inherent eminent domain power allows a taking for "public use," there cannot be a taking by government for "private use" even if just compensation is paid. The issue is what is meant by the words "public use." Is it a public use and thus an allowable exercise of the eminent domain power for a municipality to condemn private property, paying compensation to the owners who do not voluntarily want to sell it, and then transfer that property to another private owner like the General Motors Corporation? Quite clearly, if a municipality were to condemn private land for a park to be used by the public, that would be a taking for public use. Our General Motors question would appear to be a taking for private use and thus not within the eminent domain power. But let us add some additional facts. If the municipality were the City of Detroit, and General Motors were going to use the property to build a new plant, thereby promoting industry and commerce and adding badly needed jobs and taxes to the economic base of the city and the state, do we now have a "public use?" A narrow interpretation of the words "public use" would still result in our answer being no. The use is a private use—use by General Motors. The courts have not, however, always given the words "public use" a narrow interpretation. Public use has been held to include serving "public purposes" or providing "public benefits," and, so long as the public interests are dominant, the fact that private interests will also benefit from the condemnation does not necessarily mean that the condemnation is outside the scope of the

---

62. "Oregon's Vistas May Get Less Scenic," *Christian Science Monitor* (December 3, 2004), available at www.csmonitor.com/2004/1203/p02s01.

eminent domain power. In the General Motors example, the Michigan Supreme Court said:

> The power of eminent domain is to be used in this instance primarily to accomplish the essential purposes of alleviating unemployment and revitalizing the economic base of the community. The benefit to a private interest is merely incidental.[63]

Public takings in which private property is condemned and transferred to new, private owners were also approved by the United States Supreme Court in *Hawaii Housing Authority v. Midkiff*.[64] In *Hawaii*, the state legislature found that, because 47% of the state's land was owned by 72 private landowners and the federal and state governments owned another 49%, concentrated land ownership skewed the real estate market, inflated land prices, and injured public tranquility and welfare. The legislature, in response to the land oligopoly, provided for the condemnation of residential tracts and the transfer of ownership to existing tenants. The tenants also were provided with state assistance in financing the land purchases. The Supreme Court held that the "public use" requirement does not mean that the government must possess and use the property during a taking. The Court found that, despite incidental private benefits incurred by the purchasing tenants, the dominant public interest of reducing the concentration of land ownership statewide demonstrated that the land reforms were constitutional exercises of the state's eminent domain power.

Twenty-three years after the Michigan Supreme Court determined in the General Motors case that the public use requirement of the eminent domain power could be satisfied by the finding of a "public purpose," the Michigan Supreme Court reversed its position or at least severely narrowed it. In the 2004 case of *County of Wayne v. Hathcock*,[65] it held that government's

---

63. *Poletown Neighborhood Council v. City of Detroit*, 304 N.W.2d 455.

64. 467 U.S. 229.

65. 684 N.W.2d 765.

attempt to take private property and transfer it to other private parties for redevelopment as a business and technology park was not a public use and thus violated the taking clause. It would only allow such a transfer if there were an extreme public necessity and the property would remain subject to public oversight after the transfer. Also in 2004, the Connecticut Supreme Court, in *Kelo v. City of New London*,[66] moved in the opposite direction. It held that private property taken by government and transferred to another private entity satisfies the requirement for public benefit if the resulting economic benefits run to the public. In 2005, the United States Supreme Court, in a 5-4 decision, agreed, finding that the "public use" aspect of the taking clause is satisfied where government is acting for a "public purpose" and that economic development is a well-established public purpose.[67]

Most recently, the U.S. Supreme Court in 2013 expanded the scope of the takings clause, holding that regardless of whether property was actually taken from a private landholder, "extortionate demands for property in the land-use permitting context run afoul of the Takings Clause not because they take property but because they impermissibly burden the right not to have property taken without just compensation."[68] In *Koontz v. St. Johns River Water Management District*, a local land use planning committee denied a permit when the landowner refused to comply with the committee's conditions to develop the land. Previously, the takings clause prevented land-use agencies from demanding a concession of property or property easements in exchange for a development permit. The decision in *Koontz* prevents agencies from asking for money as well.

Recent increases in foreclosures, population loss, and declining property values, have resulted in a large number of abandoned properties in many locations. Some local governments have suggested relying on the post-*Kelo* "public purpose" definition of

---

66. 843 A.2d 500.

67. 125 S.Ct. 2655.

68. 133 S.Ct. 2586 (June 25, 2013).

eminent domain to acquire mortgages in an effort to prevent vacant lots. In Detroit, where an estimated 40 square miles of land is vacant, residents have annexed vacant lots, either buying them or fencing off areas as big as a city block in an effort to stabilize neighborhoods and bring the lots back onto the tax rolls. Municipalities have granted residents the opportunity to purchase adjacent empty lots at low cost in order to achieve this goal. As a preventative mechanism, local governments have considered relying on eminent domain to prevent mortgage defaults by acquiring under-water mortgages (mortgages where the value of a home is below the amount of the mortgage debt).[69] The government would pay investors fair market value for the mortgages, below face value, allowing it to issue new mortgages with smaller balances to the homeowners. By seizing the property, with fair compensation to owners, the public interest would be served with a reduced likelihood of mortgage defaults and abandoned property.

Since *Kelo*, the question whether the Supreme Court allows states and local governments to use the power of eminent domain to take private property for economic development by other private entities to achieve a public benefit has been answered. Whether states and local governments will act in such a manner is an entirely different question. After the Court's decision in *Kelo*, many states have enacted legislation limiting the power of eminent domain. Limitations have been strong, significantly limiting a state's eminent domain powers;[70] intermediate, imposing some limits on

---

69. Shiller, R., "Reviving Real Estate Requires Collective Action," *New York Times* (June 23, 2012) http://www.nytimes.com/2012/06/24/business/economy/real-estates-collective-action-problem.html?smid=pl-share (last visited December 26, 2012).

70. In 2006, the Michigan Legislature passed an amendment to the state constitution to limit the eminent domain power. The amendment prohibits "the taking of private property for transfer to a private entity for the purpose of economic development or enhancement of tax revenues." The Michigan Legislature also modified procedures for condemnation and calculation of compensation through the Uniform Compensation Procedures Act, which raised the statutory cap for individuals' moving expenses, provided attorney's fees for low-income individuals in the event of an unsuccessful condemnation challenge, and clarified the process for surrendering property. The Act also narrowly defines the public uses for which private property may be condemned. Virginia voters approved a constitutional amendment to limit the state's power to seize private property for redevelopment.

state powers with exceptions;[71] weak, where state powers have remained essentially the same;[72] or non-existent where the pre-*Kelo* status quo has been retained.[73]

The future of the use of eminent domain power to foster economic development to increase a community's tax base is a topic of great dispute. When we discussed the line between what is a police power regulation and what is an eminent domain taking, we concluded that government can go quite far in restricting property use and still be on the regulation side of the line. If government is, however, acting under its eminent domain power, it also has substantial latitude with respect to what it chooses to call a public purpose or public benefit to satisfy the public use requirement of the taking clause. Clearly, economic development is sufficient, and in *Berman v. Parker*, the United States Supreme Court decided that aesthetics is a valid public purpose. The Court said: "It is within the power of the legislature to determine that the community should be beautiful as well as healthy. . ."[74] There are legal limits on public control of land use, but at least if government is willing to pay compensation, the legal limits are not very limiting. Perhaps the more significant limits are political and/or economic.

---

71. Utah has passed numerous procedural measures to limit use of eminent domain, including creating special taxing entities and procedural requirements for urban redevelopment and economic development takings and allowing local governments to take private property for blight, allows condemnation, and imposes some procedural and notice requirements on condemning authorities. The Utah Legislature adopted the Private Property Protection Act requiring state agencies to adopt guidelines to help them identify constitutional takings issues, to prepare assessments when the agencies have identified projects with constitutional takings issues, and to minimize the risk of takings wherever possible.

72. Washington's legislature adopted a bill requiring that a government seeking condemnation notify affected property owners by certified mail at least fifteen days before the public meeting at which the authority will make a final decision on the condemnation.

73. For example, Idaho, Illinois, Kentucky, Maine, Nebraska, Alaska, Maryland, Missouri, Montana, California, Rhode Island, Tennessee, Vermont, Arkansas, Hawaii, Mississippi, New York, Oklahoma, and Connecticut.

74. 348 U.S. 26.

D. THE PUBLIC TRUST DOCTRINE

In addition to police power regulations and eminent domain takings, a third doctrine provides some restrictions on private ownership and use of land. Originating in English law, the public trust doctrine held that title in the land under the sea belonged to the public but was managed in trust for the public by the king. Although the king, or today the state, can convey this land to private owners, the state cannot convey or "alienate" the land free of public trust obligations or rights of use by the public such as for navigation or fishing. The legislature may thus convey public trust lands to private parties, but some public rights in the land will continue to exist, and grants of property subject to the public trust doctrine may even be revoked. The source of the modern public trust doctrine in the United States is the 1892 case of *Illinois Central Railroad v. Illinois*, where the U.S. Supreme Court allowed Illinois to revoke its grant to the railroad of the title to an area of the bed of Lake Michigan bordering Chicago. The Court found that the conveyance violated the public trust with respect to public rights in navigable waters. The court said:

> The state can no more abdicate its trust over property in which the whole people are interested . . . than it can abdicate its police powers in the administration of government and the preservation of the peace.[75]

As the public trust doctrine has evolved, its applicability and operation have expanded and become more defined.[76] Let's first consider what types of land or natural resources, although privately held, may be subject to public rights, and what public rights or benefits may exist with regard to that land. We will then discuss the scope of the limitations or "encumbrances" that these rights place

---

75. 146 U.S. 387.

76. Callies, D. and Breemer, J., "Selected Legal and Policy Trends in Takings Law: Background Principles, Custom and Public Trust 'Exceptions' and the (Mis)Use of Investment-Backed Expectations," 36 *Valparaiso University Law Review* (Spring 2002) pp. 355-361.

on the private ownership of land.

Traditionally, the king's trust responsibilities extended to lands under the sea for use by the public in navigation, commerce, and fishing. Subsequently, the public trust doctrine has been extended to include other navigable waters such as lakes and rivers, and also tidelands and wetlands. For example, when the state of Mississippi began issuing oil and gas leases on land underlying a bayou and streams which were several miles from the Gulf of Mexico and non-navigable, the state's ownership of the land was contested by private parties claiming ownership. The United States Supreme Court held that Mississippi's public trust rights extended not only to lands under navigable waters, but also to those under tidal waters because of public interests including geographical, chemical, and environmental qualities of non-navigable tidal waters.[77]

Although the concept of an inalienable public trust originally was used to protect public rights concerning navigation, commerce, and fishing, the public trust doctrine approach manifests itself today in numerous other conflicts ranging from the regulation of grazing land in national forests[78] to the protection of and recovery for damages to natural resources. Where an oil spill destroyed 30,000 birds, a court held that the government had a right and duty to protect the public interest in preserving wildlife resources.[79] Legislatively, Congress has provided, in the Superfund Act (CERCLA), that government "shall act on behalf of the public as trustee of such natural resources to recover for . . . damages."[80] Natural resources are defined as "land, fish, wildlife . . . ground water . . . and other such resources belonging to, managed by, held in trust by . . . the United States . . . State or local governments . . ."[81]

---

77. *Phillips Petroleum v. Mississippi*, 484 U.S. 469.

78. *Light v. United States*, 220 U.S. 523.

79. *In re Stewart Transportation Co.*, 495 F. Supp. 38.

80. 42 U.S.C. § 9607(f).

81. 42 U.S.C. § 9601 (16).

The types of lands and natural resources which may carry with them rights of the public as a whole appear to be expanding, and that expansion can be seen not only in federal court cases and legislation but also in state court decisions. The New Jersey Supreme Court has expanded the public trust doctrine beyond water resources to include dry-sand beach areas.[82] Over 100 years after the recognition of the public trust doctrine by the U.S. Supreme Court with respect to navigable waters in *Illinois Central Railroad*, the Hawaii Supreme Court, in 2000, extended the doctrine to include the entire fresh water supply of the state without any regard to navigability.[83] Pursuant to the public trust doctrine, land that is in the hands of a private landowner may still be subject to the public's rights in that land or in natural resources related to it.

Once we determine that a parcel of land is covered by the public trust doctrine, we must next examine what constraints the public trust doctrine places on the interests of the private landowner. The scope of the encumbrances that the public trust doctrine may establish on the ownership of applicable lands can extend to restrictions on the use, development, and alienability of the land, and can lead to the modification or revocation of ownership interests. The legislature, as trustee, has the discretion to impair public uses of trust lands, but it also has an affirmative obligation to consider public interests and to minimize harms done to those trust interests. For example, where water rights to a lake have been granted to a municipality, the legislature retains an obligation of continued supervision and a power to revoke or modify the conveyed water rights.[84] Thus, the municipality acquires the water rights subject to the trust and can assert no vested right which would do harm to the public's interests such as by draining a lake beyond certain levels. Also, development of lands adjacent to trust lands may be restricted to a greater extent than other lands. State courts have determined that, because lands adjacent to navigable

---

82. *Matthews v. Bay Head Improvement Assn*, 471 A.2d 355.

83. *In re Water Use Permit Application*, 9 P.3d 409.

84. *National Audubon Society v. Superior Court of Alpine Cty.*, 658 P.2d 709.

lakes, streams, or oceans have a special relationship to public trust lands, to permit the development of these adjacent lands would degrade or deteriorate public trust lands and would contravene the intent of the doctrine.[85] Therefore, more restrictive land use regulations may be imposed on lands adjacent to trust lands than on other lands without exceeding the police power authority and creating a compensable taking.

Perhaps the most restrictive public trust constraint on private land ownership would involve a prohibition on sale of the land or on converting it to other than its present use. Assume that local government condemns some private land for a public purpose and pays just compensation to the owners. It then transfers the land to another private owner to achieve that public purpose. What if the new private owner discontinues its initial public interest use—can it put the property to another use or sell it? This issue could arise with respect to the city of Detroit/General Motors situation discussed in Section C above. Since, in that example, no trust land was involved, General Motors may be allowed to subsequently use the land for other purposes or to sell it. The situation could be different, however, for a private landowner who was granted public trust land upon which to build a wharf for navigation and commercial uses. If the owner later wants to develop the property into a hotel or apartment building, courts may require that the changed use be consistent with the public trust. The Massachusetts Supreme Judicial Court has stated that public trust land "can be granted by the State only to fulfill a public purpose and the rights of the grantee to that land are ended when that purpose is extinguished."[86]

Another example involving changing use and ownership of public trust land concerns federal military installations. Assume that the federal government purchases public trust lands from the state for use as a naval base. If the Navy subsequently ceases operation of its base, may it sell the land to another private owner, or does the public trust doctrine require that the land revert back to the state? Federal courts in California and Massachusetts, both of which

---

85. *Graham v. Estuary Properties, Inc.*, 399 So.2d 1374.

86. *Boston Waterfront Dev. Corp. v. Commonwealth*, 393 N.E. 2d 356.

confronted questions similar to this, reached opposite results. The Massachusetts court decided that federal condemnation did not extinguish the public trust; instead, the federal government assumed the trustee responsibilities.[87] In effect, the public trust is administered jointly by the federal and state governments, and the public trust requirements persist. Conversely, the California court focused on the supremacy of federal law over state law.[88] That court decided that federal condemnation of the land extinguished the state's public trust because the federal power of eminent domain is supreme over the state duty of public trust. Therefore, the federal government was free to convey the land, after ceasing its naval base operations, to a private concern. The federal government periodically undertakes to close military facilities. Whether a federal public trust obligation in this context will be recognized remains to be seen. Though the public trust doctrine has recently received considerable support both academically and judicially, the doctrine often remains rather vague and obscure in its definition and application.

As a possible further expansion of the public trust doctrine, one may speculate about whether, in the future, the act of taking land by government through the eminent domain process might be found, by itself, to have made land that is not otherwise public trust land into public trust land. Such a result could be supported by arguing that, since the eminent domain process can only be used for the public interest, once it is so used, the public acquires permanent rights in the land that has been obtained under that process. This would be a significant expansion of the public trust approach. With a growing number of environmentally concerned plaintiffs embracing the public trust doctrine for protecting land and other environmental interests, it is not clear whether the courts will continue to expand the scope of a state's public trust rights and duties, or whether the doctrine, even as it currently stands, will be found to be too restrictive of private interests in the ownership and use of land.

---

87. *United States v. 1.58 Acres of Land*, 523 F. Supp. 120.

88. *United States v. 11.037 Acres of Land*, 685 F. Supp. 214.

E. EMERGING ISSUES IN LAND USE

1. Alternative Energy, Farm Subsidies, and Land Use Change

U.S. policy has been to support the production of ethanol as an alternative fuel to be blended with and thereby reduce the use of gasoline, and the U.S. is the largest single producer of ethanol fuel.[89] The policy of encouraging ethanol has been implemented with laws including mandated use as fuel and subsidies to farmers. The Energy Independence and Security Act requires that fuel producers must use at least 36 billion gallons of bio-fuels by 2022, 15 billion of which must be corn ethanol,[90] and Congress has provided subsidies for crops at varying levels for many years.[91] Increased demand based on mandated use and the payment of subsidies tends to result in higher potential profits which lead farmers to plant more acreage. Farmers converted more than 23 million acres of grasslands, wetlands, and shrub lands to cropland between 2008 and 2011.[92] Approximately one-third of the converted land has been used to produce corn, converting forest or grassland, which function as natural carbon dioxide sequesters. The conversion thus contributes to climate change. The 2012 U.S. corn harvest was estimated at 11.8 billion bushels, 4.3 billion bushels of which will be converted into fuel. The increase in demand for ethanol for fuel has diverted almost half of the domestic corn supply from animal feedlots to ethanol refineries and driven up corn prices leading to concerns about future prices of livestock feed and the

---

89. Statistics: Annual World Ethanol Production by Country, Renewable Fuels Ass'n, http://www.ethanolrfa.org/pages/statistics/ (last visited Dec. 29, 2010).

90. Congressional Research Service, Report for Congress, Energy Independence and Security Act of 2007, P.L. 110-140, H.R. 6 A Summary of Major Provisions (Dec. 21, 2007) (finding that ethanol can be produced from a large variety and combination of biomass products including wheat, corn, animal waste, soybeans, and sugarcane).

91. Peterka, A., "Farm Bill Stokes Fear of Long-Term Price Decline," *Climate Wire* http://stevens.vermontlaw.edu:2073/EEDaily/2012/05/23/archive/2?terms=corn+subsidy (last visited Jan. 2, 2013).

92. *Ibid.*

effects on prices of milk, eggs, and meat both domestically and globally since the U.S. supplies 70% of the world's corn exports.[93]

Support for ethanol production has resulted in land use changes in the U.S., and some of the effects of those changes are noted above. Global land use patterns can also be affected indirectly by ethanol production.[94] For example, when U.S. farmers sell a large percentage of their corn for ethanol production, the price of corn rises as supply decreases. More grain farmers choose to dedicate their cropland to corn, which in turn increases demand for less profitable grains. That causes Brazilian cattle farmers to fill the demand for these grains by converting pastures to farmland, requiring land in the Amazon to be converted to cattle pastures. Indirect land use changes were relied on by the California Air Resource Board (CARB) when it assigned a carbon intensity value to ethanol made from corn, and a court agreed that CARB could base carbon intensity values on the indirect land use theory.[95] Because it is a relatively new issue, there has been little litigation regarding the indirect-land use theory. It is but one factor in the ongoing debate about whether government policy favoring ethanol is ultimately more beneficial than harmful.

2. State and Local Government: Combating Climate Change

The uses of land affect climate change, and climate change will impact local governments in many ways, including increased hurricanes and tornados, flooding and draught, loss of biodiversity, and soil degradation. State and local governments have the power to act in many ways to combat climate change and simultaneously improve daily life with respect to matters such as air and water

---

93. Grunwald, M., "The Clean Energy Scam," *Time Magazine* (Mar. 27, 2008), available at http://www.time.com/time/magazine/article/0,9171,1725975,00.html.

94. Zeller, T, "The The Biofuel Debate: Good, Bad or Too Soon to Tell?" *New York Times* (Nov. 3, 2008), available at http://green.blogs.nytimes.com/2008/11/03/the-biofuel-debate-good-bad-or-too-soon-to-tell/?scp=10&sq=Clean%2520energy%2520scam%2520Time%25202008&st=cse.

95. *Rocky Mountain Farmers Union v. Goldstene*, 719 F.Supp.2d 1170 (E.D. Cal. 2010).

quality, traffic congestion, and availability of natural resources. Let's consider what state and local governments can do and have done in the land use context to address what is perhaps today's dominant environmental issue—climate change.

States have the power to focus on sustainable development and renewable energy by requiring that local governments consider conservation and reductions in greenhouse gases. Municipalities can require that building projects utilize energy efficient building techniques and can facilitate the implementation of sustainable energy by providing financial or other incentives for the use of solar energy. Local governments have adopted rules requiring that all public sector decisions consider the impact of those decisions on climate change. If, however, local land use controls or covenants would stand in the way of projects that would help combat climate change, state law could remove those obstacles. For example, Arizona's Solar Rights Act overrides local ordinances or covenants that would otherwise prohibit the installation of solar panels.[96]

Another land use approach to combating climate change works through what is generally known as comprehensive planning. State enabling statutes that empower local governments to control land use by zoning often require that zoning be done in accordance with a comprehensive plan. States can require that local comprehensive plans address ecological building projects, preserve rural areas and farmland, and reduce emissions by planning for urban development. Local government, in turn, could restructure its zoning by using "mixed use zoning" rather than traditional zoning which separates residential, commercial, and industrial uses. Mixed use zoning allows ground level commercial uses with residential uses on the stories above, which tends to reduce sprawl, transportation, and emissions, each of which contributes to climate change. Marin County in California has a policy utilizing mixed use development to help reduce emissions from vehicles.[97] Other examples of utilizing the comprehensive planning requirement to address

---

96. Ariz. Rev. Stat. Ann. §33-439 (2012).

97. Marin County Community Dev. Agency, Marin Countywide Plan (2007), available at http://www.co.marin.ca.us/depts/cd/main/fm/cwpdocs/CWP_CD2.pdf.

climate change include the Colorado and Pennsylvania enabling statutes that emphasize reliance on strategies to facilitate energy conservation and the use of alternative energy sources as part of comprehensive land use planning.[98] In addition to having general comprehensive land use planning with climate change components, states and municipalities can adopt specific "climate action plans."[99] By assessing local emission of greenhouse gases and setting reduction targets, states and municipalities can implement land use policies that assist them in meeting their goals. Denver, Colorado's climate action plan suggested policies to reduce emissions produced in various sectors of the city, including preventing construction of a coal power plant.[100]

Climate change is a, and many people say the, big environmental issue. With what is generally thought to be not enough action on climate change at the international and national levels, perhaps numerous state and local actions, taken together, can have a meaningful impact on combating climate change and also serve as a catalyst for national and international efforts. The land use control powers of state and local governments give them a wide array of approaches to take the lead in addressing climate change and its related issues.

---

98. Colo. Rev. Stat. § 30-28-106(3)(a)(VI) (2008); 53 Pa. Con. Stat. § 10301.1 (2009).

99. U.S. Environmental Protection Agency, *Climate Change Action Plans*, available at http://www.epa.gov/state.local.climate.

100. City and County of Denver, *Denver Comprehensive Plan 2000* (2000), available at http://www.denvergov.org/Portals/650/documents/CompPlan2000.pdf.

Photographs by Michael J. Firestone

ADDITIONAL READINGS

Aubrecht, C., et al., *Land Use: Planning, Regulations, and Environment* (Nova Publishers, 2012).

Blake, W., Pipes, C., Will, R., *The Law of Eminent Domain: Condemnation, Zoning and Land Use Committee* (Chicago: First Chair Press; American Bar Association, 2012).

Brewer, R., *Conservancy—The Land Trust Movement in America* (Lebanon, NH, Dartmouth College, University Press of New England, 2003).

Dietrich, D.J. and Dietrich, C., *Conservation Easements: Tax and Real Estate Planning for Landowners and Advisors* (Chicago: American Bar Association, Section of Real Property, Trust, and Estate Law, 2011).

Exner, A., et al, *Land and Resource Scarcity* (Routledge: 2013).

May, J., *Principles of Constitutional Environmental Law* (Chicago: American Bar Association, Section of Environment, Energy, and Resources, 2011).

Miller, C., *Public Lands, Public Debates: A Century of Controversy* (Oregon State University Press, 2012).

Nolan, S., *Land in Conflict: Managing and Resolving Land Use Disputes* (Lincoln Institute of Land Policy, 2013).

Randolph, J., *Environmental Land Use Planning and Management* (Island Press, 2011).

Shuford, S., *Planning For a New Energy and Climate Future* (American Planning Assoc., 2010).

CHAPTER 5
WASTE AND RESOURCE RECOVERY

A. THE SCOPE OF THE WASTE PROBLEM

"Gee whiz mom, my bicycle finally fell apart, and now I need a new one. What should I do with this junker?" "Put it out in front son, and the garbage man will take it away," she said. And take it away he did, just like that garbage has been taken away for decades and just like your municipal government or the waste disposal company you hire takes your garbage away. But, as we observed in Chapter 1, you cannot always take it away and put it someplace else. We are a part of that someplace else. There is no external environment. So, where do we put it? "It" is really a collection of stuff for which we no longer have a use or we simply do not want. It is defined by our federal government under the general heading of solid waste. According to federal statute, the Resource Conservation and Recovery Act (RCRA), we define "solid waste" as;

> . . .any garbage, refuse, sludge from a waste treatment plant, water supply treatment plant, or air pollution control facility and other discarded material, including solid, liquid, semisolid, or contained gaseous material resulting from industrial, commercial, mining, and agricultural operations, and from community activities, but does not include solid or dissolved material in domestic sewage, or solid or dissolved materials in irrigation return flows or industrial discharges which are point sources subject to permits under section 1342 of the Clean Water Act, or source, special nuclear, or byproduct material as

defined by the Atomic Energy Act of 1954, as amended.[1]
As shown in Tables I and II,[2] in 2010, we generated almost 250 million tons of municipal solid waste, about 4.43 pounds per person per day.

Table I.
GENERATION, MATERIALS RECOVERY, COMPOSTING, AND DISCARDS OF MUNICIPAL SOLID WASTE, 1960-2010

Millions of tons							
	1960	1970	1980	1990	2000	2005	2010
Generation	88.1	121.1	151.6	205.2	237.6	245.7	249.9
Recovery for recycling	5.6	8.0	14.5	29.0	52.7	58.4	64.9
Recovery for composting	Neg.	Neg.	Neg.	4.2	16.5	20.6	20.2
Total Materials Recovery	5.6	8.0	14.5	33.2	69.1	79.0	85.1
Combustion with energy recovery	0.0	0.4	2.7	29.7	33.7	33.4	29.3
Discards to landfill, other disposal	82.5	112.7	134.4	142.3	134.8	133.3	135.5

Our per capita generation has remained stable for more than a decade; however, our total generation has shown an increase of 20% since 1990 and 180% since 1960.

On the bright side, our recovery of materials for both recycling and composting has been increasing both in total and per capita amounts. Only 54 percent of all waste generated ends up in landfills, compared to 89 percent in 1980. Also, the amount of waste recovered reduces total waste generation per person to less than 3 pounds per day. Almost 65 million tons of waste is recovered

---

1. 42 U.S.C. § 6903(27).

2. "Municipal Solid Waste in the United States: 2010 Facts and Figures," (2013), available at www.epa.gov.

through recycling and over 20 million tons of waste is recovered through composting, and we combusted about 12 percent of all waste for energy recovery. While waste combustion for energy production has its positive side, one might question the overall environmental soundness of the waste to energy process. Combustion of waste, in addition to causing air pollution, leaves a residue—ash. This ash may have high concentrations of heavy metals, which, without extremely careful handling, could have severe environmental impacts such as leaching into and contaminating ground water.

Table II.
GENERATION, MATERIALS RECOVERY, COMPOSTING
AND DISCARDS OF MUNICIPAL SOLID WASTE, 1960-2010

	Pounds per person per day					
	1960	1970	1980	1990	2000	2010
Generation	2.68	3.25	3.66	4.50	4.63	4.43
Recovery for recycling	0.17	0.22	0.35	0.64	1.03	1.15
Recovery for composting	Neg.	Neg.	Neg.	0.09	0.32	0.36
Total Materials Recovery	0.17	0.22	0.35	0.73	1.35	1.51
Combustion with energy recovery	0.00	0.01	0.07	0.65	0.66	0.52
Discards to landfill, other disposal	2.51	3.02	3.24	3.12	2.62	2.40
Population (millions)	179.98	203.98	227.26	249.91	281.42	309.05

When we think of solid waste, we think of paper, glass, plastics, food scraps, grass clippings, etc. But there is another "species" of solid waste, known as "hazardous waste." Hazardous waste is generally identified by the federal government as a solid waste (defined above) that may cause or significantly contribute to increased mortality or illness or threaten human health or the environment when improperly handled[3] *and* can be measured using a standard test or reasonably detected by generators of hazardous waste.[4] Most hazardous waste is further characterized as a solid waste that is ignitable, corrosive, reactive or toxic.[5] In 2011, EPA estimated that 16,000 large quantity generators collectively generated 35 million tons of hazardous waste. Comparisons with earlier data would show a tremendous decrease, but that would be highly misleading. Between 1995 and 1997, the reporting system changed to exclude wastewater from the data. In fact, between those 2 years, hazardous waste generation increased by 4.4 million tons.[6] In addition to the wastewater exclusion, it should be noted that radioactive waste is not covered by the hazardous waste control mechanisms of RCRA. Is radioactive waste hazardous? Yes. Is radioactive waste "hazardous waste?" No. In order to be within the definition of "hazardous waste" under RCRA, the waste must be a "solid waste" as defined above, and the end of that definition excludes radioactive materials. Radioactive waste is controlled under other statutes.

Industries that generate hazardous waste include makers of cosmetics, petroleum products, leather, and plastics. While we keep track of what hazardous wastes these industries are putting where, hazardous wastes generated in our homes when we discard materials like drain cleaners, solvents, and garden pesticides are usually either unregulated or regulated by local law with little or no enforcement. We cope with industry-generated hazardous waste by incineration, disposal in a landfill, deepwell/underground injection, or recovery. Incineration of hazardous waste raises similar, but perhaps greater, problems of air pollution and water pollution than

---

3. 42 U.S.C. § 6903(5).

4. 42 U.S.C. § 6903(5), 40 CFR § 261.10.

5. 40 CFR § 261.21-24.

6. EPA, "The National Biennial RCRA Hazardous Waste Report (Based on 2011 Data), Exhibit 1.2, www.epa.gov, (December 2012).

the ash problem noted above with respect to solid waste. Less than 3 percent of our hazardous waste is incinerated, some for the energy that can be recovered. The majority of hazardous waste, 59 percent, is managed with deepwell or underground injection.[7] Storing hazardous wastes until methods are developed to render them nonhazardous or, hopefully, to make use of them, causes significant concern that, in the meantime, leakage will result in the poisoning of our drinking water. When considering hazardous waste, even more than with respect to nonhazardous solid waste, there is no good answer yet. Progress has, however, been made under the Resource Conservation and Recovery Act (RCRA).[8] At least we now know where most hazardous waste is going, and that reduces its potential for contamination of land and water. Efforts are also being made under the Superfund Act,[9] which we will discuss later, to remedy the hazardous waste contamination that occurred in earlier years.

The volume of ordinary, nonhazardous solid waste continues to increase, and finding appropriate disposal sites or developing other approaches to dealing with waste continues to be a major concern of many local governments. No area of the United States is immune from the pressing environmental and economic problems of solid waste disposal. New England towns with populations of a few hundred people are faced with having to close their landfills pursuant to state laws that require plastic-lined landfills in order to protect ground water against the leachate from waste. These lined landfills are very expensive, and small towns are exploring ways to join together to provide environmentally sound landfill sites at costs that are within their financial capabilities. Urban areas have been faced with the issue of where to put their trash for many years, but the magnitude of today's concern can be highlighted by noting the extremes which are being considered for coping with the urban solid waste problem. Cities on the west coast of the United States

---

7. *Ibid.*, Exhibit 2.6.

8. 42 U.S.C. § 6901 et seq.

9. 42 U.S.C. § 9601 et seq.

once discussed paying millions of dollars to send millions of tons of trash by boat to the Marshall Islands. Today, trash is one of the nation's leading exports.[10] New technologies are constantly developed, producing vast amounts of electronic waste, about 80 percent of which is sold as "scrap" to foreign countries like China, Nigeria, India, Vietnam, and Pakistan.[11]

The environmental problems of waste are numerous. Waste disposal is related to air pollution (smell and the pollutants created by the burning process), water pollution (leaching from dump sites), and the aesthetic pollution of disposal sites. Hazardous waste raises the level of concern even higher. In addition, the whole approach of disposal results in the loss of resources that have a potential for future use. Whether it be by incineration or by the mixing of wastes in a landfill, future use is precluded. We next look at how the problems associated with waste disposal are addressed by the legal system and what the law is doing to provide alternatives to disposal.

B. MECHANISMS FOR CONTROLLING WASTE DISPOSAL–LOCAL, STATE, NATIONAL, AND INTERNATIONAL

The two interrelated facets of the solid waste problem are, as noted in Section A, collection and disposal of solid waste and the fact that waste "disposal" results in the depletion of resources. Both the disposal and resource depletion aspects of the problem have received substantial attention at all levels of government—local, state, national, and international. This section will consider regulatory mechanisms which are addressed to disposal. Mechanisms addressed to the resource depletion problem will be discussed in Section C.

---

10. Edward Humes, "Grappling with Garbage Glut," *The Wall Street Journal* (April 18, 2012), available at http://online.wsj.com/article/SB10001424052702304444460457733 7702024537204.html.

11. "After Dump, What Happens to Electronic Waste," *NPR* (Dec. 10, 2010), available at http://www.npr.org/2010/12/21/132204954/after-dump-what-happens-to-electronic-waste.

1. Nonhazardous Waste

Collection and disposal of solid waste was a local government function until the 1960s. There was little federal involvement other than studies and advice. The mechanisms which regulated disposal were local health laws, other local ordinances such as zoning to restrict where a dump could be located, and private lawsuits. If you were bothered by a disposal activity, your recourse was to bring a nuisance action against those private parties who were interfering with your use of your property or against the local government that ran or planned a dump near your property.[12] Your remedy might take the form of receiving money damages to compensate you for the harm you suffered, a court-issued injunction to prevent the harmful conduct from continuing, or the imposition of a wide variety of conditions which the disposing party must adhere to in order to be allowed to continue the disposal activity. Examples of such conditions might be time periods when burning is prohibited or requiring treatment of certain types of waste prior to disposal. While a wide array of private law remedies was available, they were generally only available with respect to harm inflicted on real estate. Also, the remedies tended to come into play after a harm had been done rather than as a preventative measure against harm, and those harmed had to go through the process of a lawsuit to attempt to obtain a remedy. Local legislative efforts to control waste disposal encountered enforcement problems and a lack of technology to provide a sound disposal system. Perhaps of greater significance with respect to local efforts was the lack of funds to effectively deal with waste disposal. The costs are high and, since there was little political glamour involved with promising a strong waste disposal program, waste disposal never got proper local funding.

In the 1960s and early 1970s, the federal government entered the picture. The first federal statutes had minimal federal involvement such as providing states with technical assistance and funding for research and demonstration projects. These statutes

---

12. See Chapter 3 for a discussion of nuisance actions and remedies.

were the wedge that opened the door to serious federal regulation of solid waste disposal. They helped set the stage for public and Congressional acceptance of federal control over what had been historically a local matter.

In the Resource Conservation and Recovery Act of 1976 (RCRA),[13] Congress undertook to impose a broad federal scheme for regulating solid waste disposal. That statute, with amendments, is the heart of waste disposal law today. It seeks to control the disposal of solid wastes by providing financial incentives for the adoption of state or regional plans which will comply with federally established requirements. In addition to dealing with "general" solid wastes through the use of an incentive approach, the statute also established a mandatory regulatory system for the management of "hazardous" wastes.

With respect to nonhazardous solid wastes, if a state adopts a solid waste plan which is approved by the federal government (EPA), then the state qualifies for federal financial and technical assistance involving many facets of the development and implementation of the state plan. In order for a state plan to be approved, it must meet federal requirements for approval which include a prohibition on the establishment of new open dumps and a phasing out of existing open dumps. Approved plans must also provide that disposal be in sanitary landfills, through resource conservation and recovery methods, or by other environmentally sound methods. In order for a disposal site to be a "sanitary landfill," there must be "no reasonable probability of adverse effects on health or the environment from disposal of solid waste at such facility."[14] The design criteria for a site to be a new sanitary landfill include that it be lined with a material such as heavy plastic and have a leachate collection system.[15] In addition to the high cost of the liner/leachate requirement, one might question whether plastic liners will really work in the long run.

A point of contrast between the Resource Conservation and

_____

13. 42 U.S.C. § 6901 *et seq.*

14. 42 U.S.C. § 6944(a).

15. 40 CFR § 258.40.

Recovery Act and both the Clean Air Act and the Clean Water Act is that, while the latter two statutes provide that, in the absence of an approved state implementation plan, EPA will impose a federally prepared plan on the state, no such federal imposition takes place with respect to solid waste. The only sanction in the event of state noncompliance with the federal requirements for state plan approval is the state's ineligibility to receive federal financial and technical assistance. Why then, without compulsion, do the states go along with the federal objectives and requirements? The answer is twofold: money and money. First, the offer of a significant amount of federal money is hard for a state to pass up. Federal money provides jobs and other elements of economic well-being. Furthermore, state administrations passing up "free" federal dollars usually take a sound beating in the press for doing so. Being efficient in bringing federal money to the state is good politics for state officials. Perhaps a more substantive money argument for states accepting the federal solid waste disposal requirements is awareness that, sooner or later, the waste disposal problems will have to be faced. States may feel that they might as well address the problem while the federal government is picking up a good share of the bill rather than wait to address the problem after other states have gotten federal assistance and the federal program is no longer available to help.

Although there is now substantial federal prodding and federal assistance, nonhazardous solid waste management is still largely a matter of state and local control. One step that some states took to attempt to reduce the magnitude of their solid waste problem was to prohibit the disposal within the state of waste which originated or had been collected outside of the state. New Jersey had such a prohibition, and the validity of the New Jersey law was challenged repeatedly in the courts until a final decision was reached by the United States Supreme Court.

The first attempts to have the out-of-state prohibition declared invalid were made in the New Jersey state court system in a case called *City of Philadelphia v. New Jersey*.[16] The major grounds on which invalidity was alleged were (1) that the enactment of solid

---

16. 68 N.J. 451 and 73 N.J. 562.

waste disposal legislation by the federal government preempted the field of solid waste disposal regulation and thus the state law was invalid under the Supremacy Clause of the United States Constitution, and (2) that the New Jersey statute was invalid because it violated the Commerce Clause of the United States Constitution by unjustifiably discriminating against articles of commerce coming from outside of the state. Let's consider the preemption and Commerce Clause issues one at a time.

The Supremacy Clause, contained in Article VI of the United States Constitution, says that the "Constitution, and the Laws of the United States... shall be the supreme Law of the Land;... any Thing in the Constitution or Laws of any State to the Contrary notwithstanding." It is thus clear that state laws which are in direct conflict with federal law are invalid. The Supremacy Clause has, however, been given broader scope by the courts. If it is found that Congress intended to *exclusively* control or "preempt" the field of regulation of certain subject matter, state laws which seek to regulate the same subject matter are invalid even though they do not directly conflict with federal law. Whether Congress has intended to preempt a field of regulation is often analyzed in terms of how pervasive is the scheme of federal regulation which Congress has created and whether Congress has indicated in that legislation that it is willing to accept additional, non-conflicting state legislation.

In the New Jersey Supreme Court cases decided both before and after the federal Resource Conservation and Recovery Act was enacted, the New Jersey Court found that Congress' statutes, rather than evidencing a hostility to state regulation, affirmatively encouraged state action with respect to the disposal of solid waste. Thus there was no Congressional intent to preempt the field of regulation, and the state law prohibiting out-of-state waste was not invalid under the Supremacy Clause. When *City of Philadelphia v. New Jersey* went to the United States Supreme Court, the United States Supreme Court agreed with the New Jersey Supreme Court on the issue of preemption.[17]

The New Jersey Supreme Court had also determined that the out-of-state prohibition did not violate the Commerce Clause of the

---

17. 437 U.S. 617.

United States Constitution. The Commerce Clause, contained in Article I, Section 8 of the Constitution, gives Congress the power "To regulate Commerce... among the several States. ..." In addition to the Commerce Clause giving power to Congress, as discussed in Chapter 3 in the context of water pollution, the courts have interpreted this constitutional grant of power to Congress to preclude states from enacting laws which discriminate against articles of commerce coming from outside the state unless there is some reason, apart from their origin, to treat them differently. This interpretation is consistent with the policy of preventing a state from engaging in protectionism by treating out-of-state commerce in a less favorable way than it treats its own commerce. That policy was much on the minds of the drafters of the Constitution who were well aware that many of the economic woes of the country under the Articles of Confederation were a result of states practicing protectionism.

The New Jersey Supreme Court had found that the out-of-state prohibition advanced vital health and environmental objectives with no economic discrimination against and with little burden upon interstate commerce. The United States Supreme Court reversed that judgment. It decided that solid waste is an item of commerce and is thus under the protection of the Commerce Clause. Even if an object of interstate trade is valueless, it is not outside the scope of the Commerce Clause. Furthermore, unlike diseased cattle, there are no dangers inherent in the movement of solid waste from one state to another which would justify a prohibition against its crossing a state line. The Court found that while it was true that some items of commerce may be validly subjected to state regulation, such regulation cannot take place where the purpose is basically protectionism. Although New Jersey may have an interest in conserving its remaining landfill space, it may not attempt to isolate itself from a problem common to many states by erecting a barrier against interstate movement of an item of commerce such as solid waste. The New Jersey statute prohibiting disposal of out-of-state waste in New Jersey was unconstitutional, and, while Congress has given the states a large role to play under the Resource Conservation and Recovery Act, states may not seek to limit their solid waste problems by prohibiting the entry of out-of-state waste.

If a state cannot limit the entry of out-of-state waste, and if the volume of its own waste is growing rapidly, and if its' existing landfills are full and/or a threat to ground water, what can the state do? After doing all that can be done to minimize the creation of solid waste and to recycle or reuse what would otherwise be solid waste, the problem of disposing of the remainder becomes unavoidable. Incineration results in air pollution and in needing to dispose of the ash that may contain substances that have become especially hazardous due to concentration by the process of incineration. There is great resistance to locating an incinerator or ash disposal site anywhere. So what are the choices? Let's consider an alternative that addresses the shortage of landfill space and the disadvantages of incineration: export.

Given the lack of willing sites in the United States, proposals for disposing of American solid waste in foreign nations have been presented. These proposals, such as the one for a site in the Marshall Islands noted in Section A above, raise many interesting issues. While most of the discussion about and opposition to international transport of waste for disposal has focused on radioactive or hazardous waste,[18] the Marshall Islands proposal involved nontoxic trash from west coast cities. The Marshall Islands were part of the Trust Territory of the Pacific Islands administered by the United States under United Nations auspices after World War II. In 1986, the Republic of the Marshall Islands became an independent nation. It is a Third World country and also has virtually no economic base. It is almost wholly dependent on funds from the United States which come from rent for a missile testing facility and foreign aid under a compact that was part of the independence process. The prospect of receiving $56 million annually as a nonhazardous waste disposal site is enticing to a Third World nation with a population of about 50,000 and an extremely high rate of population growth; however, the money received is not the only advantage that might be derived from being a disposal site.

The Marshall Islands consist of narrow coral atolls that barely rise above the high tide mark. Land is very scarce, and a solid waste

---

18. Nee, V. and Sewall, B., "Can Kazakhstan Profit from Radioactive Waste," 15 *Georgetown International Environmental law Review*, 429 (2003).

landfill placed in a lagoon of an atoll means more usable land. In addition, the existing land is very close to sea level, and a landfill brings the possibility of raising the elevation, something that sounds very attractive to people concerned about rising sea levels due to global warming. Another advantage that must be acknowledged is that waste disposal is an industry that will provide jobs and perhaps the beginning of an independent economic base. The waste disposal industry might also provide, as a "by-product," the means for establishing other industries on the Marshall Islands because the boats that bring the waste may be available to transport freight to the United States at a reasonable price since they would otherwise be returning empty. The availability of cheap transport could make the isolated Marshalls competitive as an exporter. All of these advantages led the government of the Marshall Islands to tentatively endorse the waste disposal proposal. There are, however, numerous disadvantages that should be very carefully considered prior to any nation agreeing to accept waste from another nation for disposal.

Although waste may be of the "nonhazardous" type, it does bring with it the likelihood of significant adverse effects on the ecology of an area. This is especially true of an ecologically fragile coral reef which is used as a source of food for the local people and which may also have the potential to be developed for export of reef products and for tourism. Also, even nonhazardous waste can easily cause pollution of drinking water, and that is one of the main reasons for opposition to sites in the United States. Besides the environmental problems that nonhazardous waste might cause in developing countries, the establishment of the waste industry might work to psychologically preempt other business and industry in those countries. Tourism certainly would not benefit by the image of countries as waste disposal areas. Consider the economic desirability of real estate in the United States that is located near "the dump" or on the "Dump Road." In addition, how can a Third World nation adequately monitor the waste it receives to be sure it is "nonhazardous," or can it trust those bringing the waste to do this monitoring for them?

Our discussion of the export of waste has so far focused on export to developing countries for recycling, but the future could see waste being exported to developed countries and for a very different purpose: energy production. Oslo, Norway, and many other places in Northern Europe are generating large amounts of heat and electricity by burning trash. The waste-to-energy incinerating plants can handle more than 700 million tons of waste, but Northern Europe produces only 150 million tons. Oslo now imports garbage from England and Ireland and is eying the American market. While some champion trash-to-energy as renewable energy reducing the use of fossil fuels, other caution that the over capacity of the plants creates pressure for producing more waste and undermines efforts at waste reduction, reuse, and recycling.[19]

Another example of exporting waste is electronic waste, or e-waste. According to EPA, the United States produces more than 2.5 million tons of e-waste each year.[20] This includes a variety of products, such as cell phones, computers, televisions, and washing machines. E-waste contains both non-hazardous materials and hazardous substances, including lead, mercury, and arsenic. The United States does not have an adequate e-waste recycling program, mainly due to a lack of federal regulation and the high cost of e-waste recycling. While RCRA covers both disposal and recycling of hazardous solid-waste, it does not cover waste labeled for "re-use." Compounded by the fact that RCRA allows generators to determine whether waste is "hazardous," and not the exporter,[21] the majority of e-waste is exported overseas for recycling.

The United States' failure to recycle e-waste domestically is largely the result of the statutory language of RCRA. For example, RCRA specifically excludes solid waste that can be recycled, including circuit boards and cathode ray tubes (CRTs), but does not

---

19. Tagliabue, J., "A City that Turns Garbage into Energy Copes with a Shortage," *New York Times* (Apr. 29, 2013), available at http://www.nytimes.com/2013/04/30/world/europe/oslo-copes-with-shortage-of-garbage-it-turns-into-energy.html.

20. "Statistics on the Management of Used and End-of-Life Electronics," *EPA* (2009) available at http://www.epa.gov/wastes/conserve/materials/ecycling/manage.htm#report.

21. 40 C.F.R. § 262.11 (2010).

address other forms of e-waste.[22] As a result, federal regulation of e-waste exports is limited. The Government Accountability Office has suggested amending RCRA to include the export of e-waste posing health or environmental risks by expanding the scope of the rule for CRTs or revising the definition of hazardous waste.[23] This would only be effective if EPA tested e-waste prior to shipment to verify whether it is suitable for reuse, which they do not currently do.[24] An alternative would be to expand on EPA's voluntary certification and collection programs, including Responsible Recycling Practices (R2), and the e-Stewards® standards, which establish standards for exporting e-waste.[25]

In the absence of federal standards for e-waste, twenty-five states have placed controls on the disposal of e-waste. However, state regulation could lead to a lack of uniformity, and in turn a "compliance burden" for electronics manufacturers, retailers, and recyclers operating in those states. For example, California established a fund, charging a fee for the purchase of new electronic products, to pay for the collection and recycling of used electronics, while in Maine, Minnesota, Texas, and Washington the manufacturer pays for the cost of recycling, based on the manufacturer's relative market share or through requiring take-back or collection programs.[26] A state-by-state approach is inadequate to address an issue as large as e-waste management, particularly

---

22. Luther, L., "Managing Electronic Waste: Issues with Exporting E-Waste," *Cong. Research Serv.*, R40850 (2010), available at http://www.fas.org/sgp/crs/misc/R40850.pdf; 40 C.F.R. §§ 261.4, 261.6.

23. "Electronic Waste: EPA Needs to Better Control Harmful U.S. Exports Through Stronger Enforcement and More Comprehensive Regulation," *U.S. Gov't Accountability Office*, GAO-08-1044, 14-21 (2008).

24. "Electronic Waste: Considerations for Promoting Environmentally Sound Reuse and Recycling," U.S. *Gov't Accountability Office*, GAO-10-626 (2010).

25. "Certification Programs for Electronics Recyclers," *U.S. EPA*, available at http://www.epa.gov/osw/conserve/materials/ecycling/certification.htm.

26. CAL. PUB. RES. CODE §§ 42464, 42476 (2011); ME. REV. STAT. ANN. tit. 38 § 1610.5(D) (2011); MINN. STAT. § 115A.1214 (2011); TEX. HEALTH & SAFETY CODE ANN. §§ 361.955, 361.978 (2011); WASH. REV. CODE § 70.95N.030-.090(2011).

considering the fact that the majority of e-waste is exported.

Under the Basel Convention (a comprehensive global environmental treaty on hazardous waste), exporting e-waste to developing countries is banned. More than 175 nations have ratified the treaty, but the United States is not one of them.[27] In the United States, prior to exporting hazardous waste for recycling, an exporter must notify EPA prior to the initial shipment and at a minimum every twelve months thereafter, providing EPA with the name and address of the recycler and an alternate recycler, the transit route and a description of the waste being exported and how it will be recycled.[28] If the waste is exported for reuse, the requirements are far less. As a result most e-waste is disposed of in landfills or exported[29] overseas for "recycling," often to countries like China, India and Latin America, which lack the adequate infrastructure to safely recycle the waste.[30]

The temptation for a developing nation to provide a waste disposal site in exchange for large amounts of money and the hope of other related benefits is quite understandable and may or may not be the right decision. Assuming that a developing country decided that it would accept solid waste from the United States, should the United States allow its waste to be exported, or should it enact a statute prohibiting the export? On one hand, not to allow such commerce might be viewed as an undue interference by the U.S. with the right of another sovereign country to decide for itself what is best for it. On the other hand, can sending waste to an impoverished, Third World country in exchange for money be anything short of exploitation of the developing nations by the

---

27. A list of parties to the Basel Convention is available at Parties to the Basel Convention <www.basei:int/Countries/Statusofratifications/PartiesSignatories/ tabid/1290/language/ en-US/Default.aspx#16>.

28. 40 C.F.R. § 261.39(a)(5) (2011).

29. "Electronic Waste: Considerations for Promoting Environmentally Sound Reuse and Recycling," *U.S. Gov't Accountability Office*, GAO-10-626 (2010).

30. "Electronic Waste: EPA Needs to Better Control Harmful U.S. Exports through Stronger Enforcement and More Comprehensive Regulation," *U.S. Gov't Accountability Office*, GAO-08-1044, 14-21 (2008).

industrialized nations? Similar arguments have been raised concerning the export of unregistered pesticides from the United States. Although there has been significant opposition both within the U.S. and in the international community, the U.S. does allow unregistered pesticides to be exported.[31] Beyond questions about the export of nonhazardous solid waste, a further question is what should be allowed or prohibited when the issue is the export of hazardous waste or even nuclear waste?[32] Under RCRA, export of hazardous waste from the U.S. is allowed if the receiving country consents.[33] Is allowing the export of hazardous substances to less developed countries an appropriate recognition of the sovereignty of those countries,[34] or is it immoral exploitation of the people of those countries because, due to factors such as corruption and/or economic need, their governments cannot choose to prohibit the import of those hazardous substances?[35]

In considering our thoughts about the export and import of waste, especially hazardous waste, we ought to be aware that hazardous waste can be imported into the U.S. About 300 tons of mercury contaminated material was sent from India to the United States in 2003.[36] Should this highly toxic material have been kept out of the United States? Is there any relevance to the facts that: 1) India has no recycling facilities for mercury-contaminated material, and the material was going to the world's largest mercury-recycling facility, 2) the mercury in India had been imported primarily from the U.S., and many of the thermometers that were made in India

---

31. See Chapter 6.

32. In 1989, the Marshall Islands did offer to be a storage site for high-level nuclear waste from the U.S. That offer was withdrawn, but there are those in the Marshall Islands government who continue to favor the idea.

33. 42 U.S.C. § 6938.

34. This is the position advocated by the consensus of one group of law students in Mysore, India, in 2004, during a discussion with the author of this text.

35. This is the position vigorously advocated by faculty members at a law school in Cochin, India, in 2007, during a discussion with the author of this text.

36. Rai, S., "Hazardous Waste Is Shipped from India to U.S. Recycling Plant," *New York Times* (May 7, 2003) p. A13.

using the mercury were exported to the U.S., and 3) the thermometer factory in India had actually been moved there from the U.S. after it had been dismantled? While the facts may make the recycling activity sound like a good idea, would it not be better if the mercury were permanently stored instead of being recycled, sold again, and continuing the cycle of poisoning developing countries? Mercury is being phased out in developed countries and, after recycling, it would likely be sent to a developing country.[37]

Our discussion of waste disposal led us to consider the shortage of domestic sites willing to dispose of waste, and alternatives of incineration and export, especially from large cities. At the other end of the spectrum from the large cities with grandiose plans for massive waste disposal projects like export are the small American towns that, until recently, simply had some vacant land and used bulldozers to cover what was trucked into their "sanitary landfills." Today these towns are having to confront the question of how to better handle their solid waste. The vacant land and the bulldozer do not protect the ground water from contamination, incineration problems have been discussed above, and plastic-lined landfills are extremely expensive. Although there is some doubt about the environmental effectiveness of lined landfills, federal and state law now require that new municipal solid waste landfills be lined.[38]

Historically, waste disposal in rural and suburban communities was handled by each town separately or by some towns contracting to have others dispose of their waste for them. Today, largely due to the high costs of disposal and waste reduction facilities, smaller governmental units are forming independent, multi-town entities for waste management and affiliating with them. The creation of multi-town facilities raises issues of siting and costs. The affiliation efforts have raised the fundamental question of whether representation on and decision-making power within a multi-town waste control district should be based on the population of the member towns. While population is the norm for representation in the United States, smaller towns are concerned about being

---

37. "Activists Demand Halt on Trade of Mercury from India," *U.S. Newswire* (May 29, 2003).

38. 40 CFR § 258.40.

outvoted by those with greater population and are especially concerned about being "elected" by the other towns to be the "host" town for a multi-town dump. This brings with it the tension-filled issues of whether to empower the multi-town district to acquire land by the forced sale eminent domain process and whether a small town without much business or industry will be selected as the disposal site for waste from larger towns that generate what is perceived as much riskier types of waste. Site selection for a landfill is, without doubt, the waste disposal issue that creates the highest level of emotional involvement among the general public—the NIMBY (not in my back yard) syndrome is very strong. The costs of disposal are also, however, in the forefront of the voters' thoughts when they are asked to decide whether their town will join in forming a multi-town waste district.

Much of the impetus behind affiliation of smaller units is to achieve economies of scale—one larger facility being more economical than several smaller facilities for handling the same volume of trash or for sorting and marketing recyclable materials. The opposing view is that large facilities will lean in the direction of high cost, high technology solutions which would be less economical and less environmentally sound than a greater number of smaller alternative approaches such as waste stream reduction through consumer education and curbside recycling by individual households. If landfills are all required to be lined, a strong argument can be made in favor of the economies of scale because the costs of constructing a lined landfill (or an incinerator) are enormous. The district must be able to pay the cost, and that usually entails financing the construction through the borrowing or "bonding" process and paying off the lenders over a period of time such as the expected useful life of the facility. In order for a lender to be willing to finance landfill or incinerator construction, the lender wants to be assured that the loan will be repaid. This requires that the facility take in a predetermined amount of revenue each year to cover the loan payments for the year as well as the operating expenses. A waste facility generally derives its revenues by charging "tipping fees" based on the amount of trash that someone brings to it. If tipping fees are to be reasonable and still provide enough revenue to repay the loan, at least a certain minimum amount of trash must come to the facility. This minimum is based on the annual volume that the facility was built to handle and the facility's lifespan and loan repayment period.

If less trash arrives than was predicted in planning for what size facility to build, one alternative to produce the needed revenue is to charge a higher rate to those who are bringing the trash. This approach worries the users of the facility because it exposes them to higher charges for what they do bring. It also worries the lenders because, with higher charges, the trash might go elsewhere and endanger the repayment of the loan. Alternatively, the district could require that all its members bring all their trash to the facility, but an overall reduction of the amount of trash generated within the district, such as by successful recycling efforts, could still lead to higher tipping fees than people are willing to pay and a possible default in loan repayment. This need for at least a minimum amount of trash to feed the facility, or an amount of revenue equivalent to what would have been collected if that amount of trash had been brought in, has led to lenders requiring, and some district members advocating, "put or pay" clauses in agreements among the member communities of a multi-town district.[39]

"Put or Pay" clauses obligate a member community to "put" at least a certain amount of trash in the facility and be charged the tipping fee or to "pay" the full tipping fee as though it had put in the trash. This assures that there will be revenue for paying the lenders without having to raise the tipping fee for those whose trash arrives at the facility. It also, however, removes a significant incentive for individuals and communities to undertake very important environmental efforts like reducing the amount of waste generated or recycling wastes. These efforts are sound for purposes of both conserving resources and lowering environmental risks from waste disposal, but communities are told that if there is waste reduction and a community does not "put," it will still have to "pay." Once again in the environmental context we see a circular problem. If we do not commit our money to financing a good landfill, we cause

---

39. Authorization for "put or pay" clauses typically appear in the organizational charter of a district. See, for example, Article I, § 5h and Article IV, § 2c of *Agreement for the Formation of the Greater Upper Valley Solid Waste Management District*, available from the Two Rivers Regional Commission, Woodstock, Vermont 05091.

large environmental risks; however, when we commit our money to financing a good landfill, we may remove the incentive and the available funds to promote waste reduction that would, in turn, reduce our need for landfills and the risks associated with them.

2. Hazardous Waste

A primary focus of the Resource Conservation and Recovery Act (RCRA) is how to manage those wastes which, because of their hazardous nature, raise problems that might not be raised by nonhazardous wastes and are so significant in character that they must be controlled by a stricter regulatory approach than that used for nonhazardous wastes. We will begin by looking at RCRA's system for preventing harm from hazardous wastes and then consider the Superfund legislation addressing issues that arise in cases where RCRA did not prevent harm.

Hazardous waste, as defined in the statute, is waste which because of its quantity, concentration, or its physical, chemical, or infectious characteristics may significantly contribute to an increase in mortality or serious illness or may, when improperly managed, pose a substantial hazard to human health or the environment. Thus, while a pesticide could be a hazardous waste, and a chemical substance under the Toxic Substances Control Act could be a hazardous waste, the definition of hazardous waste under RCRA is much broader and can also include many other types of wastes. Among the factors that EPA and the states use to determine whether a material is hazardous are toxicity, corrosivity, flammability, and potential for bioaccumulation. Examples of what are hazardous wastes are industrial wastes containing heavy metals, infectious hospital wastes, waste oils like crankcase oil, and waste paint.

The two main operative mechanisms used by RCRA for controlling hazardous wastes are the "manifest system" and the requirement of permits for the treatment, storage, or disposal of hazardous wastes.[40] RCRA focuses on the disposal stage in the life of a hazardous substance; however, its methodology for ensuring proper disposal is to provide a tracking of the substance through its

---

40. 42 U.S.C. § 6921 *et seq.*

entire life or what is commonly referred to as from "cradle to grave." This tracking approach is called the manifest system. In addition, those who handle the hazardous waste at various stages after it has been created will have to have a permit and/or conform to federal standards in order to be allowed to handle the substance. By knowing who has the hazardous waste at every point in time, and by controlling who can have the waste and making those who have it be responsible for what they do with it, Congress hopes that improper and hence environmentally unsound disposal will be avoided.

The tracking process begins with the generator of a hazardous waste. If you generate something which falls within the statutory definition of "hazardous waste," unless you are exempted, you are part of the manifest system for tracking the material's location at any time. You must initiate the manifest process by completing the "Generator Completes" section of the Hazardous Waste Manifest and Shipping Paper, a sample of which is shown in Figure 1. The manifest has multiple copies. The original stays with the waste from the point of generation until it reaches the hazardous waste facility where the waste will be disposed of, treated, or stored. Other copies are kept by those who come into contact with the waste during its journey to the hazardous waste facility, and copies are also sent to the state where generation took place and the state of destination. The idea is to keep track of who has the hazardous waste, with the intent that it ultimately end up in a proper hazardous waste facility for treatment, storage, or disposal.

One important exemption from the manifest system should be noted because, to some extent, it cuts back on the protection which the system was designed to provide. That exemption is for "small generators" of hazardous waste and acute hazardous waste. Under federal regulations, one is not required to comply with the manifest system if one generates less than 1000 kg per month of hazardous waste that is to be reclaimed at a recycling facility.[41] Also, if one generates less than 100 kg per month of hazardous waste and does not accumulate over 1000 kg or generates less than 1 kg per month of acute hazardous waste, that generator is exempt from the

---

41. 40 CFR § 262.20.

Please print or type. (Form designed for use on elite (12-pitch) typewriter.)   Form Approved. OMB No. 2050-0039

UNIFORM HAZARDOUS WASTE MANIFEST	1. Generator ID Number VTD555666777	2. Page 1 of 1	3. Emergency Response Phone 800-222-3344	4. Manifest Tracking Number ABC999999999

5. Generator's Name and Mailing Address
ACME AUTO SALES & SERVICE
PO BOX 99999
WATERBURY, VT 05676
Generator's Phone: 802-555-1212

Generator's Site Address (if different than mailing address)
ACME AUTO SALES & SERVICE
9999 SOUTH MAIN STR
WATERBURY, VT 05676

6. Transporter 1 Company Name
ROGERS TRANSPORT SERVICE   U.S. EPA ID Number VTZ000999888

7. Transporter 2 Company Name
ONEWAY TRANSPORT SERVICES   U.S. EPA ID Number MAZ111222333

8. Designated Facility Name and Site Address
FINAL STOP ENVIRONMENTAL SERVICES
100 AVENUE Z
MOODUS, CT 06088
Facility's Phone: 888-657-0001   U.S. EPA ID Number CTZ333444555

9a. HM	9b. U.S. DOT Description (including Proper Shipping Name, Hazard Class, ID Number, and Packing Group (if any))	10. Containers No. Type	11. Total Quantity	12. Unit Wt./Vol.	13. Waste Codes
	1. WASTE OIL & ABSORBENT MIXTURE NON RCRA REGULATED	3 DM	1200	P	VT02
	2. USED OIL FOR RECYCLING NON DOT REGULATED MATERIAL	1 DM	55	G	VT99
X	3. RQ WASTE PAINT RELATED MATERIAL 3 UN1263 PGII	2 DM	150	P	D001
X	4. RQ WASTE COMBUSTIBLE LIQUID (PETROLEUM NAPHTHA) NA1993 PG III PARTS WASHER	1 DM	55	G	D001 D018 D039

14. Special Handling Instructions and Additional Information

15. GENERATOR'S/OFFEROR'S CERTIFICATION: I hereby declare that the contents of this consignment are fully and accurately described above by the proper shipping name, and are classified, packaged, marked and labeled/placarded, and are in all respects in proper condition for transport according to applicable international and national governmental regulations. If export shipment and I am the Primary Exporter, I certify that the contents of this consignment conform to the terms of the attached EPA Acknowledgment of Consent.
I certify that the waste minimization statement identified in 40 CFR 262.27(a) (if I am a large quantity generator) or (b) (if I am a small quantity generator) is true.

Generator's/Offeror's Printed/Typed Name GEORGE WASHINGTON	Signature George Washington	Month 02	Day 01	Year 06

16. International Shipments   ☐ Import to U.S.   ☐ Export from U.S.   Port of entry/exit:
Transporter signature (for exports only):   Date leaving U.S.:

17. Transporter Acknowledgment of Receipt of Materials

Transporter 1 Printed/Typed Name ROGER CLARKE	Signature Roger Clarke	Month 02	Day 01	Year 06
Transporter 2 Printed/Typed Name JOHN ONEWAY	Signature John Oneway	Month 02	Day 03	Year 06

18. Discrepancy
18a. Discrepancy Indication Space ☐ Quantity ☐ Type ☐ Residue ☐ Partial Rejection ☐ Full Rejection
Manifest Reference Number:
18b. Alternate Facility (or Generator)   U.S. EPA ID Number
Facility's Phone:
18c. Signature of Alternate Facility (or Generator)   Month Day Year

19. Hazardous Waste Report Management Method Codes (i.e., codes for hazardous waste treatment, disposal, and recycling systems)

1. H050	2. H101	3.	4.

20. Designated Facility Owner or Operator: Certification of receipt of hazardous materials covered by the manifest except as noted in Item 18a

Printed/Typed Name JOHN FINAL	Signature John Final	Month 02	Day 08	Year 06

EPA Form 8700-22 (Rev. 3-05) Previous editions are obsolete.   DESIGNATED FACILITY TO DESTINATION STATE (IF REQUIRED)

Figure 1. Sample hazardous waste manifest and shipping paper.

manifest system.[42] While it is clear that many small, and thus exempt, generators of hazardous wastes can, in the aggregate, have very significant effects on the environment, the federal government has decided that to require small generators to be part of the

---

42. 40 CFR § 261.5.

manifest system would be placing an excessive administrative burden on them which would not be justified by the potential for harm which they may cause. RCRA does place treatment and disposal requirements on the small, exempt generators. It just exempts them from the manifest system. This is the balance that the federal government has made; however, states, if they choose, can tighten up on the exemption for small generators and impose additional regulations on them. State control which is stricter than federal control is specifically allowed by RCRA with respect to hazardous wastes.

The complementary mechanism to the manifest which tracks the hazardous waste to its ultimate location is RCRA's requirement that the ultimate location be one which has a permit evidencing that it meets specific standards with respect to such matters as recordkeeping, satisfactory treatment, storage, or disposal methods, contingency plans for minimizing unanticipated damage, proper personnel, and financial responsibility. Unless the applicable standards are met, the facility will not receive a permit and, unless the facility has a permit, a generator of hazardous waste may not send the waste to the facility. Violations of the federal control mechanisms which we have discussed can subject the violator to sanctions including EPA compliance orders and criminal penalties of large fines and imprisonment.

As mentioned above, Congress' goal is to have hazardous waste find its way to a "proper" facility. A practical problem which bears on the fulfillment of that goal is the availability of "proper" facilities. Realistically, no one wants a hazardous waste facility in his or her backyard even if it is financially responsible and has contingency plans for unanticipated damage due to the activities of the facility. State and local governments or the federal government will have to work out an approach which will result in an adequate number of proper facilities being sited.

Waste disposal facilities, along with polluting factories, uranium enrichment plants, incinerators, and other high risk/high burden operations, are part of a class often known as locally undesirable land uses (LULUs). These LULUs are generally recognized to be disproportionately located in poor and minority communities. Among the factors claimed to have brought about this result are economic issues of property values, political power or the lack thereof, and racial and/or class discrimination. Which factors and to what extent they have contributed to the disproportionality is subject to debate, but the need to consider matters of "environmental justice" has been recognized and made applicable in numerous contexts.[43] One is a Presidential Executive Order which directs that:

> [t]o the greatest extent practicable and permitted by law . . . each Federal agency shall make achieving environmental justice part of its mission by identifying and addressing, as appropriate, disproportionately high and adverse human health or environmental effects of its programs, policies, and activities on minority populations and low-income populations in the United States.[44]

The environmental justice discussion with respect to siting waste disposal facilities in the United States would contain many of the same points that would be raised in addressing the question of whether waste should be exported to developing nations.

The specific hazardous waste control mechanisms of the Resource Conservation and Recovery Act are designed to prevent hazardous waste problems. RCRA's preventative efforts have not always worked, and, in addition, hazardous wastes that were disposed of prior to RCRA have resulted in numerous dangerous situations. This is where the Superfund Act, CERCLA, enters the picture. Congress enacted CERCLA to clean up sites contaminated with hazardous substances and established the Agency for Toxic Substances and Disease Registry (ATSDR) to provide information about exposure to toxic substances. In addition to ATSDR, Congress enacted the Emergency Planning and Community Right-to-Know Act (EPCRA) to provide the public and local governments with information concerning potential chemical hazards present in

---

43. Guana, E., "Environmental Law, Civil Rights and Sustainability: Three Frameworks for Environmental Justice," 19 *Journal of Environmental and Sustainability Law* 34 (Summer, 2012).

44. E.O. 12898, 59 Fed. Reg. 7629, 3 CFR 859.

their communities. EPCRA requires facilities to submit information on releases of toxic emissions, which are compiled in a public database known as the Toxic Chemical Release Inventory (TRI). TRI aggregates data from more than 20,000 facilities, reporting on more than 4 billion pounds of toxic chemicals released into the environment, an increase of 8 percent between 2010 and 2011.[45]

Under CERCLA, the process of cleaning hazardous waste requires potential hazardous release sites be assessed and placed on the National Priority List, which ranks the known releases or threatened releases of hazardous substances, pollutants, or contaminants throughout the United States and its territories. Once on the National Priority List, CERCLA authorizes EPA to identify the potentially responsible parties (PRP), which includes all parties responsible for contaminating the site, past and current operators or owners as well as any party responsible for sending hazardous material to the site. EPA then orders the parties to clean up the site.

CERCLA is an example of the "polluter pays" principle, which holds that industries and companies that used hazardous substances and purchasers of products that generate hazardous wastes should bear the cleanup costs. If the responsible party cannot be found, EPA is authorized to clean the site using a trust fund established under CERCLA. In the mid- 1980s, the Superfund Amendments and Reauthorization Act (SARA) amended CERCLA, increasing both state involvement and the size of the Trust Fund, from $1.6 to $8.5 billion. Additional revenue for the Trust Fund came from excise taxes on oil and hazardous chemicals, and an environmental corporate income tax. These taxes expired in 1995, and by 2005, the amount of unobligated money in the Trust Fund had slowly declined to zero. Operating at a deficit of $1.8 billion a year, the Fund received an influx of cash in 2009 with the passage of the American Recovery and Reinvestment Act, which allocated $600 million, enough to clean up 51 Superfund sites.[46] Despite the

---

45. "Amount of Toxins Released in the U.S. Increased for the Second Year in 2011," *Center for Effective Government* (January 29, 2013), available at www.foreffectivegov.org.

46. Pub. L. 111-5 (2009).

additional funding, the ten-year deficit had slowed the clean-up process.

The remedial provisions of CERCLA[47] held out great promise for cleaning up hazardous waste sites[48] but the Superfund process has been widely criticized for the cleanups themselves and getting responsible parties to pay. Concerning the cleanups themselves, EPA's National Priorities List contained 1312 final sites and 54 proposed sites in 2013.[49] The major obstacle to cleaning up Superfund sites has been the lack of adequate funds for full and timely cleanups. Even though the "mixed funding concept" allows EPA to settle with parties willing to settle, use the Trust Fund to pay the share of the resistant parties, and later sue them for their share, this only works if EPA can establish that a potentially responsible party is clearly liable and that the liable party has the ability to pay. Another issue is whether the costs of clean-up are covered by insurance, often a question of state law, revolving around the interpretation of the terms "sudden and accidental" and "damages" in general liability coverage. In *Industrial Enterprises, Inc. v. Penn America Ins. Co.*, the First Circuit held that the commercial liability policy did not require an insurance company to indemnify the insured for costs incurred while remediating a Superfund site on the insured's property.[50] The court reasoned that the policy provides indemnity for sums the insured is legally obligated to pay as damages, but *not* sums under regulatory liability, like the costs for remediation under CERCLA. If insurance companies are unwilling to pay, many PRP's will be unable to pay the high cost of clean-up. This, combined with the under-funded Trust Fund, has encouraged both the President and EPA to call for a re-instatement of the excise taxes, arguing that imposing these taxes

---

47. Comprehensive Environmental Response, Compensation, and Liability Act, 42 U.S.C. § 9601 et seq.

48. 42 U.S.C. § 9611.

49. February 2013, www.epa.gov/superfund/sites.

50. 637 F.3d 481, 490 (1st Cir. 2011).

again may discourage the use of toxins while helping to clean the nation's Superfund sites.[51]

Two issues often litigated under CERCLA are how to allocate liability when there are multiple PRPs and what constitutes an appropriate cleanups. Lawsuits among PRPs (and also involving government) have both slowed the cleanup process and led to huge litigation costs with respect to the topic of what constitutes a technically appropriate cleanup. Should a site be restored to the status under its previous use, which can vary depending on whether the site was used for industrial purposes or as farmland? Should PRPs be required to restore a site to a level that would enrich the current owner who purchased the property very cheaply as a hazardous waste site? What should be the ultimate status of the property? The statute requires a permanent remedy, including the removal of hazardous substances that threaten the public's health or the environment.[52] Removal actions are "those taken to counter imminent and substantial threats to public health and welfare," while remedial actions "are longer term, more permanent responses."[53] However, this raises other questions, such as should a site that contains vinyl chloride, benzene, toluene, and numerous other toxic substances be capped by EPA with a clay dome to prevent the entry of water? Already contaminated water in the site would be pumped out and treated to remove the dangerous water from the ground water system. Some would say that this is not the correct approach and that, unless EPA excavates and removes the toxic materials themselves, it is not adequately cleaning up a source of cancer and birth defects.

Scientifically, there are many different possible solutions for hazardous waste cleanup problems, and, even if cost were not a

---

51. "2010 Budget Tax Proposals: Reinstate Superfund Tax," *Tax Policy Center*, http://taxpolicycenter.org/taxtopics/2010_budget_superfund.cfm and Press Release, "EPA Supports Superfund 'Polluter Pays' Provision," (June 21, 2010), available at http://yosemite.epa.gov/opa/admpress.nsf/0/6e61eb7ab20b163c8525774900592657?OpenDocument.

52. 42 U.S.C. § 9601(23)(24).

53. *Minnesota v. Kalman W. Abrams Metals, Inc.*, 155 F.3d 1019, 1024 (8th Cir.).

factor, there will seldom be full agreement on to what extent a property should be "clean" and what is the appropriate method for achieving that level of cleanliness. Cost is, however, a very significant factor, and CERCLA seeks to make those who caused the contamination liable for its cleanup wherever possible. Sometimes the responsible party no longer exists, and government cannot pass the cost of cleanup on to it, but, assuming the business enterprise that caused the problem does exist, the question has been raised of whether that business should be liable for the cleanup costs. The argument is made that if the business had been negligent in not acting as a reasonable business would have done at the time it dumped its waste, then it should be liable. If, however, the business was acting legally and also in accordance with the generally accepted business practices of the time, then it should not now be held liable for the high cleanup costs. This retroactive liability puts a business at a serious competitive disadvantage that is unfair because, at the time of the action for which it is now being held liable, it was not doing anything then known to be wrong. A possible result of accepting this argument is that government, meaning all taxpayers, would have to pay the cost of cleanup. Congress rejected that approach and clearly answered the question of liability for the party who caused the contamination—it is liable—but what about other "potentially responsible parties?" These become especially important if the party that caused the contamination cannot pay for the cleanup. As examples, might successor companies who buy real estate from or stock of the party that caused the contamination be liable for the costs of cleanup? Might lenders to borrowers with contaminated property be liable for cleanup costs?

Successor companies have been held liable,[54] and that has spawned the practice of companies signing indemnification agreements whereby the seller agrees to indemnify the buyer of the property for environmental liabilities such as cleanup costs that the buyer might incur with respect to the property. Banks that become involved with borrowers or property subject to Superfund have also

---

54. *United States v. Davis*, 261 F.3d 1.

been seen as sources of cleanup funds. Banks that become the owners of hazardous sites when they foreclose on a mortgage or that exercise control over their borrowers may be liable for cleanup costs. In *U.S. v. Fleet Factors Corp.*,[55] the court said that a bank's "capacity to influence" hazardous waste decisions may make it liable under Superfund. The banks, as have the insurance companies who had never heard of cleanup liability when they wrote policies long before Superfund, raise the issue of fairness. They contend that, as lenders, they have done nothing to warrant liability and are only being found liable because they have "deep pockets." After the *Fleet Factors* case, EPA provided some protection for lenders,[56] but those rules were invalidated in *Kelley v. EPA*.[57] Congress then amended CERCLA in 1996 to exclude lenders from liability if they do not actually participate in management. Only having the "capacity to influence" operations would not make them liable.[58]

While many of the issues concerning who might be a responsible party and thus liable for cleanup costs have been answered, other ambiguities remain under CERCLA. For example, what statute of limitations might apply to cleanup responsibility and when does a time limit under a statute of limitations begin to run? Can a contributor of only trace amounts of hazardous waste be held liable for the entire cleanup costs at a site? If, 1) multiple parties contributed to the contamination but in vastly varying amounts, 2) they acted at points in time with very different levels of awareness about contamination, and 3) their ability to pay cleanup costs and still survive is also very different, how should we determine who contributes how much to the cost of cleanup? This type of litigation continues[59] and raises yet one more major criticism of CERCLA— too much money and time spent in the legal process of deciding

---

55. 901 F.2d 1550.

56. 57 Fed. Reg. 18343 et seq.

57. 15 F.3d 1100.

58. 42 U.S.C. § 9601(E) and (F)(i).

59. Fitzgerald, D., "Helca to Pay for Site Cleanup," *Wall Street Journal* (June 13, 2011), available at http://online.wsj.com/article/SB1000142405270230384810457 6384001297880430.html.

who pays and how much, and not enough spent actually doing the cleanups.

C. CONSERVATION AND RESOURCE RECOVERY

In addition to the many control mechanisms that affect the disposal of waste materials, there are mechanisms that attempt to mitigate the need for disposal. This is the "reduce, reuse, recycle" trio, and it is the alternative strategy to the "dump it or burn it" approach. "Reduce" says that if the item to be displayed on the shelf in the drugstore is in a plastic bottle, perhaps it does not also need to be put in a cardboard box. "Reuse" says that if you receive a mail order item in a padded mailer, perhaps you can use that padded mailer when you send a gift to your friend. The reducer and the reuser can feel good environmentally, but they also reap a direct financial benefit from reducing or reusing packaging. That financial incentive is not generally present for recycling. "Recycling" says that this is a material we no longer want, but we will process it to turn it into something we do want rather than dispose of it. After we have reduced and reused, reality is we still have a huge volume of material that no one wants, at least not in its current form. Some of it may have a market value as a "raw material" to be processed into something else, but much of it is truly unwanted. If this unwanted material is to be kept out of the waste disposal stream and not add to landfill and incinerator capacity problems and environmental burdens associated with those facilities, it will need to be recycled. Let's look at some alternative approaches to how recycling can be done physically and then consider how law can and does encourage recycling.

RCRA defines "recycled" material as that which is "used, reused, or reclaimed."[60] Recycling involves materials that range from glass bottles and beer cans to newspapers and magazines to sludge application on forests and crops—the recycling method depending on the resource in question. The two basic approaches to solid waste recycling are the centralized approach using high technology (Figure 2) and the decentralized approach using low

---

60. 40 C.F.R. § 261.1(c)(7).

technology (Figure 3). Centralization involves collecting all the solid waste from an area such as a large city and bringing this material to a central location where separating and sorting takes place. There are several claimed advantages to this system. The weight and volume of materials needing a landfill will be drastically reduced while, at the same time, a municipality can use revenues gathered from resource separation (iron, aluminum, glass) to pay for the operation of the program. The biodegradable remainder could be burned to heat water and get steam to make electricity or heat for municipal offices or, using a more efficient energy recycling strategy, the biodegradable portion could be properly digested under low-oxygen conditions. Using this process, methane gas is produced and burned to heat water and provide heat or electricity. If properly executed, the above plan could reduce the tax burden on residents of the municipality participating in such a program; however, the initial cost of such a facility is high, and the amount of organic waste needed on a continuous basis for the energy recovery portion of such an undertaking is very large.

The other strategy for recycling municipal solid waste is source separation (Figure 3). The object of this alternative is to convince consumers to voluntarily separate paper, glass, metals, plastics, and organic material before collection or to mandate that they do so. Once this separation is complete, a municipality could either collect the resource or attempt to get the consumer to deliver the resource to a recycling center. The center then sells the resource and uses revenues to keep the center operating. This type of system was originally established, used, and operated by volunteers. Today, as recycling has become widely accepted by the public as both environmentally sound and economically and physically necessary to reduce problems of waste disposal, communities the size of New York City and Barnard, Vermont (population 958) have legally mandated recycling (at least for some materials).[61] Source separation has the advantage of requiring much less initial capital investment; however, it relies heavily on consumers acting properly in situations where they gain no financial advantage and where

---

61. Rodgers, W., "State Waste Reduction and Recycling Laws," 4 *Rodgers Environmental Law* 7:34 (2012).

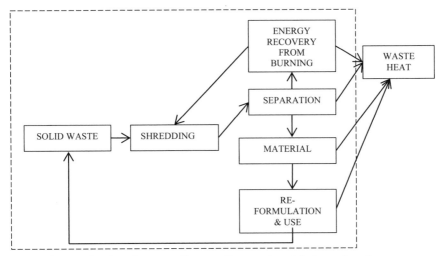

Figure 2. A scheme of recycling using high technology.

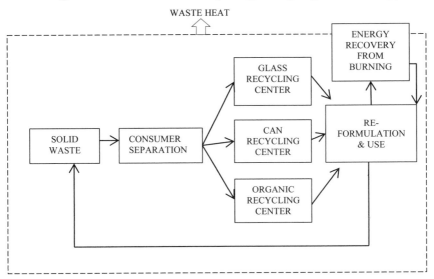

Figure 3. A scheme of recycling using low technology.

enforcement of any mandatory scheme would be very difficult. Neither of the above approaches to recycling or any of their incarnations will likely provide the complete solution to the problem of recycling consumer solid waste. A combination of the approaches, using each where it is most appropriate, is serving as a basis to increase our recycling efforts. Of course, the most certain way to make recycling successful is to have new technology and new personal habits result in recycling being economically as well as environmentally sound. Those with waste need to find it financially rewarding to recycle rather than dispose, and those who are buying need to find products made from recycled materials that are competitive in quality and price.

Let's next consider some examples of how government has acted to encourage conservation and resource recovery. Subchapter V of the Resource Conservation and Recovery Act[62] assigns certain duties to the Secretary of Commerce, designed to encourage resource recovery. The Secretary is given the responsibility of stimulating the development of markets for recovered materials by identifying existing or potential markets and identifying economic and technical barriers to the use of recovered materials as well as encouraging the development of new uses for recovered materials. It would appear that taking such steps should lead to a reduction in the amount of waste which will have to be dealt with by disposal and also should result in a reduction in the amount of virgin materials which would be used in the absence of those steps. Consistent with these goals, the Secretary is directed to promote resource recovery technology by evaluating its commercial feasibility, publishing the results of the evaluation, and assisting those interested in making a choice of a recovery system. The Secretary is further charged with initiating the process of developing specifications for secondary materials. If reliable specifications are available for secondary materials, it is hoped that users will be more likely to avail themselves of such materials because they will be confident about how the materials will function.

A summarizing phrase for the above-described federal mechanisms relating to stimulating resource recovery might be "information dissemination." A more direct approach to resource recovery is contained in that part of RCRA which addresses itself to federal procurement policy.[63] Under RCRA, federal agencies are

---

62. 42 U.S.C. § 6951 et seq.

63. 42 U.S.C.A. § 6962.

required to purchase items composed of the highest percentage of recovered materials practicable consistent with maintaining a satisfactory level of competition. Unless such items are not reasonably available, fail to meet quality standards, or are unreasonably priced, their procurement is mandated if it is consistent with administrative guidelines prepared to achieve Congress' objectives. An Executive Order titled "Greening the Government through waste prevention, recycling, and Federal acquisition" provided for waste prevention and recycling in each agency's daily operations.[64] This "taking the lead" approach could spur the use of recovered materials in various ways including providing a substantial demand for a product and thus encouraging someone to become a supplier. In turn, that supplier may very well attempt to find other buyers for the product that it is now producing in order to satisfy its large customer, the federal government. Also, having large amounts of items made from recovered materials in general use throughout the country may serve to reduce psychological barriers to the use of secondary materials. Thus, with respect to resource recovery, Congress sought to achieve its goals using relatively non-coercive mechanisms—information dissemination and the use of the federal purchasing power.

How have these approaches worked? Not well at all. With no data to verify compliance and a low level of awareness among federal employees with contracting responsibilities, there were no mechanisms to determine whether products purchased were environmentally preferable.[65] As a result, the federal procurement policy has had some, but not a huge, practical impact, and while some industry organizations have published specifications for secondary materials, government has done little in this area. Congress named the centerpiece of its solid waste and resource recovery effort the Resource Conservation and Recovery Act (RCRA), but that is clearly a misnomer. Although RCRA does

---

64. E.O. 13101.

65. "Federal Procurement: Better Guidance and Monitoring Needed to Assess Purchases of Environmentally Friendly Products," *U.S. General Accounting Office* GAO-01-430 (June 2001).

occasionally address conservation such as by requiring an "energy and materials conservation" component in state plans,[66] RCRA is primarily and almost exclusively a disposal statute. Resource conservation and recovery has grown extensively in recent years, but this has been due to greater public awareness and voluntary action[67] and because local governments, faced with dwindling disposal sites, have mandated recycling. Additionally, some business entities have found that recycling is profitable. The real boom in resource conservation and recovery will likely be the result of the free enterprise system as many resources become more limited in supply and recovery technology makes recovery economically profitable. In many situations, products such as gypsum wallboard and poultry bedding made from recycled materials are performing functions better and as cheaply or cheaper than the products they are replacing. Ultimately, resource conservation and recovery will probably turn out to be plain good business.

---

66. 42 U.S.C. § 6943(c).

67. Increasing public awareness and facilitating voluntary action has been a mission of many non-governmental organizations (NGOs). For example, a wealth of information about paper products containing recycled materials and how to purchase those products is easily accessible at www.conservatree.org.

ADDITIONAL READINGS

Applegate, J., *Environmental Law: RCRA, CERCLA and the Management of Hazardous Waste* (New York: Foundation Press, 2006).

Cole, L. and Foster, S., *From the Ground Up: Environmental Racism and the Rise of the Environmental Justice Movement* (New York: New York University Press, 2001).

Hathaway, C.R., et al., *TSCA Deskbook* (Washington, DC: Environmental Law Institute, 2nd ed., 2012).

Hazardous Waste Cleanup (LandMark Publications, 2013).

Hill, B., *Environmental Justice: Legal Theory and Practice* (Washington, DC: ELI Press, 2012).

Pichtel, J., *Waste Management Practices: Municipal, Hazardous, and Industrial* (Boca Raton, FL: CRC Press, 2014).

Porter, R., *The Economics of Waste* (Washington, DC: Resources for the Future, 2002).

RCRA/CERCLA Case Management Handbook (Washington, DC: BiblioGov, 2013).

Redelegation of Authority under CERCLA and SARA (Washington DC: BiblioGov, 2013).

Rogers, H., *Gone Tomorrow: The Hidden Life of Garbage* (New York; London: New Press Distributed by W.W. Norton & Company, 2005).

Superfund: CERCLA, SARA (LandMark Publications, 2012).

CHAPTER 6
PESTICIDES AND TOXIC SUBSTANCES

A. WHERE DO THEY COME FROM AND WHY DO WE NEED THEM?

While pesticides are considered to be toxic substances, there are other toxic substances which are not pesticides. The regulatory scheme is different for pesticides than for other toxic substances, so let's begin by considering pesticides separately with respect to their origins and uses.

1. Pesticides

A pesticide can be defined as a chemical agent that can be used to cause the death of, or the regulation of, nonhuman organisms that people consider detrimental. Thus, the intended target species of pesticides are the insects, plants, fungi, rodents, mites, and any other organisms that negatively affect humans. These effects are usually in the form of reduced crop yields, disease infestation, general nuisance situations (flies, mosquitos), or real estate destruction (termites, powder post beetles, nematodes).

To illustrate the extent of pesticide development, let's take a look at the history of three forms of pesticides: herbicides, fungicides, and insecticides. Herbicides (chemicals to control plant growth, usually resulting in death) were first noted about 100 years ago with the use of arsenic compounds as soil sterilants. Arsenic compounds work by degrading cell membranes and thereby disrupting normal cell metabolism, resulting in death of the organism. About the end of World War II, the first organic herbicides (phenoxy herbicides), 2, 4-D and 2, 4, 5-T, and silvex were developed. These three herbicides act like plant auxins (growth stimulators) and virtually cause the plant to grow itself to death. The two latter compounds are commonly known to contain dioxin, sometimes known as Agent Orange. Later, in the 1950s and 1960s, urea base nonselective soil sterilants were developed. These act by inhibiting the photosynthetic process. Durion and linuron are examples. Still later came the desiccant herbicides diquat and paraquat that disrupt plant membranes and cause the plant to dry up, and the glyphosate herbicides (such as Roundup developed by Monsanto) that disrupt the critical biochemical pathways for forming essential amino acids that are necessary for plant growth.

Fungicides (chemicals that destroy fungi) were first used in modern times in France in the 1850s, with the use of lime-sulfur on ornamental plants. Later, Bordeau mixture, mainly copper sulfate, was used to protect the French grapes. In the early 1900s, mercurial fungicides were developed to protect seeds. Some of these are still used today. Organic fungicides (PCP) were developed in the World War II time period. These fungicides alter enzyme action in cells and thus kill the fungus. The fungicide business really came of age with the appearance of captan, a foliar (leaf) spray, and systemic fungicides. The systemic fungicides are carried in the transport vessels throughout the plants, giving a more certain effect. These fungicides inhibit chemical reactions and eventually leave cells unable to breathe.

By far the most researched pesticides are the insecticides. The first insecticides (1860s) were arsenic compounds which are stomach poisons that eventually cause muscle paralysis and death to organisms that eat it. In the 1880s came the cyanide insecticides and a natural insecticide, rotenone (still used today). In 1939, the most widely recognized insecticide ever developed, DDT, was placed on the market. DDT is a long-term, highly effective, broad-spectrum insecticide that causes repetitive nerve discharges and eventually kills the insect. The cyclodiene insecticides (chlordane, dieldrin, aldrin) were developed about 1945 and are all neurotoxins operating on the junction between sensory and motor neurons, causing a malfunction resulting in death. Then came the organophosphorus insecticides, parathion and malathion, which cause muscles to keep tensing and never relax, eventually causing death. Recently the juvenile hormone insecticides, which disrupt metamorphosis, and the chitin synthesis inhibitors, which make exoskeleton formation difficult, have been developed to combat insects. Today, with the increasing popularity of organic farming, extensive use is being made of the protein from Bacillus Thuringiensis (Bt). This works by breaking open the digestive tract of the target insect resulting in its death. Bt has generally been sprayed or dusted onto the infested plant, but the gene for this protein has also been incorporated into genetically modified crops such as corn and soybeans.

The passage of time has seen not only the development of new classes of pesticides but also new versions of and uses for existing pesticides. An example of a new version and use in the herbicides area is the creation of a solid form of glyphosate like Roundup. Roundup has been applied as a liquid in agriculture for decades. It has now been made as a solid polymer which might prove useful as a herbicidal paint or other growth-inhibiting coating.[1] Over $12.5 billion worth of pesticides are sold in the U.S. annually.[2]

The fact that we have pesticides has resulted in the widespread belief that we need pesticides and, ironically, the availability of pesticides has led to the need to constantly create new pesticides. A look at how we raise our food crops should illustrate this situation. Our crop raising efforts are primarily concentrated in a few families of plants, the grasses (corn, sorghum, barley, oats, rice, wheat), the nightshades (tomatoes, potatoes, peppers), and the legume family (beans, peas, peanuts). Also, we have found it to be more economical to plant large areas in a single crop (monoculture) so we can easily plant, cultivate, fertilize, protect, and harvest the crops; however, this allows pests that prey on a particular crop to thrive because we have provided a concentrated food source. We make these crops even more susceptible to pest attack by selecting genetic strains that maximize food output at the expense of producing

---

1. Fountain, H., "One Solid Herbicide," *New York Times*, (March 27, 2007). www.nytimes.com/2007/03/27/science/27observ.html.

2. "Pesticide Market Estimates: Sales," *Environmental Protection Agency* http://www.epa.gov/opp00001/pestsales/07pestsales/sales2007.htm; http://www.epa.gov/oppfead1/cb/csb_page/updates/2011.

defense mechanisms. Therefore, the crops we have created through genetic selection require protection from various pests and necessitate the use of pesticides so we get abundant food and the farmer makes a reasonable profit. Since pests themselves have a varied genetic make-up within the pest species population, some individuals of the species population will be resistant to the pesticide, and we therefore help or "select" in favor of these individuals when we apply the pesticide. These resistant members of the species population breed, and eventually a pest species population will be present that resists the previously effective pesticide to such an extent that the pesticide is considered useless and a new one is needed.

Although pesticides create many evils and also perpetuate dependency on pesticides, there certainly are sound arguments favoring their use. One example of our need for pesticides is the economic need. If one assumes that pests destroy 10% of a crop and this reduces profit by an amount X, and if the use of pesticides will cost less than 100% of X, then pesticides would probably be used to increase profits and yields (see Table I). The table indicates it is generally more profitable in terms of food yield and money to use a pesticide and thus many people are satisfied that there is a real need for pesticides. As the risks associated with eating food produced with pesticides have become more understood and knowledge about the risks has become more widely disseminated, some farmers are rethinking the economics of using pesticides. If consumers are willing to pay a higher price for food produced without pesticides, the economic advantage to the farmer who uses pesticides could disappear.[3] Some would argue that we could wean ourselves from the use of pesticides and that food production and farm profits would not be reduced, at least not after a short startup time. Others claim that without protection, losses of some crops would increase to near 80% of attainable yield.[4] This argument depends, however,

---

3. Skevas, T. et al, "Can economic incentives encourage actual reductions in pesticide use and environmental spillovers?" *Agricultural Economics* 43, 267–276 (2012).

4. Zalom, F., "Pests, Endangered Pesticides and Processing Tomatoes," *VIII International Symposium on the Processing Tomato* (Leuven, Belgium: International Society of Horticultural Science, 2003).

on the inability of crops to tolerate damage without yield reduction, but research indicates that some crops can tolerate as much as 50% defoliation or 25% destruction of stems without any crop loss.[5] Another factor to consider is that pesticides are indiscriminate, targeting all insects, and have contributed to, but are not likely to be the sole cause of,[6] a collapse of bee colonies in the U.S. Farmers have relied on bees to pollinate crops, and without their help, farmers have been faced with almost $15 billion per year in additional costs.[7] It is uncertain whether these and other costs caused by widespread pesticide use tip the balance in favor of reduced reliance on pesticides.

Table I. HYPOTHETICAL RELATIONSHIP BETWEEEN USE AND NO USE OF PESTICIDES ON PROFIT FROM RAISING SILAGE CORN

	Pesticide	No Pesticide
Yield/acre	30 tons	27 tons
Selling price/ton	$20	$20
Total price	$600	$540
Cost pesticide/acre	$5	$0
Profit/acre	$595	$540

2. Toxic Substances

In the broadest sense, a toxic substance can be defined as any chemical or mixture which could, under proper circumstances, do harm to health or the environment. Congress has, through its findings at the outset of the Toxic Substances Control Act (TSCA),[8] implicitly defined a toxic substance as any chemical or mixture

---

5. "Integrated Pest Management Guidebook: Damage Tolerance," *World Bank*, available at http://web.worldbank.org.

6. Broden, J., "Study finds no single cause of honey bee deaths," *New York Times* (May 2, 2013), available at http://www.nytimes.com/2013/05/03/science/earth/government-study-cites-mix-of-factors-in-death-of-honeybees.html?_r=0.

7. "Evidence is growing that commonly used pesticides, even when employed carefully, are bad for bees," *The Economist* (Mar. 31, 2012) available at http://www.economist.com/node/21551451.

8. 15 U.S.C.A. § 2601 et seq.

whose manufacture, processing, distribution, use or disposal may present unreasonable risk of injury to health or environment.[9] Pursuant to TSCA, and procedures established under it and other statutes,[10] prior to production or import of a new chemical substance, EPA must receive pre-manufacture notice (PMN) at least 90 days prior to the manufacture or import of the chemical. EPA must also compile, update, and publish a list of each chemical manufactured or processed in the U.S.[11]

There are many chemicals of great concern, such as mercury, dioxins, and PCBs, but toxic substances are much more common than these listed items. Toxic substances include almost everything we use in modern manufacturing. After the proliferation of chemicals following World War II, we became a society dependent upon chemicals for our way of life. We need motor oil, plastics, paint, pesticides, and car batteries. Because of the way we live, the occurrence of toxic substances in our environment is inevitable. This is not to say that our lifestyle is totally wrong, nor is this to say that such products ought not to be used. What the reader should have is an awareness of the scope of the toxic substances situation such that the following sections of this chapter can be understood. Toxic substances are with us. Our problem is to ensure that the least amount of damage to health and environment occurs during the process of making, using, and disposing of these chemicals and mixtures.

B. WHY WE NEED TO REGULATE THEM

Let's first consider some statistics about pesticides and toxic substances. The annual conventional pesticide usage level in the U.S. is approximately 857 million pounds of *active* ingredients.[12]

---

9. 15 U.S.C.A. § 2604(f).

10. Can be accessed at http://www.epa.gov/tri/ (established under §113 of the Emergency Planning and Community Right-to-Know Act and the Pollution Prevention Act).

11. See §8(b) (15 U.S.C.A. § 2606(b)), data is available at https://explore.data.gov/Geography-and-Environment/TSCA-Inventory/pkhi-wvjh.

This is approximately 3 pounds of active poisons for each member of our population. Agricultural pesticide use accounts for about 80% of conventional use[13]—about 2.5 pounds of active poison per person is being used to grow crops. There are approximately 100 producers, 1600 formulators, and 13,500 distributors of pesticides,[14] 78 million households using pesticides, 25,000 commercial pest control firms, and almost one million certified applicators[15] who have access to our most dangerous pesticides, the ones we will later be referring to as "restricted use pesticides." With respect to non-pesticide toxic substances, the numbers are also staggering. The EPA Toxic Release Inventory (TRI) shows 4.09 billion pounds of toxic releases for 2011, although that is down from 7.88 billion pounds in 1988.[16] The huge variety of pesticides and other toxic substances, the vast quantities of them in use, the things we use them for, and the large number of people with access to them is alarming. We normally use pesticides to increase crop yield, to control weed growth on rights of way and lawns, and to kill disease-carrying or annoying pests. While all of this use creates an environment seemingly pleasant to live in, there are other effects of pesticide application besides cheap food, beautiful lawns, and freedom from insect bites. These effects force us to consider regulation.

Pesticide application in agriculture is viewed today as a necessity. Because we have genetically selected for strains of crop plants that maximize the yield of usable product, we have removed the plants' natural defenses against most pests. GMO technology increased annual herbicide use by 527 million pounds from 1996

---

12. EPA, *Pesticide Industry Sales and Usage: 2007 Market Estimates*, Table 3.3, available at http://www.epa.gov/pesticides/pestsales.

13. *Ibid.*, Table 3.4.

14. *Ibid.*, Table 4.1.

15. *Ibid.*, Tables 4.1-4.4.

16. *EPA, 2011 TRI National Analysis Overview*, available at http://www.epa.gov/tri/tridata/tri11/nationalanalysis/index.htm.

(when Roundup Ready crops were introduced) to 2011.[17] Therefore, we continue to apply more and more chemicals because if we did not, marketable yields would be drastically reduced, possibly causing pockets of starvation and definitely causing reduced profits. One reason we produce so many different pesticides is because target species become resistant to a pesticide after long-term exposure. For example, resistant weeds eventually developed after years of exposure to Monsanto's Roundup Ready technology, which dominates corn, soy, and cotton farming. Resistant individuals produce many offspring that are resistant to that particular pesticide. In response, farmers have either used more of the same pesticide per unit area, hoping that quantity will kill, or have shifted to other, more toxic, pesticides, such as 2,4-D, and used them until the same resistance is evidenced. Agriculture and the prevention of disease and annoyance are the main reasons we use pesticides. The reasons we need to regulate pesticides are scattered among several topics which we will consider now.

One case usually made for regulation of pesticides deals with the notion of United States industry wanting to make a profit by selling products without any care as to the effects of those products on non-target species, including humans. While industry might argue that all their pesticides are properly labeled, many unregistered and banned pesticides, as well as regulated pesticides, are currently sold outside this country. These unregistered pesticides usually do not meet United States standards; however, many of the crops sprayed with these pesticides may be raised by foreign agriculture for export to the United States. Although we do inspect our imported food, it is still likely that some of that imported food contains levels of registered or unregistered pesticide residue far above what is allowed by United States law. It appears in this situation we need to regulate to protect us from ourselves.

Other concerns of regulation proponents deal mainly with biological effects on non-target species and long-term effects of pesticide application. We know that when pesticides are applied, species other than the target species are killed. In many instances,

---

17. Philpot, T., "How GMOs Unleashed a Pesticide Gusher," *Mother Jones* (Oct. 3, 2012), available at http://www.motherjones.com/tom-philpott/2012/10/how-gmos-ramped-us-pesticide-use.

the other species are predators on the target species (natural controls) or economically useful species such as bees, which we discussed above. Thus, the benefit of the pesticide may be outweighed by the unintended harm it causes. Persistence of pesticides is also a concern. Ideally, a pesticide should eliminate a target species and dissipate into a harmless end product. However, many of the early pesticides, DDT in particular, did not degrade for a long period of time, and consequently were consumed along with any crop on which they were applied.

Two very significant environmental concerns with respect to pesticides are the biological effects of pesticide degradation products and the phenomenon of biological magnification. Probably the most publicized pesticide degradation product is DDE, a decay product of DDT. DDE has been implicated in the decline of many carnivorous bird species such as the brown pelican and the peregrine falcon because DDE affects the shell gland in these birds to such a degree that the egg shells of chicks are so fragile the mother crushes them during incubation. The Centers for Disease Control has found DDT in amniotic fluid, placentas, fetuses, umbilical cord blood, and human breast milk, even in those born long after the chemical was banned in the United States in 1972. Many people believe that in order to prevent exposure to possible degradation products of today's chemicals we should test for decay products before allowing chemicals to be put on the market. Another major concern is biological magnification, where organisms higher on the food chain have higher concentrations of pesticide residue in their systems. This is caused by chemical residue that accumulates in tissue over time. For example, suppose that zooplankton contains 1 parts of mercury. If a very small fish eats 100 zooplankton, the fish could theoretically contain 100 parts of mercury, and if a trout or whitefish eats two of these small fish, it could contain 200 parts of mercury. If you were to eat a trout or whitefish, your tissue could absorb that 200 parts of mercury—this is called biological magnification.

Many arguments similar to those we have seen with respect to pesticides can be applied or analogized to other toxic substances. While Agent Orange is a pesticide, benzene, napthalene and other possible carcinogens are not. These and other toxins are used in huge volume and have tremendous potential for effects on human health. In addition, we have recently become more aware of the heightened effects that toxic materials have on children over and above the effects on adults. Children's environmental health has emerged into scientific prominence. Children have increased exposure and increased susceptibility to toxicants.[18] They breathe, eat, and drink more for their body weights than adults—they also behave differently, living closer to the ground, touching and putting things in their mouths—which also increases their exposure. Children's susceptibility to the effects of exposure are also heightened because developing bodies react differently to toxicants than adult bodies. Children are less able to metabolize foreign compounds and often absorb them at a higher rate than adults; their immune systems are immature, their bodies and minds are still developing, and they have more time in their lives to accumulate toxicants. Government has begun to address some of the special impacts associated with child exposure to pesticides and other toxic substances.

Pesticide residue was traditionally regulated by the Food, Drug and Cosmetic Act under the Delaney Clause. The Delaney Clause was extremely protective of pesticide residue in foods consumed by children, prohibiting any residue that had been shown to cause cancer in humans *or* animals.[19] In 1996, Congress passed the Food Quality Protection Act,[20] replacing the Delaney Clause with a risk-benefit standard for all pesticide residues on food. All residues must be "safe." In other words, there must be a reasonable certainty that aggregate exposure to the levels of pesticides commonly found on food will not result in harm. Despite a lack of sufficient data on the effects of chemicals on children, EPA has selected several chemicals of concern, the majority of which are frequently found in food, including organochlorine chemicals (dioxins, dibenzofurans,

---

18. "Children's Health Protection," *Environmental Protection Agency* (2013) available at http://yosemite.epa.gov/ochp/ochpweb.nsf/content/homepage.htm; Firestone, A., "Why Children Are Vulnerable," *Clean Air Council: Children's Environmental Health*, available at www.cleanair.org.

19. 21 U.S.C.A. § 348(c)(3)(A).

20. 21 U.S.C.A § 346a(b)(2).

PCBs and organochlorine pesticides), and organophosphates,[21] and restricts use of the organophosphate pesticides azinphos methyl, chlorpyrifos, and methyl parathion on certain food crops and around the home, due largely to concerns about potential exposures of children. Agricultural crops commonly consumed by children, like apples, corn, oranges, rice, and wheat, can retain residues of these pesticides, and have been shown to have adverse effects on children's neurological development and immune responses. The Food Quality Protection Act required EPA to determine whether pesticide residue on foods presented "reasonable certainty of no harm" to infants and children, and even with these protective measures, studies have found pesticide residues of at least one organophosphate pesticide in 14 percent of samples of fruits, vegetables, and juices commonly served to children.[22]

C. THE ORGANIC ALTERNATIVE TO PESTICIDE USE

After a brief decline, pesticide use in American agriculture appears to be on an upswing. In 1979, farmers applied 843 million pounds of pesticides; by 2011, that number had risen to 857.[23] It is encouraging to note, however, that the number of organic farms continues to grow and non-organic farms are using pesticides to a much lesser degree. Instead of making regular applications of pesticides, many farmers are now applying them only when and where there is a clear need. Also, the need for pesticides is being reduced by alternative control mechanisms such as the release from airplanes of beneficial insects that are bred and sold for controlling harmful insects. Regardless of trends in pesticide use, it is important to consider that the average American is exposed to seven to ten different pesticides from food and water daily. While the

---

21. *"America's Children and the Environment," Environmental Protection Agency* (2013), available at http://www.epa.gov/envirohealth/children/.

22. Lu, C., F.J. Schenck, M.A. Pearson, and J.W. Wong., "Assessing children's dietary pesticide exposure - direct measurement of pesticide residues in 24-hour duplicate food samples." *Environmental Health Perspectives* 118 (11):1625-30 (2010).

23. "Pesticide Industry Sales and Usage: 2011 Market Estimates," *Environmental Protection Agency*, Table 5.3 (2011).

majority of this exposure comes from conventionally grown fruits and vegetables, 65 percent of which contain chemical residue, as much as 16 percent of organic fruits and vegetables also contain traces of pesticides. This is most likely due to cross-contamination in cold storage facilities, during trucking, or in grocery stores.[24] Organic crops are also often inadvertently exposed to non-organic pesticides that have drifted from other farms. This raises the question faced by many farmers seeking organic certification–how can organic and conventional crops co-exist in the same areas? And who is responsible for the drifting pesticides, the conventional farmer, or the organic farmer? A California court ruled that an applicator has a duty not to apply pesticides if there is a "reasonable possibility" that post-application drift will damage another farmer's crops, but what constitutes "damage?"[25]

Consumer demand for organic foods is the driving force behind reductions in pesticide use. In response to this demand, sales of organic goods have grown exponentially, from $7.4 billion in 2001 to $31.5 billion in 2011.[26] There are more than 17,000 certified organic farms on over 4.1 million acres of U.S. land. 9000 farms have been certified in the past ten years. The sudden expansion has contributed to increased sales of organic produce, accounting for more than 9% of retail sales annually. Despite the growing demand for organic produce, converting from conventional to organic farming is no easy task. Organic certification requires farmers to prove that their soil is free of certain substances and that those substances haven't been used on the farm for at least three years. This delay, combined with reductions in yield during the first five years after transition to organic farming practices, can create tough economic hurdles to "going organic."

Organic farming is regulated by private organizations under federal, and sometimes state, law. Under the Organic Food

---

24. *Ibid.*

25. *Jacobs Farm/Del Cabo, Inc. v. Western Services, Inc.*, Cal.Rptr.3d (6th Dist.).

26. "Organic Farming for Health and Prosperity," *Organic Farming Research Foundation* (2012), available at http://ofrf.org.

Production Act, [27] the National Organic Program (NOP) within the U.S. Department of Agriculture can amend existing regulations, promulgate new standards, clarify regulations and policies, and amend the National List of Allowed and Prohibited Substances for organic farming. Not surprisingly, most synthetic pesticides are prohibited, as well as some toxic natural substances, like arsenic. Also not surprisingly, most natural substances are permitted, including bacillus thuringiensis, microbial pesticides, copper fungicides, garlic products, neem pesticides (containing the active ingredient azadirachtin), pheromone products (used in traps or to disrupt insect mating), various repellants, soap-based products, and a relatively new biochemical insecticide called spinosad. One major difference between conventional and organic farming is that organic farmers are required to both follow the label and adhere to additional restrictions imposed by organic certifiers, including reporting which pesticides they will be using before they are applied. To encourage consumer confidence in the integrity of organic farming practices, USDA requires organic certifying agents to test products from at least 5 percent of the organic farms and businesses that they certify each year. [28] NOP can also take measures to ensure the integrity of the certification process, and has issued 34 civil penalties to those in violation of the organic farming regulations totaling more than $428,500.

The Organic Foods Production Act (OFPA) does not prevent states from supplementing federal standards. [29] Several states have their own organic farming statutes, but they generally adopt the provisions under OFPA. For example, California adopted NOP standards under the California Organic Foods Act. [30] The state certification body, accredited by the USDA, is California Certified Organic Farmers (CCOF). California has more certified organic acres in production than any of the other states, with more than 2300 producers on 718,450 acres. The small state of Vermont has

---

27. Organic Foods Production Act 7 U.S.C.A. § 205.

28. Available at http://bit.ly/residue-final-rule.

29. *In re Aurora Dairy Corp.*, 621 F.3d 781 (8th Cir.).

30. Cal. Food & Agric. Code § 46000.

582 certified organic producers and 100,000 acres in production. Vermont has a USDA accredited certification body, Vermont Organic Farmers (VOF), to verify that agricultural products are raised in accordance with standards under NOP, but it does not have a state statute.

Perhaps if advances in alternative pest controls continue, and if consumers require farmers to use fewer pesticides, the need for extensive government regulation of pesticides may also decrease. Similarly, if the Toxic Release Inventory numbers continue to decline, concern and government control might not be as prominent. Pesticides do continue, however, to be in widespread use and to pose increasingly troublesome environmental problems such as leaching into ground water. Other toxic substances also continue to cause severe environmental problems, and the problems they cause for children may be greater than we ever anticipated. It therefore appears likely that extensive regulation of pesticides and toxic substances will remain with us in the foreseeable future.

D. HOW WE REGULATE THEM

Having considered the benefits which society derives from pesticides and other toxic substances as well as the harms that such products might create, we next turn to how we try to keep the benefits while reducing or eliminating the harms. How far we should go in controlling our use of pesticides and toxic substances is a question to be left for the reader's own determination. The question that will be addressed here is what the law has given us in the way of control mechanisms. We will first focus on control through the private law mechanism of a lawsuit where someone (a plaintiff) will be asking a court for relief without the request for relief being based on any action of a legislative body. Relief will thus be based on the "common law" or judge-made law. We will then examine public law control mechanisms in the form of legislation directed at pesticide use and at the manufacturing and use of toxic substances.

1. Private Controls—Negligence Actions, Nuisance Actions, and Inverse Condemnation

Our primary example of a private control mechanism will be where a plaintiff seeks a remedy for harm caused to the plaintiff by someone's (the defendant's) improper use of a pesticide. The plaintiff's lawsuit will likely be a negligence action since injuries caused in pesticide cases are usually one-time occurrences such as aerial spraying of pesticides in high winds or failure to stop spraying when the defendant's airplane has flown over the plaintiff's land. A brief description of the theory of negligence is that: (1) society has established a duty of care, e.g., do not spray in a high wind, (2) the defendant has breached or acted inconsistently with that duty (sprayed in a high wind), (3) the defendant's breach of its duty caused harm to the plaintiff, (4) the harm was of a type which was foreseeable, and (5) the defendant had no justifiable excuse for its conduct. If the plaintiff is successful in establishing these elements of negligence by the defendant, the court will award plaintiff money damages to compensate for the harm that has been suffered. The defendants in negligence suits involving pesticides are usually applicators of pesticides or the person or company for whom the applicator is working, but other defendants might be manufacturers of pesticides. Manufacturers might be responsible for breaches of duties of care such as failing to warn the user of possible harms to the health of the user or of harms which would occur to species other than those which were intended to be adversely affected by the pesticide. Manufacturers might also be found liable under various state consumer protection laws.

Negligence actions and consumer protection actions are usually matters of state law. Since pesticides are subject to extensive controls by the federal government, as will be discussed later in this chapter, manufacturers have asserted that federal law has "preempted" state law and thus made them immune from suit under state law.[31] In the 2005 case of *Bates v. Dow Agrosciences*,[32]

---

31. The issue of federal preemption is discussed more extensively in Chapter 3 in the context of noise pollution control.

32. 544 U.S. 431.

farmers claimed that their peanut crop was severely damaged by a weed control pesticide recommended by its manufacturer for use on peanuts. With respect to the manufacturer's preemption defense, the U.S. Supreme Court held that federal law with respect to pesticide labeling did not preempt all state law actions and give pesticide manufactures virtual immunity from certain forms of tort liability. Thus manufacturers as well as applicators of pesticides may be liable by way of the private law control mechanism of the "common law" lawsuit.

While the theory of negligence is available to an injured party with respect to improper pesticide use situations, there are hurdles to be crossed before that theory leads to an actual remedy. The hurdle of establishing "causation" (number 3 above) is especially difficult in some pesticide cases because the plaintiff must show that the defendant's actions are connected to the resultant injury to the plaintiff. There are substantial problems in proving such a connection when the manifestation of the injury is delayed or if the injury could have resulted from other causes in addition to or instead of the defendant's actions. For example, if the lifespan of dairy cattle that were subjected to negligent crop-spraying activity is reduced by three years, that effect will likely not make itself known until a time in the future when demonstrating the cause of the reduced lifespan is difficult. Similarly, if a beekeeper's bees die over the winter, it may be difficult to determine whether they died due to negligent pesticide spraying the previous spring or due to climatic conditions or due to a combination of both. Although not all cases present problems of proof such as those noted here, many of them do. Situations where the cause of harm is in doubt can result in a worthy plaintiff being left without a remedy, but can also result in a defendant being found responsible and liable for a harm which the plaintiff has suffered but which the defendant did not cause.

In addition to negligence suits, private lawsuits based on the theory of nuisance, discussed in Chapter 3, have been used to obtain relief from environmental harm, especially where the harm is of a continuing nature rather than a one-time occurrence. Many of these cases have concerned harm due to toxic substances. Historically, the usual subject matter of nuisance suits was someone interfering with your use and enjoyment of your land. Today, toxic substance personal injury in the form of discomfort, annoyance, irritation, and anguish, as well as injury to property, can be compensated in a nuisance action. In *Wilson v. Key Tronic Corp.*,[33] where the defendant private company had disposed of a cleaning byproduct containing an extremely hazardous waste in a landfill, and the waste had leached into the plaintiff landowners' well water, the landowners were compensated not only for the loss in the market value of their real estate, but also for mental anguish caused by the threat and actual ingestion of contaminated water. They also were given compensation for the inconvenience of having to haul water and for the disruption of ordinary activities of family life.

In *Wilson*, Spokane County, as well as the private defendant, was also found liable for the harm to the landowners. The county's liability was based on the theory of "inverse condemnation." The Washington Constitution provides that: "No private property shall be taken or damaged for public or private use without just compensation having been first made. . . ." Where a governmental entity with eminent domain power[34] acts in a planned way that results in property being "taken or damaged," even though the entity did not intend that the property be "taken or damaged," the property has been "inversely condemned." Spokane County operated the landfill and had asked that the chemical waste be dumped in it rather than at another site. This planned action by the county amounted to an inverse condemnation, triggering the landowners' right to compensation for damages under the Washington Constitution.

Through use of private lawsuits, the common law seeks to provide help for those harmed by pesticides or other toxic substances and to deter people from acting in ways that cause harm. Deterrence will hopefully result from one's knowing that causing harm will mean one will have to pay damages. While the common law mechanisms have proven somewhat helpful, they have been criticized as inadequate deterrents due to the ability of parties to

---

33. 40 Wash. App. 802, 701 P.2d 518.

34. The eminent domain power and taking or condemnation are discussed in Chapter 4, Section C.2.

pass on to their customers the costs of paying damages or to insure themselves against liability. In addition, compensatory damages come after the harm has been inflicted. Thus, they are remedial rather than preventative. For these reasons, it has been felt that additional protective mechanisms are needed to prevent harm from happening rather than to merely compensate for harm after the fact. Harm also needs to be prevented in a more certain way than through the deterrence mechanism which is weakened by the uncertainty of obtaining a judgment for damages. To answer this need, public controls in the form of statutes were enacted, but private lawsuits continue to be an important tool for relieving those who have suffered from toxic activities. State courts appear to be quite interested in having private lawsuits compensate those who have not been protected by statutory preventative mechanisms. For example, one's reasonable fear of contracting cancer due to exposure to asbestos has been recognized as an allowable factor in assessing damages from exposure.[35] The scope of protection offered by private lawsuits to victims of toxic materials may be increasing. After years of success in defending lawsuits involving harm to people from lead in paint, paint manufacturers were found liable by a jury in Rhode Island on the theory that lead paint constituted a public nuisance. The result, however, did not hold up on appeal. The Rhode Island Supreme Court found that because the state failed to allege that the paint manufacturers' conduct interfered with a public right, or that defendants were in control of lead pigment at the time it caused harm to children in Rhode Island, they failed to show a public nuisance.[36] Most Federal Courts of Appeal have likewise rejected the idea of products as a public nuisance, reasoning that the result would be an overwhelming expansion of public nuisance law.

---

35. *Sorenson v. Raymark Industries, Inc.*, 51 Wash. App. 954, 756 P.2d 740.

36 *Rhode Island v. Lead Industries Association*, 951 A.2d 428, 443 (R.I. 2008).

2. Public Controls—Pesticide Control Act; Food, Drug, and Cosmetic Act; Toxic Substances Control Act

a. Pesticide Control

The major tool for public control of pesticides is the registration system established in the Federal Insecticide, Fungicide, and Rodenticide Act (FIFRA).[37] Under FIFRA, a pesticide may not be sold unless it is registered with EPA, and who may use a registered pesticide depends on the type of registration that the pesticide receives. FIFRA defines "pesticide" very broadly. Substances intended to prevent, destroy, repel, or mitigate any "pest" (a term also very broadly defined) or to be used as a plant regulator, defoliant, or desiccant are all pesticides. The prerequisites for approval of the registration of a pesticide by EPA (and thus to its qualifying to be lawfully sold) are that the pesticide composition is such that it will do what it is claimed that it will do, that its labeling complies with the law, that "it will perform its intended function without unreasonable adverse effects on the environment," and "when used in accordance with widespread and commonly recognized practice it will not generally cause unreasonable adverse effects on the environment." If these criteria are met without any need for limiting who can use the pesticide and without any need to place restrictions on its use, then the pesticide will qualify to be registered as a "general use" pesticide. "General use" pesticides are readily available to anyone in hardware stores, supermarkets, etc. If, however, unreasonable adverse effects on the environment may generally result unless restrictions on who may use the pesticide or other restrictions on its use are imposed, the pesticide may still be registered, but it will be as a "restricted use" pesticide. If the pesticide cannot satisfy the criteria even with restrictions placed on its use, its registration will be denied.

In those situations where a pesticide has been classified as a restricted use pesticide, unreasonable adverse environmental effects are sought to be avoided by restricting who may use the pesticide or

---

37. 7 U.S.C.A. §§ 136 to 136y.

placing other restrictions on its use. Pesticides which the EPA Administrator has classified as "restricted use" because they present a hazard to persons due to the pesticides' acute dermal or inhalation toxicity may only be applied by or under direct supervision of a "certified applicator." If the pesticide has been classified as "restricted use" because it may cause unreasonable adverse effects on the environment other than the toxicity to humans mentioned above, then application is allowed by or under the supervision of a certified applicator or subject to whatever other restrictions on use EPA may impose by administrative regulation.[38]

From the above description of the registration system and the fact that the most dangerous pesticides are restricted to use by certified applicators, we can see that a key mechanism of public control and protection with respect to pesticides is the process by which applicators are certified. Applicators may be certified either by federal certification or by state certification under a state plan approved by EPA. In either situation, Congress has established that the standard for qualifying for certification is that the applicator be "competent." The factors affecting competency are determined administratively by EPA and include topics like safety, equipment use, and application techniques. For "commercial applicators," those who are in the business of applying pesticides for others, competency is determined by written examinations and performance testing;[39] however, FIFRA exempts "private applicators" from federal requirements to take an examination to establish competency in the use of the restricted use pesticide. A "private applicator" is one who uses the restricted use pesticide on property owned or rented by the applicator or the applicator's employer or on property of another person if done without compensation other than trading of personal services between producers of agricultural commodities. Under an approved state plan, a "private applicator" can certify himself/herself merely by completing a certification form. While EPA can require a private applicator to affirm that he/she has completed a training program,

---

38. 7 U.S.C.A. § 136a(d).

39. 40 CRF § 171.4(a).

EPA may not require that a private applicator be examined to establish competency.

The above-described self-certification provision, supported by agribusiness, was added by an amendment to the original FIFRA.[40] That amendment recognizes that farmers working on their own land or that of their neighbors in an agricultural services exchange will likely be very careful in their use of pesticides and are also probably quite knowledgeable concerning pesticide use. Congress has thus been satisfied that such people need not pass examinations to determine their competency. It is true that farmers have strong motivations to use pesticides properly. In addition to the protection of their own health and land, and the health and land of their neighbors (items which will likely be of importance to them even without the possibility of sanctions), they are also motivated to be careful by the possibility of lawsuits against them if they are not careful. It is also true that examinations would be bothersome to many farmers. Yet the same or similar motivations for care are present for commercial applicators and have been present for many years, and still Congress found that these motivations need supplementation in the form of a system which restricts the use of our most dangerous pesticides to those people we are sure are competent to use them. Farmers (and agribusiness) are large users of pesticides, and, if Congress was concerned enough about the environmental hazards of pesticide use to create the "restricted use" classification, one may want to question the wisdom of allowing such large users of "restricted use" pesticides to use them without a real check on their competency. The words of the statute allow a large agribusiness corporation to have its many employees apply restricted use pesticides on the corporation's land without those employees being examined as to their competence.[41] The corporation may be motivated to make sure its employees are competent in order to protect itself against lawsuits and to protect the quality of its land and its crop, but if those motivations had successfully controlled the problems associated with pesticide use,

---

40 7 U.S.C.A. § 136(i).

41. 7 U.S.C.A. § 136(i)(a)(1).

FIFRA would not have been needed. Some states have closed the "private applicators" loophole by providing, as a matter of state law, that all users of restricted use pesticides, private applicators as well as commercial applicators, may be given a competency examination.[42] The following is a question that appeared on a state examination for commercial applicators:

> Q: If a 100-gallon sprayer sprays 5 acres per tank-full and the spray recommendations call for 2 pounds actual per acre, how many pounds of 50WP pesticide must be added to the sprayer?
>
> A: 50WP means 50% active; to get 2 pounds actual, you need 4 pounds of product. The sprayer treats 5 acres per load and you want 2 pounds actual per acre, so you add 4 pounds of product for each acre treated or 20 pounds of product.

Another protection under FIFRA is the set of mechanisms for ending registration and thus ending the sale of a pesticide. First, FIFRA establishes the goal that EPA review registration every 15 years.[43] This automatic review provision determines the pesticide's continued acceptability under the criteria for registration. Second, EPA may cancel registration or change a classification from general to restricted use if the EPA Administrator determines that the registration criteria (labeling, performance, unreasonable adverse effects on the environment) are no longer being met.[44] Procedural requirements for notice and hearings protect the registrant against unjustified cancellation or classification changes, which can take months or even years. If, however, the Administrator determines that action is required to prevent an "imminent hazard," a third mechanism may be triggered—an order to "suspend" registration. The process of suspension still carries with it the procedural safeguards of notice and hearing, but the process is much shorter,

---

42. Vermont Regulations for Control of Pesticides, IX.

43. 7 U.S.C.A. § 136a(g).

44. 7 U.S.C.A. § 136(d).

taking days and weeks, rather than months and years. An imminent hazard can be to human health or the environment, as well as situations presenting a risk to the survival of a species listed as endangered or threatened under the Endangered Species Act.[45] The final option, for "emergency" situations, permits an immediate ban on sales or use without a notice or hearing.[46]

As an example of the process, after the manufacturer of rodenticides failed to adopt new safety standards to prevent accidental exposures of children and pets, EPA initiated an action to cancel and remove twelve of their products from the consumer market.[47] Once EPA publishes the Notice of Intent to Cancel in the Federal Register, the company has the opportunity to voluntarily remove the products from the market, or EPA will cancel the product's registration. The cancellation therein is effective 30 days after the notice is published, unless the manufacturer requests a hearing. Under FIFRA, hearings are chaired by an administrative law judge, who will make both procedural and substantive decisions about the products. A final cancellation order after an administrative hearing is subject to judicial review within 60 days after entry of the order.

In addition to FIFRA, Congress has sought to protect the public health from problems associated with pesticide use by enacting provisions of the Food, Drug, and Cosmetic Act (FDCA) to limit pesticide residues on food.[48] If an amount of residue in excess of a federally established "tolerance level" is present in or on the food, that food is considered "adulterated." Introducing adulterated food into interstate commerce is a criminal offense, and the food is also subject to seizure. EPA establishes "tolerance levels" that are the maximum amounts of residue consistent with protecting the public health, and they vary for each pesticide and for each food on which that pesticide is used. For example, the tolerance level for the

---

45. 7 U.S.C.A. § 136(l).

46. 7 U.S.C.A. § 136(k).

47. News Release (2013), available at http://www.epa.gov.

48. 21 U.S.C.A. §§ 346, 346(a).

insecticide malathion is eight parts per million on apricots and one part per million on sweet potatoes.[49] The tolerance level for the fungicide 2, 6-dichloro-4-nitroaniline is 20 parts per million on apricots and 10 parts per million on sweet potatoes.[50]

The above-described system of legislative and administrative control of pesticides under FIFRA and the FDCA has been in place for many years. Amendments that have made significant changes include: (1) making it easier for EPA to ban a registered pesticide by altering the "indemnification" requirement under FIFRA and (2) requiring that the special needs of infants and children be considered when tolerance levels are set under the FDCA. Areas where federal legislative amendments have been attempted but have not been enacted include: (1) prohibiting the export of unregistered pesticides and (2) providing specific protection for ground water from pesticides. Let's first consider the indemnification provisions of FIFRA and how they relate to the pesticide export issue. We will then address ground water protection and end our pesticide control discussion with how the special needs of children are considered with respect to food safety.

Prior to the amendments to FIFRA, EPA could only suspend or cancel the registration of a pesticide if it paid financial compensation to the manufacturer or other owner of the banned pesticide for their existing stock. The heavy cost of indemnification that came along with a pesticide ban was felt to be a major disincentive for EPA to take a suspension or cancellation action. It was also thought that the taxpayers should not be the ones to bear the loss if a registered pesticide was subsequently found to be unsafe and had to be banned. The FIFRA amendments preclude EPA from paying indemnification to a manufacturer for a banned pesticide unless Congress were to take the highly unusual step of providing a specific line item appropriation for payment.[51] If, however, the owner of the banned pesticide is an end user, such as a

---

49. 40 CFR § 180.111.

50. 40 CFR § 180.200.

51. 7 U.S.C. § 136m.

farmer, and cannot be reimbursed by the manufacturer, then indemnification from EPA is available.

Since EPA will not be paying manufacturers for existing stocks of banned pesticides, which lack of indemnification raises the question of what will happen to the existing stocks of pesticides in the hands of the un-indemnified manufacturers. Although notices of EPA's cancellation or suspension of a pesticide registration must be given to foreign governments, federal pesticide legislation specifically and affirmatively allows unregistered pesticides intended solely for export to be sold to foreign purchasers.[52] Manufacturers are merely required to package the substance according to the specifications of the foreign purchaser, and the foreign purchaser must acknowledge that the pesticide is not registered for use in and cannot be sold in the U.S.[53] Without indemnification, and with the high costs of disposal, manufacturers have significant incentives to sell existing stocks of banned pesticides, as well as newly manufactured supplies of unregistered pesticides, in other countries.

The exporting of pesticides from the U.S. that have been deemed unsafe for use in the U.S. is troublesome. First, some of the unregistered pesticides end up in the American food supply. The United States imports much of its fruit and vegetable supply, and the U.S. Department of Agriculture inspects less than one percent of all import shipments. A study of the top 20 most commonly imported produce items found pesticide levels in excess of U.S. tolerances.[54] Over a quarter of all shipments that are inspected are rejected when the U.S.D.A. detects unlawful pesticide residue—the majority of violations are caused by residue of unregistered pesticides. Second, when pesticides are exported, the U.S. loses track of procedures for handling and disposal of often times hazardous chemicals. Even assuming that an unregistered pesticide never finds its way to the United States, the wisdom of allowing its

---

52. 7 U.S.C. § 136(o)(a).

53. 58 Federal Register 9062, 9089.

54. Neff, R., et al, "A comparative study of allowable pesticide residue levels on produce in the United States" *Globalization and Health* (Jan. 2012).

export has been questioned.[55] Some argue that it is immoral for the United States to allow its manufacturers to sell pesticides for use in other countries when those pesticides are not safe enough for use by Americans. Unregistered pesticides are often sold to developing nations whose governments lack the expertise or the resources to properly regulate them or to appropriately train the people who will use them. Pesticide poisonings and deaths are said to be widespread, and poor countries have little economic choice but to buy and use the older, cheaper, and less safe unregistered pesticides that are prohibited from use in the rich countries. If safer pesticides are available, poor countries should be given access to them and not be purposely poisoned due to their poverty. In the face of these facts, are profits from the export of unsafe pesticides warranted?

On the other hand, the arguments in favor of allowing the export of unregistered pesticides cannot be viewed as wholly unreasonable. Other sovereign nations should have the right to choose for themselves whether the benefits from the use of a given pesticide outweigh the detriments. So long as a foreign government has been told that a pesticide it is importing is not allowed in the United States, it is claimed that it would be paternalistic for us to interfere further with that sovereign nation's decision. Also, if another country wants this product and it is not internationally banned, it will obtain it even if it is not sent from the United States. Production facilities can be set up in many other countries, and they will not even be subject to safeguards such as the strict hazardous waste disposal and employee protection provisions contained in American law. The use of the unregistered pesticide would continue, with additional risks being created that would not be present if the pesticide were manufactured in the United States. Furthermore, the needs of other countries, especially the developing countries, are far different than ours. Consider food and disease. Poor countries have a great need for food for consumption and for the help that increased food production gives their economies. The harm associated with lower productivity from not using a pesticide may outweigh the harm attributable to increased health risks. While

---

55. Holley, M., "The EPA's Pesticide Export Policy: Why the United States Should Restrict the Export of Unregistered Pesticides to Developing Countries," 9 *New York University Environmental Law Journal* 340 (2001).

the U.S. may be able to afford to reduce agricultural productivity, other nations may not be so fortunate. Are long term risks of possible cancer relevant in societies with short term problems of malnutrition and starvation, when those contemporary problems can be mitigated by the use of a potentially carcinogenic pesticide?

Disease is also different in developing countries than in developed countries. Malaria, carried by mosquitoes, kills over one million people a year and at least 2,000 children each day, costing approximately $12.5 billion in lost income per year.[56] The U.S. and Europe both used DDT to eradicate malaria, but that was before the health effects were widely known and it was banned. Alternatives, like drug therapies for treatment are available but costly, and programs to distribute mosquito nets have been widespread but largely unsuccessful. There is little incentive to create new and safe pesticides—the developing world is not a lucrative market. In 2000, the United Nations exempted DDT for malaria use in an international treaty that would have included the substance in a list of banned persistent pollutants. Furthermore, in 2006, the World Health Organization said it would encourage the use of DDT in areas at highest risk of malaria,[57] and in 2008 the United States sanctioned DDT to combat uncontrolled malaria outbreaks in African countries.[58] As a result, over 50,000 certified organic farms were contaminated, and the Ugandan government issued an injunction against further use of the chemical.

The battle over whether to allow the export of unregistered pesticides has been fought in the Executive Branch of government as well as in the Congress. Pursuant to the President's asserted power over the conduct of foreign policy, President Carter issued an Executive Order that could, under certain circumstances, have resulted in prohibitions on the export of unregistered pesticides

---

56. "World Malaria Report," *World Health Organization* (2012).

57. McKay, B., "WHO Calls for Spraying Controversial DDT to Fight Malaria," *Wall Street Journal* p.B1 (September 15, 2006).

58. Kron, J., "As an Insecticide Makes a Comeback, Uganda Must Weigh Its Costs," *New York Times* (May 18, 2011), available at http://www.nytimes.com/2011/05/19/world/africa/19uganda.html?pagewanted=all.

even though export is allowed by Congressional legislation.[59] President Reagan revoked that Executive Order with his own Executive Order about one month later.[60] Legislation has been repeatedly introduced by Congress to prohibit the export of unregistered pesticides, but it has never passed, and the export of unregistered pesticides continues to be legal. The most significant changes in recent years have been clarifications of regulations about the transfer of unregistered pesticides to ensure appropriate handling as they move in commerce before they actually leave the United States.[61]

At the same time as FIFRA was being amended to remove the need for EPA to pay the manufacturer for existing stocks of its pesticide if that registered pesticide were subsequently banned, Congress considered, but did not act on, the issue of protecting ground water from contamination by pesticides. Under FIFRA, waterways are not specifically protected. EPA had ruled that regulated pesticides, applied according to federal label, were not pollutants under the Clean Water Act, but the Sixth Circuit Court of Appeals disagreed, holding that pesticide users must comply with the Clean Water Act.[62] Applicators will need, therefore, a permit to apply aquatic pesticides into, around, and over water, unless the pesticide does not leave a residue or contaminate the water. The decision indicated that all pesticides should be regulated under the Clean Water Act as point source pollutants. In response, EPA issued a final rule for general permits for pesticide application as a point source pollutant. Under the rule, pesticide users must submit a Notice of Intent (NOI) for discharges to receive a Pesticide General Permit (PGP) for mosquito and other flying insect pest control, weed and algae control, animal pest control, and forest canopy pest

---

59. Executive Order 12264 of January 15, 1981, 46 Fed. Register 4659.

60. Executive Order 12290 of February 17, 1981, 46 Fed. Register 12943.

61. 78 Federal Register 4078 (Jan. 18, 2013).

62. *National Cotton Council v. EPA*, 553 F.3d 927.

control.[63] Whether or not this system will be effective likely depends on whether "general" permits can prevent contamination of water supplies, or whether it will become necessary to institute a system of site-specific permits to prevent significant harm.

In the absence of comprehensive federal protection of ground water from pesticide contamination, some states have taken their own measures to protect ground water. They are using "action limits" in an effort to prevent contamination. For example, Wisconsin law requires that the Wisconsin Department of Natural Resources monitor and sample ground water. It must also establish "enforcement standards" and "preventative action limits" with respect to ground water contamination.[64] The "enforcement standard" for a substance is the maximum allowable concentration of that substance in ground water, and, if it is exceeded, the department *must* require that the owner or operator of the activity take corrective actions to bring the contamination level below the enforcement standard. In addition, if contamination of ground water reaches a "preventative action limit," which is a percentage of the enforcement standard, then the department *may* require corrective action, but it must at least be given notice by the owner or operator of the activity that this preventative level of concern has been reached and that the department should consider greater vigilance in monitoring the ground water quality.[65]

The concern over ground water contamination from pesticides has been largely driven by agricultural pesticide use. There is, however, some concern that ground water contamination could result from non-agricultural pesticide use on golf courses or lawns. In addition, health issues have been raised related to simply coming into personal physical contact with pesticides that have been applied in landscaping situations. States have begun greater regulation of non-agricultural pesticide use by requiring landscaping companies to post conspicuous signs warning that they have recently applied

---

63. "Notice of Final Permit, Final National Pollution Discharge Elimination System (NPDES) Pesticide General Permit for Point Source Discharges from the Application of Pesticides," 76 Federal Register 68750 (Nov. 7, 2011).

64. Wisconsin Statutes Annotated, §§ 160.07, 160.09, 160.15, and 160.27.

65. Wisconsin Administrative Code, §§ NR 140.24 and 140.26.

pesticides on areas including not only golf courses and public athletic fields, but also on the lawns and landscape plants of single or multi-family residences.[66] Golf courses are also being required to get permits prior to applying pesticides, with those permits being conditioned on the applicant establishing buffer strips to protect surface waters and environmentally sensitive areas and doing periodic sampling and analysis of ground and surface water. Additionally, the proposed golf course must be built in accordance with the construction plans presented in its pesticide permit application.[67] The states, rather than the federal government, appear to have taken the lead in expanding public control of pesticide use, especially with respect to ground water protection.

The most significant federal changes in recent years in the area of pesticide control is the acknowledgment by Congress that children are subject to special and/or heightened risks due to pesticide exposure. Congress amended the Food, Drug, and Cosmetic Act to mandate greater protection for infants and children with respect to their exposure to pesticide residues on food.[68] Addressing the issues of increased exposure and increased susceptibility discussed in Section B of this chapter, the FDCA requires that tolerance levels for pesticide residues on food be based on "consumption patterns among infants and children that are likely to result in disproportionately high consumption of foods," "special susceptibility . . . including neurological differences . . . and effects of in utero exposure," and "cumulative effects." The tolerance level is required to "ensure that there is a reasonable certainty that no harm will result to infants and children from aggregate exposure. . . ." Of course, one cannot expect full agreement at the scientific or administrative levels about issues like what are the effects of in utero exposure or what is a reasonable certainty of no harm. Furthermore, expressly focusing on children in the area of tolerance levels for pesticides does not solve problems of their

---

66. Vermont Regulations for Control of Pesticides, § IV.8, Vermont Department of Agriculture.

67. Id. § IV.9.

68. 21 U.S.C. §346a(b)(2)(C).

increased exposure and increased susceptibility in other situations like common air pollutants, lead, mercury, and second hand tobacco smoke.[69] It is, however, encouraging to see federal legislation moving in the direction of including the need to protect special populations with special needs like children.

b. Toxic Substances

There are currently more than 84,000 chemicals in U.S. commerce, 7,000 of which are produced at volumes of 25,000 pounds or greater.[70] Many substances that would certainly qualify as "toxic" are regulated under laws other than the Toxic Substances Control Act (TSCA).[71] We just discussed legislation directed at pesticides, and examples of other legislation controlling "toxics" include the Clean Air Act, regulating hazardous air pollutants, the Atomic Energy Act, regulating nuclear materials, and the Resource Conservation and Recovery Act, establishing controls on hazardous waste disposal. In enacting TSCA, Congress focused on newly developed chemical substances. It took the position that chemical substances were being developed and introduced into the marketplace in such high volume and with such a high degree of potential for harm that they should be the subject of a particularized regulatory framework. Many argue that TSCA lacks the teeth necessary to protect the public, and there is agreement among stakeholders that reform is long overdue. Some suggest that the EPA adopt REACH, the European Union's innovative chemical regulatory program, as a model for more effective and complete review of existing and future toxic substances. REACH places the burden of proof of safety on the manufacturer, and REACH has reduced the costs and inconsistencies in chemical regulation,

---

69. Firestone, A., "Hazards Facing Children," *Clean Air Council: Children's Environmental Health*, available at www.cleanair.org.

70. Existing Chemicals Program: Strategy, U.S. EPA 1 (2012).

71. 15 U.S.C.A. § 2601 et seq.

obstacles that have plagued toxics regulation in the U.S. for decades.[72]

The basic operative mechanism of TSCA is that new chemical substances may not be manufactured unless a notice of intention to manufacture is filed with EPA at least 90 days before manufacture.[73] This is generally called a pre-manufacture notice (PMN). The manufacturer must submit information, including test data it has on health and environmental effects, estimated volume of manufacture, methods of manufacture and disposal of the substance. The thrust of the legislation is to provide EPA with the opportunity to review risks to health or the environment in advance of the manufacturing of the chemical substance rather than leaving such review until sometime after the substance has been manufactured and when harm may already have occurred. If EPA does not take action within the 90 days to prohibit or restrict manufacture of the substance, manufacturing may commence unless EPA, for good cause, extends the review period for up to 90 additional days. If EPA concludes that the new substance presents or will present an unreasonable risk of injury to health or the environment, it may prohibit or limit the manufacture of the chemical. Action to temporarily prohibit the manufacture of the chemical may be taken where EPA finds that it needs additional information in order to evaluate the potential effects of the new chemical. EPA also has regulatory power with respect to existing chemical substances. If there is a finding of unreasonable risk to health or the environment, EPA may invoke remedies, ranging from labeling requirements and notifying purchasers of risks to prohibitions on manufacture and distribution of the product.

Although TSCA provides an increased level of protection for the public, our TSCA discussion should not end without expressly noting some potential costs of that protection. Obviously, there are the administrative costs of establishing, implementing, and enforcing the regulatory scheme. Less obvious costs might be the

---

72. "The Commission's Extended Impact Assessment in 2003, accompanying its proposal for REACH legislation," *European Chemicals Agency* 11 (2003), available at ec.europa.eu/enterprise/reach/docs/reach/eia-sec-2003_1171_en.pdf.

73. 15 U.S.C.A. § 2604.

disincentives for the chemical industry to provide new products. This could result in society not having the benefit of valuable and safe new chemical products. One rather direct potential disincentive may be that companies which have choices to make between investing in new product development or using their capital in other ways will be deterred from developing new chemicals because the cost and the time needed to get a new product on the market may be substantially increased. A less direct disincentive may lie in the fact that going through the TSCA process of information disclosure can result in a company's competitors acquiring the company's trade secret concerning its new product. Since the trade secret may represent a substantial share of the worth of the new product, the risk of losing trade secrets may dilute the profit potential of developing new chemicals and thus shift companies away from chemical product development.

While TSCA does seek to protect the confidentiality of information submitted to EPA, not all information submitted will remain confidential, either because of exceptions to confidentiality allowed by the statute or merely through inadvertence by agency employees. Hence, there is a price for TSCA's protection, but Congress has determined that the health and environmental protection provided by TSCA are worth the decrease, if any, in new chemical development and availability to the American public. As it stands, there are more than 65,000 substances of concern in commerce. Concerns that these substances are potentially hazardous to human health are in large part due to inadequate information about their toxicity. Estimates indicate that even the most basic toxicity data is unavailable for 75 percent of substances used in commerce.[74] In 2009, EPA implemented new strategies to improve its chemicals management program, including the Existing Chemicals Program Strategy, which addresses enhanced risk assessment and reduction, data collection and public access. As one component, EPA identified 83 chemicals for further review under TSCA. In 2011, the President issued an Executive Order calling for an amendment to TSCA that protects public health, welfare, safety,

74. "Toxic Ignorance," *Environmental Defense Fund*, available at http://www.edf.org/search/google_cse_adv/toxicity.

and our environment while promoting economic growth, innovation, competitiveness, and job creation.[75] In response, the most recent attempt to amend TSCA, the proposed bi-partisan Chemical Safety Improvement Act, would, like the European REACH approach, shift the burden of proving the safety of existing chemicals from EPA to industry, increasing the agency's capacity to review new and existing substances.

In addition to the federal statutes designed to protect against toxic substances, states are also heavily committed to the control of toxic substances through state legislation. In response to growing scientific evidence of harm, strong public demand, and the failure of Congress to amend TSCA, Washington approved laws requiring that industry provide up-to-date information on toxicity for priority chemicals;[76] Connecticut created a program to fund development of green chemicals;[77] and California passed legislation permitting action on the most hazardous chemicals.[78] State laws targeting chemicals posing a threat to children's health, including BPA, lead, cadmium, toxic flame-retardants, and phthalates, received the greatest support. For example, Maine passed the Kid-Safe Products Act, and Illinois introduced the Child-Safe Chemicals Act in 2011, creating the BPA-Free Kids Act which prohibits the sale or distribution of reusable children's food or beverage containers that contain bisphenol-A.[79] At the federal level, however, TSCA is not an effective way to regulate toxic substances because of the lack of capacity to review the majority of chemicals before they go to market. Whether Congress will enact the proposed Safe Chemicals Act, and whether it will better protect the public and the environment from toxic substances, remains to be seen.

---

75. Executive Order No. 1356376.

76. Children's Safe Product Act, Wash. Rev. Code. Ann. § 70.240.

77. Chemical Innovations Institute at the UCONN Health Center, Public Act 10-164.

78. Green Chemistry Initiative, Hazardous Materials and Toxic Substances Evaluation and Regulation, AB 1879.

79. 2011 Il. H.B. 1269.

ADDITIONAL READINGS

Angelo, M., *The Law and Ecology of Pesticides and Pest Management* (Burlington, VT: Ashgate Pub Co., 2013).

Bianchi, R.M., *Pesticide Use in the U.S.: Law and Fee Issues* (Hauppauge, NY: Nova Science Publishers, 2010).

Carson, R.L., *Silent Spring* (Boston: Houghton Mifflin, 1962); *see also* Carson, R.L., *Silent Spring: 50th Anniversary Edition* (Boston: Houghton Mifflin, 2012).

Cranor, C., *Toxic Torts: Science, Law, and the Possibility of Justice* (Cambridge; New York: Cambridge University Press, 2006).

Davies, K., *The Rise of the U.S. Environmental Health Movement* (Plymouth, UK: Rowman & Littlefield Publishers, 2013).

Hall, D. and Moffitt, L., *Economics of Pesticides, Sustainable Food Production, and Organic Food Markets* (Kidlington, Oxford, UK: Elsevier Science, Ltd., 2002).

Harrison, J.L., *Pesticide Drift and the Pursuit of Environmental Justice* (Cambridge, MA: MIT Press, 2011).

Lichtfouse, E., *Alternative Farming Systems, Biotechnology, Drought Stress and Ecological Fertilization* (Dordrecht; New York; Springer, 2011).

McDonnery, Shannon M., *Toxic Substances Control Act: Summary, Challenges, and Reform Proposals* (Hauppauge, N.Y: Nova Science Publisher's, Inc., 2012).

CHAPTER 7
ENERGY

A. AN ENERGY PERSPECTIVE – WHAT WE USE, WHERE IT COMES FROM, AND FORMS OF USABLE ENERGY

United States' energy consumption and production over time are shown in Figure 1,[1] with the 2011 level of energy consumption being 97 QBtus or "quads." One quad is equal to 1,000,000,000,000,000 British thermal units (Btu), and one Btu is the amount of energy required to raise the temperature of one pound of water by one degree Fahrenheit. In 2011, each American consumed enough energy to raise the temperature of over 300 million pounds of water one degree Fahrenheit. Expressed in different terms, the 2011 level of energy consumption was equivalent to 13 tons of coal or 2300 gallons of oil per year for each person in the United States. Let's make some observations about historical and future trends in our consumption, production, and supply of energy.

Total U.S. energy consumption increased significantly in the 1950s, 60s, and early 70s. Then, based largely on measures taken in response to the oil embargo against the U.S. from some of the oil exporting nations, consumption remained relatively stable through the mid-1980s. Since then, consumption has generally been rising.

---

1. U.S. Department of Energy, Energy Information Administration, *Annual Energy Review 2012*, available at www.eia.doe.gov/emeu/aer.

Per capita energy consumption and consumption per dollar of Gross Domestic Product (GDP) give us a much more optimistic perspective as shown in Figure 2.[2] Per capita consumption has remained relatively level and consumption per dollar of GDP has dropped dramatically. Yet, we should be aware that U.S. per capita energy consumption is over twice that of Europe and over ten times that of the developing countries.[3]

With respect to production and supply, our energy sources are either renewable or nonrenewable and either domestic or imported. Nonrenewable energy is viewed as a resource base that is depletable on a time scale measured in generations. Renewable energy is an energy supply that is always there and is not considered finite (exhaustible). Nonrenewable energy generally refers to fossil fuels, while renewable energy supplies are thought of as including solar energy, water power, ocean tides, wind, plant biomass, and geothermal energy from heat deep in the earth. Figure 3[4] shows how heavily we have relied and do rely on fossil fuels, and Figure 4[5] indicates a continued decline in reliance on fossil fuels—the share of energy consumption is predicted to fall from 82% in 2011 to 79% in 2040.

Problems with nonrenewable energy include what their name expressly states—they are nonrenewable and thus may run out or become scarce enough to cause severe economic problems. In addition, procuring them raises numerous environmental issues involving topics like mining, drilling, pipelines, and supertankers. Renewable energy has the distinct advantage of its name—it won't run out, but renewables also raise both economic and environmental issues. Economic concerns include the cost per unit of energy (solar and wind), the dependability of the source (wind and hydro), and the amount of space devoted to the source conversion (solar, tides, and biomass). Environmental issues include the effects of

---

2. *Ibid.*

3. *Ibid.*

4. *Ibid.*

5. U.S. Department of Energy, Energy Information Administration, *Annual Energy Outlook 2013*, available at http://www.eia.gov/forecasts/aeo/er/early_fuel.cfm.

hydroelectric facilities on fish and the aesthetics of windmills on ridgelines or as part of an oceanfront sunrise or sunset.

The dependence of the United States on fossil fuels leads to the question of where we get them. Figure 1 shows that of our 97 quads of consumption, 28.6 quads were imported. After the oil embargo noted above, and after measures aimed at energy independence took hold, energy imports declined, but since 1985, oil imports have nearly tripled

Overview, 1949-2011

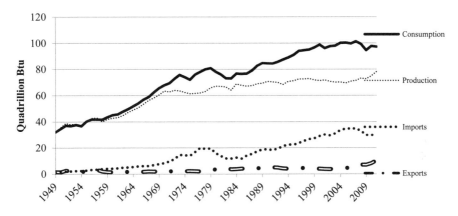

Figure 1. U.S. Consumption and Production of Energy 1949-2011.

(Figure 5[6]) and total energy imports have approximately doubled (Figure 1). Perhaps with the growth of the global economy and more emphasis on free trade, the energy independence that the United States was striving for in earlier years is not necessary. Yet the status of global violence and global politics do not appear to be any less disruptive than they were when we made a "commitment" to energy independence. The combination of our continuing increase in total energy consumption and our high level of reliance on imported petroleum may be forgetting a lesson we should have learned.

6. U.S. Department of Energy, Energy Information Administration, *Annual Energy Review 2012*, available at www.eia.doe.gov/emeu/aer.

U.S. Primary Energy Consumption Per Capita, 1949-2011

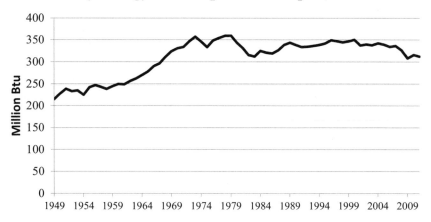

Energy Consumption per Dollar of Gross Domestic Product, 1949-2011

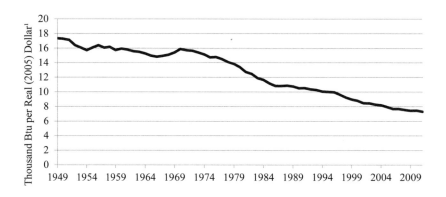

Figure 2. U.S. Per Capita and Per Dollar of GDP Energy Consumption.

By Fossil Fuels, Nuclear Electric Power, and Renewable Energy, 1949-2011

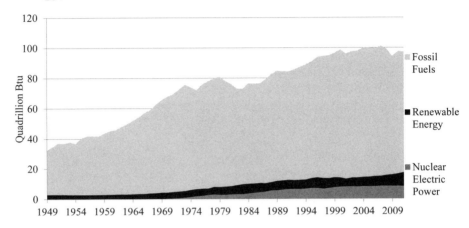

Figure 3. U.S. Energy Consumption by Source, 1949-2011.

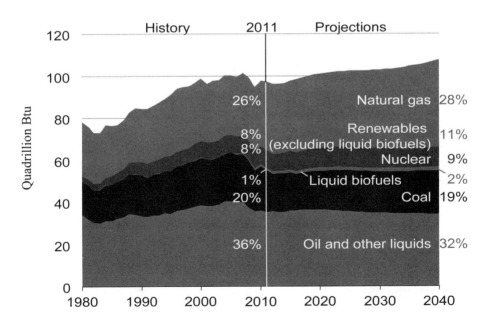

Figure 4. U.S. Energy Consumption, History, and Outlook, 1949-2040.

Energy Imports and Exports

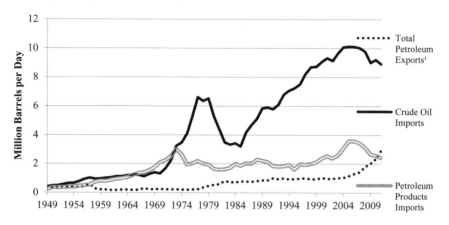

Figure 5. U.S. Petroleum Imports and Exports, 1949-2011.

B. STUMULATING ENERGY SUPPLYING

The American public has been acutely concerned about energy issues since the 1970s when supplies of oil became unreliable, prices of energy increased drastically and almost instantaneously, and gasoline and heating oil were rationed. Today, the issue appears to be balanced between the need for energy, the desire for energy independence, and environmental protection. Renewable energy resources such as wind, solar, biomass, and hydroelectric power have their own set of environmental problems; however, those problems may be of less significance and more easily solvable than the ones caused by our continued reliance on fossil fuels. A bigger hurdle to greater use of renewable energy has been the large investment of time and money to develop the technology to make it work and the risk of failure that deters people from making the effort. Congress has tried to address the issue by guaranteeing that producers of renewable energy would be able to sell that energy via the national power grid[7] and by subsidizing the development of

---

7. See section C, below.

renewables. These subsidies create an artificial reduction in development and production cost, which allows for increased consumption of renewables. Congress has used tax credits for hybrid cars, which both stimulated demand for hybrid cars and increased profits for hybrid cars, which in turn encouraged further development of the technology. Another example is the Production Tax Credit (PTC), which supports renewable energy by providing an income tax credit for new facilities relying on renewable electricity production.[8] Pursuant to § 45 of the Internal Revenue Code, the Internal Revenue Service establishes an income tax credit of a number of cents per kilowatt-hour on the sale of electricity produced from qualified energy resources such as wind, biomass, geothermal, and solar. Financial incentives, such as tax credits, combined with the guaranteed market noted above, have contributed greatly to the emerging economic viability of renewable energy, but that viability is still highly dependent on government subsidies.

In addition to financial incentives, the federal government stimulates energy supply by leasing federal lands for energy production, primarily to private enterprises. The federal government owns or controls about 650 million acres of land plus the vast Outer Continental Shelf (OCS). About 30% of the physical units of fossil fuels produced in the U.S. come from these federally administered lands.[9] The conditions of the leases ensure that the federal energy resource actually creates an energy supply. For example, leases of federal land for coal mining contain provisions requiring diligent development and continued operation of the mines.[10] The Code of Federal Regulations defines "diligent development" as developing the coal source such that coal is actually produced in commercial quantities (1% of the reserves of the source) by the end of the tenth year of the lease. "Continued operation" requires that an average of

---

8. P.L. 109-432, Section 201 amending Section 45 of the Internal Revenue Code.

9. U.S. Department of Energy, Energy Information Administration, *Annual Energy Review 2012*, www.eia.doe.gov/emeu/aer.

10. 30 U.S.C.A. § 207(b).

1% of the reserves be produced in succeeding years.[11] Thus, those who might seek to enter into a long-term lease of the federally owned coal source for the purpose of speculating on increasing prices rather than to bring the coal to market are discouraged from doing so.

The OCS is comprised of land that extends from the coastline under the ocean to the point where the slope flattens and becomes the ocean floor. Congress drafted leases with the intent to encourage greater production of energy. Congress also amended the Outer Continental Shelf Lands Act declaring that it is national policy that the OCS should be made available, subject to environmental safeguards, for expeditious and orderly development.[12] The legislative history of the statute, as contained in the report of the House of Representatives, reasoned that U.S. dependence on foreign oil must be reduced, and that the basic purpose of the legislation was to "promote the swift, orderly and efficient exploitation of our almost untapped domestic oil and gas resources in the Outer Continental Shelf."[13] The amendment provided new bidding procedures for leases, designed to encourage expeditious development. Prior to the amendments, all leasing used a "front-end bonus system" that required a potential lessee to secure a large amount of capital immediately upon acceptance of the winning bid for the lease. The amendment permits alternative bidding and leasing procedures that do not require large front-end payments, making leasing more attractive to producers and encouraging greater production.[14] Whether in part because of the above legislation or for other reasons, the Secretary of the Interior reported that lease sales have continued to increase domestic oil and gas production and reduced foreign oil imports, with over 155 million

---

11. 43 CFR § 3400.0-5.

12. 92 Stat. 629 at 635.

13. The material referred to here is from Vol. 3, 95th Congress, Second Session, p. 1460 of *United States Code Congressional and Administrative News*. A substantial amount of the history behind a piece of legislation may be found in the *United States Code Congressional and Administrative News*.

14. 43 U.S.C.S. § 1337(a) and (b).

acres leased since 1960, accounting for more than 50 percent of the oil consumed in America–the highest level since 1995.[15] The federal government also has used the OCS to stimulate the supply of renewable energy, opening 277,550 acres of the OCS to lease sales for development of wind power able to support more than 4,000 megawatts of wind generation and to power an estimated 1.4 million homes.

C. ENCOURAGING CONSERVATION OF ENERGY

We have discussed ways in which the federal government uses economic incentives to stimulate the energy *supply*. Now let's turn our attention to the numerous legal mechanisms at both the federal and state levels of government that seek to encourage energy *conservation*. Some of the approaches reduce the amount of energy being used by reducing demand, like fuel economy standards and rate setting. Other approaches focus on reducing the impact of energy use by changing the form of energy used from a less available supply to one that is more abundant or from a supply with bigger environmental problems to one with smaller environmental problems, like developing solar energy arrays. These approaches will be discussed in more detail in section D.

Consumers dictate the amount of energy required based on their usage, while usage is simultaneously affected by energy policy. The government has relied on energy policy to decrease demand for fossil fuels, both by restricting the supply of traditional sources and encouraging demand for alternative sources. For example, federal standards require that the average of fuel economy of all the cars manufactured by an individual manufacturer shall not be less than a stated number of miles per gallon in a given year.[16] The average fuel economy standard was 27.5 miles per gallon for thirty years before rising to 30.7 miles per gallon.[17] In response, more efficient

---

15. "Federal Lease Offerings and Acerage Leased since 1960," *Bureau of Ocean Energy Management* available at http://www.boem.gov/BOEM-Newsroom/Offshore-Stats-and-Facts/OCS-Leases.aspx.

16. 49 U.S.C.A. § 32902.

17. 49 CFR § 531.5.

vehicles have resulted in a decline in gas consumption, which peaked in 2007 at 9.3 million barrels per day and has fallen to roughly 8.5 million barrels per day.[18]

Another example of encouraging conservation is the Public Utility Regulatory Policies Act (PURPA), which Congress believed would reduce the demand for traditional fossil fuels by stimulating investment in small power production facilities and cogeneration facilities. A "co-generation facility" produces both electric energy and steam or some other form of useful energy, such as heat, and has higher efficiency than traditional electric power producers. A "small power production facility" has a production capacity not exceeding 80 megawatts and produces electricity from biomass, waste, geothermal resources, or renewable resources such as wind, water, or solar energy.[19] Congress directed FERC, the Federal Energy Regulatory Commission, to prescribe rules requiring that traditional electric utilities buy electricity from the co-generators and small producers. FERC acted by (1) requiring the utilities to make the interconnections that would be necessary to accomplish the sale and (2) requiring that the utilities actually buy from the small generators and co-generators at the "full avoided cost" (the cost the traditional utility paid to generate the purchased power itself or to purchase the power elsewhere).[20] This established a guaranteed market and a potentially high profit to incentivize further investment. The utilities challenged these regulations, contending that if they were required to purchase power from these small facilities, they should pay less than full avoided cost and any savings should be passed to customers in the form of direct rate savings. They argued that the language in PURPA required the purchase to be "just and reasonable to the electric consumers of the electric utility and in the public interest," and that the interest of the

---

18. "Estimated U.S. Gasoline Consumption Low Compared to Five-Year Average," *U.S. Energy Information Administration* (Aug. 12, 2012), available at http://www.eia.gov/todayinenergy/detail.cfm?id=7510#.

19. 16 U.S.C. § 796(18)(A) and (17)(A).

20. 18 CFR § 292.303 and 292.304(b)(2).

consumers would be served if the utilities could buy at lower rates from the co-generators and small power producers, permitting them to charge consumers lower rates. The United States Supreme Court, in *American Paper Institute, Inc. v. American Electric Power Service Corporation*,[21] upheld the "full avoided cost" purchase price regulation because it was a reasonable exercise of FERC's authority to provide an incentive for cogeneration and small power production facilities. Any savings would be insignificant for the individual consumer, but the profit to small generators could be a significant incentive for them to develop cogeneration and alternative energy technology. Also, in the long run, consumers of power would benefit from the decreased reliance on fossil fuel energy and the greater efficiency of energy production. Thus Congress, FERC, and the Supreme Court combined to use a financial incentive to stimulate the production of electricity from alternative energy sources.

The federal government has also introduced funding mechanisms to encourage energy conservation. One federal agency, the Department of Housing and Urban Development, offered low-cost loans to encourage homeowners to make energy saving improvements. Another agency, the Department of Energy, established Property-Assessed Clean Energy (PACE), enabling local governments to issue bonds to raise money to fund energy efficiency and renewable energy projects, and Power Purchase Agreements, helping property owners enter long-term contracts for renewable energy development. Critics argue that these efforts have gone underutilized. For example, Congress's Qualified Energy Conservation Bonds (QECB) made $3.2 billion in bonds available, subsidized by the U.S. Department of Treasury, to enable states to borrow money at low rates to fund clean energy projects.[22] By the end of 2012, few cities had taken advantage of the program, and only 20% of the bonds, had been issued. Whether or not the incentives are sufficient to encourage new energy projects or

---

21. 103 S. Ct. 1921.

22. U.S. Department of Energy, available at http://energy.gov/savings/qualified-energy-conservation-bonds-qecbs.

whether the issue is one of awareness, the fact that these funding mechanisms have been underutilized suggests that the government must find another way to incentivize energy conservation.

In addition to the federal government, there is potential for state laws to promote conservation of energy, but their use may be inhibited by economic needs of the state and by the doctrine of federal preemption. We will here examine state control of the price structure of electric power, or rate setting. The federal preemption issue will be discussed in Section D.2, below. Historically, those using higher quantities of power paid a lower price per unit of power than lower-quantity users. Because high volume users receive the electricity at a higher voltage, less energy is lost during transmission, making the purchase of high-voltage electricity more efficient. Lower rates for high-voltage users reward this efficiency and are known as "declining block rates." Some rate structures are more conservation oriented, like "flat rates" with a constant price per unit consumed, or "inverted rates" with a higher price per unit as consumption increases. These rate structures may more fairly account for actual costs of power production, since additional output capacity needed to meet high demands results in the cost per unit of electricity produced increasing as output increases. Thus, in setting the rate structure for electric power, states are left with a number of questions. Among them are: (1) which rate structure is economically more reflective of the true costs of supplying power to the high-volume and low-volume users; (2) whether it is fair to a high-volume user to make it pay more per unit consumed if the costs to provide power to it are lower than for a low-volume user; and (3) do flat rates or inverted rates really result in significantly greater conservation of energy than declining block rates, or are large-volume users' consumption patterns independent of the rate structure? Of course, as with many efforts at conservation, economic development issues also come into play. While raising rates for large-volume users may result in greater conservation efforts by them, it may also result in their relocating to another state. One incentive for industry coming to a state is often its low cost of electricity. Increasing the cost of electric power could encourage high-volume users to relocate to other areas, and states are rarely interested in losing industry, jobs, and tax revenues.

D. EMERGING ISSUES IN ENERGY

With our understanding of how the government uses energy policy to shape energy consumption, let's next examine various sources of energy and how they are affected by energy policy. We will also examine the impacts of each source on the environment, because finding, developing and consuming energy is never free from negative environmental consequences. For example, regarding consumption, the burning of fuel emits carbon dioxide, which contributes to global warming,[23] and the burning of high sulfur coal contributes to pollutants that cause acid rain.[24] With respect to production, bringing oil to market in tankers results in all too frequent oil pollution spills, and as methods of extraction change with innovation, deep-ocean drilling and hydraulic fracturing creates new environmental controversies. Working off the assumption that the world needs and will continue to need an energy supply, let's consider the various sources of energy, their negative environmental effects, and how the law deals with them.

1. Coal Fired Power Plants

Coal has been our largest source of domestically produced energy. Coal—be it anthracite, bituminous, sub-bituminous, or lignite—is either deep-mined or strip-mined. According to more than twenty peer-reviewed scientific studies, the public health costs of pollution from coal operations in Appalachia total $75 billion a year, accounting for rates of cancer and birth defects that are almost double those of people who do not live near strip mines.[25] Mining itself results in health problems among workers caused by the gases in mine shafts, collapse of shafts, and black lung disease from coal particulate matter.

The non-health environmental impacts of mining are also

---

23. Climate change is discussed in chapters 1 and 8.

24. Acid rain is discussed in chapters 1 and 3.

25. <http://ilovemountains.org/the-human-cost>

significant. Coal fired power plants emit almost one quarter of the country's carbon dioxide.[26] Strip mining destroys land surfaces, which are either never reclaimed or reclaimed very slowly. In geographically intricate areas like Wyoming, reclamation is difficult, and it can take years to re-establish the integrated ecosystems that were destroyed. Compounding the problem in western states is the lack of large quantities of water, without which the process of land reclamation is a long-term project. Mountaintop removal, another form of coal mining, not only implicates the physical condition of the land being mined but also that of the waterways in the surrounding area. Mountaintop removal mining uses dynamite to expose seams of coal, breaking off large areas of rock and dumping the rubble, or "overburden," into nearby valleys and streams. The process is most widely used in West Virginia and the Appalachian Mountains, where 1.1 million hectares of forest have been converted to surface mines, and over 1,200 miles of streams have been buried under overburden.[27] Damage to the environment in this area totals roughly $500 billion annually; the majority of the cost is associated with emissions and discharge into waterways.[28]

Coal mined in the eastern U.S., cheaper and burning hotter than western coal, is mostly bituminous and contains high sulfur content. When burned, the coal releases the sulfur, causing acid rain. Plant operations can control sulfur emissions with technology, but the cost is significant, and there is no consensus whether the ends justify the means.[29] Western coal, on the other hand, is sub-

---

26. "Annual Energy Outlook, 2011," U.S. *Energy Information Administration* (Dec. 16, 2010), available at http://www.eia.gov/oiaf/aeo/overview.html.

27. "The Effects of Mountaintop Mines and Valley Fills on Aquatic Ecosystems of the Central Appalachian Coalfields," *EPA* (March 2011), available at http://cfpub.epa.gov/ncea/cfm/recordisplay.cfm?deid=225743#Download.

28. "Mining Coal, Mounting Costs: The Life Cycle Consequences of Coal," *Center for Health and the Global Environment, Harvard Medical School* (Jan. 2011), available at http://chge.med.harvard.edu/resource/mining-coal-mounting-costs-life-cycle-consequences-coal.

29. The Acid Rain section of Chapter 3 discusses how the Clean Air Act is now attempting to control acid deposition.

bituminous and contains virtually no sulfur. Instead, it contains heavy metals, some of which, mercury in particular, are considered harmful to humans and can accumulate in biological systems, affecting the human nervous system, heart, kidneys, lungs, and immune system. Again, the harms can be mitigated with high cost technology, but then the question emerges of what to do with the byproducts. Our domestic coal supply clearly holds great potential, but it just as clearly leaves us with major environmental questions that cannot be ignored.

Congress, understanding that coal is essential to the nation's energy requirements but recognizing the adverse effects it has on the environment, established the Surface Mining Control and Reclamation Act (SMCRA)[30] within the Department of the Interior to regulate coal mining primarily from the viewpoint of environmental protection. The Act sets minimum standards to prevent a competitive "race to the bottom," and ensure uniformity between states. The Act uses permits for mining operations as the basic statutory mechanism to address present and future threats to the environment.[31] In a manner similar to its approach in the Clean Air Act, Congress has given the states the primary responsibility for administering permits, contingent on approval from the Secretary of the Interior. Also like the Clean Air Act, in the absence of an approved state program, the Office of Surface Mining (OSM) carries out permitting and enforcement functions.

Pursuant to the Act, permits for surface coal mining operation require a reclamation plan, which is a plan to restore the land to its approximate original contours and a condition capable of supporting its prior or suitable use. As one would imagine, reclamation is expensive and measures taken are often insufficient. In response to this shortcoming, the Act established fees for current coal production which go to fund reclamation and restoration of land and water resources adversely affected by past coal mining.[32]

---

30. 30 U.S.C.S. § 1201 et seq.

31. *Ibid.*

32. *Ibid.*

The fund receives 35 cents/ton of surface mined coal and 15 cents/ton of underground mined coal.[33] Allocations from the fund are based on the geographic area where the revenue was derived. Large scale operations, looking for a way to avoid the cost of reclamation, exploited an exemption in the Act for small surface mining operations by hiring small contractors to mine their coal in small plots of less than two acres. Another approach was skipping a few feet between two-acre sites along a seam.[34] After unsuccessful efforts by the Department of the Interior to administratively correct these abuses, Congress repealed the two-acre exemption for small operators.[35] Despite attempts to ensure reclamation, opponents of coal mining argue that the nature of mining means that reclamation plans rarely bring mined lands anywhere near their original status. For example, mountaintop removal mining requires the removal of rock, creating overburden, or excess soil and rock, which then rolls down the steep mountain slopes and accumulates in valley fills. Because the rock naturally "swells" by 15-25 percent when it is mined, what cannot be returned to its natural location remains in the valleys, creating "valley fills" that bury streams and wetlands. EPA estimates that 2,000 miles of streams have been filled in Appalachia alone because of mountaintop mining, and 120 additional miles are filled each year.[36] Discharge from valley fills has become a major environmental problem.[37] Until 2008, overburden from mountaintop removal was subject to the Clean Water Act's "buffer-zone rule," which prevented surface coal mining within 100 feet of a stream, unless "environmentally acceptable."[38] Then, in 2008, the Office of

---

33. 30 U.S.C.S. § 1232.

34. House Report No. 100-59 to accompany H.R. 1963.

35. Public Law 100-34, § 201 (deleting the two acre exemption from 30 U.S.C.S. § 1278).

36. "Congressionally Requested Information on the Status and Length of Review for Appalachian Surface Mining Permit Applications," *EPA, Office of the Inspector General* (Nov. 21, 2011).

37. Regulated under §§ 402 and 404 of the Clean Water Act.

38. 30 CFR § 715.17(d)(3).

Surface Mining released a new rule creating an exemption to the "buffer-zone-rule," effectively permitting coal companies to place mining waste directly into waterways, accelerating the rate of environmental degradation.[39]

The majority of challenges to the Surface Mining Control and Reclamation Act are based on the fact that the Act, a federal statute permitting state control, establishes a *minimum* standard. This means that a state can choose to impose more stringent land use or environmental controls on surface mining practices than required under the Act.[40] In *Hodel v. Virginia Surface Mining & Reclamation Association*,[41] the Supreme Court held that the Act "allows the States, within limits established by federal minimum standards, to enact and administer their own regulatory programs, structured to meet their own particular needs."[42] Courts have since narrowed EPA's authority to regulate mining as an environmental issue, starting with the Fourth Circuit in *Ohio Valley Environmental Coalition v. Arcoma Coal Co.*,[43] an opinion very favorable to mining operators. The court held that because the permits were administered by the state, they did not require environmental review under NEPA, and found that EPA's authority to permit discharge under the Clean Water Act did not supersede the state's authority to permit overfill discharge into streams under the Surface Mining Control and Reclamation Act.[44] The court went even further by holding that streams between valley fill and downstream sedimentation ponds were not discrete "waters of the United

---

39. "Excess Spoil, Coal Mine Waste, and Buffers for Perennial and Intermittent Streams," 42 *Federal Register* 78890 (2008), available at www.gpo.gov/fdsys/pkg/FR-2008-12-12/pdf/E8-29150.pdf.

40. 30 U.S.C.A. § 1255.

41. 425 U.S. 262 at 264.

42. "The powers not delegated to the United States by the Constitution, nor prohibited by it to the States, are reserved to the States respectively or to the people." U. S. Const., Tenth Amendment.

43. 556 F.3d 177 (4th Cir. 2009).

44. *Aracoma Coal*, 556 F.3d at 194-95.

States," and therefore did not require a National Pollutant Discharge Elimination System (NPDES) permit under § 402 of the Clean Water Act. In an attempt to circumvent this decision, EPA required that permits issued by the Army Corps undergo enhanced federal review, but in 2011, a federal district court ruled that this exceeded EPA's authority under the Clean Water Act, which was limited to developing guidelines and prohibiting issuance of specific permits.[45] The U.S. District Court for the District of Columbia further narrowed EPA's authority to regulate mining, revoking EPA's power to veto state fill permits. The decision came after EPA vetoed Arch Coal Company's Mingo Logan subsidiary's Spruce No. 1 permit under its § 404 powers.[46] The court held that §404(c) of the Clean Water Act did not grant EPA authority to veto an *existing* § 404 permit, merely those not yet authorized.

While the courts have come down in favor of limiting regulation of mining operations, not all disputes are resolved in court. In recent years, a number of coal companies have entered into settlements with EPA. For example, in 2008, Massey Energy Company, an extractor yielding about 40 million tons of coal annually, agreed to pay $20 million as part of a settlement for violations under the Clean Water Act. According to EPA, Massey routinely polluted waterways with coal slurry and wastewater and buried over 700 miles of rivers and streams, amassing fines of more than $2.4 billion.[47] This was the highest fine paid under the Clean Water Act and set a standard for future instances of abuse in coal mining. How "mountaintop removal" mining is done, the gains to be had from it, and its effects on land, water, and people, continue to provoke controversies, but today discussion of the future of coal revolves mainly around the development of "clean coal."

---

45. *National Mining Association v. Jackson*, 768 F.Supp.2d 34 (2011).

46. EPA's veto was the first § 404 permit veto of the Obama administration, the 13th in Agency history, and the first veto of a permit that had already been granted.

47. "Massey Energy to Pay Largest Civil Penalty Ever for Water Permit Violations," *Environmental Protection Agency* (2008), available at http://yosemite.epa.gov/opa/admpress.nsf/0/6944ea38b888dd03852573d3005074ba?OpenDocument.

The term "clean coal," typically used by coal companies, was developed in response to stricter regulations under the Clean Air Act, and refers to methods of carbon capture and storage to reduce emissions of carbon dioxide from burning coal for energy. The process of carbon capture and storage, or carbon sequestration, entails pumping carbon dioxide emissions underground,[48] or using chemical filters to reduce emissions. Both methods present problems. The long-term effects of sequestration are unknown and could include leaking and geological instability and/or contamination of drinking water supplies. Chemical filters require a significant amount of energy and could cost as much as $600 per ton.[49] Despite the uncertainty surrounding sequestration, the Department of Energy estimates that the United States could store as much as 3,600 billion tons of carbon dioxide underground. EPA is currently developing regulations that clarify how carbon dioxide streams injected for geologic sequestration would be classified under the Resource Conservation and Recovery Act (RCRA) hazardous waste requirements, and the President established an Interagency Task Force on Carbon Capture and Storage to explore development of "clean coal" technologies.

In light of these uncertainties, the development of clean coal has met with some resistance. For example, the Mississippi Public Service Commission approved the first "clean coal" plant in the U.S., the Kemper County Plant in the Chickasawhay flood plain, designed to gasify coal before it is burned and capturing 65 percent of the carbon dioxide emitted from the plant. In approving the plant, the Commission allowed Mississippi Power to increase rates to finance the $3 billion plant. The Sierra Club challenged the decision, alleging that the Commission failed to justify the rate

---

48. "The Illusion of Clean Coal," *The Economist* (March 5, 2009), available at http://www.economist.com/node/13235041.

49. Pulmer, B., "Sucking carbon dioxide out of the air: Neat idea, but impractical," *The Washington Post* (Apr. 5, 2012), available at http://www.washingtonpost.com/blogs/wonkblog/post/sucking-carbon-dioxide-out-of-the-air-neat-idea-but-infeasible/2012/04/05/gIQA3t8rxS_blog.html.

increase before the plant was operational as required by law.[50] The Mississippi Supreme Court agreed, unanimously holding that state law required the Commission *make decisions based on substantial evidence and that the Commission's approval of the rate increase failed to satisfy this requirement.*[51] *In response,* the Commission reissued approval for the plant, including a 21 percent rate increase. The Sierra Club immediately appealed the decision on the same grounds, adding a claim regarding the constitutionality of the state's Baseload Act,[52] which permits the Commission to factor financing costs into electricity rates before a plant is operational to encourage development in the state. For better or worse, the controversy stalled the development of clean coal and created public awareness about the issue. Even if carbon emissions from coal can be sequestered underground, the effects of mountaintop removal, groundwater contamination, and valley fill are significant environmental issues.[53] Let's now turn to another contentious source of energy, but one that at least contributes significantly less carbon dioxide to global warming.

2. Nuclear Energy

Another method of energy production, one that has often spurred passionate debate, is nuclear energy. Opposition is largely based on the presence of radioactive material and the looming potential for catastrophe. There is also a belief that nuclear reactors are unstable and inherently more dangerous in the event of a disaster than an oil spill or the valley fill from coal mining. While other issues are relevant to the dispute concerning the desirability of nuclear power, including the ability and cost to store nuclear waste,

---

50. Marshall, C., "Legal settlement reached over 'clean' coal plant in Miss.," *E&E Reporter* (Friday, January 25, 2013).

51. *Sierra Club v. Mississippi Public Service Com'n*, 882 So.3d 618, 618 (Miss. Sp. Ct.).

52. Rate determination; construction cancellation; prudence reviews; professional service contracts; appeals, Miss. Code Ann. § 77-3-105 (2008).

53. "Quit Coal," *Greenpeace*, available at http://www.greenpeace.org/usa/en/campaigns/actions/quit-coal-chicago/.

protection from radiation hazards appears to be the major item of public concern. As of 2013, there were 104 nuclear reactors in America, providing about one-fifth of the nation's electricity.[54] Some political leaders have called for continued expansion of U.S. nuclear energy supply, while others argue that energy efficiency, cogeneration, and renewable sources could just as easily meet energy needs. Also, because nuclear energy does not burn fossil fuel or contribute greenhouse gases to the atmosphere, some environmentalists support nuclear power as an alternative to fossil fuels. However, the threat of nuclear disaster tends to destabilize this fragile support base. For example, Japan's Fukushima Daiichi began to leak radioactive waste after an earthquake and tsunami caused significant damage in the area. The accident heightened awareness of public safety in the United States, where there have been a total of forty-seven serious accidents at nuclear facilities, increasing in frequency as the reactors age,[55] costing between $1.5 and $2 billion.[56]

The federal government has often relied on tax credits and subsidies to pique interest in new technology for safer nuclear power.[57] Subsidies and tax credits for nuclear development have even been incorporated into proposed federal legislation,[58] but as the price of alternative energy and natural gas continue to fall, it

---

54. "The 30 Year Itch," *The Economist*, Feb. 18, 2012, http://www.economist.com/node/21547803.

55. The Government Accountability Office found that "all 65 sites where nuclear plants are located in the United States have experienced leakage or spillage of radioactive material into groundwater, some of which is attributable to aging underground pipes." Northey, H., "Pipes Under Nuclear Plants are Leaking," *Environment & Energy Daily* (June 22, 2011), http://www.eenews.net/public/EEDaily/2011/06/22/10.

56. Herbert, B., Op.-Ed., "We're Not Ready," *New York Times* (July 20, 2010), available at http://www.nytimes.com/2010/07/20/opinion/20herbert.html.

57. Deutch, J. and Moniz, E., "How to Prevent the Next Energy Crisis," *New York Times* (Aug. 14, 2003) p. A25.

58. Johnston, D., "Size of Proposed Tax Breaks in Energy Bill Startles Experts," *New York Times* (Nov. 19, 2003) p. A18.

gets harder to argue that nuclear energy is still competitive.[59] The cost of nuclear power roughly quintupled between the 1970s and the early 1990s,[60] currently costing 12 to 20 cents per kilowatt-hour, almost double traditional fuels. There is also a concern that subsidies and tax breaks for nuclear facilities would take away from developing and providing market access for renewable energy sources.[61]

Under the Atomic Energy Act, regulation of nuclear energy facilities and protection against radiation hazards was vested in the federal Nuclear Regulatory Commission (NRC), the successor to the Atomic Energy Commission (AEC).[62] This authority includes the licensing of nuclear power facilities. In response to the above-mentioned concerns, some states have enacted various types of state legislation to provide additional control over or protection from nuclear power. The leading case on this topic is *Northern States Power Company v. State of Minnesota.*[63] In *Northern States*, the AEC had issued an operating license to a power company, but Minnesota sought to impose more stringent conditions on the allowable level of radioactive discharge. The state argued that, while the Atomic Energy Act did not expressly allow more stringent state controls with respect to the radioactive waste releases, it neither expressly nor implicitly disallowed more stringent state control; i.e., it did not preempt the state's authority to more strictly regulate such waste releases. The United States Court of Appeals for the Eighth Circuit found that, although there was no express preemption in the Atomic Energy Act, preemption was

---

59. Powers, D., "Nuclear Energy Loses Cost Advantage," *New York Times* (July 26, 2010), available at http://www.nytimes.com/2010/07/27/business/global/27iht-renuke.html.

60. Cooper, M., "Nuclear Safety and Nuclear Economics," *Symposium on the Future of Nuclear Power*, University of Pittsburgh (March 27-28, 2012).

61. Powers, D., "Nuclear Energy Loses Cost Advantage," *New York Times* (July 26, 2010), available at http://www.nytimes.com/2010/07/27/business/global/27iht-renuke.html.

62. 42 U.S.C.S. § 2011 et seq.

63. 447 F.2d 1143.

implied by Congress's intent to displace all state regulation in that field. The implication was based on the legislative history and the pervasiveness of the federal regulatory scheme. The court determined that the nature of nuclear power required uniform nationwide controls in order to effectuate the objectives of Congress under the Atomic Energy Act. States efforts to regulate nuclear power plants with respect to radiation hazards were therefore invalid.[64] The Eighth Circuit's decision was affirmed without an opinion by the United States Supreme Court.[65] However, the issue of state regulation did not end there. The issue of what control states may exercise over nuclear power facilities was further contested in the courts in *Pacific Gas and Electric Co. v. State Energy Resources, Etc.*[66] *Northern States* had said that there can be no state regulation with respect to radiation hazards. In *Pacific Gas*, the question was whether a California statute is invalid due to its having been preempted by the federal Atomic Energy Act. The California statute conditions nuclear power plant construction on findings by a state commission that adequate storage facilities and means of disposal are available for high-level nuclear waste. The Ninth Circuit Court of Appeals in *Pacific Gas* decided that this California statute was not preempted since it was based on the economic aspects of nuclear waste disposal rather than on radiation safety concerns. The United States Supreme Court, by a 9 to 0 vote, upheld California's right, as a state, to prevent nuclear power plant construction for economic reasons even if the federal government would license a plant as being safe.[67] If a state wants to regulate such areas as nuclear fuel disposal or other areas involving radiation hazards, could it not frame its statutory purposes and legislative history to show economic or other legitimate concerns rather than radiation hazard concerns and thus circumvent the federal preemption that Congress was found to have intended in the

---

64. A more detailed discussion of the issue of federal preemption is provided in Ch. 3.

65. 405 U.S. 1035.

66. 659 F.2d 903.

67. 461 U.S. 190.

Northern States case?

In 2012, the NRC approved construction of the first new nuclear reactors since the Three Mile Island accident in 1979, two each in Georgia and South Carolina.[68] The gap in construction highlights one of the major issues facing nuclear energy in the U.S.–aging nuclear energy reactors, some of which have been in operation for much longer than the forty years they were designed to last. The NRC has issued sixty-six licenses extending the operating lifetime of reactors by twenty years.[69] In response, states have attempted to block the NRC's extensions and shut down nuclear facilities within their borders, relying on their regulatory authority over environmental issues. One recent example, the Vermont Yankee Nuclear Power Plant, provides one-third of Vermont's energy. The facility was granted a forty-year license in 1972, set to expire in 2012.[70] In 2006, the Vermont General Assembly passed Vermont Act 160 to prevent an extension of the reactor's license without legislative approval. Despite the lack of state legislative approval for continued operation, the federal NRC extended Vermont Yankee's license through 2032. Entergy, the plant's operator, alleged that the Atomic Energy Act preempted Vermont Act 160, and that any decision-making power lay with the NRC, not the state. Both the District Court and the Second Circuit agreed that the Atomic Energy Act preempted Vermont Act 160, basing their decisions in part on the Vermont legislature's consideration of radiological safety concerns, which had been determined in the *Northern States Power* case, above, to be the exclusive concern of the NRC.[71] While experts contended that the Atomic Energy Act is

---

68. "The 30 Year Itch," *The Economist*, Feb. 18, 2012, http://www.economist.com/node/21547803.

69. Donn, J., "Tritium Leaks Found at Many Nuke Sites," *Associated Press* (June 21, 2011), http://www.ap.org/company/awards/part-ii-aging-nukes; see also Hurst, T., "Will Fukushima Pull a Vermont Nuclear Plant Off the Rails?" *Reuters* (March 31, 2011).

70. Metzger, G., "The Story of Vermont Yankee: A Cautionary Tale of Judicial Review and Nuclear Waste," *Columbia Law Sch. Pub. Law & Legal Theory Working Paper Grp.*, Paper No. 0592 (2005), available at http:// lsr.nellco.org/cgi/viewcontent.cgi?article=1016&context=columbia_pllt.

71. 838 F.Supp.2d 183

a "dual track regulatory process," and that the state is authorized to act on everything except radiological health and safety, which falls under the exclusive authority of the NRC,[72] the Second Circuit held that the Atomic Energy Act preempts states' ability to regulate safety, which is a federal responsibility.[73] Regardless of the outcome in the Second Circuit, the tension between state and federal regulation of nuclear power plants will likely find its way to the U.S. Supreme Court again in some case, but not in the Vermont Yankee case. After the Second Circuit opinion in its favor, Entergy announced that it will voluntarily close the Vermont Yankee Nuclear Power Plant, likely because of the large increase in the availability of natural gas and thus the reduced demand for nuclear power.[74]

3. Natural Gas

The United States is closer to energy independence than ever before, in large part due to shale gas and oil. The gas and oil, trapped under layers of shale rock, has emerged as a leading source of energy in the country. Hydraulic Fracturing, or fracking, the process of extracting natural gas and oil, could potentially release over 50 trillion cubic feet of natural gas previously thought unrecoverable within the Marcellus Shale Formation, located beneath Pennsylvania, West Virginia, New York, Ohio, Virginia, and Maryland. Other formations, like the Bakken formation in North Dakota, have attracted more than 150 gas and oil companies over a short time period. These companies use fracking to produce

---

72. Parenteau, P., "Vermont Yankee Debate Heats Up On Two Fronts," *NPR* (Oct. 24, 2012) available at http://www.vpr.net/news_detail/96334/vermont-yankee-debate-heats-up-on-two-fronts/.

73. *Entergy Nuclear Vermont Yankee, LLC v. Shumlin*, 12-707-CV L, 2013 WL 4081696 (2d Cir. Aug. 14, 2013).

74. Wald, M., "Vermont Yankee Plant to Close Next Year as the Nuclear Industry Retrenches," *New York Times* (Aug. 27, 2013), available at http://www.nytimes.com/2013/08/28/science/entergy-announces-closing-of-vermont-nuclear-plant.html?smid=pl-share.

.

660,000 barrels of shale oil a day— making North Dakota the second-largest oil producing state in America.[75] Fracking, currently used to produce 90 percent of U.S. oil and natural gas, uses injection wells to pump pressurized water and chemicals into shale bedrock beneath the earth's surface. When the pressure of the fracking liquid exceeds the tensile strength of the rock, the rock fractures, and fracturing fluid fills and extends the cracks. It is through these cracks that the natural gas and oil come to the earth's surface. Due to the cost of processing natural gas, a significant portion is flared off as developers wait for the oil to emerge. In North Dakota, where 29 percent of the natural gas is flared off in favor of shale oil, the night-time glow from the fracking fields can be seen from space.[76]

Because natural gas is technically and financially low risk and emits lower amounts of carbon than other fossil fuels,[77] it not only has the potential to increase domestic energy supply, but it could help the U.S. reduce greenhouse gas emissions and reach the standards of the Kyoto Protocol by 2020.[78] Even though the electricity generated from burning natural gas results in significantly less carbon dioxide than burning coal, it raises a host of other environmental concerns, including the safety of our groundwater and potential geological instability resulting in the release of methane, also a greenhouse gas, and previously sequestered hydrocarbons.[79] There is little agreement over the significance of the release of methane previously trapped within the

---

75. Krulwich, R., "A Mysterious Path of Light Shows up in the North Dakota Dark," NPR (Jan. 16, 2013) available at http://www.npr.org/blogs/krulwich/2013/01/16/169511949/a-mysterious-patch-of-light-shows-up-in-the-north-dakota-dark.

76. *Ibid.*

77. International Energy Agency <http://www.iea.org/topics/naturalgas/>

78. Carey, J., "How Unconventional Oil and Gas is Supercharging the U.S. Economy," *Forbes* (Dec. 13, 2012), http://www.forbes.com/sites/energysource/2012/12/13/how-unconventional-oil-and-gas-is-transforming-the-u-s-economy/.

79. Entine, J., "New York Times Blunders into Advocacy Role on the Fracking Debate," *Forbes* (Oct. 3, 2012), http://www.forbes.com/sites/jonentine/2012/10/03/new-york-times-blunders-into-advocacy-role-on-the-fracking-debate-children-are-the-victims/.

bedrock.[80] Some argue that the effects have been exaggerated, but recent data from M.I.T. indicate that well-to-burner emissions from fracking are 4 to 9 percent higher than for conventional gas.[81] As natural gas becomes an increasingly significant component of the U.S. domestic fuel supply, the uncertainty of the impacts of fracking become increasingly important. Many argue that the government should put a moratorium on fracking until scientists can confirm whether it is safe for groundwater supplies. The Department of Energy (DoE) responded to this uncertainty by establishing an advisory panel to identify any "immediate steps" that could be taken to improve the safety and environmental performance of fracking. In addition to the panel, Congress requested that EPA conduct a study on the impact of fracking on drinking water, weighing whether new federal guidelines are necessary.[82] The DoE report called for standards to limit air emissions, but failed to make recommendations on what agency or existing laws should regulate the practice. Many saw the panel's report as a governmental endorsement of fracking that would encourage domestic exploration of natural gas extraction.[83] Others felt that the panel's findings were biased because six of the seven members had financial ties to the oil and gas industry.[84] This was

---

80. Ekstrom, V., "Study: Fugitive methane from shale gas production less than previously thought," *MIT News* (Nov. 29, 2012), http://web.mit.edu/newsoffice/2012/fugitive-methane-from-shale-less-than-thought.html.

81. Vaidyanathan, G., "The entire natural gas system is driving methane emissions -- MIT study," *EnergyWire* (November 28, 2012), available at http://eenews.net/public/ energywire/2012/11/28/1.

82. Data will not be released until 2014. "EPA Releases Update on Ongoing Hydraulic Fracturing Study," (Dec. 21, 2012), available at http://yosemite.epa.gov/opa/admpress. nsf/d0cf6618525a9efb85257359003fb69d/4af0024955d936ef85257adb0058aa29!OpenD ocument.

83. Eilperin, J., "Energy Department panel to endorse shale gas exploration," *The Washington Post* (Aug. 11, 2011), available at http://www.washingtonpost.com/ national/health-science/energy-department-panel-to-endorse-shale-gas- exploration/2011/08/10/gIQAXqbh7I_story.html.

84. "Scientists Protests Makeup of DoE Natural Gas Panel," Environmental Working Group (Aug. 10, 2011), available at http://www.ewg.org/news/newsreleases/

not the first time concerns about the gas and oil industry's influences have been raised. After backing away from claims that fracking contaminated groundwater in Wyoming and Pennsylvania, E.P.A. officials have recently reported that contamination from injection wells is significantly under-reported.[85] The gas and oil industry contends that hydraulic fracturing is safe when a well is constructed correctly, but the difficulty of conducting, reporting and interpreting the results of studies on fracking has resulted in a lack of regulation of the process.

Of the numerous environmental concerns fracking raises, the most significant may be groundwater contamination. As we discussed, fracking involves large quantities of chemical laden water. Despite these huge sources of water pollution, gas companies are exempt from federal laws protecting the nation's water supply, and fracking fluids go largely unregulated. Subsurface injection wells were regulated under the Safe Drinking Water Act's Underground Injection Control (UIC) program,[86] but in 2005, the Energy Policy Act specifically excluded fracking from UIC regulation. While the U.S. government has yet to attribute water contamination to fracking operations, this may be due to the limited availability of information about the process itself. Because natural gas companies are allowed to conceal the identities of the chemicals in their fracking fluids as trade secrets, there is no requirement that the chemicals in fracking fluids be disclosed. Those that do disclose the chemicals used do so voluntarily, often disclosing groups of chemicals, but not the concentrations or amounts. What is known about fracking fluids is that they contan petroleum distillates, which include kerosene, mineral spirits and other petroleum products containing high levels of benzene. Benzene is a known human carcinogen and is toxic in water even at very low levels. Estimates

---

2011/08/09/scientists-protest-makeup-doe-natural-gas-panel (pointing out that the chairman of the panel, John Deutch, was paid more than $1.4 million by two leading natural gas companies, Schlumberger Ltd. and Cheniere Energy, from '06-'09 alone).

85. Urbina, I., "Tainted Well Water Challenges Claim of Fracking's Safety," *New York Times* (Aug. 3, 2011), available at http://www.nytimes.com/2011/08/04/us/04natgas.html?pagewanted=all&_r=0.

86. SDWA § 1421(d).

suggest that the distillates used in a single well could contain enough benzene to contaminate more than 100 billion gallons of drinking water, and the Environmental Working Group, an environmental non-profit, has linked the contamination to water in Colorado, Ohio, Pennsylvania, Wyoming and other states.[87]

The federal government has been slow to develop regulations, in large part due to the U.S. desire to be energy independent and the negative effects that regulations have on production. But without regulation or oversight, gas and oil companies will not be held accountable, and the effects of their practices cannot be examined for environmental consequences. The Bureau of Land Management (BLM) has been instructed to develop regulations for natural gas extraction on federal and tribal lands, which would cover 25 to 30 percent of existing wells and could be used as examples for state regulation. On the estimated 700 million acres of federal and tribal lands, about 3,400 wells are drilled annually, 90 percent of which use fracking. The regulations will attempt to prevent groundwater contamination. They will likely include requirements that gas and oil companies disclose which chemicals are in their fracking fluids, set standards for well construction and the disposal of fracking fluid, and establish a permitting process for new wells. With respect to air pollution, EPA promulgated new air-quality standards for oil and natural gas wells, but extended the deadline for compliance and loosened disclosure requirements after gas companies warned that the regulations would slow gas production.[88]

While states may have the authority to regulate fracking, concerns about federal preemption have hindered significant regulation. Some states, including Kansas and North Dakota, have adopted resolutions urging Congress to delegate regulatory responsibility to the states.[89] Others, like New York and West

---

87. "Drilling Around the Law," *Environmental Working Group* (Jan. 20, 2010), available at http://www.ewg.org/drillingaroundthelaw.

88. Tracy, T., "U.S. to Set Fracking Rules on Federal Land," *Wall Street Journal* (May 3, 2012), available at http://online.wsj.com/article/SB10001424052702303877604577382 460699241978.html.

89. Kansas adopted HR 6025, and North Dakota adopted HCR 3008.

Virginia, have attempted to ban fracking by state law until more is known about its environmental impact.[90] Nineteen states have introduced hydraulic fracturing legislation, most commonly related to requiring chemical disclosure and fluid regulation. Wyoming, Michigan and Texas require full disclosure of fracking chemicals. Another approach would use permitting to restrict fracking near public water sources.[91]

Until the federal government steps in, state lawmakers will continue to debate their role in the regulation of fracking. While many industry officials favor delegation to states because a lack of federal oversight allows faster development at lower costs, some environmental groups have taken advantage of state oversight, using state laws to file lawsuits to prevent fracking projects. For example, the Center for Biological Diversity has filed several claims under the California Environmental Quality Act (CEQA), California's version of the federal National Environmental Policy Act (NEPA). CEQA requires that state and local California agencies analyze and disclose the environmental impacts of proposed projects and adopt all feasible measures to mitigate those impacts, making environmental protection a mandatory part of the agency decision making process.[92] California's Monterey and Santos shale formations hold an estimated 15 billion barrels of oil, accounting for approximately two-thirds of the shale oil in the U.S, and are lucrative spots for potential fracking projects.[93] The Center for Biological Diversity and the Sierra Club used CEQA to file a lawsuit against the California Department of Conservation, Division of Oil, Gas, and Geothermal Resources, attempting to block

---

90. New York implemented a ban on high-volume, horizontal hydrofracking until July 2011. West Virginia banned hydraulic fracturing in Morgantown and within one mile of the city's limits.

91. Senate Bill 1230 would prohibit permits to be issued for hydraulic fracturing in oil or gas wells within ten miles of the New York City water supply infrastructure; Senate Bill 1234 would also prohibit fracking near a watershed.

92. 14 California Code of Regulations § 15000.

93. "Review of Emerging Resources: Overview of U.S. Oil and Gas Shale Plays," *Energy Information Agency Report* (2011) available at http://www.eia.gov/analysis/studies/usshalegas/.

approval of a new gas well by claiming that regulators had approved permits for fracking wells without conducting analysis of the risks the projects posed to the environment.[94] The Center for Biological Diversity has also attempted to stop fracking projects under the Safe Drinking Water Act,[95] and California's Underground Injection Control program.[96] The outcomes of these adversarial cases will most likely hinge on the availability of data proving the effects of fracking, but some efforts are being made between potential adversaries to reduce litigation. Energy companies, including Shell and Chevron, are working with environmental groups, such as the Environmental Defense Fund and the Clean Air Task Force, on a voluntary agreement encouraging energy companies to submit their plans for independent review for compliance with standards designed to protect the air and water.[97]

4. Oil

There are still huge volumes of oil and gas at offshore sites and on federal land, and industry remains eager to find this energy and bring it to market; however, increased public awareness of the environmental consequences of offshore drilling and land drilling in sensitive areas has led to constant controversy about the need to use federal lands for energy production and the extent of such use. While the original versions of the Energy Policy Act of 1992 provided for oil and gas leasing of land in the Arctic National Wildlife Refuge (ANWR) in Alaska, Congress removed those provisions from the bill prior to passage. Yet Congress and the President regularly consider opening the ANWR for energy

---

94. *Center for Biological Diversity v. California Dept. of Conservation*, 2012 WL 4882970 (Cal.Super.) (Trial Pleading) (October 16, 2012).

95. *Ibid.*

96. Cal. Reg. Code §§ 1724.6-10, 3013, 3106(a), 3203, 3222, 3224.

97. "Pennsylvania: Pact Reached on Fuel Drilling," *The New York Times* (Mar. 20, 2013), available at http://www.nytimes.com/2013/03/21/us/pennsylvania-pact-reached-on-fuel-drilling.html?ref=naturalgas&_r=0.

production.[98] Those who oppose drilling in the ANWR say the energy to be gained is not worth the environmental degradation. They cite the U.S. Geological Survey's estimate that the refuge contains a recoverable equivalent of only six months' worth of oil, and even that would not be available for 10 years.[99] They further contend that, while the actual extent of environmental damage may be unknown, oil drilling and wilderness cannot coexist,[100] and that history has shown that the extent of environmental damage from oil production has been greater than estimated. The environmental impact statement for Alaska's Prudhoe Bay oil field predicted the destruction of 6000 acres of wildlife habitat, but at least 11,000 acres were destroyed. Those who favor drilling in the ANWR stress the need for U.S. energy independence, and they cite studies that show exploration can be done in an environmentally safe way, and that there is extremely high promise for finding a great amount of untapped oil beneath the ANWR.[101] They also point out that most, although not all, people in Alaska support oil development and think that oil is not mutually exclusive with wildlife and wilderness.[102] Of course, opponents would be quick to point out that local support for oil development is somewhat biased in that Alaska abolished its state income tax based on oil revenues and that practically every adult and child in Alaska receives an annual check, (generally $1000 - $2000) from the state's oil royalty fund. Regardless of one's position on using federal lands in general, and

---

98. Broder, J., "New and Frozen Frontier Awaits Offshore Oil Drilling," *New York Times* (May 23, 2012) http://www.nytimes.com/2012/05/24/science/earth/shell-arctic-ocean-drilling-stands-to-open-new-oil-frontier.html?smid=pl-share.

99. "USGS Release: USGS Oil and Gas Resource Estimates Updated for National Petroleum Reserve in Alaska (NPRA)," (Oct. 26, 2010), usgs.gov (ANWR contains approximately 896 million barrels of conventional, undiscovered oil).

100. Clements, C., "No Blood for Oil? United States National Security, Oil, and the Arctic Wildlife Refuge," 28 *Wm. & Mary Environmental Law and Policy Review* 87 (Fall, 2003) p. 112.

101. *Ibid.*, p. 111.

102. D'Oro, R., "Alaskans Keen to Explore State's Resources," *Associated Press, Washington Post* (December 28, 2003), p. A9.

the ANWR in particular, for increasing our supply of energy, it is clear the controversy will continue.

Let us next use the context of oil to consider issues relating to what happens when efforts to produce energy do result in disaster. These issues include liability for the consequences of disaster and responses triggered by disaster with the goal of preventing future disasters. In 1990, largely in response to concerns over the Exxon Valdez tanker spill of over 10 million gallons of oil in the pristine Prince William Sound area of Alaska, the Oil Pollution Act (OPA) was signed into law.[103] The statute contains a liability system that covers oil spills in navigable waters, in the 200-mile coastal zone, and along the nation's shorelines. The liability limits were increased from the $150 per gross ton of the vessel amount under the Clean Water Act to $1200 per ton under the OPA. Responsible parties may also be held liable for harm above this much higher limit if the release of oil is due to gross negligence, willful misconduct, or a violation of federal operating regulations. In those situations, the statute provides for unlimited liability. In addition, the OPA does not preempt state law remedies, and thus responsible parties may be liable under state law for amounts even higher than the increased federal limits.

With respect to federal cleanup activity, the Act established an Oil Spill Liability Trust Fund, under which up to one billion dollars would be available per oil spill.[104] This fund is designed to pay for cleanups in situations such as insolvency of the responsible party or harm in excess of that party's liability limitation. It is, however, from the Oil Pollution Act's personnel and construction standards that the greatest increase in preventative environmental protection can be derived. Standards have been significantly tightened for personnel staffing, training, and licensing, with special emphasis on preventing alcohol and drug-related problems. Beyond demanding greater competence and integrity of the people running the tanker, the structural integrity of the tanker itself has been increased. Construction standards now require that all new tankers have

---

103. 33 U.S.C.A. § 40.

104. 104 Stat. 484, 26 U.S.C. § 9509.

double hulls to reduce spill possibilities, and, as of 2010, all existing single-hulled vessels were to be phased out.[105] At the time of their enactment, these construction standards set the United States apart from other nations in the international shipping community. If other countries decided not to follow the U.S. lead, many oil shipping companies could simply boycott U.S. ports. Congress apparently thought that would not happen, or, if it did, the negative effects were worth the added environmental protection to be gained. The double hull requirement raises the importance of international solutions for environmental problems of international significance, but also suggests that if international agreement is not forthcoming, perhaps an individual nation needs to lead the way where technology is available to protect the environment.

2010 brought another oil spill disaster when British Petroleum's Deepwater Horizon exploded in the Gulf of Mexico, causing one of the biggest oil spills in history at over 4.9 million barrels of oil. After paying $4.5 billion in fines and other penalties and pleading guilty to 14 criminal charges, BP may still face billions of dollars in penalties under the Oil Pollution Act or the Clean Water Act. Fines under the Clean Water Act are based on the degree of negligence and range from $5.4 to $21 billion. Under the Oil Pollution Act, BP could face additional fines of as much as $31 billion. In response to the spill, the Secretary of the U.S. Department of the Interior ordered inspections of all deepwater operations in the Gulf of Mexico, established the Outer Continental Shelf Safety Oversight Board within the Department of the Interior, and launched a joint investigation of the spill with the U.S. Coast Guard. In addition, the Department of the Interior imposed a six-month moratorium on offshore drilling and established an Outer Continental Shelf safety review board to make recommendations on offshore drilling in the Gulf. Oil companies sought and were granted a preliminary injunction forbidding the moratorium from taking effect, which was upheld by the U.S. Court of Appeals for the Fifth Circuit. While numerous attempts were made to enact legislation in response to the

---

105. 104 Stat. 517, 46 U.S.C. § 3703a.

spill, reform legislation failed to be enacted,[106] and the only changes have been safety regulations at the agency level. The Department of the Interior (DOI) restructured management of natural gas, oil, and mineral resources on the outer continental shelf (OCS), splitting the duties of the Minerals Management Services (MMS), previously responsible for those resources, into three separate divisions. The Bureau of Ocean Energy Management oversees energy leasing, the Bureau of Safety and Environmental Enforcement oversees safety and enforcement, and the Office of Natural Resources Revenue oversees revenue collection.[107] In 2011, in an effort to better enforce laws and regulations applicable to oil and gas companies drilling on the OCS, the new structure delegated safety and environmental functions to an independent unit.[108]

5. Hydroelectric Power

Hydroelectric energy is the oldest major source of non-carbon, renewable energy. Conventional hydroelectric generation uses gravity or the energy of a river's flow to produce electricity, either by storing water behind a dam or using the river's current to turn the blades of a turbine. The Department of Energy estimates that the U.S. generates over 300 billion kwh of electricity from hydropower plants, a figure that could increase by as much as 25 percent if undeveloped rivers were dammed. There are many reasons why hydropower is a beneficial source of energy, including a relatively low cost of 3 to 5 cents per kwh.[109] Without the costs associated with transporting fuel, and because hydro plants are functional for an average of 50 to 100 years, operating costs are low. Because

---

106. Schrope, N., "Lessons of Deepwater Horizon still not learned," *Nature* (Apr. 17, 2012), available at http://www.nature.com/news/lessons-of-deepwater-horizon-still-not-learned-1.10455.

107. Salazar, K., "Secretarial Order No. 3299," (May 19, 2010).

108. Salazar, K., "Salazar Launches Safety and Environmental Protection Reforms to Toughen Oversight of Offshore Oil and Gas Operations," (May 11, 2010), available at http://www.doi.gov.

109. "Use and Capacity of Global Hydropower Increases," *Worldwatch Institute* (2013), available at http://www.worldwatch.org/node/9527.

hydroelectric dams do not burn fossil fuel, their carbon dioxide emissions are low as well. However, there are a number of reasons why hydroelectric power is not entirely beneficial, the primary reason being that dams often rely on reservoirs which destroy large ecosystems, productive lowlands, marshlands, and grassland. The disruption of river flow affects many species, specifically the fish that use the river to spawn, and also scours riverbeds and riverbanks. The diversion of water has introduced numerous questions about water rights, leading to disagreements that often need to be resolved by the courts. For example, in 1963, the U.S. Supreme Court apportioned water among the lower-basin states along the Colorado River.[110] Today, the rights to the water of the Colorado River, as well as the impact of dams and canals, continue to cause controversy.

Hydroelectric power was among the types of renewable energy that Congress sought to encourage by mandating a guaranteed market that required existing utility providers purchase the hydroelectric power generated by other entities.[111] The Supreme Court validated that approach,[112] but the increase in generation was minimal, and generation continues to fall short of expectations. Most likely, this is because the environmental movement has historically opposed to the expansion of hydroelectric facilities. It is difficult to separate the environmental benefits, such as the reduction in greenhouse gas emissions, from the stigma of ecosystems destroyed by dams. Additionally, U.S. environmental law favors water conservation and river restoration, such as efforts to remove dysfunctional dams along Washington's Elwha River and multibillion-dollar restorations of the inland delta near San Francisco Bay.[113] Furthermore, dam operation often falls under

---

110. *Arizona v. California*, 373 U.S. 546.

111. The Public Utility Regulatory Policies Act of 1978, 16 U.S.C.A. § 824a *et seq.* (2000).

112. *American Paper Inst., v. American Electric Power Servs. Corp.*, 461 U.S. 402, 423.

113. "Workers Start Dismantling Dams In Wash.," NPR (Sept. 15, 2011) available at http://www.npr.org/2011/09/15/140513390/workers-start-to-dismantle-dams-in-olympic-peninsula; Sommer, L., "Resotre the California Delta!" NPR (Oct. 7, 2012), available at http://www.npr.org/2012/10/07/162393931/restore-california-delta-to-what-exactly.

environmental laws, including the Clean Water Act and the Endangered Species Act, which have been used to establish mandatory flow conditions to protect at risk species. In *PUD No. 1 of Jefferson County v. Washington Department of Ecology*,[114] the Supreme Court held that the Federal Energy Regulatory Commission (FERC) must accept conditions imposed by the state, including minimum flow or environmental flow release conditions on FERC licensees. Therefore, dam operations are currently regulated under the Clean Water Act, and must acquire discharge permits that do not violate state water quality standards.[115] There are approximately 2,400 hydropower dams in the U.S, and the Department of Energy recently funded modernization of seven hydropower projects at existing facilities. The fund, providing $30.6 million, was established to increase the supply of clean energy without having to build new facilities. While the future of energy production in the U.S. favors low-emission options, it is difficult to say whether hydroelectricity will be a big part of that future. California has called for the construction of new hydroelectric dams to help meet the state's ambitious greenhouse gas emission targets,[116] and, in Colorado, a hydropower plant built in 1910 was modernized to increase generation by 30 percent. The DoE has also begun to focus on tidal energy, funding projects in Maine and in Long Island Sound.[117]

6. Alternative Energy (Wind, Solar, Geothermal, Biomass)

Despite reliance on coal and oil, carbon emissions reached a 20-year low in 2012, partially due to alternative sources of energy.[118]

---

114. 511 U.S. 700.

115. 33 U.S.C.A. § 1312.

116. Jaffe, I., "Schwarzenegger Unveils Ambitious Building Plans," NPR (Jan. 10, 2007), available at http://www.npr.org/templates/story/story.php?storyId=6777763.

117. < http://energy.gov/articles/turbines-nyc-east-river-will-provide-power-9500-residents>

118. Ekstrom, V., "Study: Fugitive methane from shale gas production less than previously thought," *MIT News* (Nov. 29, 2012), http://web.mit.edu/newsoffice/

Alternative energy terminology differs among users and is often overlapping. Sustainable energy can be thought of as energy with little or no environmental impact and that meets current needs without compromising the ability to meet future needs. Renewable energy is energy that comes from resources like sunlight, wind, oceans, and geothermal heat. Green energy is produced from solar, wind, geothermal, biogas, biomass, or low-impact small hydroelectric sources, sources that are renewable but not necessarily sustainable. Clean energy is a combination of energy efficiency and renewable energy sources. Alternative energy has its pluses, but it is not without minuses as well. For example, not all alternative sources of energy are sustainable, and some cause environmental and economic harm. 40% of the U.S. corn crop goes toward the production of ethanol for fuel, which in turn has driven up food prices and created other environmental issues related to land use. In this section, we will discuss renewable energy and green energy. New types of energy will require innovation which will require investment of capital. Some investors appear to think that renewable energy is not only good news for society's environment but also good news for investors, yet others familiar with the business of investing have doubts and have compared the boom in investing in renewable energy to the excessive enthusiasm of the dotcom boom.[119]

a. Renewable Energy

The discussion of renewable energy starts with the premise that renewable energy is good for the environment and raises the question of whether it is economically sustainable. Does renewable energy require governmental subsidies to make it profitable? Should innovation in renewable energy be left to the private sector and the wisdom of scientists, investors and the free market? How should renewable energy be regulated? Solar energy is the most abundant energy resource on earth, but accounts for 0.03% of U.S.

2012/fugitive-methane-from-shale-less-than-thought.html.

119. "Green Dreams –The risky boom in the clean energy business," *The Economist* (November 18-24, 2006).

energy production.[120] The technology for solar power has been around since 1954, but demand continues to increase. The U.S. is the fourth largest solar market in the world, producing more than 3300 megawatts of solar power. While the cost of installing solar arrays can be high, it is not necessarily the materials or the installation, but the costs associated with zoning, permitting, inspection and hooking a system up to the grid that raise the price well above traditional energy sources.[121] The U.S. is constructing the largest solar energy project in the world in California's Mojave Desert, relying on 350,000 mirrors to reflect light onto water, which boils and creates steam to turn a turbine.[122]

Over $14 billion was invested in wind energy in 2011, accounting for 32 percent of all new U.S. electric capacity. Wind, a widely available resource, has the capacity to produce 60,000 megawatts of electricity, enough to power 12 million homes annually—or every home in California—with 66 utilities contracted for active wind-farm projects, accounting for three and a half percent of U.S. electricity generation. Not only has this increased the amount of renewable energy used, but it also supports the U.S. economy because 70 percent of the equipment installed was produced domestically. The potential for offshore wind could increase supply, but currently faces high cost, infrastructure, and regulatory challenges, specifically, the leasing and permitting processes.

Despite a record number of wind turbine installations in 2012, due to a delay in extending a wind power tax credit worth 2.2 cents for each kilowatt-hour of electricity generated, construction all but halted in early 2013. The federal subsidy for solar power, a tax credit for 30% of the cost of installed equipment, extends through

---

120. "North American Energy Inventory," *Institute for Energy Research* 17 (Dec. 2011).

121. According to the DoE, the local permitting and inspection processes adds more than $2500 to the cost of a solar energy system (http://energy.gov/science-innovation/energy-sources/renewable-energy/solar).

122. Revkin, A., "California Utility Looks to Mojave Desert Project for Solar Power," *New York Times* (Feb. 11, 2011), available at www.nytimes.com/2009/02/12/science/earth/12solar.html.

2016. Many argue that federal involvement in these industries is no longer necessary, and that wind and solar power should attempt to operate in the free market.[123] Those in favor of subsidies argue that they provide a necessary edge for the development of wind and solar power, without which they will not be able to compete with the lower cost of electricity produced from coal and natural gas. Estimates from the DoE indicate that onshore wind power will be equal in cost to the baseline price grid power by 2016, and that solar photovoltaic energy will be largely cost-competitive at the residential level in California by 2017 and in many other states shortly thereafter. Government subsidies are designed to enable new technologies to achieve price stability in challenging markets. Without the infrastructure that is already in place for energy sources like oil and gas, wind and solar need governmental help to overcome barriers to production and delivery. Government subsidies have enabled rapid technical advances and incentivized installation. Those opposed to government subsidies argue that subsidies are not making wind or solar energy affordable and are spreading the cost to taxpayers instead of producers and consumers. They also argue that subsidies mask the viability of both solar and wind power. When considering the cost of different types of energy without governmental subsidies, cost per kwh is lowest for natural gas at 6.5 cents, increases to 9.5 cents for coal and 9.6 cents for on-shore wind, and then jumps to 21.2 cents for solar power.[124] While wind energy appears to be competitive with traditional energy sources, whether or not continued subsidies of solar energy will result in competitiveness is not known.

b. Green Energy

Bio-fuels are derived from plant material, including corn, sugarcane, or grasses. The fuels can be used in vehicles, like

---

123. Tracy, R., "Wind Power Installations Set Record in 2012," *Wall Street Journal* (Jan. 30, 2013) available at http://online.wsj.com/article/SB10001424127887323701 9045782742300016130030.html.

124. "North American Energy Inventory," *Institute for Energy Research* 18 (December, 2011).

bioethanol, or biodiesel. In 2010, 28 billion gallons of bio-fuels were produced worldwide, accounting for 2.7% of the world's energy. Other sources of bio-fuel include algae and bacteria, which hold enormous potential for the future. As discussed in Chapter 4, bioethanol production challenges the assumption that renewable energy is environmentally good. Brazil's conversion of half of its sugar crop into ethanol for cars has contributed to the doubling of world sugar prices. Ethanol is not unique: rapeseed in Europe and palm oil from Malaysia are being used in increasing amounts for biodiesel instead of food. Many environmentalists think that food crops should be used to feed people, not cars,[125] and that using food crops such as corn for ethanol production provides only a marginally positive energy balance while driving up food prices.[126] In response, the government recently enacted the Energy Independence and Security Act,[127] which increases the production of renewable fuel but caps the amount of corn-based ethanol at 15 billion gallons and requires refineries to use non-grain crop sources for the remaining 21 billion gallons required under the Act. A recent study suggests that 27 million acres of marginal farmland unsuitable for food crops could be used to produce more than 20 million gallons of bio-fuels a year. Whether or not the crops would be reliable would dictate profitability.[128] Cellulose from non-food crops such as switchgrass and waste biomass could also provide a better energy balance producing twice as much ethanol per hectare as corn.[129] Others argue that because they are inefficient, bio-fuels could never account for a substantial portion of the energy produced. Some have said that even if every crop produced on earth

---

125. Brown, L., "Starving the People to Feed the Cars," Washington Post (Sept. 10, 2006) B03.

126. McElroy, M., "The Ethanol Illusion," *Harvard Magazine* (Nov.-Dec., 2006) p. 33.

127. 42 U.S.C.A. § 17155.

128. Harris, R., "Could Some Midwest Land Support New Biofuel Refineries?" *NPR* (Jan. 16, 2013) available at http://www.npr.org/2013/01/16/169538570/could-some-midwest-land-support-new-biofuel-refineries.

129. "Fuels gold–Are biofuels really the greenhouse-busting answer to our energy woes?" *NewScientist* (Sept. 23, 2006) p. 36, www.newscientist.com.

were used to produce bio-fuels, which would only produce about 14 percent of world energy needs.[130]

The future of biofuels and whether they can develop as sound alternatives to fossil fuels without infringing on the availability of food at affordable prices for all the people of the world may rest in the hands of research facilities such as the National Biofuel Energy Lab, a partnership between NextEnergy, Inc., Michigan's non-profit energy accelerator and Wayne State University. The lab, located in Detroit and funded by the U.S. Department of Energy, is the first-of-its-kind bio-fuel technology development lab.[131]

---

130. Searchinger, T., associate research scholar at Princeton University, from Harris, R., "Could Some Midwest Land Support New Biofuel Refineries?" *National Public Radio* (Jan. 16, 2013), available at http://www.npr.org/2013/01/16/169538570/could-some-midwest-land-support-new-biofuel-refineries.

131. "College Partners With NextEnergy," *Exemplar, Wayne State University College of Engineering* (Fall, 2006) p.7.

CHAPTER 8
GLOBAL ENVIRONMENTAL LAW

A. SUBSETS OF GLOBAL ENVIRONMENTAL LAW

When many people refer to environmental law in a context that encompasses matters outside their own country, they generally use "international environmental law" as the title of their topic. A better title might be "global environmental law" because international environmental law is only one of three subsets of global environmental law. The other two are comparative environmental law and extraterritorial application and effects of national environmental law. Let's begin by seeing how these parts of the global environmental law matrix are different from each other. We will then consider the importance of having environmental control mechanisms in each of the subsets of global environmental law along with specific examples of what those control mechanisms are and how they work.

International environmental law is law which is applicable to more than one country. The most common example is where nations become parties to a treaty such as The Montreal Protocol concerning stratospheric ozone depletion.[1] When the required number of countries stated in the treaty become parties to the treaty and the treaty thus "enters into force," those countries have expressly created international law. International law can also be created implicitly. This happens when there is a uniform practice followed by most nations, when general principles of law are recognized by nations, or when judicial decisions and writings by

---

1. <www.unep.org/ozone/montreal>

respected scholars indicate that nations have agreed, albeit without a treaty. This is known as customary international law.

An example of customary international law involved transboundary air pollution and the then newly discovered possibility of the phenomenon of acid rain. An arbitral tribunal was constituted to decide what should be done about the Trail Smelter in Canada whose emissions were going to the State of Washington in the U.S. and causing damage. The damage may have been greater than usual when the emissions mixed with precipitation. The tribunal said:

> [N]o State has the right to use or permit the use of its territory in such a manner as to cause injury by fumes in or to the territory of another or the properties or persons therein . . . .[2]

A nation's sovereignty over activities in its territory is therefore limited by its responsibility to not cause damage outside of its territory. This customary international environmental law principle of limiting sovereignty was also stated in Principle 21 of the Declaration of The United Nations Conference on the Human Environment which said that countries have the "responsibility to ensure that activities within their jurisdiction or control do not cause damage to the environment of other States or of areas beyond the limits of national jurisdiction."[3] Customary international law does play a role in international environmental law, but most international environmental law involves treaties. These will be discussed in Section C of this chapter.

International environmental law usually pertains to situations where activities in one country cause effects in other nations or to the global commons. Our second subset of global environmental law, extraterritorial application of national environmental law, also has effects outside the borders of the nation in which the activity takes place, but this body of environmental law is not international. It is not composed of treaties and customary international

---

2. 3 R. Int'l. Arb. Awards 1905.

3. U.N. Doc. A/Conf. 48/14/Rev. 1. This language is also part of Article 3 of the U.N. Framework Convention on Biological Diversity, www.biodiv.org/convention and 31 I.L.M. 818.

principles. Rather, it is the law of an individual country, but it may have environmental effects on other countries. Two examples of national law with extraterritorial effects that have been discussed earlier in this book are U.S. law with respect to the export of solid waste and pesticides. Concerning solid waste export, U.S. law is largely passive. By having no law, we allow the potentially adverse extraterritorial effects of export. In the pesticide area, we go beyond being passive. Our federal pesticide legislation explicitly allows unregistered and banned pesticides manufactured in the U.S. to be exported. Although this is a hotly debated topic and many efforts have been made to change this law, we do, with respect to pesticide export, specifically allow extraterritorial effects which may be adverse but which some people say are not adverse and may even be beneficial.[4] Three additional examples of national laws or non-laws with significant possibilities for extraterritorial effects will be discussed in Section B. These will be the U.S. National Environmental Policy Act (NEPA), Brazil's allowing of rainforest cutting, and the labeling laws of Austria and the European Community which have been designed to encourage environmental protection through the use of consumer buying power.

Our third subset of global environmental law is comparative environmental law. This facet of global environmental law also involves national as opposed to international law. Comparative law asks how do two or more individual nations, each using its own national law, deal with the same or similar factual situations that exist in their nations. A fact situation in a country may or may not have extraterritorial effects, but extraterritorial effects is not the focus of comparative law. Comparative law is primarily interested in the differences and similarities with respect to the approaches that nations would use to handle the situation. If an environmental dispute involving land use exists between neighbors, how will it be resolved in the People's Republic of China compared to in the United States? Will the Russian government, like the U.S. government, conduct a site specific analysis to value the actual harm that an oil spill has caused to a natural resource? Might the culture of some nations allow them to successfully achieve

---

4. 7 U.S.C. § 136(o), discussed in Chapter 6.

environmental protection without the use of law? Comparative environmental law looks at the differences and similarities in approaches and asks questions such as are the differences explainable and appropriate in view of different cultures, geography, economics, etc., or should efforts be made to determine which is the "best" approach and to encourage uniform use of that approach. These comparative environmental law examples and issues will be discussed in Section D.

B. EXTRATERRITORIAL APPLICATION AND EFFECTS OF NATIONAL LAW

There are many activities that take place within the borders of one nation but have very significant effects outside that nation—effects on other nations directly or effects on parts of the global commons such as air and oceans. Unless there is international law like a treaty, these activities are subject only to the national law of the country in which they are located. If the national law of that country does not apply to environmental effects outside the country, and if the activity does not produce environmental effects within the country that trigger environmental controls, the activity is not subject to any environmental controls. In the United States, the National Environmental Policy Act (NEPA) is one context that raises the issue of whether extraterritorial effects will trigger U.S. environmental control mechanisms.[5] As discussed in Chapter 2, NEPA requires that all agencies of the federal government prepare an environmental impact statement (EIS) for any major federal action significantly affecting the quality of the human environment. Do environmental effects outside of the United States which would result from federal agency action fall within NEPA's EIS requirement, or are those effects not subject to NEPA's environmental controls?

The extraterritorial application of NEPA issue has been

---

5. Other contexts include the Resource Conservation and Recovery Act with respect to extraterritorial disposal of hazardous waste by private parties—not applicable, *Amlon Metals, Inc. v. FMC Corp.*, 775 F. Supp. 668, and air pollution controls on greenhouse gas emissions, such as CO_2, under the Clean Air Act or otherwise.

contested for many years in numerous factual situations including highway construction in Central America involving the U.S. Department of Transportation,[6] the exporting of nuclear power plant components to the Philippines,[7] and the U.S. Army's transporting 100,000 artillery shells containing nerve gas in Germany.[8] NEPA appears to have a domestic orientation since it asks the federal government to "assure for all Americans safe, healthful, productive, and aesthetically and culturally pleasing surroundings."[9] Yet, it also says that all agencies of the federal government shall:

> ...recognize the worldwide and long-range character of environmental problems and, where consistent with the foreign policy of the United States, lend appropriate support to initiatives, resolutions, and programs designed to maximize international cooperation in anticipating and preventing a decline in the quality of mankind's world environment.[10]

Thus, the language of NEPA itself is not totally clear on the issue of extraterritorial applicability. The courts have also not provided clear answers concerning NEPA's extraterritorial applicability. An EIS was required for the military to conduct a simulated nuclear explosion on a Pacific atoll, but, at least in part, the decision was based on the site being in a U.S. Trust Territory.[11] In the cases discussed above involving export of nuclear power plant components and the transportation of nerve gas, the courts' decisions not to require an EIS reflected concern about interference with U.S. foreign policy. Making the situation even murkier is

---

6. *Sierra Club v. Adams*, 578 F.2d 389.

7. *Natural Resources Defense Council, Inc. v. Nuclear Reg. Comm.*, 647 F.2d 1345.

8. *Greenpeace USA v. Stone*, 748 F. Supp. 749.

9. PL 91-190, § 101(b)(2).

10. PL 91-190, § 102(F).

11. *People of Enewetak v. Laird*, 353 F. Supp. 811.

Executive Order 12114.[12] E.O. 12114 establishes an environmental review process for extraterritorial effects of government actions, but expressly states that the authority for the process comes from the President rather than NEPA. It therefore might be said to take the position that NEPA does not have extraterritorial applicability. This would be irrelevant if the E.O. environmental review process were the same as the EIS requirement of NEPA, but it differs significantly.

Although an EIS is required under the Executive Order for federal actions affecting the global commons (e.g. the oceans or Antarctica), lesser evaluations, "environmental studies" or "concise reviews of the environmental issues," are sufficient for effects in countries that are not participating or involved with the U.S. agency action, and no environmental evaluation is required for effects in a country that is "participating."[13] While this non-review position may be defended on the grounds of not wanting to interfere with the sovereignty of another nation, one should at least question the degree to which an impoverished Third World country, dependent on foreign aid, can be said to be "voluntarily" agreeing to a U.S. activity that may result in environmental harm.

Another important difference between NEPA and E.O. 12114 is that the Executive Order says:

> This Order is solely for the purpose of establishing internal procedures for Federal agencies . . . and nothing in this Order shall be construed to create a cause of action [in a court].

This provision led the court in the case of *Environmental Defense Fund, Inc. v. Massey*,[14] to say:

> Thus, what is at stake in this litigation is whether a federal agency may decide to take actions significantly affecting the

---

12. 3 CFR 356.

13. E.O. 12114, § 2-4.

14. 986 F.2d 528, 530.

human environment in Antarctica without complying with NEPA and without being subject to judicial review.

In *Massey*, the National Science Foundation (NSF) contended that it did not need to do an EIS prior to operating its incinerator in Antarctica because NEPA does not apply to federal agency actions outside the U.S. It also contended that E.O. 12114, which it said covers extraterritorial environmental analysis, does not create a cause of action, and, therefore, courts do not have jurisdiction to hear cases alleging that an agency has not followed the E.O. procedures. The Federal District Court granted NSF's motion to dismiss the case, clearly stating that "NEPA does not apply extraterritorially and Executive Order 12114 does not provide for a private cause of action."[15] The U.S. Circuit Court of Appeals for the District of Columbia found that NEPA did apply to the Antarctica incineration proposal, and it reversed the District Court decision.

The Circuit Court in *Massey* noted the U.S. Supreme Court's general presumption against extraterritorial application of statutes. The primary purpose of that presumption is "to protect against the unintended clashes between our laws and those of other nations which could result in international discord."[16] The court in *Massey*, however, found this presumption to be inapplicable because to apply NEPA would not tend toward international discord. First, the NEPA EIS process is designed to control decision-making by an agency, not the substance of the agency decision. The decision-making process is done in the U.S., regardless of the fact that the incineration would be in Antarctica. Thus there are no issues of international discord. Second, since Antarctica, under the Antarctic Treaty of 1961, is not subject to the sovereign rule of any nation, there is no potential for conflict between U.S. law and that of other nations. The conflict avoidance purpose of the presumption against extraterritorial application is not present.

---

15. 772 F. Supp. 1296, 1298.

16. *Equal Employment Opportunity Comm. v. Arabian American Oil Co.*, 111 S. Ct. 1227.

The Circuit Court found that NEPA is applicable to agency action in Antarctica. It barely mentioned E.O. 12114 and certainly did not find it reduced the agency's responsibility to comply with the EIS requirements of NEPA. So where does the issue of the extraterritorial application of NEPA stand? The *Massey* decision applies only to effects in Antarctica and is not a broad declaration that NEPA applies extraterritorially. In fact the court concluded: "[W]e do not decide today how NEPA might apply to actions in a case involving an actual foreign sovereign . . . ." The court also noted that NEPA's EIS requirement may yield where overriding policy concerns such as national security are present. *Massey* was cited in the case of *Natural Resources Defense Council v. U.S. Department of the Navy*[17] which held that the general presumption against extraterritorial application of U.S. statutes did not apply to the Navy sonar testing program on the open sea or in the U.S. Exclusive Economic Zone and NEPA was applicable, but the interface between NEPA's applicability and national security was raised again, as discussed in Chapter 2, in *Winter v. Natural Resources Defense Counsel.*[18] In *Winter*, national security was central to the Court exempting the U.S. Navy from preparing an Environmental Impact Statement (EIS) before conducting a series of training exercises using mid-frequency active sonar in the Pacific Ocean off the southern California coast because the exercises were essential to national security. The Court held that "the Navy's need to conduct realistic training exercises to ensure that it is able to neutralize the threat posed by enemy submarines" outweighed the "ecological, scientific, and recreational interests in marine mammals."[19]

After all the years of controversy and litigation, shouldn't NEPA be amended to clarify, one way or the other, its application to environmental impacts outside the land mass of the United States? With respect to the substance of such a clarification,

---

17. 555 U.S. 7 (2008).

18. 555 U.S. 7.

19. *Ibid.* at 33.

shouldn't the environmental evaluation required by NEPA be the same regardless of whether the environmental effects of government action will be outside or inside the borders of the United States? Indeed, Congress, in another environmentally related statute, did amend that statute to make it applicable to activities outside the United States. The National Historic Preservation Act now requires federal agencies to take into account the effects that their undertakings in other countries may have on properties that are on the World Heritage List or the other country's equivalent of the U.S. National Register of Historic Places.[20] A U.S. federal court invoked that amendment to require the Department of Defense to consider the effects of its activities in Okinawa, Japan, on the habitat of the Okinawa dugong, a marine mammal that is a protected "natural monument" on the Japanese Register established under Japan's "Law for the Protection of Cultural Properties." The Japanese Register and the U.S. Register were found to be equivalent, thus triggering the extraterritorial aspects of the U.S. National Historic Preservation Act.[21]

We should note that environmental law often operates in a larger context, and the Okinawa dugong case is a good example of that. Besides the legal issue of extraterritorial application of domestic law, the practical issue with respect to the Okinawa dugong case centers around the fact that a large percentage of Okinawans oppose U.S. military bases in Okinawa. In total, Okinawa is home to two-thirds of the 40,000 American forces in Japan, accounting for fourteen U.S. military bases on 90 square miles occupying 18% of the main island. While the Japanese government likes the U.S. military presence, in large part because it precludes Japan from spending money on national defense, the majority of the U.S. military presence is located in Okinawa.[22] The crux of the issue may stem from the fact that Okinawans and the Japanese government have not always seen eye to eye, perhaps

---

20. 16 U.S.C. §470a-2.

21. *Okinawa Dugong (Dugong Dugon) v. Rumsfeld*, 2005 U.S. Dist. LEXIS 3123.

22. Fackler, M., "Amid Image of Ire Toward U.S. Bases, Okinawans' True Views Vary," *New York Times* p. A6 (Feb. 15, 2012).

because Okinawa, originally part of the Ryukyu Kingdom, was annexed by Japan in 1879.

Another area of friction between Okinawa and the Japanese government is that Japan fought the last battle of World War II in Okinawa, resulting in the death of a quarter of the island's population. Yet another factor is that the Okinawans contend that they have long been discriminated against by the "mainland" Japanese. As a result of opposition by Okinawa, the U.S. is in the process of reducing its military presence in Okinawa by relocating many of the troops to the U.S. territory of Guam.[23] Of course, re-locating troops to Guam raises a host of issues, including a limited infrastructure and resources as well as ongoing issues stemming from the U.S. failure to provide reparations to that island's indigenous people, the Chamorros, who fought against the Japanese invasion of the island during World War II. Returning to our central topic of extraterritorial application of national law, in 2013 the U.S. Supreme Court in *Kiobel v. Royal Dutch Petroleum*, reaffirmed that absent a contrary intent of Congress, there is a presumption against extraterritorial application of U.S. statutes.[24]

Our second example of the extraterritorial application and effects of national law is the cutting and burning of the rainforest in Brazil. The topic of extraterritorial application of the national law of Brazil is much less developed than that of U.S. scenario, but the extraterritorial effects on the global commons may be more important, more difficult to ascertain, and more difficult to control than those from a relatively small incinerator activity in Antarctica. Until recently, there were virtually no controls in Brazil to prevent rainforest destruction. In fact, there were government incentives that encouraged deforestation. From the 1960s through the 1980s, Brazil tried to develop the Amazon by exempting farmers and ranchers from income and other taxes.[25] Those who cleared the

---

23. "US to return Okinawa air base area to Japan," *BBC World News* (Apr. 5, 2013) available at http://www.bbc.co.uk/news/world-asia-22039186.

24. 1325 S.Ct. 1659 (2013).

25. "Slower Rate of Amazon Deforestation Due to Economic Crisis, Expert Says," *International Environment Reporter* (April 22, 1992) p. 241.

rainforest for agriculture were the beneficiaries of the tax incentives, while the losers were global climate and global biological diversity.

Burning the rainforest has produced billions of tons of carbon dioxide which builds up in the atmosphere and traps Earth's heat. This is the greenhouse effect and results in global warming. In addition, with fewer trees due to burning or cutting of the rainforest, less CO_2 is taken out of the atmosphere and converted to oxygen in the photosynthesis process. This also contributes to the greenhouse effect. Besides global climate effects, rainforest deforestation destroys some of the world's richest areas of biological diversity. This leads to a vast array of environmental consequences, known and unknown in both types and magnitudes. Among these are destruction of the ecological processes that keep the Earth in balance and fit for life and destruction of genetic stocks which may be important for the future health and nutrition of humans. Indeed, the importance of the topics of global warming and biological diversity, both related to rainforest destruction, is underscored by their being the subject of the two treaties that came out of UNCED, the United Nations Conference on Environment and Development, held at Rio de Janeiro and known as the Earth Summit.[26]

The tax incentives that encouraged deforestation in Brazil were discontinued beginning in 1989, but the reasons that led Brazil to encourage deforestation for agricultural purposes had not disappeared. Brazil was experiencing rapid economic growth when world oil prices skyrocketed in 1973. As a huge importer of oil, Brazil was faced with scaling back its prospering economy or increasing foreign borrowing. It borrowed with hopes for lower oil prices in the future and a continuation of the increase in demand for Brazil's exports. Oil prices stayed high, global recession reduced export profits, and interest rates rose dramatically, with the result being unmanageable debt. Brazil turned to its primary asset—the Amazon rainforest.[27]

---

26. U.N. Framework Convention on Climate Change and U.N. Framework Convention on Biological Diversity, *International Environment Reporter Reference File 1*, 21:3901 and 21:4001.

27. Lazarus, A., "A War Worth Fighting: The Ongoing Battle to Save the Brazilian

Brazil contends that rainforest destruction has been brought under control, but a Smithsonian Tropical Research Institute study says otherwise.[28] If Amazon deforestation has not dropped or has not dropped enough, why, with the huge potential for global impacts, does Brazil not enact national law that would stop rainforest destruction and prevent extraterritorial adverse effects? The question is largely one of rich nations and poor nations, developed countries and the less developed countries, north and south.

The poorer, developing countries take the position that the richer, developed nations achieved their success without environmental restrictions or concern for the rest of the world. Now the "haves" want the "have nots" to be environmentally responsible for the good of all. The people of the developing countries also have a different view of what are the significant environmental problems. This is not a new conflict. In the 1972 Declaration of The United Nations Conference on the Human Environment (Stockholm Conference), it was proclaimed that:

4. In the developing countries most of the environmental problems are caused by under-development. Millions continue to live far below the minimum levels required for a decent human existence, deprived of adequate food and clothing, shelter and education, health and sanitation. Therefore, the developing countries must direct their efforts to development, bearing in mind their priorities and the need to safeguard and improve the environment. For the same purpose, the industrialized countries should make efforts to reduce the gap between themselves and the developing countries. In the industrialized countries, environmental problems are generally related to industrialization and technological development.[29]

Amazon," 9 *NAFTA L. & Bus. Rev. Am.* 399 (Spring, 2003).

28. McDonough, B., "Brazilian Government Disputes Bleak Amazon Deforestation Outlook," *NewsFactor Network* (January 29, 2002), available at http://science.newsfactor.com/story.xhtml?story_id=16038.

29. U.N. Doc. A/ Conf. 48/14/Rev. 1.

The United Nations Framework Convention on Climate Change contains a similar perspective:

> 7. The extent to which developing country Parties will effectively implement their commitments under the Convention will depend on the effective implementation by developed country Parties of their commitments under the Convention related to financial resources and transfer of technology and will take fully into account that economic and social development and poverty eradication are the first and overriding priorities of the developing country Parties.[30]

The ability to close the gap between the highly divergent standards of living in developed and developing countries is complicated by the tremendous foreign debt owed by Third World countries. This debt load puts great pressure on poor nations to expand their economies at the expense of environmental concerns. With respect to Brazil and its rainforest, transactions have taken place whereby Brazil has swapped some of its more than $100 billion in foreign debt for commitments to protect rainforest land (debt-for-nature swaps).[31] In response to the spread of debt-for-nature swaps beyond the Western Hemisphere, Congress enacted the Tropical Forest Conservation Act (TFCA) to extend debt reduction opportunities to developing countries with tropical forests around the world.[32] Swaps were originally privately funded and subsidized by grants from USAID, but are increasingly funded publically with subsidies from small NGOs. In 2009, the United States and Indonesia negotiated the largest swap under TFCA. Indonesia has one of the fastest rates of deforestation in the world. The United States pledged to forgive $30 million in debt for an

---

30. *International Environment Reporter Reference File 1*, 21:3901.

31. Knickley, J., "Debt, Nature, and Indigenous Rights: Twenty-Five Years of Debt-for-Nature Evolution," *36 Harv. Envtl. L. Rev. 79* (2012).

32. 22 U.S.C. § 2431 (2006).

agreement to protect forests on Sumatra Island. The swaps have sometimes imposed conditions of economic reform in order for the debtor country to obtain the debt reduction from the swap. To debtor nations, debt-for-nature swaps, with or without economic conditions, raise the issue of loss of sovereignty over their land, their resources, and their economy. To some people, this loss of sovereignty may be far worse than being in debt. The real answer to preventing the extraterritorial impacts from destruction of rainforests is probably enabling some form of sustainable income for the people. If a poor nation is to be expected to take action to protect its land from being depleted of its economically valuable resources, it must be able to provide for the current needs of its people and for improving their standard of living. It must be assisted in achieving sustainable development of its resources. One recent example is the UN's project, Reducing Emissions from Deforestation and Forest Degradation (REDD), designed to complement cuts in emissions in developing countries.[33] REDD offers incentives to developing countries to reduce emissions from forests and invest in low-carbon sustainable development. REDD+ introduced incentives for sustainable forest management and forest carbon stocks.

Our third example of national law with extraterritorial effects is labeling of products to indicate their consistency with environmental protection. Here we do not have to stray from our discussion of tropical forests to begin our discussion. Austrian law required a label showing the origin of tropical wood and tropical wood products. This law allowed consumers to make their purchasing choices with awareness that obtaining the wood may have contributed to adverse environmental effects. After a threatened boycott of all Austrian products by tropical timber exporting countries, Austria abandoned the labeling requirement. It is also possible that the Austrian economic labeling measure would have been invalid under world trade agreements because Austria had no tropical forests of its own to protect, and the imports would not harm anyone in Austria. It was using a purely extraterritorial

---

33. <http://www.un-redd.org/aboutredd/tabid/582/default.aspx>

measure to improve the environment in other nations.[34] On a broader scale, the European Community (EC or EU), a group of nations but acting as a single nation under law established by the Community, has adopted "eco-labeling" for most consumer products excluding foods and medical goods.[35] The eco-label will inform consumers that the product with the label is less damaging to the environment than other products. With 340 million EU consumers, there is great potential for market forces to provide significant environmental protection. In order to be awarded the eco-label, a product must have "a reduced environmental impact compared with other products in the same product group." Criteria to meet this test are established for groups of products.[36] Although these reduced impacts may be on the people or the ecosystems within the EU, they may be in other nations and affect the environmental conduct of other nations who are exporting their products to the EU. For example, foreign manufacturers or nations may decide not to use certain types of tropical wood in their furniture. The EU, of which Austria is now a member, appears to be convinced that it can use its "national law" to promote extraterritorial improvements for the environment without violating world trade agreements.

C. INTERNATIONAL ENVIRONMENTAL LAW

The most commonly discussed subset of global environmental law is international environmental law. International law also holds the greatest promise for solving environmental problems if the nations of the world can agree on what the problems are and on unified action to prevent or remedy those problems. The paramount example of international law's ability to recognize a problem, enact

---

34. Gaines, S., "Processes and Production Methods: How to Produce Sound Policy for Environmental PPM-Based Trade Measures?," 27 *Columbia Journal of Environmental Law* 383, 402 (2002).

35. Regulation (EC) No. 1980/2000 of the European Parliament.

36. Examples: tissue paper products, Decision 2001/405/EC; laundry detergents, Decision 2003/200/EC.

a solution, and apparently achieve success is the Montreal Protocol on Substances That Deplete the Ozone Layer.[37] The Montreal Protocol is a treaty, or more properly, it is an amendment ("Protocol") to a treaty (in this case, the Vienna Convention for the Protection of the Ozone Layer). Treaties, also known as "conventions," are the most meaningful form of international environmental law. We noted customary environmental law earlier as a way of implicitly establishing principles such as a nation's responsibility to not cause damage outside its territory, and we will later consider United Nations' resolutions and programs as part of international environmental law, but our focus in this section will be treaties—express agreements by more than one country that establish law that is applicable to more than one country.

There are many ways to categorize treaties such as: (1) Are they between two countries (bilateral) or are they multilateral? (2) Do they use financial liability to remedy problems or do they create a system of preventative controls? (3) Do they establish a separate entity with power to act in a situation or do they rely on the individual parties to the treaty to each act themselves? (4) Are they merely statements of cooperative intentions, are they frameworks for future treaties but non-binding in and of themselves, or do they establish substantive mechanisms to control an environmental problem? and (5) Are they treaties directed specifically at environmental issues or are they treaties that are directed at other subject matter like trade but have significant environmental implications? We will discuss a number of treaties that are examples of these various approaches of international environmental law. Let's begin with what is now projected to be a dramatic international environmental success story—The Montreal Protocol.

The significance of The Montreal Protocol begins with the magnitude and timing of the stratospheric ozone layer depletion issue. Although possible depletion of the ozone layer that shields Earth from ultraviolet radiation was raised in 1974,[38] it only became

---

37. <www.unep.org/ozone/montreal>

38. Molina, M., and Rowland, F., "Stratospheric Sink for Chlorofluoromethanes: Chlorine Atom—Catalyzed Destruction of Ozone," *Nature* (1974) pp. 910-12. Molina,

widely publicized in 1985. By 1989, a treaty to protect the ozone layer, The Montreal Protocol, had been drafted, agreed to, and formally ratified by 29 countries and the European Community—enough to have the treaty enter into force.[39] In the international environmental law timeframe, the elapsed time between acknowledging the problem and "in force" standards to solve the ozone problem is unrivaled in its brevity. Of greatest importance, the treaty appears to be working. The rate of ozone layer depletion has slowed, and scientists say that the Antarctic ozone hole could fully recover in 50 years.[40] A short explanation of the process and effects of ozone layer depletion will indicate why the international community was motivated to act so quickly.

Photochemical reactions in the stratosphere constantly create and destroy ozone, but the presence of chlorofluorocarbons (CFCs), halons, and other gases alter the balance. These gases, having been produced at ground level, migrate to the stratosphere where they are broken down due to ultraviolet radiation, and the breakdown releases chlorine from the CFCs and bromine from the halons. Chlorine and bromine atoms react with ozone to destroy the ozone without destroying themselves. They remain and continue destroying more ozone, and, therefore, a small amount of chlorine or bromine can destroy a large amount of ozone. Increased ultraviolet radiation because of lack of protection from the ozone layer has numerous possible effects. Among the more publicized are skin cancer, depression of the human immune system, and reduced crop yields due to a decrease in photosynthesis. Others include fading paint, more eye cataracts, and harm to phytoplankton which are the source of food for most fish. The type, variety, and magnitude of the effects of ozone layer depletion, especially the public's reaction to getting cancer from simply being outdoors, make it easy to understand the need for quick action and why action

---

Rowland, and Paul Crutzen who had pointed out possible ozone layer depletion in 1970, received the Nobel Prize for chemistry in 1995 for their ozone layer work.

39. Montreal Protocol, Article 16, Entry into Force.

40. Gardner, G., *State of the World 2003: A Worldwatch Institute Report on Progress Toward a Sustainable Society* (2013).

actually was taken.

The Montreal Protocol is a multilateral treaty that contains specific control measures to stop ozone layer depletion and allow its "regrowth." It requires that each party to the treaty act to create its own national law to achieve the targets and timetables established in the treaty. As amended, it has control measures and control levels in Articles 2, 2A-E, and Article 3 with respect to the production and consumption of CFCs, Halons, Carbon Tetrachloride, and other ozone depleting substances. Phaseout levels and schedules were provided, and all new CFCs are now banned in industrialized countries. Consumption in developed countries is now virtually zero, but some problems remain. These include consumption in developing countries, illegal trade, and other chemicals such as methyl bromide.[41]

In our discussion of the issue of rainforest protection, we noted the divergent economic situations and thus divergent perspectives held by the developed as opposed to the developing countries. The Montreal Protocol about ozone layer depletion sought to account for the "Special Situation of Developing Countries"—the title of Article 5. For example, a developing country whose annual level of consumption of Annex A controlled substances was less than 0.3 kilograms per capita was entitled to delay its compliance with the control measures for 10 years. In addition, Articles 10 and 10A required that developing countries be provided with financial and technological assistance including the transfer "under fair and most favorable conditions" of "the best available, environmentally safe substitutes and related technologies." Further, Article 5 notes that for developing countries to meet even the delayed compliance schedule will depend upon the effective implementation of financial co-operation and transfer of technology. The Montreal Protocol thus sought to achieve unity by not demanding uniformity for all nations regardless of their ability to take steps toward environmental protection. The grace period for developing nations has now ended, and they are in their "compliance period," but because of their high

---

41. "Remaining Challenges," *UNEP*, available at www.unep.org/ozone/public_information/.

rates of economic growth, their consumption of CFCs has been increasing.[42] It is hoped that the Multilateral Fund established in Article 10, referred to above, will help ensure phaseout in developing countries.

Illegal trade in CFCs is another continuing problem. There are millions of used but functioning refrigerators, air conditioners, etc. in the developed countries, and, while there are alternative chemicals for servicing these units instead of using CFCs, they are expensive. Also, illegally sold new CFCs are cheaper for the consumer than legal recycled CFCs. In addition to illegal CFCs, there are Montreal Protocol issues involving legal or potentially legal chemicals. One of them is methyl bromide. Methyl bromide is a pesticide used on strawberries, tomatoes, and other crops. It is banned by the Montreal Protocol for use in developed countries, but exemptions can be obtained if there is a "critical use" for the substance. The United States and other industrialized countries would like exemptions because they contend that alternatives that have methyl bromide's soil-sterilizing properties are either untested or too expensive.[43] They claim that methyl bromide can be used without endangering the recovery of the ozone layer. Critics, however, contend that alternatives are readily available. They also say the increase in the size of the Antarctic ozone hole in some years raises doubts about whether the optimism for long-term ozone layer recovery is premature. Methyl bromide continues to be used as a strawberry fumigant in the U.S. at least in part because alternative products may be even more harmful.[44] For example, methyl iodide, an ozone friendly substitute, was approved by EPA, but it poses health risks to farm workers that are worse than the risks from methyl bromide. Dissemination of information about these risks resulted in reduced use and lower profits for the

---

42. Bradsher, K., "Moving Faster on Refrigerant Chemicals," *New York Times* (March 15, 2007) p. C3.

43. Revkin, A., "U.S. to Seek Support for Ozone Exemptions at Meetings," *New York Times* (November 10, 2003) p. A12.

44. 2015 Critical Use-Exemption Nominations from the Phaseout of Methyl Bromide, www.epa.gov/ozone/mbr/2015.

manufacturer, and methyl iodide was taken off the U.S. market by its manufacturer in 2012.[45]

Assuming that the Montreal Protocol will continue to show signs of success in ozone layer recovery, perhaps that success will serve to boost our ability to solve other global environmental problems through international law. It is important, however, to remember that the evidence was quite clear with respect to ozone layer depletion and that the adverse effects would be catastrophic, would manifest themselves quickly, and would include at least one effect to which everyone can relate—cancer. With respect to the topic of global climate change, consensus about the science has been slower to emerge. Even today, there are those who contend that greenhouse gases, such as CO_2 from burning fossil fuels, cannot reliably be said to be causing global warming, but the cause-effect relationship seems to have moved toward consensus. Yet, other hurdles are impeding global controls for preventing climate change. When people think of changing agricultural patterns, they don't envision worldwide famine. Rising sea levels would be critical for some, such as inhabitants of small island nations, but most people do not feel directly threatened by rising sea levels. There is also the perception that, if it happens at all, it will be gradual and adjustments in lifestyle can be made. It's not quite like imminent cancer with nowhere to hide. Probably of greatest significance by way of comparing the world's reluctance to confront climate change with its rapid unity concerning ozone layer depletion is the matter of cost. On a relative basis, phasing out CFCs costs next to nothing compared to the economics of reducing fossil fuel burning and other causes contributing to global warming.

The Kyoto Protocol to the United Nations Framework Convention on Climate Change (UNFCCC)[46] is another example of an international treaty with binding obligations to reduce greenhouse gas emissions and thereby prevent anthropogenic global

---

45. Philpott, T, "Bye Bye, Cancer-Causing Strawberry Fumigant," *Mother Jones* (March, 2013), available at www.motherjones.com/tom-philpott/2012/03/strawberries-methyl-iodide-cancer.

46. <http://unfccc.int/kyoto_protocol/items/2830.php>

warming. Most UN member nations, with such notable exceptions as the United States, Canada, India, and China, are parties to the protocol. The Kyoto protocol has two phases, and many countries that participated in the first round have not taken on new targets for the second round, which began in 2013. This is likely due to widespread belief that the protocol is ineffective at impacting climate change because by targeting developed countries, the emissions targets only apply to a small share of global emissions. Countries with second-round targets account for less than one-fifth of the annual global anthropogenic greenhouse gas emissions. Without binding emissions reduction targets for developing countries, the treaty's effect is minimal. This has resulted in a fatal lack of political will, effectively rendering the treaty, as currently written and implemented, meaningless. At the seventeenth Conference of the Parties (COP) in Durban, South Africa, Canada, Japan, and Russia rejected further participation in the treaty. Canada articulated why so many developed countries are unwilling to commit to the Kyoto Protocol, namely, that it is an agreement affecting between thirty and fifteen percent of global emissions.[47] Additional criticisms include the emissions trading scheme, as opposed to a carbon tax.

In 2012, the UN held two major conferences on the UN Framework Convention on Climate Change[48] and the UN Convention on Sustainable Development.[49] The conference on sustainable development, also known as Rio+20, was the third international conference on sustainable development, and resulted in a non-binding document, "The Future We Want," reaffirming the political commitment to sustainable development and establishing Sustainable Development Goals (SDGs), targets aimed at promoting sustainable development picking up where the Millennium Development Goals left off. The conference on climate

---

47. Canada, Statement at COP-17/CMP 7: High Level Segment (Dec. 7, 2011), available at http://unfccc.int/files/meetings/durban_nov_ 2011/statements/application/pdf/111207_ cop17_hls_canada.pdf.

48. <http://unfccc.int/2860.php>

49. <http://sustainabledevelopment.un.org/>

change took place in Doha, Qatar, and member states agreed to extend the Kyoto Protocol for eight years, until 2020. Because of the lack of participation from the U.S., China, Canada, and India, the extended Kyoto Protocol will be limited to targeting reductions for fifteen percent of the global carbon dioxide emissions. Critics were not impressed with Doha, and many characterized the outcomes as "modest"[50] and deficient in terms of mitigation.[51]

For whatever reason, while scientists are concerned about global warming and conducting research about it, and while the issue has resulted in a Framework Convention on Climate Change and the Kyoto Protocol,[52] meaningful progress to stop global warming has been painfully slow or nonexistent. In fact, there appears to be a discernible shift in emphasis from stopping climate change to adapting to climate change. Examples of such adaptation efforts include investing in facilities to turn seawater into drinking water, constructing flood barriers and floating homes, and developing grains that will flourish even in a drought. The costs of adapting to climate change are astronomical, and the poorest nations, those least responsible for the buildup of the carbon dioxide that produces climate change, are least able to afford the costs of adapting to that almost inevitable change.[53]

Both treaties or conventions discussed above, the Montreal Protocol with respect to ozone layer depletion and the Climate Change Convention and Kyoto Protocol are multilateral treaties. A Multilateral treaty that goes back to 1975 for its "coming into force"

---

50. Harris, R., "At Doha Climate Talks, Results Modest at Best," *NPR* (Dec. 07, 2012) available at http://www.npr.org/2012/12/07/166748716/at-doha-climate-talks-modest-results-at-best.

51. Harriban, R., "UN Climate Talks Extend Kyoto, Promise Compensation," *BBC World News* (Dec. 8, 2012) available at http://www.bbc.co.uk/news/science-environment-20653018.

52. See discussion in Chapter 1, Section B.

53. Revkin, A., "Poorest Nations Will Bear Brunt As World Warms," *New York Times* (April 1, 2007) p. 1; "Confronting Climate Change: Avoiding the Unmanageable and Managing the Unavoidable," *American Scientist* (May-June, 2007) p. 283. The full report by Sigma Xi, The Scientific Research Society, and the United Nations Foundation can be found at www.sigmaxi.org.

date is the Convention on International Trade in Endangered Species of Wild Fauna and Flora, commonly known as CITES. A different treaty, the Convention on Biological Diversity[54] which came out of the Rio Conference at the same time as the Climate Change Convention, emphasizes entire ecosystems while CITES[55] emphasizes more than 30,000 individual species. The Biological Diversity Convention is of relatively recent vintage compared to CITES and has little developed law under it. CITES, on the other hand, has been in force for a long enough time to allow for the development of a substantial amount of law to implement its provisions. Let's consider the operative mechanisms of CITES and the various types of national law in the United States that implement its provisions—statutory law, administrative regulations, and court proceedings.

Endangered species often need protection because, whether for reasons of real usefulness, fashion, superstition, or just because they are rare, these species may fetch high prices in the marketplace. Estimates of the value of the illegal trade in endangered species vary widely, often in the $5 billion to $10 billion range. This has been said to be the third largest contraband business after illegal drugs and weapons. Some examples that have been used include giant pitcher plants from Borneo at $1000 each, Peruvian butterflies at $3000 each, rhinoceros horn at $13,000 per pound, and leopard coats selling for over $100,000. The Endangered Species Convention (CITES) divides those species that are to be protected into three categories according to the degree of threat to the species and lists those species in Appendices I, II, and III. Species of Appendix I plants and animals, dead or alive, may only be traded upon the granting of both an export permit and an import permit. Each of these permits may only be granted upon the advice of a Scientific Authority of the respective state which certifies that trade will not be detrimental to the survival of that species. For these most threatened species, CITES has thus provided that even if the exporting nation and its Scientific Authority succumb to economic

---

54. *International Environment Reporter Reference File 1*, 21:4001.

55. 27 UST 1087, TIAS No. 8249, 993 UNTS 243.

or political pressure to allow export, the importing nation may have an independent responsibility to prevent trade. Trade in Appendix I species is thus generally prohibited unless there are exceptional circumstances such as for scientific research.[56] For the less threatened species listed in Appendix II, an export permit, but not an import permit, is required. Therefore, with respect to the Chiroptera (bats/flying foxes) order of mammals, the Truk flying fox (*P.insularis*) listed in Appendix I is subject to a higher level of protection than the Big-eared flying fox (*P.macrotis*) which is part of Appendix II. Amendments to Appendices I and II listing additional species, or perhaps delisting species, are authorized to be made by agreement at periodic conferences of the parties to the treaty. A third list, Appendix III, consists of those species which any one party to the treaty designates as being subject to regulation within its jurisdiction and as needing co-operation of other parties to control trade. These species are not in the threatened or may be threatened with extinction categories but are listed by a country for the purpose of helping it prevent or restrict exploitation. If a species is listed in Appendix III, it may not be imported without an export permit, and an export permit will only be granted if the specimen was not obtained in violation of the laws of the exporting country and the specimen will be handled so as to minimize risk of injury, damage to health, and cruel treatment.

As discussed above, CITES has specific control mechanisms to protect endangered species. Those controls are implemented through national law in the countries that are parties to the treaty. Import and export permits are required under CITES and may be issued only upon the advice of a designated Scientific Authority of a country. U.S. statutory law designates the Secretary of the Interior, acting through the U.S. Fish and Wildlife Service, as the Scientific Authority.[57] CITES requires that the parties take appropriate measures to enforce the treaty and prohibit trade in violation thereof. These measures must include penalties for conducting such trade and provisions for confiscation or return of

---

56. "The CITES Appendices," available at www.cites.org.

57. 16 U.S.C. § 1537a.(a).

specimens traded in violation of the treaty.[58] U.S. statutory law provides for civil penalties, criminal sanctions, and forfeiture of the illegally traded plants or animals.[59] The day to day implementation of U.S. responsibilities under CITES such as issuing permits and dealing with enforcement is carried on by the Interior Department pursuant to its statutory authority. This agency is responsible for issuing import and export permits. Its regulations for obtaining a permit include the process for getting a permit and the information which must be provided such as how transport will occur, care during transport, and expertise of the persons who will provide care.[60] Enforcement proceedings are also initiated by Interior or other administrative agencies, and the U.S. District Courts and the U.S. Magistrates may issue enforcement orders.

One example of an enforcement proceeding that also involved an issue of interpretation of the U.S. law implementing CITES is *United States v. 3,210 Crusted Sides of Caiman Crocodilus Yacare.*[61] In *Crusted Sides*, 10,875 hides of partly tanned (thus "crusted sides") *Caiman Crocodilus Yacare*, an Appendix I endangered species, were being sent from Bolivia to France by way of Florida. The CITES permit described the shipment as 3,210 hides of *Caiman Crocodilus Crocodilus*, an Appendix II species. During a routine inspection by the U.S. Fish and Wildlife Service, the discrepancies were discovered. The court found that the government had established probable cause to institute a forfeiture action due to violation of CITES controls on trade in endangered species as implemented by 16 U.S.C. § 1538(c)(1) which says:

> It is unlawful for any person subject to the jurisdiction of the United States to engage in any trade in any specimens contrary to the provisions of the Convention or to possess any specimens traded contrary to the provisions of the Convention. . . .

---

58. CITES, Art. VIII.

59. 16 U.S.C. § 1540.

60. 50 CFR § 23.15.

61. 636 F. Supp. 1281.

It also found that the CITES export permit was improper regardless of which species was involved because it did not contain the proper number of hides. Forfeiture was thus appropriate. The parties claiming the hides argued that forfeiture should only be of the number of hides that exceeded the amount declared on the CITES permit. In deciding that all the hides were subject to forfeiture, the court said that the purpose of CITES is to prevent extinction of certain species by over-exploitation through international trade, and, to accomplish that aim, the penalties for violation of CITES must be stringent. Forfeiting only the offending hides, those in excess of the permit, would only serve to thwart the intent and undermine the effectiveness of CITES.

Has CITES worked? To some extent, yes. However, CITES' structure and philosophy is to prevent unsustainable use by limiting trade. It ignores possible mechanisms to promote sustainable use such as by addressing habitat loss, ecosystem preservation, or sustainable development. All of these impact endangered species, and without addressing these areas, the quest to protect endangered species will remain limited.

The treaties we have considered thus far in our discussion of international environmental law have been multilateral treaties open to all countries to become parties if they so choose. Other treaties are multilateral but are limited with respect to their membership. The Treaty Establishing the European Community (EC),[62] previously known as the European Economic Community (EEC) and subsequently as the European Union (EU), is a multilateral treaty of the Member States of Europe. This treaty also differs from the other treaties we have discussed in that it establishes institutions and confers powers upon those institutions whereas our other treaties left future action to each party individually or to a reconvening of all the parties. The major institutions of the EU are the European Parliament, a Council, a Commission, and a Court of Justice.

The original European Union Treaty (Treaty of Rome) did not

---

62. 37 I.L.M. 56.

expressly provide authority for environmental protection. However, currently, several sections of the Treaty on the European Union refer to the environment. For example, the treaty mandates balancing economic growth and the "sustainable development of Europe," and that EU States "foster the sustainable economic, social, and environmental development of developing countries, with the primary aim of eradicating poverty. It requires the EU to contribute to "the sustainable development of the Earth" through its international relationships, and requires that "[a] high level of environmental protection and the improvement of the quality of the environment must be integrated into the policies of the Union and ensured in accordance with the principle of sustainable development."[63] Most importantly, the treaty also identifies an objective to preserve, protect, and improve the quality of the environment. One example of this approach has been the regulation of chemical substances, which relies on the "precautionary principle" and errs on the side of safety when regulating chemical substances affecting health and the environment.[64] The EU enacted legislation concerning the Registration, Evaluation, Authorization and Restriction of Chemicals (REACH) in response to a complicated and confusing system of over forty different directives and regulations allowing environmentally harmful substances on the market. REACH relies on hazard-based criteria to identify "substances of very high concern" (SVHC).[65]

Our next treaty example, like the EU Treaty, involves a limited number of nations and utilizes a treaty created institution; however, that institution is administrative rather having the legislative capabilities of the EU Parliament, and the treaty is basically single issue oriented. This is the U.S.-Canada Agreement on Great Lakes Water Quality.[66] The U.S.-Canada Great Lakes Water Quality

---

63. *Consolidated Version of the Treaty on European Union Article 3(3).*

64. Treaty of Amsterdam Amending the Treaty on European Union, the Treaties Establishing the European Communities, and Certain Related Acts, art. 34 (Oct. 2, 1997), available at http://www.europarl.europa.eu/topics/treaty/pdf/amst-en.pdf.

65. Sand, P., *Transnational Environmental Law* 133 (1999).

66. 30 UST 1383, TIAS 9257, Amended by Protocol, TIAS 10798.

Treaty addresses the quality of a huge system of waters along an international boundary. It is a bilateral treaty—only two nations are eligible to be parties—and the institution that the treaty creates and uses for implementation is the International Joint Commission (IJC). The IJC is responsible for the collection, analysis, and dissemination of data and information concerning Great Lakes water quality and human activities that affect it such as toxic, nutrient, and heat discharges. The IJC is also responsible for making recommendations to the parties about legislation, standards, and other regulatory measures relating to water quality; however, legislative implementation is to be done by the parties themselves. The parties explicitly commit themselves to enacting necessary legislation in their countries, including the appropriation of funds, to implement the protection programs and measures provided for in the treaty. Those programs include abatement, control, and prevention of pollution from municipal and industrial sources, agricultural sources such as pesticides and animal wastes, and shipping activities. The programs contain components like construction of waste treatment facilities with target dates for their being operational, effluent limitations and evaluation processes to determine progress being made and identify emerging problems.

The primary thrust of the U.S.-Canada Great Lakes Water Quality Treaty and all the other treaties we have discussed thus far is to prevent harm by legislative and regulatory action. Some treaties take a much different approach to preventing harm and also have a goal besides prevention that is considered to be of at least equal importance—compensation for harm that has already taken place. The example of a compensation treaty approach that we will consider is actually a pair of treaties that provide a system of compensation for harm caused by oil pollution from tanker ships. These are the Civil Liability Convention and the Fund Convention.

Concern about oil pollution from ships has a long history. It is widely accepted, however, that the *Torrey Canyon* incident was the precipitating force in the creation of the modern international matrix for dealing with the issue of oil pollution from ships. The *Torrey Canyon*, carrying approximately 118,000 tons of oil, impaled herself on the rocks off the English coast in March, 1967, resulting in oil pollution expenses of an extent previously unknown, about

$15,000,000. Decades later, in the 2000s, the oil tanker industry itself estimates that tens of thousands of metric tons of oil are annually spilled into the marine environment by tankers, although this is down from being in the hundreds of thousands of tons through the mid-1990s.[67] The potential costs of cleanup and harm to humans and natural resources can be in the billions of dollars as was the case in the *Exxon Valdez* oil spill in Alaska. Although there are treaties that focus directly on oil pollution prevention such as by banning or limiting discharges of oil,[68] the Civil Liability Convention (CLC) and the Fund Convention (FC) provide for compensation for harm already done by tanker oil spills.

The CLC[69] and the FC[70] combine to form a system whereby damage caused by an oil tanker spill is paid for by the tanker owner and by the owner of the cargo, the oil. The CLC provides that the tanker owner is strictly liable for harm done. Strict liability means that if the oil caused damage, the tanker owner is liable for that damage even if the tanker owner was not negligent. Strict liability is liability without fault and is often the standard of liability used by the law with respect to harm that results from participating in dangerous activities like using dynamite or using toxic substances. If the activity causes the harm, that is itself sufficient to impose liability even if there is no wrongdoing like negligence and the harm came about due to an unpredicted storm blowing a tanker off course and onto the rocks. By providing for strict liability, the CLC is saying that transporting oil will inevitably result in some spills which are not the fault of anyone and that victims of those spills must be compensated by the businesses doing the transporting. The tanker owners bear the costs of compensation or of purchasing insurance that will compensate victims.

---

67. "Statistics," *International Tanker Owners Pollution Federation (ITOPF)*, Table 2., available at www.itopf.com.

68. The International Convention for the Prevention of Pollution from Ships (MARPOL), 17 I.L.M. 546.

69. 9 International Legal Materials 45.

70. 11 I.L.M. 284.

Although under the CLC the tanker owner is held liable even if it is not at fault (strict liability), the tanker owner's liability is limited. The maximum amount of liability is related to the capacity of the ship and is expressed in the treaty in terms of SDRs, Special Drawing Rights of the International Monetary Fund. Based on recent rates of exchange, the limits range from $7 million for small tankers up to $138 million for a tanker of 140,000 gross tons or more.[71] Thus, while the tanker owner is held strictly liable, the owner is given some protection with a ceiling on that liability. If, however, the owner is negligent, the limited liability protection does not apply.

The Fund Convention (FC) provides supplementary compensation to victims if they are not compensated fully under the CLC because the harm done by the oil spill exceeds the limited liability amount. The heart of the FC is the International Oil Pollution Compensation Fund that it established. The Fund is financed by contributions from the cargo owners—those who receive the oil after it has been carried on the sea. The cargo owners pay a levy of a given amount per ton of oil received, and the amount per ton is set annually so as to cover the anticipated need for revenue to keep the Fund viable. If a tanker spill incident causes harm in excess of the CLC limit of liability payable by the tanker owner, money from the Fund is used to provide supplementary compensation to victims so that the aggregate of compensation payable under the CLC and FC is about $312.6 million.[72] The combination of the CLC and the FC thus results in the sharing of the cost of compensating victims between the tanker owner whose ship was involved in the incident and the Fund composed of money collected from all cargo owners of all oil transported.

As of 2013, 111 countries are parties to both the CLC and the FC, but the United States is not a party to either treaty. Instead, the U.S. has its own national liability system to cover oil spills. This is

---

71. "Oil Spill Compensation," *ITOPF*, available at www.itopf.com (amounts as of October, 2012).

72. A Supplementary Fund Protocol which entered into force in 2005 can take the aggregate compensation to $1.2 billion in states that opt to ratify and that require receivers of oil in the State to finance the Supplementary Fund.

the Oil Pollution Act discussed in Section B of Chapter 7. A number of reasons have been advanced for why the U.S. should not be a part of the international system of oil pollution liability, and prominent among them is the amount of the limits on liability. There are many people who think that the U.S. should not, however, refuse to join an international arrangement that has won widespread international acceptance and which would likely be joined by many more nations if the U.S. became a party. These people contend that if the U.S. wants to obtain overall international cooperation from other nations, it must be willing to go along with reasonable international law about a specific topic even if it is not necessarily what the U.S. would prefer. Of course, this argument is vigorously advanced by many nations with respect to the U.S. refusal to ratify the Kyoto Protocol concerning global climate change.

Our discussion of international environmental law has focused on examples of categories of treaties such as preventative vs. compensating for harm, multilateral vs. bilateral, and working through an independent entity vs. working through nationally enacted laws. A far less binding form of international environmental law exists as formal documents that are not treaties. One example of this is United Nations Conference reports and resolutions, which can form the basis for the later creation of a treaty. With respect to the issue of desertification, which came into widespread recognition primarily due to problems in Africa, initial conferences, resolutions, and Plans of Action[73] resulted in a U.N. Convention to Combat Desertification.[74] Desertification affects Africa most, where two-thirds of the continent is desert or dry lands, but one fifth of Spain is said to be at risk of becoming a desert, and severe drought in parts of the United States have also raised the desertification issue. In reality though, the emphasis of the convention is on Africa—the title of the Convention itself ends with the words "Particularly in Africa."

What leads to desertification, and why have efforts thus far failed to stop the advancing deserts? The causes of desertification

---

73. A/Conf. 74/36.

74. <www.unccd.int>

are numerous and include high population growth with accompanying deforestation due to energy needs and overgrazing due to food needs.[75] The Convention seeks to remedy the problem with mechanisms such as using area-specific plans, improving land-tenure systems, empowering women and farmers, and achieving sustainability in general. Reasons for the lack of success in the past can be thought of as the logical and the questionable. Logically, deserts offer difficult climatic conditions that discourage experts from working in the areas; political instability makes continuity of efforts difficult; and cultural considerations often inhibit change. In the questionable category of reasons, one might want to think about the following. If a white, western culture of 50 million people were similarly threatened by processes of nature, would more be done? How about if a significant trading partner of developed nations were threatened—would more money be forthcoming from those developed nations? The possibility that racial and cultural discrimination interfere with solving a technologically solvable environmental problem is not, however, all one-sided. A country that has had notable success at reclaiming desert land and putting it to profitable agricultural use is Israel. A case study, "The Negev: a desert reclaimed,"[76] which was submitted by Israel to the Desertification Conference was formally denounced by a resolution of the conference, with most nations of the desertification threatened regions in Africa voting to denounce the report.

To close our discussion of international environmental law, we should note briefly that there are treaties and global organizations whose purpose for being is not environmental but trade, yet interrelationships between environment and trade are inevitable. While the European Union was founded for trade and not environmental purposes, it is clear that environmental protection is now a large part of its mandate. The World Trade Organization (WTO)[77] appears to have less in the way of an environmental

---

75. "The United Nations Convention to Combat Desertification: An Explanatory Leaflet," available at www.unccd.int/convention/text/leaflet.

76. A/CONF. 74/20.

77. <www.wto.org>

mandate or environmental goals. The treaty known as the GATT (General Agreement on Tariffs and Trade)[78] was designed in 1947 to encourage free trade,[79] but it has had numerous environmental matters before its dispute-resolution panel, including the famous tuna-dolphin dispute involving the U.S. limiting imports of tuna based on fishing practices.[80] The North American Free Trade Agreement (NAFTA)[81] seeks to eliminate trade barriers among Canada, Mexico, and the United States. A large part of the opposition to its ratification by the U.S. was concern about environmental issues such as lack of enforcement of environmental protection standards in Mexico. The treaty was ratified with a "side accord" being put into place to help resolve environmental concerns. The Commission for Environmental Cooperation (CEC) was created by the three countries as a complement to NAFTA to address regional environmental concerns and to promote effective enforcement of environmental law. Activities of the CEC range from reports to improve the tracking of transboundary hazardous waste shipments to a "green purchasing initiative."[82]

D. COMPARATIVE ENVIRONMENTAL LAW

The comparative environmental law subset of global environmental law looks at how the national law of individual countries would handle a given environmental problem. Why is the same issue resolved differently in different countries? When should a problem be approached in different ways in different nations, and when should one nation move toward adopting the approach, and perhaps the result, of another? One comparative law example we

---

78. 55 U.N.T.S. 187.

79. "GATT," *Center for International Earth Science Information Network*, available at www.ciesin.org.

80. Tuna/Dolphin Panel Report, 30 I.L.M. 1594.

81. 32 I.L.M. 605.

82. <www.cec.org>

discussed earlier was government's source of environmental power. In Part C of Chapter 1 we noted that the constitutional framework of the European Union (EU) had been amended to provide express environmental power to the EU. That may be compared to Congress' environmental power under the United States Constitution which is derived from its economic power with respect to interstate commerce—like the EU power prior to the amendments. Let's here consider three examples of how different countries deal with specific environmental problems: (1) what should be the result of a dispute between neighboring landowners due to one having negligently caused environmentally related economic harm to the other, (2) how should we value the harm to a natural resource so that we can require the cause of that harm to pay for it, and (3) how should we get people to conserve energy?

In Chapter 6, we discussed negligence law in the U.S. We saw that if someone applied a pesticide so that it went onto his or her neighbor's property and caused economic harm such as to crops or livestock, unless compensation was voluntarily paid, the injured party would likely sue the negligent party in a court and obtain compensation for the harm that was caused. Let's consider the same situation in the People's Republic of China. In the PRC, rural agricultural workers are members of communes or collectives, but they may also have private enterprises and grow produce for individual profit. Suppose X and Y are neighboring rural operators of private adjoining plots of land. X uses a chemical pesticide in a manner that allows it to drift onto Y's land, and it destroys Y's commercial cabbage crop. In such a situation, the injured party, Y, would take the dispute to the head of the collective for mediation. While there is the right to go to court in China, one goes through mediation first, and ending up in court is rare.

China strongly emphasizes mediation to bring about a reconciliation of the parties. It is to be principled peacemaking which may use persuasion and education, but not coercion. There are many possible outcomes of the mediation process with respect to X and Y.[83] X may be responsible to pay for the entire lost

---

83. These are based on an interview with Xiao Zhi yue, lawyer and Lecturer in Law, Hangzhou University, PRC.

cabbage crop, but if X can't afford to pay the entire amount, part of the loss may be paid to Y by Y's collective. There is a notion of suretyship or insurance by the collective that says Y will be protected when another collective member harms Y but cannot be given the burden to pay. Another possible result is that the victim, Y, may be left to bear part of the loss because, as a member of the collective, one is subject to some risk from actions of other members, especially if the victim does not really "need" full compensation for the destroyed cabbages. Yet another alternative would be for the collective to provide Y (the victim) with extra work so Y could have the opportunity to recover the economic loss.

Of relevance to the mediation process and to the results concerning X and Y is the undercurrent of traditional law and Confucian ideology which stress social harmony and the restoration of society's peace rather than stressing which party is legally right or wrong.[84] The goal is to have X and Y walk away from the situation with as much harmony between themselves and between each of them and the community as possible. Ill will should be minimized. This is far different than the usual American process for dispute resolution which gives us a "winner take all" court decision or a settlement of a lawsuit based on factors like economic power of the parties—could the victim afford to wait for a just remedy, or was quick settlement a matter of economic necessity? The "winner take all" decision and the economic power settlement scenarios tend to maximize rather than minimize ill will. Is the Chinese dispute resolution process and its result as far removed from American law as it sounds? Historically, yes. More recently, no. As noted in Chapter 3, the use of environmental mediation and negotiation has grown greatly in recent years. Also discussed in Chapter 3 was the *Spur Industries* case involving an existing cattle feedlot that became a nuisance when a newly developed housing project was being built. The court ordered the feedlot to close but also ordered that its relocation costs be paid by the housing developer who stood to make large profits if the feedlot closed. The result seemed to take

---

84. Lai-Wan Chan, C., "The Cultural Dilemmas in Dispute Resolution: The Chinese Experience," *Conference on Enforcing Equal Opportunities in Hong Kong; Centre for Comparative and Public Law, University of Hong Kong* (14 June 2003).

into account many of the factors discussed in our X-Y example above and perhaps gave a result designed to minimize ill will and restore the peace of society. From a different perspective, however, as China seeks more foreign investment, it may have to provide more of the type of legal protection that is familiar to foreign investors. They may want property rights to be decided based on who is predictably legally right or wrong rather than on factors such as need, ability to pay, and social harmony.

Having considered the resolution of private disputes in different legal systems, let's, as our second comparative environmental law example, see how administrative agencies in the U.S. and in Russia answer the question of how to value damage to natural resources in order to obtain payment for those damages from the party responsible for causing the harm. The legal systems of most nations have a long history of methodologies for valuing economic harm done to individual victims, but only recently has the law tried to value harm to natural resources like a coastal ecosystem or wildlife habitat. If there is an oil spill or other hazardous substance release which damages or destroys a coastal ecosystem, how can we determine the amount to charge the party responsible for the harm? If the ecosystem can be restored or replaced, perhaps the cost of the work is an appropriate measure; however, not all ecosystem losses can be replaced, and there is often a long time lag even if replacement is possible. How then do countries assess the monetary value of natural resource damages resulting from an oil spill?

The Russian system that was established under the former Soviet Union, gave a quick answer and cost very little to administer.[85] First, the amount of oil spilled was determined such as by looking at the documents to see how much the ship was carrying and then noting what remained in the ship. The spilled oil was then assumed to disperse to a concentration of 50 parts oil to one million parts water, and the hypothetical volume of impacted water was determined. The 50 parts per million concentration was considered

---

85. "Summary and Analysis of State and Selected Foreign Procedures for Determining the Costs of Natural Resource Damages From Releases of Oil or Hazardous Materials, " *Washington, DC: Office of Ocean Resources and Assessment, National Oceanic and Atmospheric Administration*, p. A-193.

to be 1000 times greater than acceptable, and the cost to restore a unit volume of impacted water to acceptable condition was obtained from cost tables which specified restoration costs for waters in different coastal regions. The amount of damage was calculated by multiplying the volume of impacted water by the restoration cost for each unit volume. The above process was done by a government administrative agency and, once you knew how much oil was spilled, it was basically a simple arithmetic problem to get the damage amount. Data gathering at the site is not needed.

The U.S. system for assessing damages to natural resources is provided in the Superfund Act[86] and Department of Interior regulations.[87] For "minor" releases of hazardous materials, a "Type A" assessment is required. This is to be done with minimal fieldwork and is to use existing data and computer models relating to units of discharge or units of affected area. This approach sounds quite similar to the former Soviet Union system described above; however, in the U.S., when a release is large or unusually damaging rather than minor, site-specific damage assessment is undertaken. In these situations, the individual site is evaluated to determine the type and extent of short- and long-term injury, destruction, or loss. Factors to be considered include "replacement value," "use value," and "the ability of the ecosystem or resource to recover." While some aspects of site-specific damage assessment such as replacement or restoration costs can be relatively precise, others are more questionable. For example, in determining "use value" of a natural resource, "travel cost methodology" may be employed. Peoples' travel costs to an area are used as a proxy for the value of the services of that area, and damages to the area are the difference between its value with and without the hazardous substance release. Presumably, if fewer visitors are willing to pay the price of getting to the area, the decrease in expenditures for traveling to the area will help measure the lost use value of the area. The cost of travel and people's interest in visiting particular areas are, however, subject to many variables other than the damage to the area caused

---

86. 42 U.S.C. § 9651(c).

87. 43 CFR Part 11.

by a substance release. Does the "travel cost methodology" described above contribute to a more precise valuation of natural resource damage, or is there only an increase in the time and money spent on valuations with no meaningful increase in the precision of the amount determined?

The ease of the Soviet and Type A U.S. approaches to natural resource damage assessment allow available time and money to be spent on environmental enhancement instead of on bureaucratic investigation of the amount of loss. On the other hand, if site-specific evaluation is done, the ability to accurately determine actual loss in a given situation may develop over time. Also, discussing the issues involved in site-specific evaluation may lead to a better understanding of what should be considered "natural resource damage." Furthermore, much of the work done to value the resource loss may provide information that can be used in the process of deciding what to do with the damaged site and in implementing that decision. Perhaps the question of spending money on site-specific evaluation of natural resource damage is a question of a country's ability or willingness to spend the capital to do such an evaluation. Or perhaps the evolution of environmental awareness makes the expense of trying to accurately value natural resource damage more justifiable. In the post-Soviet era, Russia has reformed its environmental laws and, like most countries, is making much greater efforts to consider environmental needs. While the method to be used for natural resource damage valuation in the case of harm caused by an oil spill is largely a matter of administrative discretion in Russia today, the Soviet approach of a formula based only on an amount of oil spilled has been abandoned. In practical application, the factors that may go into the administrative calculation include actual costs of dissipation, cleanup, and restoration; number of creatures killed; and whether those creatures were economically valuable or endangered/threatened species.[88]

Our comparative law examples thus far have involved considering different approaches that a legal system could use:

---

88. Reznikov, P. and Potapova, E., "Oil Spills in Russia: Penalties, Calculation of Damages," Unpublished memorandum.

resolve a property loss dispute by litigation or mediation, value a natural resource loss by fast, inexpensive, non-site-specific formulas or do site-specific damage assessment. Our last comparative law example raises the fundamental issue of whether law in any form is the way to solve environmental problems or whether societies should use other means instead of law to achieve their desired environmental ends. If the environmental goal were conservation of energy, law could impose penalties on use that would result in conservation. An example would be a "gas-guzzler" tax on low mileage automobiles.[89] Law could instead use the incentive approach such as providing a tax credit for qualified electric vehicles.[90] There are those, however, who contend that law is often not the best way to deal with environmental problems, and that other tools such as culture, tradition, and religion may be better suited to achieving environmental goals.[91] Islam teaches that humankind is the Viceregent of Allah on earth, and, as such, humankind has a trustee's responsibility to live in harmony with nature. Confucianism and Taoism link the divine, human, and natural worlds. The Judaic concept of a covenant between God and humanity and the Christian focus on sacrament and incarnation can be extended to all the natural world. Hinduism and Buddhism emphasize fulfillment of duty which often includes environmental preservation of sacred rivers and forests. Indigenous traditions have environmental ethics embedded in them, and living sustainably in their homelands is a basic part of their culture.[92] Perhaps these perspectives could be used to raise social consciousness and, without using law, encourage individuals and businesses to voluntarily conserve energy. Concerning other topics of environmental protection, perhaps some aspect of culture, religion,

---

89. 26 U.S.C. § 4064.

90. 26 U.S.C. § 30.

91. Gardner, G., "Engaging Religion in the Quest for a Sustainable World," *State of the World 2003: A Worldwatch Institute Report on Progress Toward a Sustainable Society*, Chapter 8.

92. Tucker, M. and Grim, J., "Series Forward" in Chapple, C. and Tucker, M., *Hinduism and Ecology* (Cambridge, MA: Harvard University Press, 2000).

or the tradition of family farming might be called upon to raise the social consciousness of surface mine owners so that they would respect prime agricultural land rather than our having to rely on the Surface Mining Control and Reclamation Act to keep prime agricultural land from being turned into wasteland. If we are willing to learn from Native American culture, wildlife conservation could be increased while at the same time decreasing the administrative and enforcement costs of wildlife conservation. Can social consciousness-raising work along with or maybe better than law to solve environmental problems? It is at least arguable that non-smokers may be exposed to less tobacco smoke due to the heightened social awareness of smokers than due to laws that restrict smoking and that more materials are recycled due to environmental consciousness raising effects than due to mandatory recycling ordinances. Law is critical to environmental protection, but attention should be paid to non-law approaches which might significantly contribute to that protection. In some situations, non-law approaches may be less costly and even more effective.

ADDITIONAL READING

Boyd, D., *The Environmental Rights Revolution: A Global Study of Constitutions, Human Rights, and the Environment* (B.C., Canada: UBC Press, 2012).

Environmental Discourse in Public and International Law (Cambridge, UK: Cambridge University Press, 2012).

Environmental Policy: New Directions for the Twenty-First Century (California: CQ Press, 2013).

Guruswamy, L.D., *International Environmental Law in a Nutshell* (St. Paul, MN: West, 2012).

Hoffmann, M., *Climate Governance at the Crossroads: Experimenting with a Global Response after Kyoto* (New York, NY: Oxford University Press, 2011).

Lee, T., *Global Cities and Climate Change: The Translocal Relations of Environmental Governance* (Routledge, 2014).

Massai, L., *European Climate and Clean Energy Law and Policy* (New York, NY: Earthscan, 2012).

Park, M., *European Perspectives on Environmental Law and Governance* (Routledge, 2013).

Sands, P. and Peel, J., *Principles of International Environmental Law* (New York: Cambridge University Press, 3rd ed., 2012).

The Global Environment: Institutions, Law and Policy (Washington, DC: CQ Press, 2011).

Watson, J., *The WTO and the Environment: Development of Competence Beyond Trade* (Routledge, 2013).

APPENDIX A
EXECUTIVE SUMMARY FOR
ENVIRONMENTAL IMPACT STATEMENT ON
LOON MOUNTAIN SKI AREA PROJECT

EXECUTIVE SUMMARY

BACKGROUND AND PURPOSE AND NEED

Loon Mountain Recreation Corporation (Loon) operates Loon Mountain Ski Area under a special use permit located in part on the White Mountain National Forest (Figure 1.1). Loon has applied for an amendment to their permit to allow an expansion onto South Mountain, an area of National Forest System land located on the west side of the existing ski area.

A Draft Environmental Impact Statement (Draft EIS) was prepared and released to the public in February 1989. Following review and comment, a Supplement to the Draft EIS was released in November of 1989 and addressed issues not included in the Draft. A Revised Draft EIS was issued in January 1991 and replaced the previous Draft and Supplement to the Draft and contained all information found in those two documents, as well as additional information on alternatives, alternatives considered but eliminated from detailed consideration, and cumulative impacts.

The Final EIS contains two volumes. Volume I updates and clarifies the Revised Draft EIS, and Volume II is the public comments, and response to comments, on the Revised Draft EIS. The Record of Decision will be issued approximately 45 days following release of this Final EIS.

The White Mountain National Forest Land and Resource Management Plan (Forest Plan-USDA-Forest Service 1986a) and Record of Decision (USDA-Forest Service 1986b) determined that future skier demand on the Forest would exceed supply, and that the Forest would meet the demand by expanding existing downhill ski areas rather than building new areas. A more recent study has indicated that demand may be greater than predicted. The Forest Plan designated part of the forest adjacent to existing ski areas, including South

Mountain, as 9.2 Management Areas, which are set-asides for potential ski area expansion. The Forest Plan states that future ski area expansion could result in environmental impacts and that it will be necessary to assess the impacts on a case-by-case basis in accordance with the National Environmental Policy Act.

This document evaluates the potential impacts of Loon's proposed expansion on the environment. The decision to be made is whether or not to approve the proposed action, and, if not, whether to offer an alternative kind or degree of expansion. The decision will be made in a Record of Decision which will be released approximately 45 days after issuance of this Final EIS.

The purpose of the proposed expansion is to meet the increased demand for downhill skiing at Loon Mountain Ski Area on the White Mountain National Forest. In the last few years, Loon has averaged over 20 sell-out days from mid-December to mid-March. Use of lifts and runs has been 5 to 10 percent over the rate used by the ski industry to indicate when expansion is needed to provide a quality skiing experience.

SCOPING AND IDENTIFICATION OF ISSUES

The White Mountain National Forest conducted scoping and initiated an environmental analysis in 1987. Based on public response, the Forest Service announced its intent to prepare an EIS on March 14, 1988. In preparation for the EIS, a Joint Review Committee comprised of federal, state, and local agency representatives was formed. Environmental groups and individuals were also invited to participate in the joint review process.

Additional scoping meetings were held in May 1988, and issues and concerns were received from the public and the Joint Review Committee. A total of 284 letters were received following publication of the original Draft EIS. Additional letters were received following publication of the Supplement. These comments were included as part of scoping for this EIS. Following release of the Revised Draft EIS, 218 individual comment letters were received and about 80 people spoke at public meetings. Although the comments were extensive, and are responded to in Volume II of the Final EIS, no new issues were raised in comments on the Revised Draft EIS The issues considered significant for this Final EIS, therefore, did not change from those of the Revised Draft EIS, and are summarized as follows:

Water Resources - There is a concern that the construction and operation of additional facilities would reduce the water quality and quantity of the East Branch of the Pemigewasset. Specifically, there is concern about sedimentation from ski slopes, roads, water lines, housing, and base facilities. Other concerns are that runoff from parking lots would result in heavy metal, salt, or petroleum contamination of the river. Another concern is the effect of snowmaking withdrawals on aquatic habitat, especially for the Atlantic salmon and brook trout. Still others are concerned about the effects of Loon's total water needs competing with other water uses such as municipal use by the town of Lincoln.

Socioeconomics - A number of those who commented are concerned about the increased rate of growth both at Loon and in surrounding communities, particularly Lincoln and Woodstock. Some people see the expansion as an acceleration that would detract from the quality of life. People are concerned about increased traffic, noise, demand for housing, and demand for public services such as drinking water, solid waste disposal, sewage treatment, schools, and police and fire protection. Others see this as an opportunity to increase job choices, expand secondary services, and increase the local tax base. Some see this as an opportunity to improve the quality of life through added recreation facilities and cultural opportunities that accompany the type of development proposed. Several people expressed concern when they started businesses, remodeled or expanded existing ones, or started new regional attractions such as the North Country Center for the Arts that they had relied on the Forest Plan and Loon's expressed intention to grow. Failure to increase skier capacity may threaten the viability of these endeavors.

Skier Demand - Some of the public are concerned whether there is sufficient future skier demand to warrant the Forest Service's permitting further development of the Loon Mountain Ski Area. People want to know what the options are and whether the demand is real. Others want to see Loon expand so they too can enjoy the quality of recreational experience Loon now provides without concern of overcrowding or being denied a ticket.

Alternative Sites for Meeting Skier Demand - A number of people think that skier demand on the Forest could be met at sites other than Loon. Some are concerned that the alternatives considered in detail should include expansions at other sites in New England, or the White Mountain region in general, and not be restricted to Loon Mountain. Other people indicated that skiers had site-specific preferences and that other sites would not be reasonable alternatives to expansion at Loon Mountain.

Wildlife Resources - In addition to the potential impacts on aquatic habitat from changes in water quality and quantity, several people are concerned that there may be a loss of deer habitat, bear mast trees, or other impacts due to the conversion from a forest to open slopes.

Competing Uses - Some people express concern that further ski development would so change the area's aesthetics that visual quality would be reduced; that there would be a major shift in the type of recreation experience in this part of the Forest; or that it would change the land's character, reducing local residents' quality of life.

ALTERNATIVES

The following six alternatives were analyzed in detail: No Action, Loon's Proposed Action, Limited Development, Smaller Permit Area, Expansion on the Existing Permit Area Only, and Consolidated Development. A number of other alternatives were considered including sites off the White Mountain National Forest, sites considered in earlier Forest Service planning studies, and other existing ski areas on the Forest. In addition, other alternatives at Loon Mountain were suggested during scoping, including night skiing, no snowmaking, other configurations on South Mountain, and other configurations on the existing permit area. All of these other potential alternatives were eliminated from detailed analysis because they were not reasonable or feasible alternatives. Still other alternatives were suggested but eliminated because they had already been analyzed in the Forest Plan. These other potential alternatives included whether or not skiing was an acceptable use of National Forest System lands, whether or not skier demand could best be met on National Forest System lands, or whether demand should be met by expansion of existing facilities or development of new facilities.

Alternative 1 - No Action

If this alternative were selected, the special use permit amendment would be denied. It is assumed that recreation-oriented growth would occur in the Lincoln-Woodstock area. Existing ski area operations would continue as in the past. Loon could develop some of their private land for recreation or for increased recreational housing.

Alternative 2 - Loon's Proposed Action

Under this alternative the Forest Service would grant Loon a 930-acre permit expansion onto South Mountain. Loon's expansion would be conducted in two phases (Figure 2.8). Phase I facilities on National Forest System lands would include three lifts, thirteen trails, a new snowmaking system using Loon Pond, and an up-mountain lodge. Facilities on private land would include one lift, a South Mountain base lodge, maintenance buildings, parking lots, a golf course, and additional housing units. Additional facilities on National Forest System lands during Phase II would include four more lifts (one on the existing permit area) and sixteen trails. Loon would also build a small base area lodge and more housing on private land. The Proposed Action would provide for a variety of skiing terrain from beginner to advanced. Skiing between the existing area and South Mountain would be facilitated by crossover trails.

Water for snowmaking for the proposed expansion would come from Loon Pond. Loon would drill into the side of the pond 15 feet below the top of the dam (Figure 2.9) and use gravity to provide water to the ski trails. Loon would continue to use the East Branch, Boyle Brook, and Loon Pond as the sources of snowmaking water for the existing ski area (Figure 4.1). Loon Pond would be refilled from the East Branch if needed.

In total, Phases I and II would add 7,600 skiers to Loon's present capacity of 5,800 skiers while expanding the base area facilities. Cost of the total expansion would be approximately $27 million, and would create 180 winter jobs and 40 full-time jobs at Loon. Summer use in the Lincoln area would be slightly greater than under No Action. If the Forest Service permitted full expansion, the decision on the timing and extent of Phase II would involve several factors, including economics, skier demand, available water, and the successful mitigation of Phase I impacts.

Alternative 3 - Limited Development

This alternative has been substantially revised since the Draft EIS was issued in order to reflect public concerns about the size of the proposed South Mountain expansion. A major difference between this alternative and the Proposed Action is limitations on withdrawals of water for snowmaking use from the East Branch and Loon Pond. When flows in the East Branch are above 85 cfs, Loon would use the East Branch and Boyle Brook to make snow on the existing mountain and withdraw water from Loon Pond for South Mountain and the upper portion of the existing ski area. When flows in the river drop below 85 cfs, Loon would withdraw snowmaking water only from Loon Pond for all portions of both the existing ski area and South Mountain (Figure 4.1). Loon would not be able to draw Loon Pond down below 15 feet from the top of the dam, and would ensure that the pond is full during the first week of December and by May 15 of each year. It assumes that only Phase I of Loon's Proposed Action would be permitted, but limited to an additional 3,200 skiers at one time and with a reduced South Mountain base area development. This alternative would involve a 930-acre ski area permit expansion. Housing development on Loon's private land would still continue at the same level as in their Proposed Action. The alternative would include three lifts, thirteen trails, a new snowmaking system, and an up-mountain lodge on National Forest System lands. One lift, parking lots, a golf course, and housing development would be on private land. This expansion on South Mountain would be connected to the existing ski area with ski trails to go both directions, and would provide a mix of skier terrain from beginner to advanced intermediate. The cost of construction would be about $17 million.

Alternative 4 - Smaller Permit Area

This alternative was developed due to concerns that the Limited Development Alternative was too large of an expansion. This alternative would allow an increase of 2,600 skiers at one time, and would include three lifts and nine trails. The ski area permit expansion would be about 370 acres. Skiers could ski from Loon to this expansion, but would need to take a shuttle bus back. Skier terrain would be primarily beginner and low intermediate. A lodge would be constructed at the base of the expansion, along with a maintenance building and a 750-car parking lot. This alternative would also include the private housing and golf course located on private land as discussed for the Proposed Action. Snowmaking water for the expansion would come from Loon Pond and limitations on withdrawals from the pond and the East Branch would be the same as included in Limited Development.

Alternative 5 - Expansion on the Existing Permit Area Only

This alternative represents the smallest expansion possible at Loon Mountain Ski Area and was developed in response to concerns that existing demand could be met within the existing permit area. This alternative would include one lift and two advanced trails on the eastern side of the ski area that would provide an additional 900 skiers at one time. Additional parking and limited base area facilities would be provided at the South Mountain base area. A shuttle bus would take skiers from the South Mountain parking lot to Loon. Additional snowmaking water would come from Loon Pond. Limitations on withdrawals from the pond and the East Branch would be the same as discussed for Limited Development.

Alternative 6 - Consolidated Development Alternative

This alternative was developed following release and comment on the Revised Draft EIS. It responds to concerns about meeting the demand for additional skiing capacity at Loon and about the magnitude of potential impacts related to expansion on South Mountain. To meet skier demand, this alternative would include improving and upgrading most of the existing lifts at Loon Mountain, widening many existing trails, developing six new trails, and one new lift on private land on the existing ski area. This would reduce the need for a large expansion on South Mountain, and resulted in only lift G and associated trails being proposed on South Mountain adjacent to the existing ski area. The special use permit area would be enlarged by 581 acres. Existing lodge/restaurant facilities would also be enlarged, a lodge would be built at the base of lift G, and parking would be provided at the base of South Mountain. Shuttle buses would transport skiers from the parking lot to lift G and the existing base area. This alternative would increase skier capacity to the same level (9000 CCC) as

Alternative 3. The snowmaking system and water withdrawal limitations would be the same as Alternative 3, but the intake system to Loon Pond would use the current pumping facilities rather than drilling through the side of the pond. Construction would likely occur over a 5 to 7 year period and cost would be about $17.5 million.

ENVIRONMENTAL IMPACTS AND MITIGATION

The alternatives vary in the level of development on National Forest System lands and private land. The major variables are summarized by alternative in Table 1.

Numerous issues were identified during the environmental analysis review and public scoping. Six of these issues were determined critical to the permit expansion decision. They are Alternative Sites for Meeting Skier Demand, Water Resources/Aquatic Biology, Socioeconomics, Skier Demand, Wildlife Resources, and Competing Uses. This section summarizes the six major issues and how they were addressed in this EIS. The issue of alternative sites was discussed in Chapter 2 of the Final EIS. The impact analysis presented in Chapter 4 of the Final EIS indicates that impacts between the six alternatives analyzed in detail differ considerably. The alternatives vary in the amount and location of land area that would be impacted, and therefore, the resources that would be affected. Hence, these six alternatives also vary in how the six major scoping issues would be resolved.

Alternative Sites for Meeting Skier Demand

The alternatives analysis in this chapter indicated that there were no other reasonable or feasible alternative sites for meeting the skier demand at this time. A thorough analysis using existing information indicated that expansion of other ski areas on the White Mountain National Forest may meet some of the skier demand, but none of these sites would have substantially less environmental impact associated with its expansion, none are ripe for a decision, none would meet the demand better than at Loon, and all four other ski areas may be permitted to expand in the future even if Loon or another area were permitted to expand.

Water Resources/Aquatic Biology

Water quality in the East Branch and mainstem is excellent at present except for occasional periods in the summer. Alternatives 2, 3, 4, and 6 have the potential to create water quality impacts due to increased erosion and sedimentation of the tributary streams that drain South Mountain. Of the South Mountain alternatives, Alternative 4 would have the least impact since only one crossover trail would cross Loon Pond Brook. Alternative 6 would have less impact on Loon Pond Brook than Alternatives 2 and 3 since it would cross the stream in a less sensitive area. Alternative 5 would have the lowest potential sedimentation impact of any of the action alternatives since it would not involve construction on South Mountain, or cross Loon Pond Brook. Best management practices and a State Alteration of Terrain Permit would reduce water quality impacts under all alternatives to acceptable levels. A monitoring program would assure that water quality remains excellent in the rivers and streams.

Under the No Action Alternative (Alternative 1), Loon would deplete water from the East Branch and Boyle Brook for snowmaking at a maximum combined rate of 3 cfs (1 cfs from Boyle Brook, 1 cfs from the East Branch, and 1 cfs from the Loon Pond system). This maximum rate of depletion would remain the same under all of the other five alternatives since no new snowmaking pumping system is planned. What would vary between alternatives is the total amount of water used per ski season, varying from the 67 million gallons used at present and for Alternative 1, to the 193 million gallons used under full development of Alternative 2 (Loon's Proposed Action). Alternative 3 would require 134 million gallons; Alternative 4, 118 million gallons; Alternative 5, 77 million gallons; and Alternative 6, 138 million gallons. This rate of depletion would potentially impact Atlantic salmon habitat in the East Branch, but a 32 cfs minimum flow mitigation measure would minimize impacts to fish for Alternative 2. The 85 cfs minimum flow (after the phase-in period) of Alternatives 3, 4, 5, and 6 would provide even better protection for Atlantic salmon. The total amount of water used would, under all alternatives, not affect downstream users since the amount is a very small percent of the total flow of the stream, even under Alternative 2. Under Alternatives 2, 3, 4, 5, and 6, Loon would deplete the East Branch by a maximum of 4 cfs while refilling Loon Pond (3 cfs from the East Branch and Boyle Brook combined plus 1 cfs from the Loon Pond system).

The amount of water withdrawn from Loon Pond would also vary among alternatives. Under Alternative 2, Loon could draw the pond down 10 feet below the normal full level of the pond, with another 5 feet reserved for an emergency supply for the town of Lincoln. Under Alternatives 3, 4, 5, and 6, Loon would have the potential of drawing the pond down 15 feet, with an additional 5 feet for the Town. This would be accomplished by drilling a pipe into the side of the pond under Alternatives 2, 3, 4, and 5, and by pumping the water out under Alternative 6. The 10-foot drawdown limit for Alternative 2, and the 15-foot limit for Alternatives 3, 4, 5, and 6 would protect the ecology of the pond since most of its inhabitants would not be affected by a winter drawdown. Alternative 5 would use very little additional water from Loon Pond, so withdrawals would generally be about the same as present operations (No Action).

TABLE 1
COMPARISON OF ALTERNATIVES FOR MAJOR VARIABLES

	Current	Alt 1	Alt 2	Alt 3	Alt 4	Alt 5	Alt 6
Additional comfortable carrying capacity	0	0	7,600	3,200	2,600	900	3,200
Total comfortable carrying capacity	5,800	5,800	13,400	9,000	8,400	6,700	9,000
Acres of National Forest under permit	785	785	1,715	1,715	1,155	785	1,366
Additional acres of clearing for ski area	0	0	400	200	125	32	150
Additional acres served by snowmaking	0	0	354	189	99	32	195
Total acres served by snowmaking	185	185	540	374	284	217	380
Total annual snowmaking water demand (million gallons)	67	67	193	134	118	78	138
Peak snowmaking water demand (cfs)	3	3	4**	4**	4**	4**	4**
Lifts on South Mountain	0	0	8	4	3	0	1
Winter peak visitation	14,500	22,000	25,000	25,000	25,000	22,000	25,000
Additional cars in lots	0	0	1,800	900	700	250	900
New base facilities (ft^2)	0	0	51,000	37,500	10,000	5,000	43,500

* *cfs = cubic feet per second, No Action domestic water demand will increase if the town used the river for more water than at present.*
** *This number reflects conditions when pumping to refill Loon Pond.*

The town of Lincoln is planning a new water treatment system that would utilize the East Branch as its primary water source. The rate of withdrawal of water from the East Branch would be 3 cfs under all six alternatives, and all alternatives would have a 5-foot emergency water supply in Loon Pond for the town of Lincoln. The total amount of water withdrawn would be greatest under Alternative 2, especially during the winter, due to increased numbers of skiers. All alternatives would see greater water usage in the future, but this usage would be relatively minor in comparison to the total flow of the river and would not affect downstream users. The Corps of Engineers has placed a 30 cfs minimum flow requirement for withdrawals by the town to protect Atlantic salmon habitat.

Socioeconomics

The towns of Lincoln and Woodstock, and to a much lesser degree, surrounding towns would grow under all alternatives. The primary source of the growth is a projected continued increase in summer recreation associated with this area of the White Mountains. Alternatives 2, 3, 4, 5, and 6 would have increased winter growth also due to expansion of the ski area. Under No Action (Alternative 1), the area is projected to have about 25,000 peak summer visitors within 20 years. This level of summer visitation would be reached in 15 years under both Alternatives 2, 3, and 6, and in between 15 and 20 years by Alternatives 4 and 5. Winter visitation would reach 25,000 also under Alternative 2 in 15 years, and about 20,000 under Alternatives 3 and 6 in 15 years. Alternatives 4 and 5 would see lower numbers of winter visitors. Hence, the infrastructure in the Lincoln-Woodstock area would need to support 25,000 visitors under all alternatives, but this level of visitation would be reached much sooner under Alternatives 2, 3, and 6. This rate of growth would stress local planning, traffic, demand for housing, and the demand for public services. Both Lincoln and Woodstock officials have indicated they are prepared for the growth, but other members in the communities are not as sure. Present problems with Lincoln's sewage treatment lagoons and water supply system suggest these areas may not be able to handle the rapid growth, although state and local officials feel the town's systems can handle the growth.

The Forest Service would work closely with the state and the towns to ensure that the rate of growth of the ski area does not exceed the capacity of the towns to keep up with the growth. If needed, the Forest Service would delay or deny portions of the ski area expansion to prevent serious problems with the infrastructure.

The growth of the area would provide additional jobs in the area, both summer and winter. Alternative 2 would provide the best balance between winter and summer jobs, with a greater likelihood that people could use two or three seasonal jobs to provide year-round employment. The tax base generated by the development proposed in Alternatives 2, 3, and 6 would support the infrastructural needs of the communities, although taxes would lag behind the need for the services requiring bonding or other methods to provide services.

Alternative 4 would also provide additional winter jobs but due to its small size and poor skier mix, would be the least likely of the alternatives to be financially feasible. Recent trends in the ski industry show that skiers favor larger resort-type areas with a good balance of skier mix. Alternative 4 would provide only beginner and lower intermediate skiing, not the type of skiing most of Loon's present customers are seeking. Alternative 5 would add little economic benefits or adverse impacts due to the small size of its expansion, and its poor skier mix. Alternative 5 would add only expert skiing terrain to Loon, rather than a mix of skiing terrain. Alternative 6 would add skier capacity to the present ski area, which is presently quite crowded. Planned trail widening, improvements in the lifts and facilities should reduce the crowding.

Skier Demand

Skier demand studies have shown there is sufficient skier demand to warrant construction of Alternative 2, which would provide for an additional 7600 skiers at one time. None of the other alternatives would meet this demand better than Alternative 2, since the increase in skiers at one time for Alternatives 3, 4, 5, and 6 are 3,200, 2,600, 900, and 3200, respectively. Alternatives 2, 3, and 6 would provide the best opportunities to add additional skiing similar to that presently provided at the existing ski area since these alternatives would provide beginner to advanced intermediate skiing. Alternative 4 would provide novice and intermediate skiing only, and Alternative 5 would provide advanced skiing only, but would add to present congestion and parking problems at the ski area.

Wildlife Resources

Alternatives 2, and 3 would directly impact a deer wintering area along lower Loon Pond Brook through construction of a crossover ski trail. This deer wintering area has been impacted by past ski area development and would be indirectly impacted to a lesser degree by housing construction on Loon's private land under all Alternatives. Mitigation of enhancing and protecting a nearby deer wintering area would mitigate the impacts under Alternatives 2, 3, 4, and 6. Bear mast trees and cavity trees would also be lost due to clearing of ski trails under all alternatives except No Action, with the greatest loss in Alternative 2. This impact would be minimized by avoiding cavity trees and mast trees to the extent possible during the layout of trails. Clearing for ski trails under Alternatives 2, 3, 4, 5, and 6 would increase fragmentation of dense forested areas that is preferred by some bird and mammal species. Clearing would provide additional edge habitat for other species of birds and mammals. Alternative 2 would result in the most habitat fragmentation, and greatest loss of bear mast and cavity trees, and the amount of these habitats lost would be reduced in Alternatives 3, 4, 5, and 6.

Competing Uses

Alternative 2 would create the greatest change in visual resources, as well as the greatest change in character of the land since it is the largest expansion of the four action alternatives. Alternatives 3, 4, and 6 would also have substantial visible change on South Mountain since they would all develop portions of the mountain that are most visible from the Lincoln area and I-93. Alternative 5 would be hardly noticeable to most visitors in the area. A major expansion of the ski area as proposed in Alternatives 2, 3, and 6 would have the most potential for changing the recreational experience of visitors to the area, although the type of growth that would occur under Alternative 1 is unknown and could result in considerable change to the private lands in Lincoln for additional summer tourist attractions. Some residents would feel their quality of life was reduced under Alternative 1, and others' quality of life would be reduced under Alternatives 2, 3, 4, or 6.

Mitigation

The impact analysis indicates that without mitigation, environmental consequences from permitting expansion of ski facilities onto South Mountain could result in significant impacts due to degradation of water quality in the East Branch by non-point sources, likely loss of deer winter habitat along Loon Pond Brook, accelerated growth in the Lincoln-Woodstock area, and traffic and parking problems in the Lincoln area. Permitting the expansion would also have beneficial consequences, including meeting present skier demand and some of the future skier demand, and increasing the local and regional economic activity by creating a year-round resort balance.

A number of other impacts were also noted in the analysis that were not significant, but were adverse. These impacts included small amounts of erosion to Loon Pond Brook; disturbance to less than one acre of wetland; noise from snowmaking which would affect a few people; water quality degradation would occur more frequently when flows are reduced below the seven-day, year low flow (7Q 10) on the East Branch; disturbance to raptor nests, cavity trees, and mast trees during construction of ski trails; alteration of the area's visual characteristics; and some social dissatisfaction. Beneficial impacts would include some social satisfaction, especially among skiers, and alleviation of present skier congestion at Loon.

On the other hand, the impact analysis indicates that denial of the expansion could result in continued skier congestion at Loon, failure to meet the current and projected skier demand at Loon, additional impacts to deer winter habitat that would not be mitigated, and less economic activity in Lincoln-Woodstock and the region, as well as a less balanced year-round economy.

A number of mitigation measures were developed that, in combination with Forest Plan standards and guidelines, would minimize or eliminate adverse impacts of the five action alternatives. Most of the mitigation measures have been successfully applied by Loon and other ski/resort permittees on the White

Mountain National Forest. The Forest Service will monitor the effectiveness of the proposed mitigation measures.

ENVIRONMENTALLY PREFERRED ALTERNATIVE

The environmentally preferred alternative would be the No Action Alternative, Alternative 1. Substantial impacts would still occur under this alternative, primarily due to the continued growth in the summer recreation-based economy of the Lincoln-Woodstock area. Therefore, many of the socioeconomic and infra structural impacts would occur under this alternative, although they would occur later than under any of the other alternatives.

FOREST SERVICE PREFERRED ALTERNATIVE

Alternative 6 (Consolidated Development) is the Forest Service's preferred alternative. This is a change from the preferred alternative described in the Revised Draft EIS. This alternative, if implemented, would result in conversion of Loon's special use permit to a new permit and adoption of Alternative 6 as the Master Development Plan for the ski area. This alternative would allow Loon, subject to the mitigation discussed with the alternative, to expand its downhill ski facilities. New facilities on National Forest System lands would include one lift, fifteen trails, expanded lodges, and a new snowmaking system. Facilities on private land could include one lift, expansion of existing base facilities, a base lodge at lift G, parking lot at South Mountain, and additional housing units.

A final decision will follow public review of this Final EIS.

Mitigation for the Preferred Alternative

Erosion/Sedimentation

Loon will obtain a New Hampshire Alteration of Terrain Permit prior to construction or disturbance in order to determine and implement best management practices for sedimentation and non-point pollution sources as outlined in Appendix G.

The Forest Service will have an employee on-site during construction activities to insure that mitigation measures are being fully implemented and are effective.

Noise

Loon will use the best available technology to reduce noise impacts from snowmaking operations.

Water Resources

No construction on National Forest System lands will be allowed until the town of Lincoln has installed a new water treatment facility or suitable alternative approved by the state of New Hampshire.

Until Loon's snowmaking system has been converted, by 2003 or twelve years after issuance of the permit at the latest, water withdrawals for snowmaking will cease at river flows of 40 cfs, and withdrawal for refilling Loon Pond will cease at 62 cfs. Water withdrawals from the East Branch of the Pemigewasset River will not be permitted when flows are less than or equal to 85 cubic feet per second (cfs) following Loon's conversion of their snowmaking system, by 2003 or twelve years after issuance of the permit at the latest. Depletion from the East Branch and Boyle Brook combined will not exceed 2 cfs for snowmaking and 3 cfs for refilling Loon Pond. Maximum depletion of the East Branch will, therefore, be 3 cfs for snowmaking and 4 cfs for refilling Loon Pond when 1 cfs depletion due to use of Loon Pond is added to the depletion amounts for snowmaking and refilling Loon Pond.

Loon will develop a water quality monitoring program in cooperation with the Forest Service, state of New Hampshire, Environmental Protection Agency, town of Lincoln, and other interested agencies to document future water quality changes and to determine if predictions in this environmental impact statement were accurate. Should water quality problems be identified, the Forest Service will require Loon to conduct appropriate additional mitigation.

Loon will install recording strip charts or their equivalent to meter snowmaking water pumps and will cooperate with the town of Lincoln in installing a gauge in the East Branch in order to monitor withdrawals and flows.

Loon will assure the Forest Service that Loon Pond will be filled each year it is used for snowmaking during the first week of December and by May 15 to prevent wetland or visual impacts, and there will be a drawdown limit on Loon Pond of 15 feet for snowmaking.

Loon Pond refill withdrawals will not be permitted when turbidity in the East Branch exceeds 5 nephelometric turbidity units, or the coliform bacteria count is above 50 per 100 ml., or other requirements prescribed by the State to prevent degradation of Loon Pond are not met.

Loon, the New Hampshire Department of Environmental Services, and the town of Lincoln will develop an acceptable plan for assuring an adequate emergency water supply for the town from Loon Pond.

Wildlife

The Loon Pond Brook deer wintering area will be replaced with a suitable alternative site, and be managed according to the mitigation plan.

Cavity trees and mast trees will be avoided during clearing operations, where feasible.

Raptor nest surveys will be conducted prior to forest clearing. Nesting areas will be left undisturbed until nesting and rearing is complete.

Visual Resources: All structures and clearings will meet Forest Service visual quality objectives.

Socioeconomics/Transportation

The Forest Service may delay or deny authorization of construction of any component of the expansion if, in consultation with Lincoln-Woodstock and the state, the group determines that the area's infrastructure is unable to meet any increased demand for municipal services which would result from such construction.

The Forest Service will not approve clearing of land or construction of facilities until the state of New Hampshire certifies that the town of Lincoln's sewage lagoons are operating properly.

Loon will build the new proposed South Mountain access road to be serviceable as soon as practical but in no case later than the start of the third season of operation of South Mountain, subject to the approval of the town of Lincoln and the state of New Hampshire.

Loon will be required to continue to use a traffic officer during peak use times at the Loon Mountain Road/Highway 112 intersection. The Forest Service will not approve additional development of the ski area if other intersections in Lincoln fall below a LOS C due to Loon Mountain traffic and are not mitigated to the satisfaction of the New Hampshire Department of Transportation.

Additional detail on these mitigation measures can be found in Chapter 4 of the Final EIS, and in the detailed mitigation plans included in the Appendix of that document. This detail includes estimated costs, agencies responsible for the mitigation, locations for the mitigation, and implementation plans for all of the mitigation proposed. The Forest Service will monitor the effectiveness of the mitigation measures.

APPENDIX B
STATUTE AND REGULATIONS FOR MOTOR
CARRIER NOISE EMISSION STANDARDS.
STATUTE: NOICE CONTROL ACT
42 U.S.C.S. 4917
REGULATIONS: 40 CFR, PART 202

42 USCS 4917

4917. Motor carrier noise emission standards

(a) Regulations; standards; consultation with Secretary of Transportation

(1) Within nine months after October 27, 1972, the Administrator shall publish proposed noise emission regulations for motor carriers engaged in interstate commerce. Such proposed regulations shall include noise emission standards setting such limits on noise emissions resulting from operation of motor carriers engaged in interstate commerce which reflect the degree of noise reduction achievable through the application of the best available technology, taking into account the cost of compliance. These regulations shall be in addition to any regulations that may be proposed under section 4905 of this title.

(2) Within ninety days after the publication of such regulations as may be proposed under paragraph (1) of this subsection, and subject to the provisions of section 4915 of this title, the Administrator shall promulgate final regulations. Such regulations may be revised from time to time, in accordance with this subsection.

(3) Any standard or regulation, or revision thereof, proposed under this subsection shall be promulgated only after consultation with the Secretary of Transportation in order to assure appropriate consideration for safety and technological availability.

(4) Any regulation or revision thereof promulgated under this subsection shall take effect after such period as the Administrator finds necessary, after consultation with the Secretary of Transportation, to permit the development and application of the requisite technology, giving appropriate consideration to the cost of compliance within such period.

(b) Regulations to insure compliance with noise emission standards. The Secretary of Transportation, after consultation with the Administrator shall promulgate regulations to insure compliance with all standards promulgated by the Administrator under this section. The Secretary of Transportation shall carry out such regulations through the use of his powers and duties of enforcement and inspection authorized by subtitle IV of Title 49 and the Department of Transportation Act. Regulations promulgated under this section shall be subject to the provisions of sections 4909, 4910, 4911, and 4915 of this title.

(c) State and local standards and controls.

(1) Subject to paragraph (2) of this subsection but notwithstanding any other provision of this chapter, after the effective date of a regulation under this section applicable to noise emissions resulting from the operation of any motor carrier engaged in interstate commerce, no State or political subdivision thereof may adopt or enforce any standard applicable to the same operation of such motor carrier, unless such standard is identical to a standard applicable to noise emissions resulting from such operation prescribed by any regulation under this section.

(2) Nothing in this section shall diminish or enhance the rights of any State or political subdivision thereof to establish and enforce standards or controls on levels of environmental noise, or to control, license, regulate, or restrict the use, operation, or movement of any product if the Administrator, after consultation with the Secretary of Transportation, determines that such standard, control, license, regulation, or restriction is necessitated by special local conditions and is not in conflict with regulations promulgated under this section.

(d) "Motor carrier" defined.

For purposes of this section, the term "motor carrier" includes a motor carrier and motor private carrier as those terms are defined in section 13102 of Title 49.

PART 202C MOTOR CARRIERS
ENGAGED IN INTERSTATE COMMERCE

Subpart A General Provisions

Sec.

202.10   Definitions.

202.11   Effective date.

202.12   Applicability.

Subpart B Interstate Motor Carrier
Operations Standards

202.20   Standards for highway operations.

202.21   Standards for operation under stationary test.

202.22   Visual exhaust system inspection.

202.23   Visual tire inspection.

Authority: Sec. 18, 36 Stat. 1249, 42 U.S.C. 4917(a)

Subpart A
General Provisions

202.10 Definitions.

As used in this part, all terms not defined herein shall have the meaning given them in the Act:

(a) "Act" means the Noise Control Act of 1972 (Pub.L. 92-574, 86 Stat. 1234)

(b) "Common carrier by motor vehicle" means any person who holds himself out to the general public to engage in the transportation by motor vehicle in interstate or foreign commerce of passengers or property or any class or classes thereof for compensation, whether over regular or irregular routes.

(c) "Contract carrier by motor vehicle" means any person who engages in transportation by motor vehicle of passengers or property in interstate or foreign commerce for compensation (other than transportation referred to in paragraph (b) of this section) under continuing contracts with one person or a limited number of persons either (1) for the furnishing of transportation services through the assignment of motor vehicles for a continuing period of time to the exclusive use of each person served or

(2) for the furnishing of transportation services designed to meet the distinct need of each individual customer.

(d) "Cutout or by-pass or similar devices" means devices which vary the exhaust system gas flow so as to discharge the exhaust gas and acoustic energy to the atmosphere without passing through the entire length of the exhaust system, including all exhaust system sound attenuation components.

(e) "dB(A)" means the standard abbreviation for A-weighted sound level in decibels.

(f) "Exhaust system" means the system comprised of a combination of components which provides for enclosed flow of exhaust gas from engine parts to the atmosphere.

(g) "Fast meter response" means that the fast dynamic response of the sound level meter shall be used. The fast dynamic response shall comply with the meter dynamic characteristics in paragraph 5.3 of the American National Standard Specification for Sound Level Meters, ANSI S1. 4-1971. This publication is available from the American National Standards Institute, Inc., 1420 Broadway, New York, New York 10018.

(h) "Gross Vehicle Weight

Rating" (GVWR) means the value specified by the manufacturer as the loaded weight of a single vehicle.

(i) "Gross Combination Weight Rating" (GCWR) means the value specified by the manufacturer as the loaded weight of a combination vehicle.

(j) "Highway" means the streets, roads, and public ways in any State.

(k) "Interstate commerce" means the commerce between any place in a State and any place in another State or between places in the same State through another State, whether such commerce moves wholly by motor vehicle or partly by motor vehicle and partly by rail, express, water or air. This definition of "interstate commerce" for purposes of these regulations is

(n) "Muffler" means a device for abating the sound of escaping gases of an internal combustion engine.

(o) "Open site" means an area that is essentially free of large sound- reflecting objects, such as barriers, walls, board fences, signboards, parked vehicles, bridges, or buildings.

(p) "Private carrier of property by motor vehicle" means any person not included in terms "common carrier by motor vehicle" or "contract

the same as the definition of "interstate commerce" in section 203(a) of the Interstate Commerce Act. [49 U.S.C. Section 303(a)]

(l) "Motor carrier" means a common carrier by motor vehicle, a contract carrier by motor vehicle, or a private carrier of property by motor vehicle as those terms are defined by paragraphs (14), (15), and (17) of section 203(a) of the Interstate Commerce Act [49 U.S.C. 303(a)].

(m) "Motor vehicle" means any vehicle, machine, tractor, trailer, or semitrailer propelled or drawn by mechanical power and used upon the highways in the transportation of passengers or property, or any combination thereof, but does not include any vehicle, locomotive, or car operated exclusively on a rail or rails. carrier by motor vehicle", who or which transports in interstate or foreign commerce by motor vehicle property of which such person is the owner, lessee, or bailee, when such transportation is for sale, lease, rent or bailment, or in furtherance of any commercial enterprise.

(q) "Sound level" means the quantity in decibels measured by a sound level meter satisfying the requirements of American

National Standards Specification for Sound Level Meters S1.4-1971. This publication is available from the American National Standards Institute, Inc., 1430 Broadway, New York, New York 10018. Sound level is the frequency-weighted sound pressure level obtained with the standardized dynamic characteristic "fast" or "slow" and weighting A, B, or C; unless indicated otherwise, the A-weighting is understood.

202.11 Effective date.

The provisions of Subpart B shall become effective October 15, 1975, except that the provisions of ' 202.20(b) and ' 202.21(b) of Subpart B shall apply to motor vehicles manufactured during or after the 1986 model year.

202.12 Applicability.

(a) The provisions of Subpart B apply to all motor carriers engaged in interstate commerce.

(b) The provisions of Subpart B apply only to those motor vehicles of such motor carriers which have a gross vehicle weight rating or gross combination weight rating in excess of 10,000 pounds, and only when such motor vehicles

are operating under the conditions specified in Subpart B.

(c) Except as provided in paragraphs (d) and (e) of this section, the provisions of Subpart B apply to the total sound produced by such motor vehicles when operating under such conditions, including the sound produced by auxiliary equipment mounted on such motor vehicles.

(d) The provisions of Subpart B do not apply to auxiliary equipment which is normally operated only when the transporting vehicle is stationary or is moving at a speed of 5 miles per hour or less. Examples of such equipment include, but are not limited to, cranes, asphalt spreaders, ditch diggers, liquid or slurry pumps, air compressors, welders, and trash compactors.

(e) The provisions of Subpart B do not apply to warning devices, such as horns and sirens; or to emergency equipment and vehicles such as fire engines, ambulances, police vans, and rescue vans, when responding to emergency calls; or to snow plows when in operation.

(f) The provisions of ' 202.20(a) and ' 202.21(a) of Subpart B apply only to applicable motor vehicles manufactured prior to the 1986 model year.

(g) The provisions of ' 202.20(b) and ' 202.21(b) apply to all applicable motor vehicles manufactured during or after the 1986 model year.

Subpart B Interstate Motor Carrier Operations Standards

202.20 Standards for highway operations.

(a) No motor carrier subject to these regulations shall operate any motor vehicle of a type to which this regulation is applicable which at any time or under any condition of highway trade, load, acceleration or deceleration generates a sound level in excess of 86dB(A) measured on an open site with fast meter response at 50 feet from the centerline of lane of travel on highways with speed limits of 35 MPH or less; or 90 dB(A) measured on an open site with fast meter response at 50 feet from the centerline of lane of travel on highways with speed limits of more than 35 MPH.

(b) No motor carrier subject to these regulations shall operate any motor vehicle of a type to which this regulation is applicable which

at any time or under any condition of highway grade, load, acceleration or deceleration generates a sound level in excess of 83 dB(A) measured on an open site with fast meter response at 50 feet from the centerline of lane of travel on highways with speed limits of 35 MPH or less; or 87 dB(A) measured on an open site with fast meter response at 50 feet from the centerline of lane of travel on highways with speed limits of more than 35 MPH.

202.21 Standard for operation under stationary test.

(a) No motor carrier subject to these regulations shall operate any motor vehicle of a type to which this regulation is applicable which generates a sound level in excess of 88 dB(A) measured on an open site with fast meter response at 50 feet from the longitudinal centerline of the vehicle, when its engine is accelerated from idle with wide open throttle to governed speed with the vehicle stationary, transmission in neutral, and clutch engaged. This ' 202.21 shall not apply to any vehicle which is not equipped with an engine speed governor.

(b) No motor carrier subject to these regulations

shall operate any motor vehicle of a type to which this regulation is applicable which generates a sound level in excess of 85 dB(A) measured on an open site with fast meter response at 50 feet from the longitudinal centerline of the vehicle, when its engine is accelerated from idle with wide open throttle to governed speed with the vehicle stationary, transmission in neutral, and clutch engaged. This paragraph shall not apply to any vehicle which is not equipped with an engine speed governor.

202.22 Visual exhaust system inspection.

No motor carrier subject to these regulations shall operate any motor vehicle of a type to which this regulation is applicable unless the exhaust system of such vehicle is (a) free from defects which affect sound reduction; (b) equipped with a muffler or other noise dissipative device; and (c) not equipped with any cut-out, bypass, or similar device.
is conducted at a speed of 65 MPH.

202.23 Visual tire inspection.

No motor carrier subject to these regulations shall at any time operate any motor vehicle of a type to which this regulation is applicable on a tire or tires having a tread pattern which as originally manufactured, or as newly retreaded, is composed primarily or cavities in the tread (excluding sipes and local chunking) which are not vented by grooves to the tire shoulder or circumferentially to each other around the tire. This ' 202.23 shall not apply to any motor vehicle which is demonstrated by the motor carrier which operates it to be in compliance with the noise emission standard specified for operations on highways with speed limits of more than 35 MPH in ' 202.20 of this Sub-part B, if the demonstration is conducted at the highway speed limit in effect at the inspection location, or, if speed is unlimited, the demonstration

APPENDIX C
PORTIONS OF A DISCHARGE PERMIT
FORM FOR WATER POLLUTANTS

Permit No._____

File No._____

AGENCY OF ENVIRONMENTAL CONSERVATION
NPDES Permits Section State Office Bldg.
MONTPELIER, VT 05602

Application Number:_____

Name of Applicant:_____

Expiration Date:_____

DISCHARGE PERMIT

In reference to the above application for a permit to discharge in compliance with the provisions of the Vermont Water Pollution Control Act as amended (hereinafter referred to as the Act),_____

_____

_____

(hereinafter referred to as the permittee) is authorized by the Secretary, Agency of Environmental Conservation, Montpelier, Vermont, to discharge from_____

_____

to_____

in accordance with the following general and special conditions:

I. SPECIAL CONDITIONS

A. *Effluent Limits*

1. Until _____, the permittee is authorized to discharge from _____
to the _____ an
effluent whose characteristics shall not exceed the values listed below

Discharge Limitations						
	(specify units)					
Effluent Characteristic	Monthly Average	Week-ly Averag e	Maximu m Day	Month-ly Averag e	Weekly Average	Maxi-mum Day
Flow, cu. M/day (MGD)	**	**	**	(1)	**	**
Biochemical Oxygen Demand, 5-day, 20E C						
Total Suspended Solids						
Settleable Solids						
Total Coliform Bacteria						
	(1) Annual Average					

2. From _____ until _____, the permittee is authorized to discharge from _____ to the
_____ an effluent whose
characteristics shall not exceed the values listed below.

Discharge Limitations						
	(specify units)					
Effluent Characteristic	Monthly Average	Week-ly Average	Maximu m Day	Month-ly Average	Weekly Average	Maxi-mum Day
Flow, cu. M/day (MGD)	**	**	**	(1)	**	**
Biochemical Oxygen Demand, 5-day, 20E C						
Total Suspended Solids						
Settleable Solids						
Total Coliform Bacteria						
	(1) Annual Average					

a. The pH of the effluent shall not be less than 6.0 nor greater than 8.5 at any time.

b. The chlorine residual shall not be greater than 4.0 MG/L. The total chlorine residual of the effluent shall not result in any demonstrable harm to aquatic life or violate any water quality standard which has been or may be promulgated. Upon promulgation of any such standard, this permit shall be reviewed or amended in accordance with such standard, and the permittee shall be so notified.

c. The effluent shall contain neither a visible oil sheen, foam, nor floating solids at any time.

d. The discharge shall not cause visible discoloration of the receiving waters.

e. The discharge shall not cause a violation of the water quality standards of the receiving waters.

f. The monthly average concentrations of BOD and total suspended solids in the discharge shall not exceed 15 percent of the monthly average concentrations of BOD and total suspended solids in the influent into the permittee's wastewater treatment facilities. For the purposes of determining whether the permittee is in compliance with this condition, samples from the discharge and the influent shall be taken with appropriate allowance for detention times.

g. When the effluent discharged for a period of 90 consecutive days exceeds 80 percent of the permitted flow limitation, the permittee shall submit to the permitting authority projected loadings and a program for maintaining satisfactory treatment levels consistent with approved water quality management plans.

h. Maintenance activities or emergencies which cause reductions of effluent quality below effluent limits as specified herein shall be considered a violation of the conditions of the permit, unless the permittee shall immediately apply for an emergency pollution permit under the provisions of 10 VSA Chapter 47, Subchapter 1, Section 1265 (f). Application shall be made to the Secretary of the Environmental Conservation Agency, State Office Building, Montpelier, Vermont 05602.

i. Any action on the part of the Agency of Environmental Conservation in reviewing, commenting upon or approving plans and specifications for the construction of wastewater treatment facilities shall not relieve the permittee from its responsibility to achieve effluent limitations set forth in this permit and shall not constitute a waiver of, or act of estoppel against any remedy available to the Agency, the State of Vermont or the federal government for failure to meet any requirement set forth in this permit or imposed by state or federal law.

II. GENERAL CONDITIONS

A. All discharges authorized herein shall be consistent with the terms and conditions of this permit. The discharge of any pollutant more frequently than, or at a level in excess of, that identified and authorized by this permit shall constitute a violation of the terms and conditions of this permit. Such a violation may result in the imposition of civil and/or criminal penalties as provided for in Section 1274 and 1275 of the Act. Facility modifications, additions and/or expansions that increase the plant capacity must be reported to the permitting authority and this permit then modified or reissued to reflect such changes. The permittee shall provide notice to the Secretary of the following:

1. any new introduction of pollutants into the treatment works from a source which would be a new source as defined in Section 306 of the Federal Water Pollution Control Act if such source were discharging pollutants;
2. except as to such categories and classes of point sources or discharges specified by the Secretary, any new introduction of pollutants into the treatment works from a source which would be subject to Section 301 of the Federal Water Pollution Control Act if such source were discharging pollutants, and
3. any substantial change in volume or character of pollutants being introduced into the treatment works by a source introducing pollutants into such works at the time of issuance of the permit.

The notice shall include:

1. the quality and quantity of the discharge to be introduced into the system, and
2. the anticipated impact of such change in the quality or quantity of the effluent to be discharged from the permitted facility.

B. After notice and opportunity for a hearing, this permit may be modified, suspended, or revoked in whole or in part during its term for cause including, but not limited to, the following:

1. violation of any terms or conditions of this permit;
2. obtaining this permit by misrepresentation or failure to disclose fully all relevant facts; or
3. a change in any condition that requires either a temporary or permanent reduction or elimination of the permitted discharge.